THE GOSPELS

THE GOSPELS

A new translation by
SARAH RUDEN

MODERN LIBRARY

NEW YORK

Published in the United States by Modern Library, an imprint
of the Random House Publishing Group, a division of Penguin
Random House LLC, New York.

MODERN LIBRARY and the TORCHBEARER colophon are
registered trademarks of Penguin Random House LLC.

LIBRARY OF CONGRESS CATALOGING-IN-PUBLICATION DATA
Names: Ruden, Sarah, translator.
Title: The Gospels / translated by Sarah Ruden.
Other titles: Bible. Gospels. English. Ruden. 2021.
Description: First edition. | New York: Modern Library, 2021.
Identifiers: LCCN 2020032892 (print) | LCCN 2020032893 (ebook) |
ISBN 9780399592942 (acid-free paper) |
ISBN 9780399592959 (ebook)
Classification: LCC BS2553 .R83 2021 (print) | LCC BS2553 (ebook) |
DDC 226/.05209—dc23
LC record available at https://lccn.loc.gov/2020032892
LC ebook record available at https://lccn.loc.gov/2020032893

Printed in the United States of America on acid-free paper

modernlibrary.com
randomhousebooks.com

10 9 8 7 6 5 4 3 2 1

FIRST EDITION

Book design by Simon Sullivan

To the Quakers

It seemed now as if, touched by human penitence and all its toil, divine goodness had parted the curtain and displayed behind it, single, distinct, the hare erect; the wave falling; the boat rocking, which, did we deserve them, should be ours always. But alas, divine goodness, twitching the cord, draws the curtain; it does not please him; he covers his treasures in a drench of hail, and so breaks them, so confuses them that it seems impossible that their calm should ever return or that we should ever compose from their fragments a perfect whole or read in the littered pieces the clear words of truth. For our penitence deserves a glimpse only; our toil respite only.

VIRGINIA WOOLF, *To the Lighthouse*

CONTENTS

INTRODUCTION

As a Quaker—a member of perhaps the least theological, most practical religious movement in the world—I'm supposed to be open to looking first at a thing in itself, whether it's a head of Swiss chard, money, a gun, a book, a belief, or anything else. As a Quaker translator, I would like to deal with the Gospels more straightforwardly than is customary, to help people respond to the books on their own terms. Yet never before, in nearly forty years of translating, have I found texts so resistant to this purpose.

But first of all, what *are* the Gospels? Scholars of ancient literature (I'm one of those too), who are used to classifying works within well-defined categories (known as genres), tend to feel that the Gospels are not quite like anything else. This is signaled by their shared name. In the original Koinē ("Common") dialect of these Greek texts, the title that emerged is *euaggelion* (the double *g* is pronounced *ng*), meaning "good news." Our word "Gospel" comes from an Old English word for that, and "Gospels" is used in the title of this book and in all parts of the book outside the translations themselves, in order to avoid confusion.

The title is unusual in being so general. Ancient books normally got their permanent names (a process that might take some time) from the author's (or purported author's) name or other designation, or from the subject matter or the form of the writing. Ezekiel, Kings, and Proverbs are biblical examples. In contrast to all this, "good news" is extremely broad and confident, as if four short narratives carry a revelation sweeping aside all others.

The four texts are differentiated up front by authorial names, as "the good news according to" Matthew, Mark, Luke, and John, but that is not the usual way of ascribing authorship in antiquity. People were normally considered to have *composed* works, with far-reaching originality, even if they happened to credit the Muses, another deity, or the literary tradition itself, and even if the name of the author is a prestigious pseudonym. But the four "evangelists," or good-news-ists, are presented right away, by that "according to" wording in the Gospel titles, more as four *witnesses* to the same events, or as four *messengers* bringing different reports on these.

Their role in this is startlingly impersonal by comparison. Perhaps the most similar of the major fields of pagan literature, historiography and biography, saw authors regularly vouching for their own reliability: "I was there," or "I reported in this way, for these reasons," or just "These are the principles I bring to this task." (The comic writer Lucian, of the second century C.E., was so sick of these conventions that in the preface to his *True History* he boasts, in the conventional style, of writing pure lies out of empty-headed conceit.) Long stretches of the Hebrew Bible can seem rather detached, but Hebrew prophets and other scriptural authors and speakers are preoccupied by their qualifications to purvey divine messages, or perhaps this preoccupation was written into the text by others.

In contrast, with the exception of the four-verse introduction to Luke and the last two verses of John, the Gospels' writerly point of view is omniscient with a vengeance. In fact, as far as we know, none of the texts was even attributed to a specific writer until around the end of the second century—that is, about a century after the latest Gospel, John's, appeared: for all the time intervening, apparently, all four works could do without the normal clear signal of a controlling human "voice" in the background. Mark and Luke the persons are so obscure as to appear only in the titles of "their" Gospels.

Of course, eyewitness testimony, at whatever remove, was vital to the existence of the Gospels; strong oral traditions helped to form them. Two of the versions, "Matthew" and "John," carry names of Jesus' followers who appear (in flashes) as actors in the narrative; but claims that they were the actual authors are far-fetched, serving mainly to promote these texts as direct, if reverently passive, testimonies to Jesus' mission. Mark and Luke, particularly because of their association with the spread of proto-Christianity, are better candidates for having had styluses in hand. A John Mark is named in the New Testament Acts of the Apostles (covering about thirty years after Jesus' death) in connection to another original follower of Jesus, Simon or Peter. Luke, an associate of the early missionary Paul, was quite probably the author of the Gospel credited to him as well as of Acts. (The Pauline letters, or Epistles—some genuine, some pseudonymous—are discursive works that counterbalance in the New Testament the mainly narrative Gospels and Acts.)

In the Gospels' content, the contrast is even sharper. In these new works, there is really only one figure, and only one voice. Just to consider the realm of scripture, the Hebrew Bible contains a variety of compelling personalities, sometimes shown in intricate counterpoint to one another. But in the Gospels no one is essential but Jesus. (The name is a later form of Joshua, the Hebrew Bible hero of the conquest of Canaan.) Very nearly everyone else who speaks and moves in the texts does so only in relation to him and is defined by the degree of either fervor for or opposition to him. Until the crucifixion, he is largely above opinions and events, choosing purposes, companions, and destinations for no stated reason and performing a widely varying set of miracles with an odd mix of publicity and (mostly ignored) requests for secrecy, most of the time without the traditional prophetic crediting of God; the most frequent basis cited is that the beneficiary had faith in himself, Jesus. He enjoys hospitality without asking for it and eludes violence without effort. He appropriates even expensive conveyances—on several occasions a boat, and one day a beast that is probably a donkey in all four Gospels—without consequence.

He also hovers outside an author's responsibility, though he discourses very often. He can be almost whimsical in his assertions. He answers many questions analogically, cryptically, not at all, or with a joke or a scolding. He preaches about the fate of the world and of individuals through stories that sometimes baffle even his own followers, and he occasionally states that the obscurity is deliberate. What is clearly set out in one Gospel may be contradicted in another, or even in another passage of the same Gospel.

Judaism of course had its established modes of public discourse, but they appear to have been circumscribed by clear purposes. Jews learned from experts how to conduct their lives by the scriptures' precepts; in the early first century C.E., the Pharisee sect was active and influential in this domain. There were also intellectual debates and metaphysical tenets arising from the scriptures; the elite Sadducees seem to have been more at home here, but it was far from an exclusive magisterium within Judaism. Near at hand to Judea, the Jewish community in Egyptian Alexandria had long been enthusiasts for pagan literature and philosophy, and for syncretic innovation. For comfort and inspiration during these harrowing times for the Jews, there were visions of the end of the present world and the triumph of God's kingdom, a strain of thought called apocalyptic and associated particularly with the Essenes, who formed purist devotional communities to prepare themselves to face the final judgment. Jesus' words in the Gospels reflect influences from all over this religious world around him but never allow him to be pinned down. The composite Jesus can in fact appear ambivalent on a subject as important as the applicability of Jewish law: he tends to advocate for a more moralistic development of it, but also to denounce the religious authorities responsible for enforcement. If his own person is somehow an alternative for enforcement, then it is problematic that this person himself is so elusive.

As to this very elusiveness, a possible pagan contributor was the Cynic diatribe, which was a contrarian and countercultural performance (the rough ancient equivalent of stand-up comedy); popular Stoic and Epicurean discourse can also partake of the contrarian, and in this can sound a little like Jesus. In the Gospel of John, his rhetoric can on occasion sound positively Sophistic, with rapid one-upmanship on the verbal level. Who *is* this speaking?

But with a crash, Jesus' arrest, trial, flogging, and brutal execution break the impression of arrogance and mercurial impenetrability resembling God's. The resurrection restores the impression; in fact, the mystery is redoubled. This was the purpose all along—but why? Since he does not answer, there *is* no real answer—because the Gospels are not *about* Jesus; they *are* Jesus. A normal kind of explication is in himself or nowhere, so it is nowhere.

———

Behind the Gospels' challenging character are arcane origins and complex interrelationships, so that scholars who do not take the texts for granted are hard put to describe them generally—which would suggest the need for clearer criteria for translating them. The following is only an outline of the (rough) consensus description.

The first text was the Gospels of Mark, likely completed around 70 C.E., more than thirty years after Jesus' death. Mark might have been based mainly or only on oral narratives. It is also the shortest Gospel. It begins with Jesus' baptism as an adult, sets out a number of his miracles (mostly healings), gives a detailed and continuous account of the last few days of his life and some events immediately after his resurrection, and then offers two alternative concluding passages: neither looks decisively more authentic according to the manuscript evidence, so both are left in the standard edited Greek text. My translation of Mark, for historical reasons, comes first in this book, though it comes second, after Matthew, in the canonical arrangement of the New Testament.

The second Gospel to appear, probably after 80 but before 90 C.E., was Matthew. Like Mark, it deals at length with the Last Supper, the trial, the crucifixion, and the resurrection. It also includes not only many incidents from Mark, similarly worded, but material from a hypothetical collection of Jesus' sayings that modern scholars call Q (for *Quelle,* German for "source"). Matthew also contains the long "Sermon on the Mount," which in part affirms and in part disputes contemporary Jewish law, morality, and outlook toward the future. Matthew is the Gospel most concerned with Jewish religion and culture.

Matthew, unlike Mark, offers details on where Jesus came from. The book opens with a genealogy going back to Abraham through the male line—which is odd, as Joseph is, here and in the birth story or nativity that follows, plainly shown as only Jesus' publicly supposed father: the true father is God, through the "Holy Spirit" (traditional translation) at work in the young girl Mary. This nativity connects Jesus, who was known to contemporaries as a native of the village Nazareth in the remote region of Galilee, to the town not far from Jerusalem where David was born and grew up, Bethlehem; the Hebrew Bible (Micah 5:2) indicates that David's heir the Messiah is to come from Bethlehem. In Matthew, Jesus is born in Bethlehem to a couple living there, taken to Egypt to escape the jealous King Herod (a client ruler on behalf of the Romans), then taken to Nazareth to be safe from one of Herod's successors.

Luke, apparently later than Matthew, is most similar to that book. Luke's Gospel encompasses many shorter incidents found in Mark and Matthew and substantial Q material (some for a "Sermon on the Plain") but greatly expands the account of Jesus' origins. There is not only a genealogy—varying from Matthew's yet making the same point about the inheritance of David's kingdom—but also a story of John the Baptist's own divinely appointed birth, as extended background to the scene of Jesus' baptism shared by all four Gospels. In Luke, John is a relative of Jesus, and Mary makes a visit to John's pregnant mother during her own pregnancy. Trailing hymns in the style of Hebrew scriptural poetry celebrate God's providence. Jesus is now connected to Bethlehem by being born there during a journey Joseph and Mary make from Nazareth, where they live, to the town from which Joseph originated. Luke includes an incident when Jesus is twelve years old, part of the biographical tradition that expanded into the noncanonical (that is, not accepted by the church establishment) "Infancy Gospels," about Jesus' childhood, including the important Protoevangelium of James.

Luke seems to have a stronger connection than Mark and Matthew, the other two Synoptic ("Seen Together") Gospels that inhabit the same basic tradition, to an array of noncanonical Gospels, many of them serving the populous Gnostic ("Knowing") sector of early Christianity. The narrative problem that apparently worsened over time to incite more and more explanation in the Gnostic direction (as well as in other directions) was the contrast between Jesus' humble status and his mission among ordinary people on the one hand, and the astonishing events reported at his life's end on the other. The tendency over time was therefore to depict him more and more insistently as self-conscious in his true identity and power, and superior and withholding in his attitude—hence all the events could be shown to serve one momentous but secret plan, known best to the favored followers closest to him. The Gnostics tended to identify with these followers.

Among the four canonical Gospels, John evinces the strongest of such mystical impulses, and apparently the strongest links with Gnosticism. This text is generally considered to have been completed before 110 C.E. It is not Synoptic, because of the amount of unique material it contains, but it deals with the same historical conundrum in the same fundamental way, by distancing and heightening the person of Jesus—a process by then strikingly advanced from its known beginnings. In Mark, for example, though early in his mission Jesus is already a miracle worker, he is shown as unable to perform any miracle except a few healings among the people of his hometown—who have rather humiliatingly (and with impunity) rejected him (6:3–5). Mark shows signs that Jesus' own family was baffled and embarrassed by his calling. In John, Jesus' siblings or brothers actually urge him to travel to Jerusalem at the time of the Passover to gain a wider audience; after hanging back for a while, he goes in secret to avoid the religious leaders threatened by his existing fame (7:3–13).

In John, interest in Jesus' mundane life and his role in the Jewish nation's destiny greatly diminishes, no doubt in part because the cataclysmic destruction of the Jerusalem Temple (70 C.E.) was now at least a generation in the past. Judaism was remaking itself out of the ashes, and Christians were going their separate ways. On the evidence of John (and innumerable documents that followed), the new religion tended toward a much more superhuman Jesus, much less confined by the roles of preacher, healer, prophet of the kind known through the scriptures, and even kingly Messiah, God's anointed savior of his chosen people, the Jews.

John is an account deeply occupied with abstractions. There is no nativity, and little practical morality, but instead a great striving to frame the mystery of Jesus' existence and destiny symbolically and idealistically. Themes to move the reader's imagination in this direction are the rejection of spiritual distinctions between the sexes and among nationalities; the forgiveness of even criminal offenses; the love and duty between a father and son; trust and loyalty among friends; and sincerity and truth in thoughts and words. All of these are ideas in previous Gospels; in John, there is a fever pitch of exhortation to accept them, without argument or reservation, as shorthand for the inconceivable and the all-sufficient. The mystery therefore remains in the center of the frame.

The voice of John's Gospel is the most urgent one for reducing life's necessities—and the necessity for eternal life in God's presence—to the reliance on Jesus' being who and what he says he is, God's actual son, as finally certified by his resurrection and ascension to heaven. As I've indicated, all the Gospels have extensive and similar "Passions" (from a Latin word for "suffering")—that is, narratives of how the crucifixion came about and took place—along with scenes of its aftermath. In John, those events almost devour the story. The long sermon is given not to crowds of all comers about how to live, how to worship, and what to expect at the end of the world; instead, it is given at the Last Supper, and it is about the ineffable oneness of God, Jesus, and those who love him and each other unquestioningly. In the final scene, Jesus is with a few of his followers, first unrecognizable, then performing a miracle that, at least in its results, looks rather prankish, then redoubling the teasing, which merges with momentous if not very clear commands, rebukes, and warnings. What does it all mean? Don't ask the author, who merely avers that his testimony about "these things" is true.

—

The words of the Gospels themselves are well suited to this strange textual enterprise. Normal authorship and subject matter are replaced with a singular yet complexly presented mystery, while the language and style—though superficially plain and not literary—manifest an almost impenetrable set of interweavings.

The Gospels are in fact something of a linguistic chimera. A lingua franca covering much of the ancient Near East was Aramaic, a relative of Hebrew; this is apparently the language Jesus spoke. Words attributed to him in his death agony on the cross (Mark 15:34, Matthew 27:46) are Aramaic versions of a Psalm verse (22:1). He would have known such verses from an Aramaic targum, or paraphrase and interpretation of the Hebrew scriptures (and a version of them that at this period would likely have been oral only).

Yet, except for the rare Aramaic interpolations in their texts, all four canonical Gospels are written in Koinē Greek, a lingua franca in use over thousands of miles of the Roman Empire. But it is an open question how much Greek of any kind Jesus' own circle understood or used—perhaps not much. Nearly all the words attributed to them are thus in a language they may never have voluntarily uttered, belonging to a cosmopolitan civilization they may well have despised. Moreover, Jesus' story is told almost entirely in this language. Further, some clunky in-text notes (indicating, for example, that the Passover is a Jewish festival) suggest that many of the Gospels' original multiethnic readers needed a primer on the religion Jesus belonged to.

It is not that Koinē Greek itself didn't have some Jewish background—and foreground. It was actually the language of the Septuagint, the Greek translation of the Hebrew Bible that was the late-antique Jewish Diaspora's basis for worship and religious study possibly until well into the second century C.E.; the Septuagint is imitated, alluded to, and quoted throughout the Gospels. It is through the Septuagint that Semitic scriptural modes of expression keep breaking through in the basically Indo-European Gospels: "it happened that" (the King James's "it came to pass"), repetitive and pleonastic verbal structures used for emphasis (I have tried to represent these instead of gliding over them, which is why I write, for example, "stunned almost beyond their capacity to be stunned" at Mark 5:42), and in general a refrain-like syntax seemingly more concerned with narrative formulae than with the representation of events.

But the Septuagint, the first major translation project in the West that is still extant, is hardly a precise or nuanced rendering of Classical Hebrew. The Gospels, themselves an awkward rendering of all their linguistic and cultural sources, cite and quote the awkward Septuagint translation with redoubled awkwardness, and the results can set the teeth on edge. The authors not only take verses far out of context but also sometimes seem to be merely guessing at the verses' original content.

Yet—again—there is nothing daunting about the Gospels' text in its basic components, on the surface. The text is even used in modern classrooms as an introduction to ancient Greek; as in a Dick and Jane reader, easy language and a set of simple stories are presented at the same time. The Gospels' short sentences, limited vocabulary, and pared-down grammatical structures were well suited to the limited schooling of the first, less advantaged waves of converts to the Jesus movement around the Mediterranean. Exposed to a passage or two at a time—probably all that poor working people had a chance for—the Gospels' first readers and hearers would likely have intuited no problem in the choices made by the new sect's leadership of what to present and how to interpret the whole—as far as anyone perceived a whole, that is: for some time, the Gospels circulated separately. The stage was thus set in the first century C.E. for the fragmentary, liturgical, and heavy-handed treatment of the Gospels in the long term.

But as I have laid out, the Gospels are hardly simple below their surface. They are ruggedly composed, defensively hermetic, yet stumbling over themselves in their ambition. These challenges would have been daunting enough. When, quite early, the administrators of the texts (that is, the solidifying church hierarchy) began to put more space between themselves and the audiences of the texts, the texts began to veer out of control, like any authoritarian project.

Among the further unstable loads they acquired over the centuries were questionable translations (like "the Word," whereas *logos* nowhere in past or contemporary ancient literature means a single vocable as such) and interpretations (like "Holy Trinity," a theological construct based on a few enigmatic New Testament verses). And not only were large, fascinating portions of them ignored because they did not serve—or because they actually opposed—the needs and wants of powerful institutions; the text itself was also comprehensively scrambled when men at great cultural and linguistic distances from its origins copied by hand only one another's handwritten copies. By far the most manuscripts to survive come from the late medieval period, when even the means to picture antiquity, except through other poorly understood texts, were gone, and doctrines and worship practices supporting an essentially feudal church urged anachronistic changes to scripture as it was being reproduced. In Western Europe, these changes were made on the basis of a Latin and not a Greek Bible—that is, at one long extra step from the original writings.

Modern papyrology, the study of surviving ancient paper documents (much rarer than later vellum, or animal-skin, manuscripts as testimonies to literary tradition), allows for fragmentary glimpses back toward the original Gospels texts. There are also early Gospels surviving in Coptic (late Egyptian), Syriac, and other languages of the Near East. Inscriptions and other archaeological finds can also be brought to bear. But a diversity of older evidence hardly unites to produce a buffed-up, clean, certain version of the text.

The critical apparatus of a properly edited ancient text in the original language is a listing, at the bottom of each page of the modern book, of what has been done to restore the text to something the authors at least could have written. But included in the apparatus are pleas of what philologists call *loci desperati*, "places without hope," or indefensible content left in because no credible alternative could be either found in any manuscript or posited. In the Gospel of John, the apparatus often takes up a third of a page, sometimes half—and of course it omits all the obvious mistakes, the innumerable throwaway absurdities: the Gospels cannot, for example, refer to customs that did not exist before monasticism. The edition shows only the furthest refinement so far of all the excavated gold, but it still sometimes leaves the translator stuck with nothing coherent to render in the target language.

The problems that the Gospels pose in these circumstances can hardly be overstated. It would be one thing if the books were trivial, or generally regarded as fantastical or cranky. But their outsized importance and prestige did as much to confirm their original and added strangeness as to encourage rational interpretation and correction.

In fact, in the phalanx of intellectual history, these books were from the start pushed hard toward ultimate, self-defining, all-encompassing meaning, and they became a basis for projects as big and wicked as the Crusades, and as startlingly decent as campaigns for humanitarian relief; meanwhile, and not coincidentally, they became almost unreadable as mere writing.

The Gospels were the first of the truly power-hungry Truth writings; epics of divinely directed national destiny like Vergil's *Aeneid* and the Hebrew Bible were humbler, more specific, more confined in their audiences and their programs. A collection like the Gospels could arise only after the start of the essentially modern world, when the apparatus of material power had become so huge, so well organized, so distant, and so inexorable that nothing but a sweeping assault of words against it was acceptable to the rage, not of the poorest and weakest and most ignorant, but of those who at least had words at their command. Like *Das Kapital* and the works of Nietzsche, the Gospels are a poetry of Truth in which the assertions take over the poetry and the sense as well, making the text suitable as a basis for force, reform, or both. But even Nietzsche is friendlier to ordinary engagement and interpretation.

Here is just one example of what the Gospels (and their institutional proponents) ask us to take without any synthetic analysis or even synthetic awareness, because the passages are usually presented in isolation from one another, from the narratives in which they are embedded, and from basic historical data. All four Gospels tell of a slave's having his ear sliced off—presumably not by someone in the high priest's retinue to which the slave belongs, or by someone in the attendant mob—during

Jesus' arrest. In Mark (14:47), the mutilation is merely cited. In later Gospels, there are explanations—sometimes radiating far into the surrounding story—for how one of Jesus' followers (who were all native civilians) came to be wearing a sword, impossible to conceal, in a land under foreign military occupation. Mitigations are also cited: in Luke the disciples are actually shown to ask permission to use their swords, and Jesus is shown not only to deplore the assault but also to heal the ear (22:49 and 51); in John, the victim has a name, Malchus (18:10), as if he were a willing witness to events and not an obscure and pathetic victim of them. During the Gospels' very composition, a great deal of energy apparently went toward such repair work on the foundations of the platform for the metaphysical claims: for example, any fissures indicating that someone other than Jesus got hurt must be cemented up. The edifice as a whole seems designed to be unspeakably untouchable, a looming demonstration of how many people made it that way, and the determination with which they acted. In itself, in its own structures (to say nothing of the guardians around it), the text dares you to touch it.

Such writing binds itself not to describing either reality or what is imagined, but instead to insisting that reality has been reshaped entirely and that the words must somehow tag along, whether absurdities or sublime moral and spiritual formulations result. And the inconsistencies do not hide, but brazen it out, as if defying readers to challenge them. It is in a way an appealing defiance; whole classes of previously disregarded people, represented by generations of authors oral and literate, anonymous and pseudonymous, are taking the world into their hands through language. But it is a disturbing defiance nevertheless, as if the tract and the revolution are chaotically coming into being at the same time.

In the face of all this, I have done what I can to reconstitute the Gospels as *books*—to be read, understood, interrogated, enjoyed, and debated *as they are*. Fundamentally, I make for this translation the plea I have made for all my others: I love significant writing, and I try to love it for the best, which means calling every word as I see it, after the requisite research. How can anyone claim to love something—be it a book, a child, a country, a faith, or anything else important—that in its essence relies on her honesty, and yet try to keep that thing outside the reach of reality? This is particularly important for translating scripture. Reality is what God is, if there is a God.

This principle is in fact related to the ancient, basic image and analogy of the Greek philosophical term *logos* (again, badly translated as "the Word"): the lexicons point me toward the idea of a mathematical accounting that can be checked against real objects and events and must come right in the end. The Hebrew prophets are eloquent and touching in showing God as the enforcer of reality, sometimes with a vengeance. It seems to me that the best role for scripture is to induce us to think more clearly about what language actually represents—with descriptions (or mere assertions) of "truth," "service," "repentance," "sacrifice," "evil"—so that we can think more clearly about what we do in the world and avoid that vengeance. I hope that American Christians in particular find my fresh cast of the Gospels' language helpful for this purpose.

—

As for methodology, at least I knew from the start that, for a more objective translation, the Gospels' original first-century C.E. Greek texts—or the best restoration of these texts, in the Nestle-Aland edition of the New Testament—needed to be extricated to the degree possible from everything that would have bewildered the authors and the early audiences. But I immediately ran into a difficulty: the shortage of vital beliefs and experiences I could be confident those people would have affirmed.

It's clear that they didn't even think of "the way things are" (let alone have a name for it, "Christianity"), but the reverse: they thought that all conventional assumptions should be adjusted or replaced. Great jolts were thus given to the meanings of words, so that a translator has constantly to aim at moving targets. The following is just a summary of the inherent but fluid contradictions that dominated the Gospels before the texts were even finalized. And here I've come to the core of the unachievable for a Gospels translator: people were, on the evidence, questioning, positing, and affirming wildly at almost the same moments. How can *that* contribute to a readable modern English version, in the mood of the original but at least comprehensible to our (officially) rationalist culture?

Here, in any case, is my impression of the convulsions in popular didacticism and belief that did the most to shape the Gospels. Because Jesus' known provincial origin, unremarkable family, and humiliating trial and death did not at all accord with his ultimate significance as it was insistently reported, it became more plausible that certain predictions of the world's end, with known powers turned upside down, were true—though the heavenly warfare, the salutary natural disasters, and the other divine interventions pictured in apocalyptic literature had almost nothing in common with events like the crucifixion and the resurrection. It appeared, then, that a brand-new and yet somehow authoritative sense had to be made of these events, even if it meant turning language upside down as well.

In Judea, the main fountainhead of authority was the Hebrew Bible (though it was not yet even in the final stage of canonization). Certain passages in it could, at a stretch, be made to explain how God's providence played out in this impressive new instance. The providence of the single, all-powerful God was supposed to play out with perfect if not perfectly comprehensible justice; traditional Jewish piety could not imagine anything else—but traditional Jewish piety was now going to be stressed to the breaking point and beyond.

The biblical book of the prophet Isaiah—actually the work of at least three authors responding to major Judean military and political crises—was already a beloved resource for those grappling more than half a millennium later with what Greek and then Roman hegemony had meant for Judaism. By turns a great poem of the natural as opposed to the built-up and institutional world, a cry for equality and fairness, an indictment of the establishment's folly and selfishness, and a fervent testimony to God's justice and mercy, Isaiah suggested why an oppressed man should become the saving leader. "We need the opposite of the powerful operators who got us into this" is in fact an intuitive sentiment at a time of national catastrophe. Isaiah even contains passages about a "suffering servant" (42:1–4, 49:1–6, 50:4–7, and 52:13–53:12)—which seems to have meant Israel itself, victimized by more powerful nations around it but chosen by God for a special role in the world. In Isaiah and other Hebrew prophets, however, validation of the underclass and the middling classes, as people, tends to be noblesse oblige, and generalizing. In the Gospels, which quote Isaiah often but usually askance, the exaltation of the lowly individual becomes quite literal, and has a special application to Jesus: this downtrodden nobody is the one we've been waiting for—it's *him,* exactly *because* he's nobody. The Gospels quote other prophets in the same vein.

Also helpful for making sense of Jesus were, paradoxically, certain linguistic barriers. A Hebrew and Aramaic idiom, "son of mankind" (basically "human being," though it was eventually to yield that portentous English phrase "Son of Man"), was replicated in Greek in connection to Jesus as his story spread. The phrase probably sounded rather peculiar to anyone—that is, to practically the whole Roman Empire—unfamiliar with the languages of Jews in their homeland. The Diaspora itself had been using the Greek Septuagint Bible translation for worship and study for many generations, but "son of mankind," rendered (more or less) literally in that work, is hardly natural Greek phrasing and so may have remained one of those wordings in sacred literature that sit waiting for an explanation in a new direction.

Through any version of scripture the phrase "son of mankind" could be linked to the biblical Book of Daniel, which contains the only substantial concentration of apocalyptic writing in what Christians call the Old Testament. In Daniel 7:13–14, the prophet has a vision of someone "like the son of mankind" coming on clouds to reign everlastingly over all peoples, not just the Jews. Here was fundamental and authoritative testimony for how Jesus could, through being a person, be much more than a person.

Daniel does not indicate here whom he is writing about, but the man is widely identified elsewhere as the Messiah or "Anointed One." (The Greek translation is *Christos,* the origin of the English word "Christ.") The Messiah was to be the successor of God's chosen ruler, King David, who had presided over a powerful and united kingdom and passed it intact to his son Solomon, the builder of the First Temple.

This was stinging history to Jews enduring Roman occupation in their homeland, whose only taste of anything approaching both unity and independence within the past eight or nine centuries had been under the recent, self-destructive Maccabean dynasty. The Dead Sea Scrolls, a cache of Jewish literature discovered in the mid-twentieth century, contains messianic passages indicating that the Jewish nation's glory will be restored through a preeminent kingly or priestly figure. But particularly interesting in the Dead Sea Scrolls, as far as the Gospels are concerned, is the so-called Messianic Apocalypse, which pictures a healer, liberator, bringer of good news to the poor, and raiser of the dead; these elements are not original, but the combination of them makes for a striking similarity to Jesus as portrayed in the Gospels: someone remarkable not so much for the position he inherits and holds, but for the comprehensively benevolent and powerful things he does; he might be seen as a sort of apotheosis of the common man.

By such routes, Jesus' identification in the Gospel accounts as "the son of mankind" could be the ultimate dual coding. It could mean the obvious, that this was a person—he wouldn't even necessarily stand out; it could also mean that this was the sovereign leader of the Jews and, in that role, the savior of the world. The phrase, in the context of the Gospels, has so much sonority, so much special weight, that I write "son of mankind" instead of "son of a human being," which was my initial choice. (In addition, the change helped me navigate the nightmare range of *anthrōpos,* "human being" in Greek: it can—and in the Gospels does—mean anyone from Jesus, a human being in an indescribably elevated sense, to a "person," a "guy," or a "you there." Pilate uses it with pitying contempt of Jesus: "Look at this guy," *not* "Behold the man!")

The extreme flexibility, and frequent vagueness, of the Hebrew and Aramaic words for "son" (sometimes "son of" looks like a mere expansion or intensification of "of") allowed another important interpretive journey. "Son of God" had long meant a special servant of God; it was probably never meant literally, at least never during the historical period:* even the greatest kings and prophets and miracle workers in the Hebrew Bible are shown as strictly human. But with the help of the translated Greek phrase used among followers of Jesus with Diaspora or pagan backgrounds, "son of God" came to mean a single human offspring of the omnipotent and omnipresent deity. Children of divinities were staples of pagan mythology and hero cult, and the Roman emperor himself was styled "son of god" and worshipped accordingly, so commonsensical and religious outrage must have been lulled in many minds when it came to similar claims about Jesus—but the Jewish establishment, especially in and around Jerusalem, plainly thought that all such claims were blasphemy.

The clash between Jewish and early Christian thought on this score was therefore a sort of cosmological drama, the intellectual version of the apocalyptic contest between incompatible

---

* In Genesis 6:1–5, a passage likely influenced by foreign mythology, "the sons of God" are male creatures who mate with "the daughters of men" to produce heroic warriors before Noah's flood. But the verses apparently never disrupted Jewish monotheism.

worlds. In the Gospels, again, the conflict saw the stretching of traditional language past the breaking point. What was the result really like?

To keep my balance in the face of this question, I had to resist evaluating the later historical, social, and intellectual spectacles enacted around the Bible—though my Quaker predecessors have been players in them. I had to try to be just a translator, concentrating on the texts as messages from the authors to the earliest readers. This is in no way to reject sectarian uses of the New Testament, but merely to confess that I have no hope of contributing to them. Anyone who asks me about ritual or theology—the latter word, by the way, did not exist until many generations after the latest Gospel—will find me even more ignorant than most Quakers. I am not equipped to deal with any later abstractions, rationalizations, or syntheses; I can only try to communicate in English what is in the ancient texts.

—

In general, I have had to be more blunt and literal than I would have liked. Various concessions to modern accessibility were of course essential. As noted above, I use the word "Gospels," and not a direct translation of the Greek word for "good news," in my book title and my exposition. I use the conventional system of numbering verses and chapters, though it was not instituted in full until the sixteenth century; without these numbers, it would be hard to compare my translation with others', which would be untransparent and very irritating to readers.

But nearly all my proper names are transliterations of the names as they appear in the Greek text. What we are used to seeing in English translations as "James," for example, appears in the Greek as Iakōbos, so I write Iakōbos. Jesus is Iēsous; the letter J was a Renaissance invention. Jerusalem is sometimes Hierosoluma and sometimes Ierousalēm. The Greek forms of words are not always consistent, even within a given episode; Mary is either Maria or Mariam: one is more like a Greek name, the other closer to the common Aramaic women's name. But nothing could be precisely what was heard in Judea, in a different language family and represented by a different alphabet. I feel that the halfway nature of the names in Greek is itself a good reminder that the text was, even in its rudiments, a squinting struggle to see Jesus' world. But I don't carry this original phonology into my own discussions and explanations; again, that would be an annoyance. A list of these new spellings, keyed to the standard ones in English Bibles, follows the Glossary below and has its own introductory note.

The edited Greek text itself contains special markers of editorial process and judgment where the issues are worth noting—and this means virtually everywhere. I have decided to include only square brackets that are placed around words of questionable authenticity (and I include the brackets only when there is a direct enough relationship between the Greek and English words to make such inclusion practical). My reasoning is threefold. First, it seemed wrong to follow all the Bible translations I know and not include any of the markers. My retained brackets are a periodic reminder that the Greek text I use—the best text available—*is* an artifact of modern scholarship, not (like an unearthed mosaic, for example) the real, original thing. Second, doubt about authenticity is among the most important reactions that an editor signals. Third, these are the least distracting and puzzling of the various markers; it is common knowledge that square brackets mean weaker authority for the words they enclose.

I've also kept to practices of capitalization as I see them in the Nestle-Aland edition of the Greek text. "Temple" is not a capitalized word there; neither is "God" or "Lord"; neither is the word for Passover, usually. Sometimes scholarly opinion diverges as to whether a Greek word should be capitalized; I follow Nestle-Aland rather than the lexicons.

I mean no offense; and in my discussions, I do follow the English conventions. But I shrink from obscuring what I might call a "lowercase understanding" of certain terms in ancient minds, particularly when the terms are common and critical. The word *theos* for "god" tended to be generic in Greek; the Jewish deity was not sharply distinguished through the use of this particular word from a multitude of ordinary pagan male deities, or from any conception outside Judaism of a singular or supreme deity. Granted, in the New Testament, it is usually "the god," with the definite article, but pagans were capable of referring to "the god" too. Also granted, both the Gospels and the Septuagint translation of Jewish scripture *allude* to the Hebrew proper name for God, Yahweh, representing it by the Greek word *kurios,* or "lord," in parallel to the Hebrew *adonai,* for "my lord," which was (and still is) substituted, in reading aloud, for the unutterable "Yahweh." But the sense of a proper name in either *theos* or *kurios,* a sense that would need to be borne out by capitalization, was apparently not discernible to the modern editors of the Greek text, who did go as far as to capitalize *christos* in instances when they judged it to be part of Jesus' name (and I follow their usage there). I trust these editors to show what the authors most likely meant, and what the earliest audiences thought they were reading and hearing, much more than I trust later customs for presenting scripture.

When a Gospel author merely transliterates a Hebrew or Aramaic word, I do the same, and if that word isn't a capitalized name, I place it in italics. This would have been, after all, a foreign word, unfamiliar to many contemporary readers—perhaps a little strange to the author himself. The word used for Passover, for example, is *pascha,* which I retain.

I have tried to keep the pages as directly communicative and uncluttered as possible. The original physical form of the Gospels was a set of papyrus rolls with only the text on them. Of course, a modern translation can't be that self-contained and self-explanatory, but it is easy for readers to access maps, specialized indexes, appendixes, and so on elsewhere if they want them; such guidance tends to all be in one nearby volume, a modern Bible—not to mention scholarly resources on the Internet. But I hope readers will pursue my translation almost without pausing, which is what a scroll invited: you would unwind it at one side while you wound it back up at the other, like a roll of film. As with a film, it was a chore to hop around between different parts, and much more natural to have a continuous experience—though, as I've written above, few members of the early Jesus movement would have had opportunities to take in an entire scroll.

Particularly noxious to a vivid experience of the Gospels is constant reference to the "harmony" (and lack of it) of the four texts, that plague of scholarly biblical footnotes. The Gospels—the first three most of all—tend to share episodes, and the variations in detail can be interesting. But for my purposes here, I need a special reason—something that will enliven understanding of the whole work—to go into a commonality or contrast that is mapped anyway in innumerable charts online and in print for anyone who wants to make such a detour.

The above are mere matters of presentation, the easiest part of calling it as I see it. The heart, and the trick, of any ancient literary work is the nexus of content and style. A translator must get a plausible sense not only of what was performed, but how, as the how was usually integral to the what. In translations of the pagan Greek and Roman Classics, the nexus has, as a rule, been ignored. In New Testament translation, it's worse: the self-expressive text has fallen under the muffling, alien weight of later Christian institutions and had the life nearly smothered out of it.

But even when I have applied the scholarly tools I have, levered up this bulk a little, and let the text breathe easier and start to speak for itself, it does not readily get with the translation program: it speaks to itself and not to me; there is no author in his familiar role, reaching out to me across the centuries and using all his training and ingenuity. The Gospels are an inward-looking, self-confirming set of writings, containing some elements of conventional rhetoric and poetics but not constructed to make a logical or aesthetic case for themselves; the case *is* Jesus, so the words don't stoop to argue or entice with any great effort, as if readers were supposed to have the choice to yawn or say "What?" or turn up their noses in the manner of an ordinary audience.

In the Gospels, densely used modes of expression, such as the words for saying and answering and coming and going, are tedious. Many speeches are flat rather than colloquial. The influence of the Septuagint translation of the Hebrew Bible can pull the language toward dutifulness and dullness.

A good example is the word that I render as the command "Look" or "See"—the old "Behold." It is so frequent, and so frequently stilted-sounding, that many translators drop most instances. The Greek is an imperative (in a few simple forms) of the commonest verb for seeing. But its ancestor is the Hebrew Bible's demonstrative particle *hinneh*, used to great effect for turns in a story and for revelatory perception, including of miraculous signs. (See Matthew 1:23, quoting Isaiah 7:14.) *Hinneh* is never an impatient or finger-pointing word, yet the abrupt command to see is used in its place in the Septuagint and the Gospels because Greek has no such word as *hinneh*—nor does English, for that matter. But there seems to be no choice except to continue the crude substitution. I am not in the business of correcting the Gospel authors in their role as translators.

Even as a literary or rhetorical project, such correction would be wrongheaded. Naturally in the Gospels exposition, which goes in its own direction away from the character and purposes of the Hebrew Bible, the Greek command to "look" takes on new uses. When Jesus introduces a story, analogy, or precept this way, he sounds much more condescending or exasperated than, say, a Hebrew Bible prophet does in interlacing his poetic sermon with *hinneh*. But this difference suits who Jesus is. He is a "teacher," but often a short-tempered, contemptuous, and withholding one—not a prophet with a passion to persuade. Moreover, Jesus' "students" seem to deserve this treatment, as they tend to be lazy, incurious, and distractible. The motif of failed instruction is integral to this work of literature; it is thematic. Jesus, who *is* the point, is above having to explain himself; he is above everything, and certainly not accountable to feeble human language. And his students are so far below him that their demands for answers verge on impious rebellion.

But I object strongly to characterizations of the Gospels as crude and lacking in charm and nuance. Both "ordinary" and exquisitely educated people have long delighted in the Gospel texts, the latter making vigorous excuses for their obvious aesthetic faults. The works, from their beginnings to their ends, somehow *work*—which is all the more remarkable in that there are four distinct authors telling the same story. These authors deserve the utmost effort to represent them to the best effect. If it seems that I have cherry-picked, with repetitious translations of words like "said" and "answered" (some translators introduce a range of variations along the lines of "remarked" and "retorted") on the one hand, and on the other hand whimsical word choices to represent slang and wordplay, I can only plead that I am a literary translator, following rhetorical performance where I see it, but not creating my own on no textual basis. I have tried hard not to impose modern standards and styles on the Gospels, but to have respect for their original tones and shapes.

In any event, I have found much more in the way of jokes, color, point, and cohesion in the Greek than in their standard English translations. Here is an example of how insensitive rendering can distort a whole episode: In standard English Bibles, Jesus seems to give a harsh scolding to a non-Jewish woman who seeks a healing miracle for her child (Matthew 15:22–28, Mark 7:24–30). But in the Greek he calls non-Jews not dogs (*kunes*), a straightforward insult, but the rare and comical "little doggies" (*kunaria*). She replies with the same word, citing the animals' tolerated scrounging under the table, a comic image in ancient pagan literature. Her implication is that, yes, dogs don't belong *at* the table, but they get their share because there's plenty to go around. Since the "eschatological banquet" of God's ultimate providence is an endless, joyful meal, why would there be no room for dogs under heaven's table? Jesus instantly concedes that the woman has effected her daughter's recovery "through what you said . . ." He may be actually congratulating her on her wit.

As usual in the Gospels, however, the tone and the point depend on a single word, not on the thoroughgoing formal structures, interwoven in the narrative or discourse, that are the norm for other ancient literature. This contrast made it clear to me what kind of research is most essential for a better translation of the Gospels: scouring lexicons and electronic databases of ancient literature. In this way, I was able to move away from one-word translations that seemed to exist only because they were traditional, such as "disciple" for the Greek word *mathētēs* (which means "student") and "angel" for the Greek word *aggelos* (which means "messenger").

But such fixes were relatively easy. Since the ancient Greek literary vocabulary was tiny yet multivalent, a bigger challenge for me was to decide which of two (or three, or seven) meanings a particular word had in a particular context, and to find an English word to approximate that meaning. Standard Bible translations tend to render an important Greek word the same way many times, with little or no attention to fit.

Sometimes the difference made by the correct translation of a single word can be shattering. In the famous passage in John, Chapter 3, about being "born again" into eternal life, the meanings "again" and "from above" (which here implies "from heaven") are equally valid for the Greek word *anōthen*. Jesus is teasing the quizzical Nicodemus with a pun, which is itself a lesson. Nicodemus never does understand what Jesus is saying about salvation; nor, apparently, is he meant to; nor, actually, can I. Through the inquirer's obtuseness and Jesus' scolding, the reader also is warned not to construe divine purposes as "Do this, get that"; everyone must simply trust Jesus. This is one place where a single rendering of a word is not adequate to the sense, so I write "born again, taking it straight from the top."

Word choices relevant to one or two passages, as in this case, are explained in footnotes. But to avoid repetitive footnotes to justify repeated new interpretations, I have included a glossary below; the entry words are the vocabulary of standard English Bibles, for easy reference.

I need, however, to reach out to those who will raise cogent objections to my more literalist word choices, among which are "the side with the blessed name" and "the better side," euphemisms for the ill-omened left. It may be said that even if the historical basis of a word was clear to the ancients, they still would not have normally been conscious of that basis when using the word. I don't, after all, picture myself physically standing under something when I say I understand it.

But I would argue that the ancients were far more self-conscious users of language than we are; wordplay (including play on etymologies and perceived etymologies) was far more common. Moreover, I think that estranging translation can be vitally informative. The ancients didn't mean what we mean by "left" and "right": for them—at least in literature—these weren't directions to be used for getting around, but an important part of the fearsome inward map of the universe: a person might believe he was to live or die according to the side of the sky on which a bird appeared. If I merely wrote "left" and "right" in translating a monumental set of their religious documents, I would not be showing as close as possible an approximation of their thought.

Moreover, as I've described them above, the Gospels must have been strange, awkward documents to the Empire-wide mass of their early audience, most of whom had extensive Greco-Roman acculturation if not actual pagan backgrounds. They would not have blinked at a euphemism for "left"—but what about when it was part of two provincial young men's request to sit on the right and left sides of a presiding, resurrected deity in heaven? Rather startling vocabulary in English is not just appropriate to give *us* a closer sense of the Gospels' different world. It isn't time alone that has made this world different, but also geography, ethnicity, language, politics, religion, and culture *from the start*. It is hard for me to imagine people—similar to any of the people I "know" from ancient literature and history—to whom the Gospels' thought and atmosphere would not have been somewhat challenging.

With all this in mind, I have often turned to a word's basic imagery as a defense against anachronism, obfuscation, and lethargy, which drain communications of their primordial electricity. Naturally it is hard—especially in such stark and peculiar texts as the Gospels—to know where a particular word, used a particular way, is in the course of its evolution; imagery never stops changing over time, it branches out, goes abstract, branches in its abstraction. But often I have felt compelled to make a bold choice.

A Discursive Glossary
of Unfamiliar Word
Choices in English

ADULTERY: I have sought a term to represent the horror that adultery (most of the time defined by the old gender double standard) provoked in the ancient world. Seducing another man's wife was a grave threat to his whole dependent family, as well as a terrible humiliation for him. "Cheat" isn't adequate, but it's better than "commit adultery." "Violate marriage" is my usual choice.

AMEN: Meaning "truly," this Hebrew-derived word in the Gospels does not conclude prayers, as in modern practice, but functions as Jesus' own formulaic assurance of truth, separate from citations of *alētheia,* truth according to the Greek term. I have italicized and transliterated to *amēn* to emphasize the difference.

ANGEL: This English word comes from the ordinary Greek word for "messenger" or "announcer," *aggelos* (pronounced "angelos," with a hard *g*), which is used throughout Greek scripture, including in the Septuagint, for heavenly functionaries who mediate God's will to mortals. I write "messenger" in all cases for this important word, to avoid confusion, even when these beings behave like guards or soldiers.

APOSTLE: The Greek text has *apostolos,* meaning an official agent or messenger. The word, sometimes used in the Septuagint for a messenger from God, was adopted in the Gospels and

Epistles to describe a human agent of the Jesus movement. "Envoy" is my choice, as it seems broadest.

APPEAR: A single Greek verb means both "to be evident" and "to shine." This makes sense when I think of the English "glaringly obvious"; and the thematic suitability to the Gospels is almost self-explanatory: light is both a sign of divine glory and a requirement for seeing anything. Slightly more complex translations than usual can cover these concepts where appropriate.

BEELZEBUB: *See* DEVIL.

BEGET: In the important genealogy of Jesus at the beginning of Matthew, I forgo the old "beget" in favor of the verb "father." The word imitated in Greek from the Hebrew Bible (through the Greek Septuagint as intermediary) means "cause to be born," which is more or less the sense: the exercise of male authority in creating a child.

BEGINNING: This is a tricky term when it is *archē*, which can indicate "firstness" in the sense of authority and governing leadership. At the opening of John's Gospel, for instance, the stately word "inauguration" (echoing similar connotations of a Hebrew word in Genesis 1) seems warranted.

BELIEVE, BELIEF (*see also* FAITH): The modern words as used in the popular media can be rather shallow, and have some connotations of magic. They also suggest mere belief in the existence of divinity, which had very little to do with the ancient experience of religion. There are passages in which a mere affirmation of divine reality seems to be sought, but elsewhere the word "trust" usually seems more appropriate.

BIRTH, GIVE/BE BORN: The relevant Greek verbs are complex, and one of them is ambiguous. *Gennaō* concentrates on the biology of birth. *Tiktō* shares with agriculture the idea of production and is concerned with obtaining heirs and prolonging a family, clan, nation, or whole chosen people. But *ginomai* means "be," "become," and "come into being," including "be born," an ambiguity sometimes wittily exploited.

BLESSED: The English adjective "blessed" represents one Greek adjective, *eulogētos* (literally "well spoken of"), acceptably well (that is, no better option has appeared) but another, *makarios* (basically, "lucky," "favored," or "happy"), relatively poorly; contextualized choices, usually "happy," have to serve there.

BOW DOWN: *Proskuneō* is not a modern European bow from the waist but an ancient Near East–style grovel, with full prostration or huddling at or grasping the feet of the object of supplication. Likely a word for "kiss," as part of the verb, comes from kissing feet or the ground, *proskuneō* is often translated as "worship," but that does not always seem vivid enough. Translations can properly concentrate on the suppliant's physical position.

BROTHER: This grammatically masculine word—especially in the plural—makes no necessary gender distinction. If it was important to class a sibling's—or a metaphorical sibling's—gender as female, a Greek Bible author used the feminine form of the word. But I avoid "siblings," because it sounds clinical, and "brothers and sisters" because women in Judea did not normally have public voices or any overt public presence.

CARPENTER: There is no reason to construe Joseph's profession so specifically. *Tektōn* means simply "skilled workman"; I choose "builder" merely because of the likelihood that Jesus' family were among local artisans employed in rebuilding the new city of Sepphoris, close to Nazareth.

CAUSE TO SIN: *See* STUMBLING BLOCK.

CHARITY: Older English translations may use this word where the Greek indicates either "love" or "mercy gift" (pious Jews' relief of the very poor). The connotations of "charity" in modern English tend to be either pejorative or institutional, so I don't think the word serves well in a Gospels translation.

CHILD: My translation tries to distinguish among different Greek words for children when they are narratively or thematically important. A *pais* (variantly masculine or feminine) can be either a boy or a girl, but the word can also refer to a slave, apparently even an adult one. *Paidion* is the neuter diminutive of *pais* and means a child too young for its gender to be of immediate importance. *Paidarion* is a slangy diminutive, used in Greek comedy, which I render as "kid." A third neuter word for child, *teknon* ("offspring"—but I don't use this word where it sounds weird), is visibly related to a word for giving birth *productively;* this word often refers to the Jews, the children of Israel and sharers of the inherited covenant.

CHRIST: This is from the Greek word *christos*—which itself translates the Hebrew word that yields our "Messiah"—and means not so much "anointed" as "smeared": the motion of rubbing on the precious holy oil of kingship is what jumps out of the original languages and texts. But "smeared" or "rubbed" are not dignified enough for the context, so "anointed" is my choice throughout.

CHURCH: The term is used far more frequently in the Epistles than in the Gospels, but in either case the modern word is wildly inappropriate for the small groups of Jesus' followers that met mainly in private homes starting a few years after his death. I write "assembly," which is already widely accepted among biblical scholars.

COMMAND (*see also* OBEY): A number of Greek expressions have widely different tones and implications—from "instruct" to "warn" to "give a [military] order." I have tried to represent both the contextual and lexicographical nuances.

CONFESS: The Greek verb is *homologeō*—literally, "I say something of the same kind"; the community of meanings covers interpersonal, forensic, and spiritual spheres and includes agreement, admission, assertion, praise, thanks, and promise. I try to cover this whole range appropriately, but sometimes the context is skimpy.

COVENANT: This is from a Greek word (*diathēkē*) commonly used in the Septuagint for the formal bond between God and the Jewish people, but the common English translation of the word is problematic. "Covenant" suggests an equal accord between God and humankind, but *diathēkē*'s primary meaning was the legal disposition of an inheritance. (See Galatians 3:15–19 for this explicit analogy.) I hope my "dispensation" addresses this distinction.

CREATION (*see also* **WORLD**): *Ktisis* is, basically, authoritative founding and building, as of a colony. Through this word choice, the Septuagint Greek translation of the Hebrew Bible obviously responded to the building imagery in Genesis 1, where God sets a barrier between an upper and lower body of water in the universe and erects a vault in the sky. I indicate that God "founded and built" the world.

CROSS, CRUCIFY, CRUCIFIXION: The cross was the perpendicular joining of two execution stakes, and the English word euphemistically emphasizes the geometry: a cross could also be an abstract cross drawn on paper. The Greeks used their word for "stake," and this carried the imagery of what was done with it, as our "stake" carries images of burning and impaling. "Hang on the stakes" for "crucify" is my habitual usage.

CROWD: Every lexicon acknowledges that *ochlos* can be a "mob" as well as any other large gathering for any purpose. On the other hand, *plēthos,* which in Classical contexts is also friendly to the construction "mob," can in the Septuagint mean the entire Jewish people, properly assembled. I try to make the correct distinctions, but often the context doesn't provide enough details to guide me.

CURSE (*see also* **SWEAR**): Standard Bibles render this way the verb *kakologeō,* which means literally "speak bad" and tends to be about ordinary interpersonal interactions, where something like the English "bad-mouth" or "insult" is more suitable. In the Greek scriptures, an actual curse refers to "offering up" or "praying over," which suggest the pagan human sacrifices that monotheistic moralism had always opposed.

DEMON: The *daimones* or personal gods of Greek folklore were a collaborative part of their hosts' personality. *Daimonion* (the diminutive, which is far more common in the New Testament) is a word I usually translate in the traditional way as "demon," but merely for lack of a better word. In traditional Jewish thought the *daimones* were part of the creation and natural history, not part of a realm of evil at war with God's realm of goodness. *Daimonia* in the Gospels function like hunting animals that could turn into parasites, like a predatory *pneuma* or "spirit" (q.v.).

DEVIL: Our word comes ultimately from the Greek *diabolos,* which literally denotes "throwing in all directions." I translate *diabolos* conservatively as "slanderer," in line with the Greek lexicon. *Diabolos* can be an ancient translation for the Hebrew Bible's Satan, who is named from the word for "opponent." As a closely adapted name in the Gospels, this is *satanas.* A more obscure name, Beelzebub or Beelzebul (*Be'elzeboul,* as transliterated from the Greek in my translation), also occurs; that he is known as "Lord of the Flies" may be due to a denigrating Hebrew pun on the name of a certain *baal,* a Canaanite deity. Beelzebub is cited in the Gospels as if he were the same, or functionally the same, as Satan.

DISCIPLE: This specialized term denoting a religious follower in modern English arose from the Latin *discipulus,* translating the Greek *mathētēs:* both mean "student" or "learner." Granted, those terms had a loftier ring in antiquity, when education was a rarer privilege; but there appears to be no way to convey that loftier ring without also implying that the young men who followed Jesus around were in a wholly different category from people under anyone else's tutelage.

DIVORCE: The Greek verbs literally denote "throwing away," "letting go," or "setting at a distance," usually (though not exclusively) when a man does it. Retention of the original harsh images seems useful because of a man's capacity to get rid of his dependent partner by means of a declaration in a single short document—a situation modern ideas of "divorce" do not cover.

ETERNITY: *See* TIME.

EVANGELIZE (*see also* **GOSPEL**): In translation of scripture, I would never use this word; the apparatus of "televangelism" alone has imposed all sorts of distracting and inappropriate images on it. The Greek word means "bring/spread good news," so I follow that meaning.

EVIL: The word commonly translated this way, *ponēros,* was not always used for destructive violence and implacable guile, but often for mere worthlessness, fecklessness, and nuisance; these may be the usual senses of the word for human beings, though contextual clues are not abundant. The real problem, however, is in the case of the devil (see above under that heading), who is also the "E/evil O/one" of standard English Bibles. I find "evil" too vague for a being who is interesting to these authors mainly for what he does, not for his nature, and I would sum these behaviors up as acts of malice; thus, for me, he is the "malicious one." The whole assortment of parasitic spirits (see "spirit" below), however, seem to be understood in terms more of the trouble they cause than of their motivations.

FAITH (*see also* BELIEVE/BELIEF): This central concept is translated too narrowly in the Gospels. Imagine daring to bank at an institution called "Federal Faith." "Trust" is usually the more appropriate translation of the noun *pistis* and of the verb derived from it, *pisteuō*, as these were powerful civic, economic, and social signifiers; they were not predominantly religious terms—not that religion could be called a separate realm in ancient societies. Our "trust" is a word that works especially well for the parent-child relationship, essential to the narrative and principles of the Gospels. A parent taking a child to the dentist and promising a reward afterward says "You have to trust me," not "You have to believe in me" or "You have to have faith in me"; the latter two are more like a child's special pleading. Occasionally, as for example when Jesus is insisting on the acceptance of specific statements as facts, "belief" may work better. Also, "faithfulness" has a special force in the Gospels as part of the metaphor of the Jewish covenant as marriage.

FLESH (*see also* LUST): We tend to associate this English word with sex, but the Greek original, *sarx,* functions quite differently in the Gospels. Death, not the body's natural desires, is the great disadvantage of mere physicality. The Jews of the Second Temple had inherited no puritanical kind of notion that the body in itself was evil, the enemy of a disembodied "soul." "Mere physical being" seems a good translation for a start.

FORGIVE: This preponderantly religious term is inadequate to render the Greek verb *afiēmi*, "throw away" or "let go" or "leave behind." (A synonym is *apoluō*, "let loose"). This verb is used both specifically for the remission of monetary debts and generally as in Mark 11:25, the command to let go "anything you have against anyone" while praying. The "letting go" is of control—whether material, emotional, intellectual, or moral—over other persons, in favor of trust in God's justice and providence. I find "pardon" and "absolve" often to be handy terms here, because their meanings are similar between the Bible and familiar modern legal contexts. Another way to say "forgive" is *charizomai*, "to be gracious" or "to do a favor": this naturally tends to be about the treatment of the weak by the strong, and it can be used of God's forgiveness as an example for mortals to follow.

FORNICATION: This word's source is the Latin for "brothel." The Greek word used in the Gospels, *porneia,* originally meant only "prostitution." *Porneia* was a particularly ugly word in connection to late-antique Judaism, which probably did not countenance any kind of commercial or extramarital sex. "Whoring" is not an outrageous translation, and it is backed up by the Hebrew verb commonly translated as "play the whore" and used for women's unchaste behavior in the text of the Torah law.

FRUIT: It has been a long time since this English word ceased to mean the noun "produce" or "harvest" in any general sense. The Greek word, *karpos,* can mean the edible fruit of a tree or ripe grain, but it is cognate with one verb for "harvest" and is often used in the context of harvesting work, so the broader meaning predominates.

GENTILES: Both the Greek and Hebrew words mean "nations [other than Jews]." From the Latin for that word, we have "Gentiles," normally capitalized in scripture translation, as if it's an ethnic or religious designation of non-Jews and not an "everyone but us" term normal for peoples whose identity has a strong tribal element.

GOD: At the risk of causing widespread offense, I am (consistent with my normal practice) dropping capitalization imposed without any warrant from the authoritative, edited Greek text. I have, however, left off the definite article that normally goes with "god," because it does not appear to have a force that the English article can duplicate: the article is sometimes used with the name Jesus, and with other personal names, and in other situations in which English does not use it.

GOOD: Ancient social and moral gradations, signified by a rich vocabulary, make such a vague word as the English "good" almost worthless. "Decent" versus "excellent" persons is a basic division to start with, but I have used other words according to context.

GOSPEL (*see also* EVANGELIZE): The Gospels are plainly labeled as the "good news" (*euaggelion*). "Gospel," from a Germanic rendering of that term, attached itself to these scriptures in English. I retain the word for the title of this book, and in expositions of the text, to avoid confusion, but I use "good news" in the actual translation.

GRACE: This is from the Latin *gratia*, meaning (basically) "gift," "favor," "goodwill," or "mercy," or something with a natural "appeal," or "thankfulness": the original Greek word, quite close to the Latin in its meanings, is *charis*. The English word has been heavily abstracted. For this translation, a variety of words for kindness, and for the proper responses to kindness, seems more useful than our theologically overwrought "grace."

HEART: The ancients did not conceive that thought took place in the brain and feeling in the heart, but rather that both the intellectual and emotional life took place in various places inside the torso. Hence the "heart" is sometimes functionally the mind, and the self's perceptions and responses may be shown in other organs that sound comical to us in these connections, mandating flexibility in translation. But "heart" works surprisingly often, because of the closer melding of thought and emotion in ancient experience.

HEAVEN: The Greek word *ouranos* refers evenhandedly to the physical sky and the place—often pictured as a royal court—where supreme divinity resides. "Sky" seems generally better, first of all in avoiding the wackier modern imagery that comes with the English "heaven." And even when a supernatural realm is meant, "sky" will often do, because the divine realm was thought to be located there, in addition to the weather and the heavenly bodies, whereas "heaven" to us is fundamentally a religious term, and the ancients did not tend to separate linguistic domains in this way. I have retained the plural "skies" where I see it in the Greek, because it is a Hebraism familiar in English translations of scripture and (I hope) not too archaic or jarring.

HELL: The Gospels text refers sometimes to the underground realm of hades, the home of all the dead in pagan mythology, but in early Christian thought a place of death and punishment for the unworthy. I write "hades," not "hell" (from an Old English word). Gehenna (in my translation, *ge'enna*) was a real valley in Judea that had ancient associations with human sacrifice and later use as a dump and incineration site.

HOLY: I originally wrote "pure and holy" and "set aside" for *hagios* throughout my translation, to express the idea of the ritual purity and set-aside condition of the flawless, acceptable sacrifice: this idea is basic to "holiness" in both the Hebrew Bible and the Gospels. My word-choice innovations in this case proved awkward and confusing, so I returned to the traditional "holy" nearly everywhere. But it should still be kept in mind that "holy" was a far less abstract designation than it is now. Also, "set aside" is a commonsense, descriptive translation in a verse like Luke 2:23, which is about the consecration of firstborn male infants to God.

HUSBAND (*see also* MAN): The Greek *anēr* can mean both "man" and "husband," an ambiguity that can be quite telling in, for example, the conversation between Jesus and the Samaritan woman in John 4.

HYPOCRITE: A *hupokritēs* is fundamentally an actor. The word has deep negativity in the Gospels on two counts: professional actors were not respectable people in the ancient world, and traditional Judaism did not countenance any kind of playacting. I write "play-actor" throughout.

IMMORTAL, IMMORTALITY: This Latinate derivative means that a being does not die; the Greek *afthartos* means that flesh does not rot. This is thematically appropriate for the Gospels.

Their promise is not the absence of death, but new life for a dead body, or else a new body. I translate literally but with some reluctance, as I understand how disturbing the imagery is.

KEEP: This is a rather vague verb for keeping in mind, respecting, and obeying commandments and other strictures. The Greek verb is the same one for "guarding" and "watching over" important objects and persons, so I translate accordingly.

KISS: This was the normal greeting between friends and relatives, including between men; it had no necessary erotic meaning. Traditional translations, however, have missed the difference between the short form of the verb, *fileō* (which also means "to be a [close] friend"), and the compound verb, *katafileō*, which is intensive, meaning a kiss that is supposed to signal special regard or emotion.

LAWYER: *See* SCRIBE.

LORD: There is no good analogy to evoke from modern Western democracies. Moreover, the relevant social situations in the ancient world varied a great deal, and in Palestine were quite unstable over history. During the first century C.E., at any rate, *kurios*, the word at issue, could mean a "Sir" on the street, the owner of a slave or other property, a local potentate, or some other person in a respected or authoritative role, as well as a deity. "Master" usually seems a better term for Jesus, as much of the deference shown being directed toward him is the kind traditionally directed toward a scholar and teacher: a teacher can be a "master" in English, but not a "lord" or "ruler." Even the analogies to divine authority in some parables use the figure of a boss or slave owner dealing with his underlings— a master and not a lord. (Another Greek word, *oikodespotēs*, "head of the household," can apparently be used almost interchangeably for this kind of *kurios*.) I do my best according to the context to judge when the exalted and revered position of a "lord" or "ruler" is meant.

LOVE: In Greek, *erōs* means sexual passion; *agapē*, affection, devotion, or benevolence of several kinds; and *filia*, friendship and other idealized bonds of individual choice—often intense and sentimental bonds between men. Cognate verbs roughly track the meanings of these nouns. Admittedly, distinctions between the last two of these words can become less precise when it comes to the New Testament. But if the word choices in Greek mean nothing, the extended teasing in John 21 would make no sense.

LUST: Biblical Greek does not have any word suggesting that sexual desire in and of itself is bad. Matthew 5:28, which in many English Bibles is about a man wrongfully "looking at a woman with lust"—really means something much more like "looking at a wife with the goal of placing intense feeling on (*epithumeō*) her": he is deliberately indulging a covetous passion for possession, which could apply to nonsexual objects too.

MAN: *Anthrōpos* has the basic meaning of "person" or "human being," not someone whose male gender is important in the context. In the Gospels, the much rarer *anēr* respectfully denotes a male. The distinction is important for breaking down the phrasing "Son of Man" (see pp. xxix–xxxi of the introduction), and in a couple of other instances, but since the default gender in scripture is male, I have backed off convoluted political correctness in phrasing: people Jesus encounters can be called men when that's obviously what they are.

MASTER: *See* LORD.

MERCY: *See* PITY.

MESSIAH: *See* CHRIST.

MONEY: Some existing translations do not divide money into even the most basic categories, though the Greek words make obvious the difference between, for example, silver coins and coins made of less valuable metals. As a rule, I give the ancient names of specific currencies mentioned in the text and explain the value in footnotes.

NEIGHBOR: The Greek term *hoh plēsion,* commonly translated in the Gospels as "neighbor"—the person to love as yourself— is literally "the one next to you." But *hoh plēsion* and its Hebrew predecessor mean, in context, something like "associate" or "compatriot" or just "another person." The proper term for neighbor, employed in a few places in the Gospels, is *geitōn.*

OATH: *See* SWEAR.

OBEY (*see also* COMMAND): There are several verbs, at home in different situations and connoting different attitudes toward the one giving the order and the one receiving it, so I have tried to maintain a careful gradation of English renderings in parallel.

OBSERVE: *See* KEEP.

OFFEND, OFFENSE: *See* STUMBLING BLOCK.

PARABLE: This term in English ordinarily refers only to an analogy or illustrative fiction presented by Jesus in the Gospels, but Greek writers applied the word to everything from logical parallels to fables. "Analogy" and "story for comparison" are the kind of wording I tend to use.

PASSOVER: The text does not use a term comprehensible in Greek to readers with exclusively pagan backgrounds, but merely transliterates the Aramaic word, *pascha.* This is therefore one of the words I transliterate into the Roman alphabet and italicize.

PEACE: The Greek word *eirēnē* translates the Hebrew and Aramaic *shalōm,* but not well: *shalōm* means health, wholeness, balance, and general well-being, as well as nonviolence; *eirēnē,* mainly nonviolence. But I don't feel entitled to correct the authors to express something they couldn't in the language they were using, even when the real speaker in the background of a passage is plainly wishing others well—not wishing them peace—in the manner his people normally employed.

PERFECT: Hebrew and Greek words rendered in English Bibles as "perfect" actually mean that things are fully developed or appropriately finished—not flawless. Standard translations have not even shrunk from various iterations of "Therefore be perfect, as your father in heaven is perfect" for Matthew 5:48 as a summing up of ethical teachings. I translate, according to context, as "fulfilled," "complete," "come to fruition," or other similar terms.

PERSECUTE: The same word (*diōkō*) means physical pursuit, harassment of all kinds, and prosecution in court, and was certainly not a word with a special application to the religious realm. I never write "persecute," which brings up images of modern religious persecution. My go-to translation is "hound," because it is so broad, suiting the many Gospels passages that use *diōkō* generally and with little or no context.

PITY: There are two different words for the two kinds: the ordinary pity that moves a powerful person to remit a punishment or give vital help, and the gut-punch kind, the experience that someone else's suffering *is* your own; this verb (the grisly-sounding *splagchnizomai*) is based on the word for "guts" and requires a stronger rendering. Mine is the inner "wrench" or "wringing" or "heart going out" of deep empathy.

POOR: In Classical Greek, *ptōchos* seems to mean not "poor" as much as "destitute" or "beggarly." Meanings do tend to become milder and more generalized in Koinē, but in this case it seems important not to allow confusion with what counts as poverty in the modern industrialized world. In the ancient Near East, debts could force the sale into slavery of the debtor's dependent relatives and then of the debtor himself. Very poor people wore not intact old or secondhand clothing, which still had substantial value, but actual rags; they were not hungry but starving.

PREACH: The Greek word (*kērussō*, cognate with the word for a herald) is not used in the prevailing modern way in the Gospels, where the messages concerned are usually delivered in public and are most urgently about the news of a new dispensation and the imminent end of history. The same verb is used for civic announcements, and so is not even necessarily religious or moral in connotation.

PURE: There was no bright line between physical, moral, and ritual purity for the Jews; this is shown by the blending of hygiene and ritual in scriptural law, and by the keen attention given this part of the law later on. In the Gospels, purity is largely sublimated to the moral and spiritual plane, but this is often done by playing off the new teachings against Jewish beliefs and practices, so the basic imagery of cleanliness and uncleanliness remains important.

RABBI (*see also* **TEACHER**): "Rabbi," literally meaning "my great one," reflects a widespread reverence for learning; people designated this way were not just teachers of young people in schools but also those who could, for example, perform ably in the public discussion of a scriptural passage. As usual with Hebrew or Aramaic words, I transliterate the Greek version, in this case retaining the Greek accent (*rabbí*) to distinguish the word from the title of modern, clerical rabbis.

RECEIVE: The verb, when used of persons, usually means "receive as an honored guest." My translation reflects this usage.

REDEEM, REDEMPTION: Our words arise from Latin ones—translating Greek ones—for the freeing of slaves and captives. The Latin is specifically about "buying back," but the Greek (*apoluō* and *apolutrōsis*) stresses not the financial transaction but the physical act of setting free. I translate in both senses, varying according to the context.

REPENT, REPENTANCE: *Metanoia* is literally a "change of mind," not a groveling moral submission; the verb is cognate. I have usually opted for changed "purpose," but occasionally it is changed "thinking": the lexicons easily support both.

RIGHTEOUS, RIGHTEOUSNESS: Not only do these English words have an archaic and pompous ring; they are also comparatively imprecise. Their Greek predecessors, based on the word for "justice" (*dikē*), seem usually to refer to the avoidance of outrageous and uncustomary behavior; in the Jewish context (the critical words are *tzedek, tzedakah,* and *tzadik*), this of course meant, first and foremost, adherence to the Mosaic law. "Lawfulness," "decency," and "uprightness" are my usual renderings. I am wary of the term "justice," because in English it tends to mean legal vindication, a preoccupation the Gospels actually warn against. As with the lowercase "god," I am not asserting my own mindset but merely trying to represent the ancient one.

RISE, BE RAISED (FROM THE DEAD), RESURRECTION: The Greek words contain mundane imagery: waking up, getting out of bed, standing up, setting out on a journey, taking a person's hand and helping him to his feet, stirring someone to action, raising a building. I hope this will justify phrasing that is more physical and specific than is usual in Gospels translation. I am, at any rate, confident in rejecting the abstract-sounding Latinate word "resurrection."

SABBATH: This, like all Hebrew or Aramaic words in the Gospels, I transliterate from the Greek version, here *sabbaton* or *sabbata.* The Greek word is not capitalized in the Nestle-Aland edition of the Gospels, so I do not capitalize it in English.

SATAN (*see also* **DEVIL**): The Hebrew means "opponent," and the Greek derivative used in the Gospels is *satanas,* which I reproduce without capitalization, since in the Nestle-Aland edition it has none. The word can concern court proceedings, which carried the terror of vicious and arbitrary prosecution in crude and freelance legal systems. The language of apocalyptic warfare provides another layer of context.

SAVE, SALVATION (*see also* **IMMORTAL, IMMORTALITY**): My "rescue" may convey a somewhat more concrete sense and is equally applicable to the most important contexts relevant here: a pagan god comes in answer to prayer and prevents a deadly shipwreck or other disaster; the Jewish God preserves his people from annihilation. "Save" will of course work, but "rescue," as a fresh word in this context, is resistant to modern theological and institutional baggage. The word "preserve" can point up the distinctive Gospel sense of immortality, literally "not-rotting."

SCANDAL: *See* STUMBLING BLOCK.

SCRIBE: "Scribe" tends to bring up images of medieval copyists. This English word traditionally translates *grammateus*, a "man of letters." People would have relied on him to interpret Jewish scriptural law for practical application; I never write "lawyer"—though *nomikos* (which I translate as "expert in the law" or "legal expert") may be roughly that: I want to avoid suggesting an official qualification or position in the modern sense. To avoid confusion with a modern *littérateur*, I translate *grammateus* as "scholar."

SCRIPTURE: The words in Greek mean "writing" and "writings." Pagans had different modes of referring to documents, but not a different basic vocabulary, so an English word like "scripture," for a class of writing that is religious only, and Jewish only, is not justified in a translation of the Gospels.

SERVANT: In Judea, servitude was sui generis and could be complicated, and accordingly the Greek vocabulary in scripture is varied. But there appears to be no basis for sugarcoating the word meaning a chattel slave in nearly all Greek literature, *doulos*. It is unlikely that the internationally oriented authors of the Gospels didn't mean what their peers meant by the word—"slave." Also, the English word "servant" is too vague for the array of servitors (including trusted house slaves and personal attendants), military and administrative subordinates, and ritual helpers the Greek of the Gospels distinguishes.

SHINE: *See* APPEAR.

SIN: This concept is sometimes dealt with in the Gospels by clear imagery. *Parabainō* is "overstep" or "go out of bounds"—more vivid than its Latin-derived English descendant "transgress." *Paraptōmata* are literally "stumbles," for which I think "blunders" can do as a translation. *Ofeilēmata*, "debts," is the only analogy to a moral deficit that has entered traditional English Bibles intact. But the very common verb *hamartanō*, with its related noun and adjective, is not strongly figurative. In Classical contexts, it tends to mean "fail of one's purpose" or "go wrong." In Jewish scripture translated into Greek, the words often carry over a sense of ritual nonconformity requiring ostracism, but in the Gospels they are applied to all sorts of wrongdoing that the early multiethnic readership could have readily understood; the specific tribal background does not obtrude, though of course it is there. This is why "sin," for us a heavily sectarian word, seems so questionable for Gospels translation. On the other hand, recent claims that *hamartanō* is merely about "mistakes" are overstated: crime, selfishness, and malice infuse the word in the Gospels. "Wrongdoing" and "offense" are my go-to translations.

SIT: Many versions of the Gospels, especially older ones, use this word for the dining posture, as if men sat in chairs for formal meals, whereas they lay on their sides on couches, propped on their elbows, sometimes with a dining companion lying in parallel. Sitting was the posture of teaching and governing, and so would have been wrong for conviviality; Jesus is repeatedly shown sitting to teach. My usual word for those dining is "recline."

SON OF MAN: The Greek is literally "son of the human being." See entry for MAN above and pp. xxix–xxxi of the Introduction for more on this critical designation, which I render throughout as "son of mankind" (or "son of humankind" to accommodate wordplay concerning other "human beings").

SOUL: *Psuchē* is the inner self or consciousness (including in animals), which may persist after death. The *psuchē* was even thought to leave the body during a faint or extreme psychological stress. But "the life within" seems a much better translation than "soul," as we consider souls as permanently separable from bodies, whereas early Christians considered life to be bound to the body, reviving along with it or not at all.

S/SPIRIT: *Pneuma* never originally meant a vague something to do with the human metaphysical potential, but instead the physical breath, the wind or breeze, a freelance minor deity, or a servant or manifestation or associate of God. The *hagion pneuma*, commonly translated in English as "Holy Spirit," was a "holy" or "pure" or "set-aside" creature—I use the adjective "holy" as more comprehensively descriptive—possibly almost like a personal divinity (*daimōn*) of God himself. My translations track the natural imagery, and I find "spirit" useful virtually nowhere except in phrases like "unclean spirit" (a demon or creature like a demon, which could possess a person), where there is no good English equivalent.

STUMBLING BLOCK: The Septuagint (see, for example, Sirach 9:5) shows that the metaphor of a trap was well established, and it fits well in some Gospel contexts; in others, where the context is unclear, I still prefer related metaphors such as "falling" or "tripping up" or "obstacle."

SWEAR (*see also* CURSE): In the context of the Gospels, swearing never means using obscenity or similar forbidden words, but oath taking. In the Hebrew of the Bible, and reflected in the Greek of the Septuagint and the New Testament, there is a special syntax of oath taking, which drops the words for the consequences if the oath is not fulfilled. I represent such sentences by circumlocution.

TEACHER (*see also* RABBI): I use this translation only for the Greek *didaskalos*, where the meaning is more straightforward, and not for the Hebrew *rabbi*.

T/TEMPLE: English translations of the Gospels usually identify *naos*, as well as *hieron*, as the "Temple." A *naos*, however, is an inner shrine. This distinction is vital in the New Testament, because of the special privacy, sanctity, and exclusivity associated with a *naos:* it can be a metaphor for the body of a faithful person, or even for Jesus' body. The enclosures of the Jerusalem Temple were increasingly restrictive going inward, and humans were barred from the inmost, most sacred part. This setup, however, necessitates care in translating *hieron* too: ancient holy places as wholes were defined not by the building but by the precinct, including outdoor spaces, and there is no indication that the adult Jesus ever enters into the exclusive ritual spaces of the Temple but rather is active in the courtyard, which was open (in different parts) to tourists, women, commercial activities, and eclectic teaching and debating. I therefore usually write "temple precinct" for *hieron*.

TEMPTATION: The word *peirasmos* refers to outward tests of all kinds, including those done on inanimate objects; but interrogation under torture could be a reference in some passages of the Gospels. Torture of noncitizens was routine in evidence gathering in the Roman legal system, and large-scale persecutions of Christians had begun before any of the Gospels' texts were finalized. "Test" or "ordeal" covers this without suggesting sexual tantalization, in which the Gospels evince almost no interest.

THIEF: The Gospels contain a word describing an ordinary housebreaker, but a *lēstēs*, such as the two shown to be crucified with Jesus, was a bandit living in a remote camp and raiding settled communities. The difference is important, because rebellious groups in the Judean province used bandits' methods, and bandits used political pretexts, and both provoked Roman crackdowns.

TIME: For the ancients, concepts of time were centered not on objective, technological measurements but on practical, ritual, and interpretive functions, so highly contextual translations are needed. *Kairos* can be a critical or important time, even a crisis, but it can also be just the time a specific thing happens. A *hōra* can sometimes be an "hour," but even then it is merely an approximate measurement, marked (if at all) by a sundial or water clock, but usually just estimated; "time" tends to be a closer English equivalent. Trickiest of all is *aiōn*, most simply an "age" or "era" but sometimes denoting either the whole present world or the whole world to come. The same word can allude to all the limits of material existence (or to dangerous worldly distractions in particular), or to their absence in the eternal age to come. Looking forward, especially to "ages of ages" (in the pattern of "King of Kings"), the meaning is "eternity."

TRIBULATION: The Greek *thlipsis* indicates, and I reflect, literal "crushing" or "wearing down," "grinding down," or even "shattering." The expression almost recedes as a figure of speech and becomes merely empirical when it refers to brutal wars, persecutions (which often included torture), or natural disasters. *Thlipsis* is the action of history's grindstone on the human body.

UNWASHED: The Greek word *koinos,* literally "common," can be used in the Gospels for the failure to wash according to the prescribed Jewish practice. The sense is of things' failing to be "set apart" or "holy" because of indiscriminate activities and associations whose taint is never cleansed away.

VIRGIN: Lack of sexual experience was assumed in a freeborn unmarried young girl, but the English word evokes some misleading expectations. The Jews included virginity testing of brides in their laws and customs, whereas the Greeks did not and had only vague ideas about the hymen; their word *parthenos* tended to mean simply "unmarried," whereas the nearest word in Hebrew—of which *parthenos* could be a translation—

concentrated on sexual ripeness and could include young motherhood. Careful contextual translation is required.

WICKED: *See* EVIL.

WISDOM: This translation works in some cases, but a strict distinction should be made between a transcendent or august understanding (the English "wisdom," I believe, is limited to that) and the earthier meanings the word *sophia* often carries in the Gospels: "shrewd," "clever," "prudent," "intelligent," "sensible."

WOMAN, WIFE: This is a single Greek word, *gunē,* its sense to be derived from context in each instance; in discussions of divorce and adultery, it is critical whether a "wife" or a mere "woman" is concerned.

W/WORD: *Logos* can mean merely "statement" or "speech," but it also has lofty philosophical uses, especially in the opening of the Book of John, where it is probably connected to the Stoic conception of the divine reasoning posited to pervade the universe. The essential connotation here is not language but the lasting, indisputable, and morally cogent truth of numbers, as displayed in correct financial accounting: this is the most basic sense of *logos.* "True account" is among the translations that can be justified on occasion. Also, *logos* appears sometimes to be related to the important *dabar* or "spoken word/matter/thing" of the Hebrew Bible: it can be the truth or commandment God imparts to his prophets or in his law. But the Greek words *rēma* and *rēthen* (both meaning "spoken thing") seem to function more reliably in this way than *logos* does. *Logos* is not capitalized in the Nestle-Aland text, so my various renderings are not capitalized either; in any case it would be impossible for me to distinguish for certain in every case how special the word is.

WORLD (*see also* CREATION *and* TIME): There are three main terms, none adequately covered by the English "world." *Kos-*

mos means the universe, the whole of what God brought into order at the beginning of history. *Oikoumenē* is the "settled/ inhabited (land)," or all of the civilized world, sometimes conceived as stopping at the boundaries of the Roman Empire. Finally, the word *aiōn*, basically "era," can refer to the conditions of human life, meaning the "worldly" sphere of passing time, imperfection, and decay, which translators have sometimes called simply "the world." But the same word can mean the *other* world, coming into existence for humankind in a future era.

WORSHIP: *See* BOW DOWN.

UNFAMILIAR TRANSLITERATIONS OF IMPORTANT PROPER NAMES IN THE GREEK TEXT

A NOTE ON PHONOLOGY

Some scholars would like to move the pronunciation of Koinē Greek closer to that of Modern Greek, which, among other changes, has merged a variety of previous vowel sounds into the sound *ee* (iotacization). In transliterating proper names and other terms for this translation, I've chosen to retain the old Attic or Athenian pronunciation that Classical scholars use.

Because a great deal of Athenian and allied literature survives, we have a reliable idea of how the words were pronounced: metrical poetry, onomatopoeia (Aristophanes mimics the voices of frogs and sheep), the remarks of contemporary scholars, and other clues are helpful in reconstructing the sounds. Koinē Greek, in contrast, is far less well attested at an early stage; the main example is Greek scripture itself, which threatens to make the question of pronunciation circular—or centrifugal, sending us off to far-flung evidence like the spelling of words on the walls of a monastery in what is now Turkey.

But I'd like to urge two things. One is some remarks in Augustine of Hippo's *Confessions,* probably written in 398 C.E. The author pictures orators' moral horror at the possibility of saying Latin words wrong—differently, that is, than the revered Roman orator Cicero had said them four and a half centuries before.

Augustine himself provides a good deal of evidence that Latin was changing, as language always does. But he also shows that mainstream resistance to change was powerful and could push back. People with enough credibility can even revive ancient linguistic norms and reestablish a "dead" language, which is what happened with Hebrew in modern Israel. I remember listening with astonishment to my teacher of Modern Hebrew as she told how, in the fifties, the decision whether to maintain the Classical Hebrew indicator of some direct objects but not others—a fussy, archaic distinction, many thought—came from the top of the government and was accepted and instituted on the ground.

The habit of pushing back against pronunciation change in formal settings could well have prevailed when the New Testament was written and first read aloud—and certain spelling variations, even in fairly early papyri and manuscripts, are not persuasive as evidence to the contrary. As a late-Imperial, cosmopolitan comparison, think of the wildly different ways people pronounce English today, sometimes unintelligibly to those at the cultural centers. "Errors," including written errors, proliferate in provincial obscurity while a hidebound, more letter-by-letter pronunciation at the BBC and in the American news media remains the formal standard and is very widely understood and accepted. Like the ancients, we are not going to hear hegemonic pronunciation slide into nowhere until its foundations, the institutions that reinforce the old-time conformity, are gone.

UNFAMILIAR TRANSLITERATIONS OF IMPORTANT PROPER NAMES IN THE GREEK TEXT

Aaron: Aarōn

Abilene: Abilēnē

Abraham: Abraam

Alexander: Alexandros

Alphaeus: Alfaios

Andrew: Andreas

Archelaus: Archelaos

Arimathea: Arimathaia

Augustus: Augoustos

Babylon: Babulōn

Bar-Jona: Bariōna

Bartholomew: Bartholomaios

Beelzebub: Be'elzeboul

Bethany: Bēthania

Bethlehem: Bēthle'em

Bethphage: Bēthfagē

Bethsaida: Bēthsaïda

Bethzatha: Bēthzatha

Caesar: Kaisar

Caesarea: Kaisareia

Caiphas: Kaïafas

Cana: Kana

Canaanite: Chananaia (feminine)

Cananean: Kananaios

Capernaum: Kafarnaoum

Cephas: Kēfas

Chuza: Chouzas

Cleopas: Kleopas

Clopas: Klōpas

Cyrenian: Kurēnaios

Dalmanutha: Dalmanoutha

Daniel: Daniēl

Egypt: Aiguptos

Elijah: Ēlias

Elisha: Elisaios

Elizabeth: Elisabet

Gabriel: Gabriēl

Gadarenes: Gadarēnoi

Galilean: Galilaios

Galilee: Galilaia

Gehenna: ge'enna

Gennesaret: Gennēsaret

Gerasenes: Gerasēnoi

Gethsemane: Gethsēmani

Gomorrah: Gomorra

Herod: Hērōdēs

Herodias: Hērōdias

Idumea: Idoumaia

Isaac: Isaak

Isaiah: Ēsaïas

Iscariot: Iskariōth, Iskariōtēs

Israel: Israēl

Israelite: Israēlitēs

Iturea: Itouraia

Jacob: Iakōb

Jairus: Iaïros

James: Iakōbos

Jeremiah: Ieremias

Jericho: Ierichō

Jerusalem: Ierousalēm *or* Hierosoluma; people of Jerusalem: Hierosolumitai

Jesse: Iessai

Jesus: Iēsous

Jew, Jews: Ioudaios, Ioudaioi

Joanna: Iōanna

John: Iōannēs

Jonah: Iōnas

Jordan: Iordanēs

Joseph: Iōsēf

Joses: Iōsēs

Judas: Ioudas

Judea: Ioudaia

Lazarus: Lazaros

Levi: Leui

Levite: Leuitēs

Lot: Lōt

Luke: Loukas

Lysanias: Lusanias

Magdalene: Magdalēnē

Malchus: Malchos

Mark: Markos

Mary: Maria *or* Mariam

Matthew: Maththaios

Messiah: Messias

Moses: Mōüsēs

Naphtali: Nefthalim

Nathan: Natham

Nathanael: Nathanaēl

Nazarene: Nazarēnos *or* Nazōraios

Nazareth: Nazara *or* Nazaret *or* Nazareth

Nicodemus: Nikodēmos

Nineveh, people of: Nineuitai

Noah: Nōe

Passover: *pascha*

Peter: Petros

Pharisee, Pharisees: Farisaios, Farisaioi

Philip: Filippos

Pilate: Pilatos

Pontius: Pontios

Quirinius: Kurēnios

Rachel: Rachēl

Rufus: Roufos

Sabbath: *sabbaton* or *sabbata* (singular and plural forms)

Sadducees: Saddoukaioi

Salome: Salōmē

Samaria: Samareia

Samaritan: Samaritēs, Samaritai (pl.), Samaritis (f.)

Satan: satanas

Sidon (city): Sidōn

Sidon (region): Sidōnia

Simeon: Sumeōn

Simon: Simōn

Sodom: Sodoma

Susanna: Sousanna

Syria, Syrian: Suria, Suros

Syrophoenician: Surofoinikissa (f.)

Thaddeus: Thaddaios

Theophilus: Theofilos

Thomas: Thōmas

Tiberius: Tiberios

Timaeus: Timaios

Trachonitis: Trachōnîtis

Tyre: Turos

Zacchaeus: Zakchaios

Zebedee: Zebedaios

Zebulun: Zaboulōn

Zechariah: Zacharias

Zion: Siōn

THE GOSPELS

THE GOOD NEWS
ACCORDING TO MARKOS

CHAPTER 1

——

¹ The inauguration of the good news of Iēsous the Anointed One, [the son of god].* ² As it is written in the prophet Ēsaïas,

> *"'Look, I'm sending my messenger ahead of you,*
> *And he will build your road.'*
> *³ The voice of someone shouting in the wasteland:*
> *'Prepare the lord's road,*
> *Make his beaten paths straight'";*†

⁴ Iōannēs [the] baptizer appeared in the wasteland, announcing baptism to change people's purpose and absolve them from their offenses.‡ ⁵ And they traveled out to him, inhabitants of the

* See the introduction, pp. xxix–xxxi, on "son of god." It is questionable whether the words are authentic here at the very beginning of the earliest Gospel.

† Isaiah 40:3. The word for "wasteland" in Hebrew is literally "the place of speaking" (*midbar*). The Greek word used here for "wasteland" (*erēmos*) itself sounds as if it has a root for "asking" or "speaking" in it. This is a special Greek word for "tracks" (*triboi*), indicating that they are worn smooth, and evoking Isaiah's special word for a broad, pleasant "highway" (*mesillah*) for the return of the exiles to their country.

‡ The basic meaning of the Greek verb we translate as "baptize" is "dip," and the verb is often used elsewhere for dyeing. In the Gospels the word describes Jewish ritual cleansing by immersion in water. It was a constant practice of the ascetic Essene sect, whose communities required it after toileting, but facilities

whole countryside of Ioudaia, and all the Hierosolumitai, and they were baptized by him in the river Iordanēs,* acknowledging their offenses. ⁶ Now, Iōannēs was dressed in unshorn camel hide, and he had an animal-skin belt covering his groin, and he ate locusts and wild honey.

⁷ And he announced this message: "The one who's more powerful than me is coming after me. I'm not fit to crouch down and untie a thong on his sandals. ⁸ I've baptized you with water, but he'll baptize you with the holy life-breath."

⁹ And it happened in those days that Iēsous came from Nazaret in Galilaia† and was baptized in the Iordanēs by Iōannēs. ¹⁰ And right when he came up from the water, he saw the skies split apart, and the life-breath coming down, like a dove, to alight on him.‡ ¹¹ And a voice came out of the skies: "You are my beloved son; in you I've taken delight."§

¹² And right away the life-breath drove him out into the wasteland. ¹³ And he was in the wasteland forty days, being tested by satanas, and he was in the company of wild animals, and god's messengers attended to him.

¹⁴ But after Iōannēs was handed over,¶ Iēsous went into Gali-

---

for immersion were connected to the Temple too. John's baptism apparently required fresh and visibly moving or "living" water, which had long-standing and important symbolism for blessing and renewal, as witnessed in many passages of the Hebrew Bible. Such baptism early on became the essential ritual for becoming a follower of Jesus.

* John is near the center of pious Judaism, in the southern region Judah or Judea (confusingly, the entire Roman province also went by the latter name), containing the Jerusalem Temple, which had been the center of the ancient Southern Kingdom.

† Galilee in hilly northeast Judea (the province, not the region around Jerusalem) was a recently rebellious backwater.

‡ The dove was among acceptable temple sacrifices and could replace a larger beast as a "sin offering" by those of modest means. See "S/spirit" in the Glossary.

§ Similar language is used by God to Abraham concerning his son Isaac, in the command to sacrifice the boy (Genesis 22:2).

¶ See Mark 6:14–29.

laia, announcing god's good news [15] and saying, "The time is ripe, and god's kingdom has come close. Change your purpose and trust in the good news."

[16] And passing along by the sea of Galilaia, he saw Simōn, and Andreas, who was Simōn's brother, and they were casting their nets into the sea, as they were fishermen. [17] And Iēsous said to them: "Come along after me, and I'll turn you into fishers for human beings." [18] And right away they left their nets and followed him. [19] Then, walking on a little, he saw Iakōbos the son of Zebedaios, and Iōannēs his brother, and they were in the boat putting their nets in order, [20] and right away he called them. And they left their father Zebedaios in the boat with the hired men, and they went away after him.*

[21] Then they traveled into Kafarnaoum.† And as soon as it was the *sabbata*, he entered the synagogue and began to teach. [22] And the people there were powerfully struck by what he taught. He was teaching them as if he had genuine authority; it wasn't the way the scholars taught.‡

[23] And right at that time in their synagogue was a man under the power of an unclean spirit, and he screamed [24] these words: "What's your business with us, Iēsous Nazarēnos? Have you come to destroy us? I know just who you are—god's holy one." [25] But Iēsous took the spirit to task, saying, "Put on a muzzle and come out of him!" [26] And the unclean spirit convulsed the man, cried out with a loud outcry, and came out of him. [27] And all the people there were amazed, so that they discussed it with each other, saying, "What's this? It must be a new teaching, carrying authority. He gives commands even to unclean spirits, and they

---

* Compare Elisha following Elijah (1 Kings 19:19–21). The detail of the hired men may indicate that Jesus' followers were not ordinary laborers but instead belonged to a class from which students could normally come.

† Capernaum was a sizable fishing town on the northern shore of the Sea of Galilee.

‡ See "scribe" in the Glossary.

obey him." ²⁸ And from that moment, news of him went out everywhere, to the whole of the surrounding Galilaia region.

²⁹ And they went straight from the synagogue to the house of Simōn and Andreas, and Iakōbos and Iōannēs went too. ³⁰ And Simōn's mother-in-law* was lying ill with a burning fever, and right away they told him about her. ³¹ And he approached and put her on her feet, grasping her hand. And the fever left her, and she began to wait on them.

³² Once evening came and the sun went down, they set about bringing him everyone who was unwell and those possessed by demons. ³³ And the whole town was gathered together outside the door. ³⁴ And he healed many who were unwell—they had various diseases—and he expelled many demons. And he kept the demons from speaking, because they knew who he was.

³⁵ And in the morning, when it was still pitch-dark, he got up and went away to an isolated place, and there he began to pray. ³⁶ But Simōn and those with him chased him down. ³⁷ And they found him and told him, "Everyone's looking for you." ³⁸ And he told them, "Let's get going somewhere else, to the country towns near here, so that I can give my news there too. This is, after all, the reason I came forward."

³⁹ And he went throughout Galilaia, giving his news in their synagogues, and expelling demons. ⁴⁰ And there came to him a man with leprosy, who pleaded with him, [falling on his knees and] telling him, "If you want, you can cleanse me." ⁴¹ And Iēsous was wrenched with pity; he stretched out his hand and touched him, and said to him, "I do want to. Be cleansed." ⁴² And right away the leprosy left him, and he was cleansed. ⁴³ And snorting a warning to him, Iēsous sent him away right then, ⁴⁴ telling him,

---

* If Jesus himself was married—which would have been expected for a Jewish man of his age at the time of his mission (he was about thirty, according to Luke 3:23)—it would not have been mentioned absent a special circumstance; Simon Peter's marriage is alluded to only because of his mother-in-law's healing. Custom prescribed that a young wife would stay at home to the extent possible, unnamed and unmentioned in public, at least until she had borne a child.

"See that you say nothing to anybody, but get going and show yourself to the priest, and make the offering for your cleansing that Mōusēs set out in the law, as proof for them."* ⁴⁵ But once the man went away, he proceeded to publicize his healing persistently, spreading the story all around, so that Iēsous could no longer go openly into a town. Instead, he remained outside in uninhabited places; but then they kept coming to him from everywhere.

CHAPTER 2

——

¹ Then a few days later, he went back to Kafarnaoum, and people heard that he was at home. ² Then so many people gathered together that the place couldn't hold them, even outside the door, while he was delivering a discourse to them. ³ But a group came, bringing to him a paralyzed man, four of them carrying him. ⁴ And since they weren't able to bring him near Iēsous because of the crowd, they turned the roof above him into no roof, digging clear through it, and lowered the stretcher on which the paralyzed man was lying. ⁵ And seeing their trust, Iēsous said to the paralyzed man, "Child, you're absolved from your offenses." ⁶ Now, some of the scholars were there, sitting and working things through in their hearts: ⁷ "What does he mean by saying that? He's blaspheming!† Who, if not god alone, can absolve a person from his offenses?" ⁸ But Iēsous, taking note right away in his own mind that they were inwardly working things through this way, said to them, "Why are you working through these things in your hearts? ⁹ Which is more efficient, to say to the

---

* See Leviticus 13–14, which probably covers a variety of skin conditions, including the effects of Hansen's disease, or leprosy.

† Blasphemy, or outrageous speech about the divine, had stoning as punishment (Leviticus 24:13–16).

paralyzed man, 'You're absolved from your offenses,' or 'Get up and pick up this stretcher of yours, and walk'?* [10] So that you know the son of mankind has authority on earth to absolve people from their offenses"— He said to the paralyzed man, [11] "I'm telling you, stand up, pick up your stretcher, and get along home." [12] And he got up, picked up his stretcher right away, and went out in front of everyone, so that they were all stunned, and they glorified God, saying, "We haven't seen anything like this, ever."

[13] Then Iēsous went out again, to the sea. And the whole crowd came to him, and he started to teach them. [14] Then as he was passing along, he saw Leui the son of Alfaios sitting at the tax booth, and he said to him, "Follow me." And he got up and followed him.

[15] And it happened that Iēsous was reclining at the table in Leui's house, and many tax-collectors and other wrongdoers† were reclining with Iēsous and his students; there were in fact many of them, and they were following him. [16] And when the scholars who were Farisaioi‡ saw that he was eating with wrongdoers, including tax-collectors, they said to his students, "He eats with wrongdoers, including tax-collectors." [17] But Iēsous, hearing this, said to them, "People who are strong and healthy don't have any need for a doctor; no, it's those who are unwell. I didn't come to call upright people, but wrongdoers instead."

[18] Now the students of Iōannēs, along with the Farisaioi, ha-

---

* The wit of this retort may hang on the comparative length of the two commands, four words in Greek in the first, eight in the second.

† Tax collectors are casually identified with the rest of the criminal class because their private contracts with the Roman Imperial government allowed them to extort and pocket additional sums.

‡ See "scribe" in the Glossary. Along with Sadducees, Pharisees were an important Jewish sect during the time of the late Second Temple. The Pharisees, as predecessors of the rabbis, were mediators between the common people and authoritative Jewish tradition.

bitually fasted. So people came and said to him, "Why is it that Iōannēs' students and the students of the Farisaioi fast, but the students you have don't fast?" [19] And Iēsous said to them, "The sons of the bridal hall can't fast as long as the bridegroom is with them. The whole time they have the bridegroom with them, they're not able to fast. [20] The days will come when the bridegroom is taken away from them, and then they'll fast, starting on that day. [21] No one sews a patch made of unshrunken cloth onto an old cloak. Otherwise, the patch would pull away from it, the new material from the old, and this would make for a worse tear. [22] And no one pours young wine into old wineskins; otherwise, the wine would burst the skins, and both the wine and the skins would be lost. Instead, people put young wine into new wineskins."*

[23] And it happened that on the *sabbata* he was passing through fields of grain, and his students began to make a path, plucking off the heads of grain. [24] And the Farisaioi said to him, "Look! Why are they doing what's forbidden on the *sabbata*?" [25] But he said to them, "Haven't you ever read what David did when he was in need, and starving—he himself and those with him? [26] How he entered the house of god when Abiathar was chief priest, and he ate the loaves of presentation, the ones no one but the priests is allowed to eat, and gave some to those with him too?"† [27] Then he said to them, "The *sabbaton* was made for the sake of humankind, and not humankind for the sake of the *sabbaton*. [28] This means that the son of mankind is the ruler even of the *sabbaton*."

---

* The Hebrew Bible has no rules for fasting, only showing through stories how it naturally suited certain occasions. Jesus uses metaphors of ill-matched items to criticize what he saw as forced and artificial fasting in his time.

† 1 Samuel 21:1–6. When David is on the run during a political emergency, he makes use of loaves that are placed as an offering to God, next to the Holy of Holies in the Tabernacle, to be eaten by priests only, after a fixed time.

CHAPTER 3

---

¹ And he came into the synagogue again, and in it there was a man with a withered hand. ² And they were watching Iēsous closely to see whether he would heal him on the *sabbata,* which would allow them to lay a charge against him. ³ And he said to the man with the withered hand, "Get up and come into the center." ⁴ Then he said to them, "Is it permitted to do good on the *sabbata* or to do evil, to save a life or to kill?" But they were silent.* ⁵ And he looked around at them with anger, deeply grieved at the lack of feeling in their hearts, and said to the man, "Hold out your hand." And he held out his hand, and it was restored. ⁶ Then the Farisaioi went out and, right away, along with men of Hērōdēs,† proceeded to come up with a plot against him, so that they could destroy him.

⁷ But Iēsous, with his students, withdrew to the seaside, and a great mass of people from Galilaia [followed him], ⁸ and from Ioudaia and Hierosoluma and Idoumaia and the other side of the Iordanēs, and the area around Turos and Sidōn—a great mass had heard of all the things he was doing and came to him.‡ ⁹ And he told his students that a boat should be placed at the

---

* Jesus' point is that to do no work, the general rule for the Sabbath, can amount to taking a life—a violation of another of the Ten Commandments, of course. The Talmud explicitly allows exertion on the Sabbath to save human life.

† These would likely be officials of Herod Antipas, a son of Herod the Great, who ruled Galilee at the time.

‡ To his own region by the Sea of Galilee, Jesus draws an audience from the Jewish heartland, Judea, and from the capital and home of the Temple, Jerusalem. Idumea, to the south, below the Dead Sea, had converted to Judaism only after conquest led by the Hasmoneans in the second century B.C.E. Beyond the Jordan to the east was the Decapolis or "Ten Cities" area, an outpost of Greek and Roman culture. Tyre and Sidon were Phoenician cities, coastal and living off international trade, and maintaining a pagan religion repellent to traditional Jews.

ready for him because of the crowd, to keep them from crushing him. [10] He had in fact healed many people, so everyone suffering from any scourges descended on him to touch him. [11] As to the unclean spirits, whenever they had him in sight, they fell down before him, screaming the words "You're the son of god!" [12] But he insistently warned them, telling them not to expose who he was.

[13] And he climbed a mountain, calling to him those he personally wanted with him, and they came to him. [14] And he appointed twelve [whom he also called envoys] to be with him, and to be sent off by him to spread the word, [15] and to have authority to expel demons. [16] [And he appointed the twelve,]* and he gave Simōn the name Petros,† [17] and to Iakōbos the son of Zebedaios and Iakōbos' brother Iōannēs he gave the name Boanērges, which means "sons of thunder." [18] And there were also Andreas and Filippos and Bartholomaios and Maththaios and Thōmas and Iakōbos the son of Alfaios, and Thaddaios and Simōn the Kananaios and [19] Ioudas Iskariōth, who actually handed him over.‡

---

* These sets of suspiciously repetitious words, bracketed by the modern editors, likely illustrate a common scribal mistake, dittography, or "twice-writing."

† This means "rock" in Greek, and behind the Greek is an Aramaic word for a rock that is rendered as Kēfas in John 1:42. The name will become significant for Peter's later role in the Jesus movement: see Matthew 16:18.

‡ The lists of the "disciples" show some variation among the Gospels. Realistic features of the passage are common names duplicated here and elsewhere (Iōannēs, Iakōbos, Simōn), nicknames not explained here (Petros, Boanērges; but see Matthew 16:18 concerning Petros), Greek names (Filippos, Andreas, Alfaios), and designations with no certain meaning (Kananaios and Iskariōth), which the author of the Gospel may not have understood. ("Kananaios" might indicate that this Simon is a Zealot, a member of a Jewish nationalist sect using violent tactics: they spearheaded an unsuccessful tax rebellion in 6 C.E. and the disastrous First Jewish–Roman War in 66 C.E. But even if that identification were historically accurate, it would not accord well at all with the Gospels' general depiction of Jesus' mission, or with the strong tendency of the Gospel authors to side with Roman interests. It has been suggested that Judas is a "man from Keriōth," but that is hardly the usual way to indicate geographical origin.)

²⁰ Then he came home, and [the] crowd assembled again, so that Iēsous and his followers couldn't even eat bread. ²¹ And when his own people heard about it, they went out to seize him, since they said, "He's out of his mind."

²² And the scholars who had come down from Hierosoluma were saying, "He has Be'elzeboul in him"; and "Through the demons' ruler, he expels demons."

²³ Then he called them over to him and spoke to them through analogies. "How can satanas expel satanas? ²⁴ If a kingdom's split in two and the two pieces of it pitted against each other, that kingdom can't remain standing. ²⁵ And if a household's split in two and the two pieces of it are pitted against each other, that household can't remain standing. ²⁶ So if satanas rises up against himself and is split in two, he can't remain standing but is going to meet his end.* ²⁷ Certainly no one can come into a strong man's house and pillage his things if he doesn't first tie up the strong man; only then can he pillage his house.

²⁸ "*Amēn* I tell you, the sons of mankind will be absolved from all their offenses, and from as many blasphemies as they've blasphemously uttered. ²⁹ But whoever blasphemes against the holy life-breath, for all of time he won't be absolved, but instead will be responsible for wrongdoing that lasts for all of time." ³⁰ He said this because they were saying, "He has an unclean spirit."

³¹ Then his mother and brothers came and stood outside, and sent someone to call him to them. ³² And a crowd was sitting around him, and they said to him, "Look, your mother and your brothers [and your sisters] are outside asking for you." ³³ And he answered them with these words: "Who are my mother and [my] brothers?" ³⁴ Then he looked around at those sitting around him in a circle, and he said, "Look, my mother and my brothers!

---

* See "devil" in the Glossary. This discourse plays on the idea of "the opponent."

³⁵ Whoever [in fact] carries out what God wants, this is my brother and sister and mother."*

CHAPTER 4

¹ And again he began to teach beside the sea; and a huge crowd gathered in front of him, so that he got into a boat and took a seat on the sea, and the whole crowd was on dry land by the sea. ² And he taught them many things through analogies, and this is what he told them in his teaching.

³ "Listen! Look, a sower went out to sow. ⁴ And as he sowed, it happened that some of the seed fell along the road, and the birds came and made short work of it. ⁵ And other seed fell on a stony place, where it didn't have much earth, and right away it sprouted and rose up, because it didn't have any depth of earth. ⁶ But when the sun rose up, the seedlings were seared, and due to their lack of roots they withered. ⁷ Still other seed fell among the thorny weeds, and these came up and strangled the seedlings, which didn't produce any grain. ⁸ But other seeds fell onto good ground and produced grain, which came up and multiplied, with one kernel yielding thirty, another sixty, another a hundred more." ⁹ And he said, "Whoever has ears for hearing had better hear."

¹⁰ But when he was in private, those around him, including the twelve, started asking him about the analogies. ¹¹ And he said to them, "To you the secret† of God's kingdom has been granted, but to those outside, everything is done through analogies,

---

* Whether his attitude is just starkly radical or outright obnoxious depends on whether he is in a home belonging to his own relatives—as Verse 20 above probably indicates—or in someone else's.

† The word *mustērion* means a holy secret: in pagan literature, it was a rite or

[12] "*'So that they definitely look, and yet don't see,*
And they definitely hear, and yet don't have any
*   understanding;*
*And they never turn around or are pardoned.'"**

[13] And he said to them, "Don't you understand this analogy? Then how will you understand all the other analogies? [14] The sower sows the true account.[†] [15] This first example is the people beside the road: when the account's sown and they hear it, satanas comes right away and takes the account that was sown in them. [16] And here next are the people sown in rocky places: when they hear the account, right away they take it in with joy. [17] Yet they don't take root, but instead are merely of the moment, so then when grinding hardship or hounding come because of the account, they instantly fall away. [18] And the next people are the ones sown among the thorny weeds: these have heard the account, [19] but the anxieties of this present life, and the false appeal of wealth, and passions for other things come in among them and strangle the account, and then it can't bear grain. [20] But then there are those sown on good ground, who hear the account and accept it, and they do produce a harvest, with every kernel yielding thirty or sixty or a hundred more."

[21] Then he said to them, "Is there any way a lamp is brought to be put under a basket or a bed? Isn't it brought in to be placed on the lampstand? [22] Nothing's hidden, you see, unless it's meant to be shown in clear light later on, and nothing's hidden away unless it's meant to come into the clear light in due course.[‡] [23] If

---

object before which an initiate in a "mystery cult" would "close his eyes" (the origin of the word) in reverent fear; in scripture, it is a secret imparted (or kept) by God. Perhaps even in this earliest Gospel, exclusivist thinking of a Gnostic strain had influence.

* Isaiah 6:9–10. The patterned, repetitive manner of the quotation in Greek reflects the Hebrew Bible's poetic language.

† See "W/word" in the Glossary.

‡ Before matches existed, it was usual to share fire among neighbors; the oil

anyone has ears for hearing, he'd better hear." ²⁴ And he said to them, "Look what you're hearing: the measure you give will be the measure you get—and you'll get a bonus besides.* ²⁵ If someone has something, more will be given to him; but if someone doesn't have something, even what he has will be taken away from him."

²⁶ And he said: "The kingdom of god is like a man scattering seed on the ground, ²⁷ and he sleeps and wakes night after night and day after day, and the seed germinates and the stalks grow tall without his knowing how this happens. ²⁸ On its own the earth produces a crop—first the shoot, and then the head, and then the full, ripe grain on the head. ²⁹ And when the crop is ready, right away he dispatches the sickle, because harvest-time has arrived."†

³⁰ And he said, "What can we say the kingdom of god is like? With what analogy can we present it? ³¹ It's like the seed of a mustard plant, ³² which, when it's sown on the earth, is smaller than all other seeds on the earth. But once it's sown, it grows up and becomes bigger than all other garden plants and puts out large branches, so that the birds of the sky can find shelter under its shadow."

³³ So with many analogies like this, he spoke to them about the true account, in ways they were able to hear. ³⁴ Unless it was by analogy, he didn't speak to them; but on his own, to his own students, he explicated everything.

³⁵ And on that day, when evening had come, he said to them, "Let's go over to the opposite shore." ³⁶ Then, once they had sent away the crowd, they took him with them, as he was already in

---

lamp with its exposed wick would be covered on the way home to preserve the flame and to keep out of sight of any nocturnal malefactors.

* The densely repetitive style (literally, "the measure in which you measure will be measured to you") suggests traditional wisdom about the marketplace.

† The harvest is important apocalyptic imagery; see, for example, Revelation 14:14–20.

the boat; and other boats were with him. ³⁷ And a great squall arose, and the waves fell on the boat, so that in no time the boat was swamped. ³⁸ But he was in the stern, sleeping on the cushion. And they woke him and asked him, "Teacher, don't you care that we're going under?" ³⁹ So he got up, scolded the wind, and said to the sea, "Be quiet! Put a muzzle on it!" And the wind broke off, and there was a great calm. ⁴⁰ And he said to them, "Why are you such cowards? Don't you have any trust yet?" ⁴¹ But their fear was an overwhelming one, and they said to one another, "Who *is* this man, then? Even the wind and the sea obey him!"*

Chapter 5

¹ Then they came to the opposite shore of the sea, to the region of the Gerasēnoi.† ² As soon as he got out of the boat, a man coming from among the tombs, who was under the power of an unclean spirit, met him. ³ He made his home among the tombs, and by this time nobody could restrain him, not even with a chain: ⁴ in the past he had often been restrained with fetters and chains, but the chains had been wrenched apart by him, and the fetters shattered, and no one had the strength to subdue him. ⁵ Now throughout the night and day he stayed among the tombs and in the mountains, screaming and mangling himself with stones. ⁶ But when he saw Iēsous from far off, he ran to him and groveled at his feet, ⁷ screamed at the top of his voice, and said, "What's your business with me, Iēsous, son of the highest god? I call on

---

* Compare this story to the first chapter of the Book of Jonah. The prophet flees his mission and, oblivious to a storm, sleeps in the hold of a pagan ship on his way to the ends of the earth.

† The location is uncertain. I have merely transliterated the name for its inhabitants in the best version of the Greek text. This lurid and derogatory story is, however, probably set in or near a place of Greco-Roman culture on the eastern shore of the Sea of Galilee, part of the Decapolis, or "Ten Cities," region.

you in god's name, don't torture me"— [8] Iēsous, you see, had said to him, "Unclean spirit, leave this man!" [9] Now Iēsous asked him, "What's your name?" And he said to him, "My name's legion: that's how many of us there are!"*— [10] and he pleaded with Iēsous fervently not to dispatch the demons out of the region. [11] In that place, on the slope of a hill, was a large herd of pigs grazing, [12] so the demons pleaded with Iēsous, saying, "Send us into the pigs— let us go into them." [13] He gave them his permission, and the unclean spirits went out of the man and into the pigs, and the herd—there were around two thousand animals—barreled down the crag into the sea, and in the sea they drowned.

[14] Then their herders ran away and brought the news to the city and the countryside. And people went to see what had happened, [15] and they came to Iēsous and saw the man who had been possessed by demons, but now he was sitting with clothes on and was clearheaded, though he'd had a "legion" of demons in him; and the people were frightened. [16] Those who'd seen it told them all about what had happened to the demon-possessed man, and also about the pigs, [17] and they began to plead with Iēsous to go away, out of their district.

[18] As he was boarding the boat, the man who'd been possessed by demons pleaded with him, wanting to go along with him. [19] But Iēsous didn't allow him to, instead telling him, "Get along to your home and family, and tell them everything the master's done for you, and how he took pity on you." [20] And the man went away and proceeded to spread the word in the Ten Cities about everything Iēsous had done for him, and everyone was amazed.

[21] Once Iēsous crossed over again to the opposite shore [in the boat], a large crowd gathered in front of him, so he stayed beside the sea. [22] And there came to him one of the synagogue leaders, whose name was Iaïros. When this man saw Iēsous, he fell at his feet [23] and pleaded with him fervently, saying, "My little daugh-

---

* A demon, like a god, must be addressed by the proper name. A Roman legion numbered around five thousand.

ter is on the verge of death, so will you come and lay your hands on her? Then she'll be cured and live." ²⁴ So Iēsous went with him, and a large crowd followed him, pushing up hard against him him.

²⁵ Now there was a woman who'd been afflicted with a flow of blood for twelve years. ²⁶ She'd suffered greatly at the hands of many doctors and spent everything she had, but found no relief—instead, she'd gotten worse. ²⁷ When she heard about Iēsous, she came up behind him in the crowd and touched his cloak, ²⁸ telling herself, "If I just touch his clothes, I'll be cured."*
²⁹ And right away, the spring of her blood dried up, and she sensed in her body that she had been healed of her scourge. ³⁰ But right away Iēsous clearly sensed in himself that power was going out of him, and he turned around in the crowd and said, "Who touched my clothes?" ³¹ But his students said to him, "You see this crowd pushing against you so hard, and you say, 'Who touched me?'" ³² But he went on looking around to see which female† had done this thing. ³³ But the woman, terrified and shaking, and knowing what had happened to her, came and threw herself at his feet and told him the whole truth. ³⁴ But he said to her, "Daughter, your trust has cured you. Be on your way in peace and be healthy after your scourge."

³⁵ While he was still speaking, people came from the house of the synagogue leader and said, "Your daughter has died. Why are you still bothering the teacher?" ³⁶ But Iēsous overheard the news being told, and he said to the synagogue leader, "Don't be afraid; only trust." ³⁷ And he didn't allow anyone to come along with him except Petros and Iakōbos and Iakōbos' brother Iōannēs. ³⁸ And they came to the leader's house, and he observed an uproar, with people crying and wailing loudly. ³⁹ Going in, he said,

---

* Back on the west side of the Sea of Galilee, this woman is presumably Jewish, and thus bound by the purity laws that would render her untouchable as long as she experiences the uncleanliness of a discharge.

† The pronoun is feminine; Jesus knows that it was a woman.

"Why are you making this uproar, why are you crying? The child hasn't died—she's just asleep." ⁴⁰ They jeered at him, but he threw out everybody, took the child's father and her mother and his companions with him, and made his way in to where the child was. ⁴¹ Then he took hold of the child's hand and said to her *"Talitha koum,"* which translates as "Little girl, I'm telling you, get up."* ⁴² And right away the little girl stood up and walked around; she was twelve years old. Then [right away] they were stunned almost beyond their capacity to be stunned. ⁴³ And he gave strict orders to them that no one was to know what had happened here, and he told them she must be given something to eat.†

CHAPTER 6

¹ And he went away from there and came to his own hometown, and his students followed him. ² And when the *sabbaton* arrived, he set about teaching in the synagogue, and many people were powerfully struck when they heard him, and they said, "Where did he get all this?" and "What's this insight that's been granted him?" and "How are such powerful things done by his hands?" ³ Isn't this the builder, the son of Maria, and the brother of Iakōbos and Iōsēs and Ioudas and Simōn? And aren't his sisters

---

* The proper, feminine form of this Aramaic verb would be *koumi,* but that is not a sufficient reason to correct the reading of the manuscripts in question; it is more likely that the author of Mark did not know Aramaic well. Notice the words he adds, "I'm telling you," to the translation to make sure readers understand that the verb is a command. This narration is not sure what to call the girl, ranging in Greek among "little daughter" and "daughter" (one time each), "child" (literally "little child," four times), and the unusual—and perhaps incorrect—*talitha* (from Aramaic), which is then echoed twice by the rather rare Greek word *korasion,* "little girl" or "little virgin."

† Eating is proof of genuine resurrection in the flesh, instead of the appearance of a ghost (see Luke 24:41–43).

here with us?"* So they were tripped up by him. ⁴But Iēsous said to them, "A prophet isn't treated dishonorably except in his hometown and among his own relatives and in his own house."† ⁵And in that place he couldn't perform any powerful act, except that he placed his hands on a few sick people and healed them. ⁶But he was amazed at their lack of trust. Then he made a circuit of the villages, teaching. ⁷And he called the twelve to him and proceeded to send them out two by two, and gave them authority over unclean spirits; ⁸and he directed them to take nothing with them on the road except a staff—not a loaf of bread, not a bag, and no copper coins in the belt; ⁹rather, they were simply to strap on their sandals and not put on two tunics.‡ ¹⁰And he said to them, "Wherever you arrive and enter a house, stay in it until you leave that locale. ¹¹And if a place doesn't take you in hospitably or listen to you, when you make your way out of it shake off the dust that's under your feet as testimony against the people."§ ¹²And the students went out and announced that people should change their purpose, ¹³and they expelled many

---

* It is not known exactly what kind of man was expected to teach in a synagogue, or to perform other religious functions in an outlying community, so it is not clear why the people would be surprised.

The death of a father would normally make no difference in someone's designation as "the son of such and such [a male]." Why is Joseph treated as if he never existed? Or is "son of the builder" as a textual variant in Verse 3 correct?

† I dispute the familiar "without honor" translation. The Greek *atimos* isn't normally a sort of blank, the simple lack of honor; it usually means conspicuous and strongly felt *dis*honor. The formulation can work, considering how badly some of the prophets of the Hebrew Bible were treated in their own communities, and in how many cases they found refuge or patronage elsewhere.

‡ These instructions resemble the rules for Essenes, members of an ascetic sect, when they traveled. They were to depend wholly on their fellow sectarians, except that they were allowed to carry weapons for self-defense. This is not an ordinary walking stick, but akin to the king's rod (for punishment) or the shepherd's staff (for defense of the herd).

§ This gesture (probably a curse) has no clear parallel; the point may be that the very dust of hostile places doesn't deserve to cling to the travelers' soles.

demons, and they rubbed olive oil on many sick people and healed them.*

[14] Then Hērōdēs the king[†] heard, since Iēsous' name grew well known and conspicuous, and they said, "Iōannēs the baptizer has awakened from among the dead, and because of this, powers are at work in him." [15] But others said, "He's Ēlias." And still others said, "He's a prophet, like one of the prophets in the books." [16] But when Hērōdēs heard all this, he said, "Iōannēs, whom I beheaded—he's awakened."

[17] Hērōdēs had in fact personally sent to seize Iōannēs, and chained him up in prison because of Hērōdias, his brother Filippos' wife, because Hērōdēs had married her. [18] Iōannēs had said to Hērōdēs, "It's not lawful for you to have your brother's wife."[‡] [19] And Hērōdias held this against him and wanted to kill him, but she couldn't, [20] as Hērōdēs had a reverent fear of Iōannēs, knowing that he was an upright and holy man; and he kept an eye out on his behalf. Having heard him, he felt he was at a dead end; yet he enjoyed hearing him.

[21] But an opportune day arrived when Hērōdēs, on his birthday, gave a banquet for his high officials and military commanders and the leading men of Galilaia. [22] And his daughter Hērōdias came in and danced, delighting Hērōdēs and the others reclining at the table with him.[§] The king said to the little girl, "Ask me

---

* Olive oil was in common use for removing dirt from skin and would probably soothe many wounds, sores, and rashes.

† This is the Romans' client ruler of Galilee and Perea, Herod Antipas, a son of Herod the Great.

‡ Leviticus 18:16 and 20:21 may have originally referred only to an adulterous relationship with a brother-in-law, but at this later period the verses were taken to forbid a divorce from one brother and marriage to another.

§ Who is the girl? The manuscripts read variously "his daughter Herodias," "the daughter of Herodias," and "Herodias' daughter herself"; I merely follow the authoritative, edited text as usual. She was probably only the king's stepdaughter. But no respectable Greek or Jewish man would have displayed any daughter of his house to his associates via such a performance. (The "entertain-

for whatever you want, and I'll give it to you." ²³ And he swore to her [repeatedly], "Whatever you ask me for, I'll give you, up to half of my kingdom." ²⁴ And she went out and said to her mother, "What should I ask for?" And her mother said, "The head of Iōannēs the baptizer." ²⁵ And she went back in right away, in a rush, to the king, and asked him in these words: "I want you to give me, here and now, on a platter, the head of Iōannēs the baptizer." ²⁶ And though the king was deeply grieved, still, because of the oaths and the men reclining at the table, he wasn't willing to refuse her. ²⁷ So right away the king sent an executioner, ordering him to bring Iōannēs' head. And the executioner went and beheaded him in the prison. ²⁸ And he brought his head on a platter and gave it to the little girl, and the little girl gave it to her mother. ²⁹ And when his students heard, they came and took up his corpse and laid it in a tomb.

³⁰ Then the envoys gathered around Iēsous and reported to him everything they had done and taught. ³¹ And he said to them, "Come on! Just you, on your own, come to a place no one lives, and rest for a little while." Many people were in fact coming and going, and they didn't even have a chance to eat.

³² So they went away on their own in a boat to an uninhabited place. ³³ But many people saw them leaving and recognized them, so they ran on foot from all the towns to assemble there and arrived before those on the boat did.

³⁴ And as he got out of it, he saw a large crowd and felt a wrenching pity for them because they were like sheep that didn't have a shepherd, and he began to teach them many things.

³⁵ By now it was late in the day, so his students approached him and said, "This is a place where no one lives, and by now it's quite late. ³⁶ Send them away, so that they can go to the farms and villages around here and buy themselves something to eat." ³⁷ But he responded by saying to them: "*You* give them something

---

ment" at an all-male banquet in the Greek style—notice that Herod's consort is not included—was barely, if at all, distinguished from prostitutes.)

to eat." But they told him, "Should we go out and buy two hundred denarii worth of loaves, and give them those to eat?"* ³⁸ But he said to them, "How many loaves do you have? Go see." And when they found out, they said, "Five, and two fish." ³⁹ Then he ordered them to have all the people recline in convivial cohorts that abutted on the verdant turf. ⁴⁰ So they reclined by fifties and hundreds, all lined up as in garden allotments.† ⁴¹ Then, taking the five loaves and the two fish, Iēsous looked up to the sky and blessed the loaves and broke them into pieces and gave them to [his] students to set before the people, and he shared out the two fish among them all. ⁴² And everyone ate until he was full, ⁴³ and they took up twelve baskets full of broken pieces of bread and fish scraps. ⁴⁴ And those who ate [the loaves] were five thousand grown men.

⁴⁵ And right away he made his students board the boat and go ahead of him to the opposite shore, to Bēthsaïda,‡ while he sent the crowd away. ⁴⁶ And he took his leave from them and went away onto the mountain to pray. ⁴⁷ And when evening came, the boat was in the middle of the sea, but he was alone on land. ⁴⁸ But when he saw them strained in their rowing, as the wind was against them, he came in their direction, around the fourth watch of the night,§ walking on the sea, and he intended to pass by them. ⁴⁹ But when they saw him walking on the sea, they thought it was a ghost, and they screamed, ⁵⁰ since they all saw him and were horrified. But right away he spoke to them and told them:

---

* That is, are they to spend what would amount to a laborer's wages for two hundred days on a single meal for a crowd of strangers?

† To depict this unconventional feast, outdoor terms are whimsically combined with terms for an ordinary indoor social gathering. The arrangement of the diners here is literally "drinking parties drinking parties," "on the green greenery," and "garden plots garden plots." Two are expressions like the modern Greek *plai plai* for "side by side."

‡ A town on the northern shore of the Sea of Galilee.

§ The hours of darkness were divided into only four "watches," so this was near dawn.

"Be brave—it's me. Don't be afraid." [51] And he got onto the boat where they were, and the wind stopped. And they were absolutely [overcome], beside themselves. [52] They hadn't understood what had happened with the loaves—just the opposite: their hearts were calloused and unfeeling.

[53] Then, crossing to the opposite shore, they came to Gennēsaret and moored there.* [54] But right when they got out of the boat, people recognized him, [55] and they ran here and there throughout that district and proceeded to put those who were unwell on stretchers and bring them here and there, wherever they heard he was. [56] And wherever he arrived—in villages or towns or rural areas—they put debilitated people down in the marketplaces and begged him to let these touch the hem of his cloak. And everyone who touched him was cured.

CHAPTER 7

——

[1] Then the Farisaioi and some of the scholars came from Hierosoluma and gathered near him, [2] and they saw that some of his students were eating loaves with hands that had been promiscuously dirtied†—which means unwashed; [3] the Farisaioi, you see, and all the other Ioudaioi don't eat unless they vigorously wash their hands, holding to what their ancestors have handed down; [4] and when they come from the marketplace, if they don't immerse themselves in water, they don't eat; and there are many other customs, received from the past, that they hold to, such as the immersion of cups and pitchers and kettles [and couches].

---

* A town on the western shore of the Sea of Galilee, not far south of Capernaum.

† The Greek here expresses the idea of purity and ritual setting aside rather clunkily with the word normally meaning "common." Routine washing is not prescribed in the Hebrew Bible but became a well-established practice later.

⁵ And the Farisaioi and the scholars asked him, "Why are your students behaving contrary to what the ancestors handed down? They eat bread with hands that have been made dirty anywhere and everywhere."

⁶ And he said to them, "Ēsaïas was right when he prophesied about you play-actors, as it's been written:

> 'This people honors me with their lips alone,
> While their heart is far away from me.
> ⁷ Uselessly they "worship" me,
> Teaching human injunctions as the teachings.'*

⁸ "Throwing away god's command, you hold to what human beings have handed down." ⁹ And he said to them, "That's a fine way to break god's command—in order to set on firm ground what *you* hand down. ¹⁰ Mōüsēs in fact said, 'Honor your father and your mother,' and 'Whoever insults his father or mother is to meet his end and die.'† ¹¹ You say, on the other hand, that if someone tells his father or mother, 'Whatever help might have come from me is *korban* (meaning an offering),' ¹² you no longer allow him to do anything for his father or mother!‡ ¹³ In this way, you cancel what god spoke by this handing down of yours that you've handed down—and you handle a whole lot else in hardly different ways."§

¹⁴ Then he called the crowd back again and said to them: "All

---

* Isaiah 29:13. Torah, the name for the five "Books of the Law," means "teaching."

† Exodus 21:17, Leviticus 20:9.

‡ This was a term for Temple offerings of all sorts. Jesus refers to an arrangement by which a man could deny the support he traditionally owed his parents on the authority of the Sixth Commandment, by directing the resources to the Temple instead.

§ The insistent repetition of the words for "hand down" (*paradidōmi*) and "handing-down" (*paradosis*, tradition) may convey sputtering anger or seething sarcasm. The Greek of the final part of this last verse has a five-word alliteration of the letter *p*, including these two words.

of you listen to me, and understand: [15] Nothing outside a person that makes its way *into* him, however indiscriminately, can make him dirty; rather, the things making their way *out* of a person make that person dirty."*

[17] Then when he came home, away from the crowd, his students asked him what this analogy meant. [18] And he said to them, "You too—do you have so little understanding? Don't you realize that nothing outside that makes its way into a person can dirty him? [19] It's because it doesn't make its way into his heart but into his belly, and then makes its way down the latrine—and that makes all kinds of foods clean!"† [20] Then he said, "The thing that makes its way *out* of a person, *that* dirties the person. [21] In fact, *out*ward, *out* of people's hearts, bad calculations make their way, and whoring, thefts, murders, [22] violations of marriage, rapacious greed, nasty vices, sneakiness, fast and loose living, the nasty stare of envy, backstabbing lies, shameless gall, moronic behavior. [23] All of these nasty things make their way from the *inside* to the *outside* and make a person dirty."‡

[24] From there he set off and went out into the region of Turos.§ He entered a house and didn't want anyone to know of his arrival, but he didn't manage to escape notice. [25] On the contrary, a woman whose little daughter had an unclean spirit in her heard about him right away and came and fell down at his feet. [26] But

* Verse 16, translated as "Whoever has ears, let him hear," is not thought to be an authentic part of the oldest manuscripts and so is excised from this edition of the Greek text.

† This is a radical proposition. The basic Jewish laws governing what kinds of food may be eaten ("kosher" is the modern term) *are* scriptural; the main sources of the laws are Leviticus 11 and Deuteronomy 14.

‡ Many Jewish decrees later than the Hebrew Bible, and some in the Hebrew Bible, do concentrate on ethical intent and inward integrity.

§ Tyre was on the Mediterranean coast, a cosmopolitan port city to the west of the rustic region of Galilee. Non-Jewish Canaanites such as the Phoenicians of Tyre were in fact the people against whose religion, including child sacrifice, the Jews had defined their own since remote times.

the woman was Greek, and Surophoinikissa by birth.* And she asked him to expel the demon from her daughter. ²⁷ And he said to her, "First let the offspring eat their fill, as it's not right to take the offspring's loaf and toss it to the little doggies." ²⁸ But she answered back, telling him, "Master, even the little doggies under the table eat some of the children's crumbs!"† ²⁹ And he said to her, "Because of what you just said: get out of here: the demon has left your daughter." ³⁰ Then she went back to her house and found her child lying on the bed, and the demon had left her.

³¹ Then he came back out of the region of Turos, going through Sidōn and to the sea of Galilaia and across the region of the Ten Cities.‡ ³² And they brought him a man who was deaf and could barely speak, and they begged him to lay his hand on him. ³³ And taking him away from the crowd to a private place, he put his fingers into the man's ears, and spat, and touched the man's tongue.§ ³⁴ Then he looked up to the sky, sighed deeply, and said

---

* Ethnic Greeks had long ago settled in many places in the Near East, where they could be well assimilated and have dual identities. To a Jew such as Jesus, the woman is of course untouchable. But she invades the home where he is a guest; and her groveling literally places him in an awkward position. One advantage a suppliant had is that her target couldn't get away from her in a dignified way—in front of the witnesses normally present.

† In the entire Greek Bible, only this passage and its mirror in Matthew (15:21–28) use this diminutive (*kunarion*) of the word for "dog," a rare and largely comical word. This word choice weakens the usual sense of dogs as dirty and uncivilized and excluded from the home, much less from the table that symbolized God's providential bounty. Also see "child" in the Glossary: in this passage the Jewish "offspring," reminiscent of the covenant, and the ordinary "children" are distinguished. The style here is also suitable to a more lighthearted narrative: *thugatrion* ("little daughter"), *daimonion* ("demon"), *kunarion* ("little doggie"), and *paidion* ("child") are four diminutive forms crowding the narrative.

‡ That is, Jesus heads north along the Mediterranean coast in Phoenicia before turning inland and to the south, passing through Galilee and then the Greco-Roman area to the east of the Sea of Galilee.

§ The saliva is probably applied to the man's tongue. The healing powers of saliva are described in ancient medical literature.

to him, *"Effatha,"* which means "Be opened."* ³⁵ And [right away] his ears were opened, and his tongue was untied and freed, and he spoke properly. ³⁶ And Iēsous gave orders to the people not to tell anyone; but the more he ordered them, the more exuberantly they spread the news. ³⁷ And they were overwhelmed and stunned, saying, "He's done everything right; he even makes the deaf hear and [the] mute speak."

CHAPTER 8

—

¹ In those days there was once more a large crowd that had nothing to eat, and he summoned his students and said to them, ² "I'm wrung with pity for this crowd, because they've lasted with me for three days already and have nothing to eat. ³ But if I send them away hungry to their homes, they'll collapse on the road; and some of them have come a long way." ⁴ But his students answered him, "Here in this place no one lives in, where will anybody be able to get enough loaves to fill these people up?" ⁵ Then he asked them, "How many loaves do you have?" And they said, "Seven." ⁶ Then he directed the crowd to recline on the ground, and he took the seven loaves, gave thanks for them, and broke them into pieces and gave them to his students to set before the crowd, and they set them before the crowd. ⁷ And they also had a few small fish. And he blessed these and said to set them before the people also. ⁸ And they ate until they were full, and they took up seven hampers full of leftover broken pieces. ⁹ And there were around four thousand people. Then he sent them away.

---

* Some magical texts instruct a drawing in and a letting go of breath to access divine power. As in the raising of the little girl from the dead (Mark 5:41), Jesus' command is shown in Aramaic.

¹⁰ Then right away he boarded a boat with his students and went to the district of Dalmanoutha.*

¹¹ Then the Farisaioi came out and began to dispute with him, looking for a sign from the sky from him, and putting him to the test. ¹² And sighing deeply with his life-breath, he said, "Why does this generation look for a sign? *Amēn* I tell you—I can't say what I stake on this: no sign will be given to this generation!"†
¹³ Then he left them, boarded the boat once more, and went away to the other shore.‡

¹⁴ But they forgot to take loaves—except for a single loaf, they didn't have any on the boat with them. ¹⁵ And he gave them a pointed order, saying, "Look out! Watch out that you look out for the yeast of the Farisaioi and the yeast of Hērōdēs."§ ¹⁶ And they tried to work it out with each other what it meant that they didn't have any loaves. ¹⁷ And perceiving this, he said to them, "Why are you trying to work it out with each other what it means that you don't have any loaves? Don't you realize, don't you understand, even now? Have your hearts become so calloused and unfeeling?

> ¹⁸ *"Do you have eyes but don't see?*
> *Do you have ears but don't hear?*¶

"And don't you remember, ¹⁹ when I broke the five loaves into pieces for the five thousand, how many baskets full of broken pieces you took up?" They told him, "Twelve." ²⁰ "When it was seven loaves for four thousand people, how many hampers full

---

* This place is unknown from any other source.

† See "swear" in the Glossary.

‡ It isn't clear which shore this refers to.

§ The bread for Passover feasting has to be made completely without yeast, so cooking implements and the home environment are thoroughly cleaned to prevent ritual contamination.

¶ See Jeremiah 5:21 and Ezekiel 12:2.

of broken pieces did you take up?" And they told [him], "Seven." 21 And he said to them, "You *still* don't understand?"*

22 Then they came to Bēthsaïda. And they brought Iēsous a blind man and begged him to touch the man. 23 And he took hold of the blind man's hand, led him outside the village, and spat into his eyes; then, putting his hands on him, he asked him, "Do you see anything?" 24 Then, seeing once more, he said, "I see people: it's as if I'm looking at trees walking around." 25 Next, he placed his hands on the man's eyes again, and he saw with his eyes wide open, and his sight was restored, and he saw everything clearly and in focus. † 26 And he sent him away to his home, telling him, "You shouldn't even go into the village."

27 Then Iēsous and his students went out to the villages around Kaisareia of Filippos,‡ but while they were on the road he questioned his students, saying to them, "Who do people say I am?" 28 And they answered him by saying, "They say [that] you're Iōannēs the baptizer, and others [that] you're Ēlias, and others [that] you're another one of the prophets." 29 But he asked them, "Who do *you* say I am?" Petros answered and said to him: "You're the anointed one." 30 And he sternly warned them to tell no one about him.

31 And he began to teach them that it was necessary for the son

---

* Jesus demands that they remember the exact scale of the miracle. Again, the verb for their ponderings, usually translated to mean mere "discussion," is cognate with *logos* (primarily a "reckoning" or "account") and is properly about *logical* discussion. In this context, this suggests that they are stuck trying to understand materially, through numbers. But the main point here must be that any concern they have with the amount of food on hand is silly, given Jesus' power to multiply food miraculously.

† See the story in 7:31–35, in which saliva is also efficacious. The narration proceeds in playful singsong, adding three different prepositions to the same verb. The first issue is whether the man can simply see (*blepein*). When he can see again (*anablepein*), his vision is blurred. Only with follow-up can he see with his eyes fully open (*diablepein*) yet (probably) focused (*emblepein*).

‡ This was one of two cities in Judea named after the Roman emperor Caesar Augustus. The Caesarea in this passage was north of the Sea of Galilee. Philip the Tetrarch was one of Herod the Great's sons and rebuilt "Philip's Caesarea."

of mankind to endure many things and to be tested and rejected by the elders and the high priests and the scholars, and to be killed, and to rise to his feet again after three days.* [32] And he was giving this discourse with confident freedom. Then Petros, taking him aside, began to speak sternly to him. [33] But he turned around and looked at his students, and castigated Petros, saying, "Get behind me, satanas! It's not the things that belong to god you're thinking of, but the things that belong to human beings."

[34] Then when he'd summoned the crowd along with his students, he said to them, "If someone wants to follow behind me, let him renounce all claim to himself, pick up the stake he'll be hung on, and follow me. [35] Whoever, in fact, wants to save his life will lose it. But whoever loses his life because of me and the good news will save it. [36] What kind of profit, tell me, does a person realize from the entire universe, if he loses his life? [37] What would someone give in exchange for his life? [38] Whoever, in fact, is ashamed of me and the things I've said among this unfaithful,† culpable generation, the son of mankind, when he comes in the glory of his father with the holy messengers, will also be ashamed of him."

CHAPTER 9

———

[1] And he said to them, "*Amēn* I tell you, there are some standing here who won't taste death until they see god's kingdom has arrived with power."

---

* This is an extreme example of what is called inclusive reckoning, which counts all units of time, no matter how partial. Jesus spends only one full day, the Sabbath, in the tomb. Yet the sum has passed into English as "three days." I have generally not drawn attention to inclusive reckoning, but in this case the difference is important.

† Literally "adulterous," an ancient prophetic image to describe the Jewish people's violation of its covenantal bond with God.

² Then after six days, Iēsous took Petros and Iakōbos and Iōannēs along with him and brought them up onto a high mountain privately, only them. ³ And his form changed before their eyes, and his clothes turned a glistening, glaring white, to a degree no laundryman on the earth could whiten them.* ⁴ And Ēlias along with Mōüsēs was seen by them,† and they were talking with Iēsous. ⁵ Now Petros responded by saying to Iēsous, "*Rabbí*, it's good that we're here, so let's make three shelters, one for you and one for Mōüsēs and one for Ēlias."‡ ⁶ He didn't in fact know how he should respond, since he and the others were terrified. ⁷ Then a cloud came and overshadowed them, and a voice came out of the cloud: "This is my son, the beloved§—listen to him." ⁸ And the next moment, when they looked around, they no longer saw anyone with them except Iēsous, him alone.

⁹ And when they came down from the mountain, he ordered them not to describe to anyone what they had seen, until the son of mankind was awakened from among the dead. ¹⁰ And they kept what he said to themselves, only arguing over what "being awakened from among the dead" meant.

¹¹ Then they questioned him, saying, "Why do the scholars say, 'It's necessary for Ēlias to come first'?" ¹² And he said to them, "Ēlias, coming first, reestablishes everything.¶ Then why has it been written that the son of mankind will endure many things

---

* Pure white clothing—difficult to produce and maintain—was associated with divinity and royalty.

† Jesus' covenantal authority is rounded out by the bringer of the Israelites to Canaan and purported author of the Torah, and the most militant and supernaturally powerful of the prophets.

‡ A *skēne* being a temporary shelter, divine beings or beings associated with divinity were supposed to have houses wherever they manifested, as the Hebrew God has his portable Tabernacle (from the Latin for "tent") as he leads his people through the wilderness after the escape from Egypt.

§ Similar wording occurs in God's instructions to sacrifice Isaac in Genesis 22:2.

¶ This language is used about Elijah in the Apocryphal book Sirach 48:10: he will return "to reestablish the tribes of Israel."

and be treated as if he were nothing?* [13] But I say to you that Ēlias too has come, and they did to him all that they wanted to—as it's been written about him."†

[14] And when they came back to the other students, they saw a large crowd around them, and scholars arguing with them. [15] And right away the crowd, seeing him, were overcome with excitement, and they ran up and greeted him. [16] And he asked them, "What are you arguing with them about?" [17] And someone in the crowd answered him: "Teacher, I've brought my son to you; he's got a spirit of muteness in him. [18] And whenever it takes hold of him, it slams him to the ground, and he foams at the mouth and grinds his teeth, and his body goes rigid. So I told your students to expel it from him, but they didn't have the power to do it." [19] And in response to them, he said, "You faithless generation!‡ How long will I be with you? How long will I put up with you?§ Bring him to me." [20] And they brought the child to him; and when it saw Iēsous, the spirit seized the boy right away, and he fell to the ground and rolled around, foaming at the mouth. [21] Then Iēsous asked his father, "How long has this been happening to him?" And the father said, "Since he was a little child. [22] And often it's thrown him into fire or into water to try to destroy him. But if you possibly can, come to our aid—if your heart goes out to us." [23] But Iēsous said to him, "That 'If you can'!—for someone who trusts, *anything* can be done." [24] Right

---

* See Isaiah 53:3.

† Elijah's wilderness mission, persecutions by royalty, and assumption into heaven are treated in 1 and 2 Kings. The story parallels John the Baptist, especially in that Elijah was hounded by the notorious royal consort Jezebel, partisan of the cult of Baal: she resembles the meddling Herodias, whose national and cultural allegiances were questionable and would have offered obvious parallels.

‡ Again, related to the metaphor of the covenant as marriage.

§ This question is somewhat similar to the one found in Psalms 13:1–2, but it looks as if it might also have been influenced by a famous rhetorical flourish in the Roman orator Cicero's speech against the traitor Catiline: *"Quo usque tandem abutere, Catilina, patientia nostra?"* ("Exactly how long in the end are you going to take advantage of our tolerance, Catiline?")

away the child's father cried out, saying, "I do trust—come to the aid of my failing trust!" ²⁵ But Iēsous, seeing that a crowd was running to the spot from all directions, berated the unclean spirit, telling it, "Mute and blind spirit, it's me ordering you, come out of him, and don't enter him again." ²⁶ And it cried out and threw the boy into long convulsions, and then came out of him. And he became like a corpse, so that most of the people said he'd died. ²⁷ But Iēsous seized his hand and roused him, and he stood up.

²⁸ Then when Iēsous had gone into the house, his students asked him privately, "Why weren't we able to expel it?" ²⁹ And he said to them, "This kind can't come out through anything but prayer."*

³⁰ Then they left that place and made their way through Galilaia, but he didn't want anyone to know it. ³¹ He instructed his students, in fact, by telling them the son of mankind was about to be given over into human hands, and they would kill him, but after he was killed he would awaken within three days.† ³² They didn't know what he was talking about, but they were afraid to question him.

³³ Then they came to Kafarnaoum. And while he was staying in a house there, he asked them, "What were you arguing about on the road?" ³⁴ But they were silent, since on the road they'd debated with each other who was greatest. ³⁵ Then he sat down and called the twelve and said to them, "If someone wants to be first, he needs to be last of all, and everyone else's attendant."‡ ³⁶ And he took a child and stood it in the center of the group, and

* Our word "epilepsy" comes from a Greek word for demonic "seizing." Pagans and Jews alike attributed this illness to demonic possession and prescribed religious remedies.

† Again, ancient inclusive reckoning expands a period with only one full day in it to "three days."

‡ Again, the verb for their discussion is based on *logos*. Is this a hint that the followers are once again trying to sort things out numerically? If so, Jesus upends the equation.

he took it in his arms and said to them, ³⁷ "Whoever takes in one child like this in my name takes me in. And whoever takes me in takes in not me but instead the one who sent me."*

³⁸ Iōannēs said to him, "Teacher, we saw somebody expelling demons in your name, and we tried to stop him, because he wasn't following us."† ³⁹ But Iēsous said, "Don't stop him, since no one who carries out an act of power in my name will be able to bad-mouth me any time soon! ⁴⁰ Whoever, in fact, isn't against us is for us.

⁴¹ "Whoever gives you a drinking cup full of water to drink, because you're under the name of the Anointed One, *amēn* I say to you, he certainly won't go without the payment due him."

⁴² And whoever sets a trap for one of these little ones who trust [in me] would do better having a millstone—a big one drawn by a donkey—hung around his neck and being thrown into the sea. ⁴³ So if your hand sets a trap for you, cut it off: it's better for you to enter into life maimed than to go with two hands to *ge'enna,* into the fire that can't be put out. ⁴⁵ And if your foot sets a trap for you, cut it off: it's better for you to enter into life crippled than to be thrown into *ge'enna* with both your feet. ⁴⁷ And if your eye sets a trap for you, pull it out: it's better for you to enter into god's kingdom one-eyed than to be thrown with both your eyes into *ge'enna,* ⁴⁸ where their worm doesn't die and the fire doesn't go out.‡

⁴⁹ "Everyone in fact will be salted with fire. ⁵⁰ Salt's a fine thing, but if salt's no longer salty, what are you going to use to

---

* See "receive" in the Glossary. Hospitality is a startling usage in connection with small children, who as a rule were not included in formal social gatherings. The widespread ancient idea of entertaining a god in disguise may figure here too.

† I.e., he is not under our religious leadership.

‡ These last two clauses are the same as the excised Verses 44 and 46. The strictures in the passage accord strongly with the Talmud, with its particular interest on control of the body and the senses to avoid temptation. See "hell" in the Glossary.

flavor *it?* Have salt within yourselves, and have peace with each other."*

CHAPTER 10

――――

¹ Then he set out from there and went into the region of Ioudaia [and] the far side of the river Iordanēs,† and again the crowds flocked to him, and he taught them again, as he was used to doing.

² And approaching, some Farisaioi asked him whether it was lawful for a man to let his wife go: they were putting him to the test. ³ But in response he said to them, "What did Mōüsēs command you to do?" ⁴ And they said, "Mōüsēs permitted us to write a notice of putting her away and to let her go." ⁵ But Iēsous said to them, "It was because your hearts were calloused and unfeeling that Mōüsēs wrote you this command. ⁶ But from the beginning, from the world's foundation, male and female he made them. ⁷ For this reason, a man is to leave his father and mother and be fused together with his wife. ⁸ And the two will be joined in a single body, so that they're no longer two people but a single body.‡ ⁹ So what god has yoked together, a human being must not separate."

¹⁰ But when they went back to the house, the students asked

――――――――

* In Leviticus 2:13, it is decreed that every sacrifice must be salted, and in the Septuagint, the Greek translation, that wording is "salted with salt." In Greek and Roman literature, "salt" can stand for the wit that prevents dullness and tastelessness. Salt was also an important preservative, while "decay" can stand in the Gospels for mortality. But why is salt, a good thing, associated with the punishment of fire? It is easy to suspect a later scribe's mistake or imposition.

† Jewish pilgrims going from Galilee to Jerusalem often crossed over to the east side of the Jordan to avoid Samaria, and then crossed back near Jericho.

‡ The Genesis verses are 1:27, 2:23–24, and 5:2. Human marriage, associated with the Creation, had an unusual degree of ethical importance for Jews.

him about this. [11] And he said to them, "Whoever lets his wife go and marries another woman violates her marriage. [12] And if she lets her husband go and marries another man, she violates marriage."*

[13] Then they were bringing him children so that he could touch them. And his students scolded them. [14] Seeing this, Iēsous grew angry and said to them: "Let the children come to me; don't stop them, because god's kingdom belongs to people like these. [15] *Amēn* I tell you, whoever doesn't welcome the kingdom of god as a child would can never enter it." [16] And he took them in his arms and blessed them, placing his hands on them.†

[17] And as he was setting off on the road, someone ran up to him, kneeled down, and asked him: "Excellent teacher, what should I do to inherit life for all time?" [18] And Iēsous said to him, "Why do you call me excellent? Nobody's excellent unless it's a single one, god. [19] You know the commands: You must not commit murder, you must not violate marriage, you must not steal, you must not give false testimony, you must not defraud, you must honor your father and mother."‡ [20] And the man said to him, "Teacher, I've observed all these commands from my youth on." [21] Looking intently at him, Iēsous felt affection for him, and told him, "You're missing one thing: come on, everything you have you need to sell and give to [the] destitute—and you'll have a storehouseful in the sky—and come and follow me." [22] And at this speech, the man's face clouded over, and he went away, distressed, as he possessed a great deal.

[23] Then Iēsous looked around and said to his students, "How

---

* The basic scriptural permission for divorce (Deuteronomy 24:1–4) opens with the condition that the husband find "indecency" in his wife, and the passage does not allude to her postmarital state except in decreeing that she may not return to her original husband.

† See the note at 9:37.

‡ See Exodus 20:12–16 and Deuteronomy 5:16–20. A stricture not among the Ten Commandments is included here: Do not defraud. This appears in Deuteronomy 24:14 and refers to cheating a worker of his pay.

hard it's going to be for those with property to enter god's kingdom!" ²⁴ And his students were astonished at the things he said.*
And Iēsous repeated his response, saying to them: "Children, how hard it is to enter god's kingdom! ²⁵ It's easier for a camel to go through [the] eye of [the] needle than for a rich man to enter god's kingdom." ²⁶ And they were overwhelmed with amazement, saying to each other, "Then who can be rescued?" ²⁷ Looking intently at them, Iēsous said, "With human beings, it's impossible, but not with god. Everything, you see, is possible with god."

²⁸ Petros spoke up, saying to him, "Look, *we*'ve left behind everything and followed you." ²⁹ Iēsous said, "*Amēn* I tell you all, there's no one who's left behind his house or his brothers or sisters or mother or father or children or fields because of me and because of the good news, ³⁰ who won't get a hundred times more now, in the present: houses and brothers and sisters and mothers and children and fields—along with hounding—as well as life throughout the ages in the age that's coming.† ³¹ But many who are first will be last, and [the] last first."

³² Now they were on the road going up to Hierosoluma,‡ and Iēsous was going ahead of them, and they were amazed; and those following him were afraid. And taking the twelve aside again, he began to speak to them about the things that were going to happen to him: ³³ "Look, we're going up to Hierosoluma, and the son of mankind will be handed over to the high priests

---

* These requirements are found nowhere in the Hebrew scripture, which emphasizes the contrary: secure wealth as God's reward for the righteous. The language with which the man has approached Jesus expresses conventional expectations along these lines: he thought he could *inherit* (Verse 17) eternal life the way he has received or will receive the family property; the "covenant" between God and the Jewish people is similarly expressed.

† The wording is playful. Obviously, one home, family, and farm are enough; a hundred would *be* a persecution.

‡ Though Jerusalem is comparatively very high above sea level and the Temple Mount itself is prominent in the landscape, "going up" to Jerusalem was also understood symbolically from ancient times, as a number of Psalms attest.

and the scholars, and they'll condemn him to death and hand him over to the other nations, ³⁴ and they'll taunt him and spit on him and flog him and kill him, but after three days he'll be on his feet again."*

³⁵ Now Iakōbos and Iōannēs, the sons of Zebedaios, approached and said to him, "Teacher, we want you to do for us whatever we ask you to." ³⁶ And he said to them, "What do you want [me] to do for you?" ³⁷ And they said to him, "Grant that we sit with you, one on your right side and one on your 'better' side, in your glory." ³⁸ But Iēsous said to them, "You don't know what you're asking for. Can you drink from the drinking cup I drink from, and can you be baptized with the baptism with which I'm baptized?" ³⁹ They said to him, "We can." But Iēsous said to them, "The drinking cup I drink from, you'll drink from, and you'll be baptized with the baptism with which I'm baptized; ⁴⁰ but as for sitting on my right side or on my side 'with the blessed name,' it's not mine to grant: no, those places belong to those they've been prepared for."†

⁴¹ When they heard this, the other ten grew upset at Iakōbos and Iōannēs. ⁴² But Iēsous called them over and said to them: "You know that in the other nations, those who look like the leaders lord it over them, and that their great men impose top-down authority on them.‡ ⁴³ But it isn't that way among *you*. Instead, whoever among you wants to be great is to be the attendant of the rest of you. ⁴⁴ And whoever among you wants to be first is to be everyone else's slave. ⁴⁵ In fact, even the son of mankind didn't come to *have* attendants but to *be* an atten-

---

* Again, inclusive reckoning's expansive way of describing units of time.

† Guests drank in turn, ritualistically, from a single cup; and Jews washed themselves before eating, using shared supplies of water. This seating will be at the "eschatological banquet," or the heavenly celebration at the end of human history that apocalyptic tradition looked forward to. Position at the table was extremely important in ancient dining, as it signified honor and social rank.

‡ In the Greek, word and sound play—including repetition of the prefix for "down"—add wit to this statement.

dant, and to give his life as the price to set a lot of other people free."*

⁴⁶ Then they came to Ierichō.† And as he was making his way out of Ierichō along with his students and a substantial crowd, the son of Timaios, Bartimaios,‡ a blind beggar, was sitting by the road. ⁴⁷ And having heard that Iēsous the Nazarēnos was there, he began to yell these words: "Son of David, Iēsous, have pity on me!"§ ⁴⁸ And many people scolded him and told him to be quiet, but he only yelled much louder: "Son of David, have pity on me!" ⁴⁹ Then Iēsous came to a standstill and said, "Call him." And they called the blind man, telling him, "Be brave! Get up, he's calling you." ⁵⁰ And he threw off his cloak, jumped up, and came to Iēsous. ⁵¹ And in response to him, Iēsous said, "What do you want me to do for you?" And the blind man said to him, "*Rabbouní*,¶ I want to see again." ⁵² And Iēsous said to him, "There you go! Your trust has healed you." And right away he could see again and followed him on the road.

* An important, well-connected man could expect to be ransomed out of captivity at a high price, not to die to rescue others.

† A city in the Jordan valley; see Joshua 6:1–21 concerning its early history. It is just south of Samaria and west of the Jordan River, and so a convenient stopping place on an apparently usual route to Jerusalem from Galilee that circled back to the west of the Jordan to avoid Samaria.

‡ "Bartimaios" also means "Son of Timaios," and is a Greek transliteration of the Aramaic.

§ The Gospel of Mark, the earliest Gospel, makes no prior mention of Jesus' human genealogy, which by the time of the Matthew (see 1:1–17) and Luke (see 3:23–38) was a matter of elaborate assertion.

¶ The man calls him not *rabbí* (see "rabbi" and "teacher" in the Glossary), but the emphatic *rabbouní*, which occurs elsewhere in the Gospels only in John 20:16. *Rabbouní* (or *rabbōni*) can actually be addressed to God.

CHAPTER 11

———

¹ And when they approached Hierosoluma and reached Bēthfagē and Bēthania near the mountain with the olive trees,* he sent off two of his students, ² telling them, "Get moving to this village ahead of you, and as soon as you enter it you'll find a colt† tied up, which nobody's ridden yet. Untie it and bring it here. ³ And if someone asks you, 'Why are you doing this?' say, 'His master needs him, and he'll send him back here right away.'"‡ ⁴ So they went and found a colt tied at a gate, outside on the street, and they untied him. ⁵ And some of the people who were standing there said to them, "What are you doing, untying that colt?" ⁶ But the students spoke to them as Iēsous had told them to, and the people allowed them to go. ⁷ And they brought the colt to Iēsous and threw their cloaks on him,§ and Iēsous sat on him. ⁸ And many people spread their cloaks on the road, while others spread there the leafy branches they had cut in the countryside.¶ ⁹ And those who went before him and those who followed him cried out,

>*Hōsanna!***
>*Blessed is the one who comes in the lord's name.*

---

* Both of these villages have been linked to the modern town Al-Eizariya, about a mile and a half from Jerusalem on the far side of the Mount of Olives.

† The universal interpretation seems to be "donkey"; here it is clear only that it is a young animal, whether a horse, donkey, or mule.

‡ The original word order makes the witticism even more definite. There is only one "of him" in the Greek, placed between the words for "master" and "need," and therefore ambiguous: as literally as possible, this is "The master/owner [of him] has need [of him]."

§ The design for a saddle was a late import from the Asian steppes.

¶ Riding could be considered prestigious and showy; see Esther 6:6–9.

** Hebrew for "Rescue [me *or* us], I beg you."

¹⁰ *Blessed is our father David's kingdom, which is coming.*
Hōsanna, in the highest places!*

¹¹ Then he came into Hierosoluma and arrived at the temple precinct, and looked around at everything. Since it was already late in the day, he went out to Bēthania with the twelve.†

¹² And the next day, when they had left Bēthania, he was hungry. ¹³ Seeing from far away a fig tree that had many leaves, he went hoping to find something on her, but once he'd gone up to her, he found nothing but leaves. It wasn't in fact the season for figs.‡ ¹⁴ But he reacted by saying to her, "No longer, for all of time, is anyone going to eat fruit from you."§ And his students heard.

¹⁵ Then they came into Hierosoluma, and once he entered the temple precinct, he proceeded to throw out the vendors and shoppers in the precinct, and he turned over the tables of the money-changers, and the backrest-chairs of those who were selling doves. ¹⁶ And he wouldn't allow anyone to carry an object through the precinct. ¹⁷ And he made this a lesson, telling them, "Hasn't it been written,

> "'*My house is to be called a house of prayer*
> *For all the nations of the world'?*
> *But you've made it a cave where bandits lurk.*"¶

---

* See Psalms 118:25–26.

† Herod the Great's expanded Second Temple rivaled the pagan "Seven Wonders" such as the pyramids of Egypt and attracted sightseers as well as worshippers.

‡ Passover is in the spring.

§ The fig tree is a traditional symbol for Israel, owing faithful productivity to its true owner, God; its destruction here looks forward to the destruction of the Temple in the year 70. But the imagery of an unpruned and overgrown tree standing for undisciplined and therefore useless human personality is widespread. Note the "hubris"—based on this very agricultural metaphor—of Greek tragedy. Since the tree's fertility is at issue, it's fitting that Jesus addresses it as a personified *female*, reflecting the feminine gender of the noun and pronouns that is visible in the Greek.

¶ Zechariah 14:21 predicts a ban on traders in the Temple. Urbanization and

¹⁸ And the high priests and the scholars heard and started seeking a way to destroy him. They in fact feared him, since the entire crowd was overpowered by his teaching.

¹⁹ And when evening came on, they made their way out beyond the city.

²⁰ And early in the morning, when they were passing by it, they saw the fig tree dried up from the roots. ²¹ And Petros remembered and said to him: "*Rabbí*, look, the fig tree you cursed has dried up." ²² And Iēsous responded by saying to them: "Have trust in god. ²³ *Amēn* I tell you: whoever says to this mountain, 'Be lifted up and thrown into the sea,' and his heart doesn't waver, but rather he trusts that what he says is about to be done, it will be granted him. ²⁴ Because of this, I say to you all, whatever you pray for and ask for, trust that you've gotten it, and it will be granted to you. ²⁵ And when you're standing at prayer, let go whatever you have against anyone, so that your father in the skies lets you go from the blunders *you*'ve made."*

²⁷ Then they came into Hierosoluma again, and while he was walking around in the temple precinct, the high priests and the scholars and the elders came up to him ²⁸ and said to him, "By what authority do you do these things—or who gave you this authority to do these things?" ²⁹ But Iēsous said to them, "I'll question you about one matter, and you need to answer me, and then I'll tell you by what kind of authority I do these things. ³⁰ Did the baptism that Iōannēs carried out come from heaven or from human beings? Give me your answer." ³¹ And they tried to

---

travel necessitated commerce in live animals for the required sacrifices. For Jews, money also had to be changed, because the Temple tax could be paid only in a single currency, Tyrian shekels. But here in Verse 16, Jesus actually enforces a Sabbath-like ban—but applied to holy *space,* not holy time—on carrying objects through the relatively freewheeling Temple courtyard. The verses quoted are Isaiah 56:7 and Jeremiah 7:11.

* Verse 26 is not included here, because it has been excised from the authoritative Greek text as not genuine. It reads, "But if you don't let go, your father in the skies won't let you go from your blunders either."

work it out among themselves, in these terms: "If we say 'From heaven,' he'll say '[Then] why didn't you trust him?' ³² But should we say 'From human beings'?"—they were afraid of the crowd; *they* all in fact held that Iōannēs truly was a prophet. ³³ So in answer to Iēsous they said, "We don't know." Then Iēsous said to them: "I'm not telling you either by what kind of authority I do these things."

CHAPTER 12

—

¹ And he undertook to speak to them through comparative stories. "A man planted a vineyard, and put a fence around it, and hollowed out a wine press,* and built a watchtower, and leased the place to farmers and went abroad. ² And at the proper time he dispatched his slave to the farmers so that he could get a share of the vineyard's harvest from the farmers. ³ But they seized him and nearly skinned him alive, and sent him away empty-handed. ⁴ And again the owner sent a slave to them, another one this time. That one too they beat, practically taking his head off, and treated him shamefully.† ⁵ And he sent them another slave, and this one they killed; and he sent many others, and some they more or less skinned alive, and others they killed. ⁶ The man had no one left but his single beloved son. He sent him to them last of all, saying, 'They'll have respect for my son.' ⁷ But those farmers said to each other, 'This is the heir. Come on, let's kill him, and the inheritance will be ours.' ⁸ Then they seized him and killed him and threw his body out of the vineyard. ⁹ [So] what will the owner of the vineyard do? He'll come and destroy the farmers and give the vineyard to other people.‡ ¹⁰ Haven't you read this, that's written:

---

* Wine presses appear to have normally been carved into the bedrock.

† Literally, "deprived him of honor," probably meaning that they raped him.

‡ I.e., the covenant of Jewish inheritance will be transferred to Gentiles.

'The stone that the builders tested and rejected—
It turned out to head up the corner:
¹¹ *The lord made it turn out this way—*
And it's amazing in our eyes?"*

¹² And they were trying to get hold of him, but they were afraid of the crowd, since they knew that they themselves were the target of the story he'd just told; so they let him alone and went away.

¹³ Then they sent to him some of the Farisaioi and some of Hērōdēs' people† to trap him in an argument. ¹⁴ And they came and said to him, "Teacher, we know you're truthful and not influenced by anybody: you don't look to people's outward distinctions, but rather on the basis of truth you teach god's path. Is it permitted to pay the individual tax to Kaisar or not? Should we pay or shouldn't we?"‡ ¹⁵ But perceiving their play-acting, he said to them: "Why are you testing me? Bring me a denarius and let me see it." ¹⁶ And they brought him one. And he said to them, "Whose image and inscription are these? And they told him, "Kaisar's." ¹⁷ And Iēsous said to them, "Pay Kaisar what belongs to Kaisar—give it right back to him—and pay god what belongs to god."§ And they were confounded by him.

---

* Psalms 118:22–23 has, literally, "for the head of the corner." This image seems thus to have been confused from the start: cornerstones are at the base of a structure, whereas a keystone is at the upper joint of an arch, and a capstone tops a flat-topped structure such as a wall. In any event, the sense of the metaphor is clear: one stone stabilizes a whole building.

† Probably courtiers or officials of the Romans' client king.

‡ The Greek word for this tax is from the Latin word *census.* An ancient census was primarily a tax roll. Jews at the time of Jesus paid two separate individual taxes, one to the Temple and one to Rome through the unregulated and very unpopular Imperial tax collectors. Galilee had been the source of a violent revolt against the institution of census taxation around the time of Jesus' birth.

§ The denarius was the iconic international currency, with the world ruler's image cast in relief on it. But only the shekels of Tyre were acceptable as taxes paid to the Jerusalem Temple, so a denarius has no essential function where Jesus

¹⁸ And Saddoukaioi came to him—these are people who say that the dead don't rise again*—and they questioned him, saying, ¹⁹ "Teacher, Mōusēs wrote down for us that if someone's brother dies and leaves behind a wife but doesn't leave a child, his brother has to take the wife and raise up seed for his brother.† ²⁰ There were seven brothers. Now the first one took a wife, and when he died, he didn't leave seed. ²¹ Then the second took her and died without leaving seed; and the same for the third; ²² and none of the seven left behind seed. Last of all, the wife died too. ²³ In the rising [when the dead rise], whose wife will she be? All seven in fact had her as a wife." ²⁴ And Iēsous said to them, "Isn't this why you're misled, that you don't know either the writings or the power of god? ²⁵ The fact is that when people rise from among the dead, they don't take wives, and they're not given as wives, but they're like messengers in the skies. ²⁶ As to the dead rising, haven't you read in the book of Mōusēs, in the passage about the bush, how god spoke to him, saying: 'I am the god of Abraam and [the] god of Isaak and [the] god of Iakōb'? ²⁷ He's not a god of corpses but of living people! You've been badly misled."‡

²⁸ Then one of the scholars approached, having heard them arguing; seeing that Iēsous had answered them well, he ques-

---

and his audience are now. The literal meaning of the Greek verb for "pay what you owe" is "give back": not only is the money owed, but it is owned, with its owner's picture and name on it: there is no question that it should be returned to him.

* We know little else about the beliefs of the Sadducees, a late, elite sect that intersected with the Temple priesthood.

† Genesis 38:8, Deuteronomy 25:5–6. The practical purposes of such "levirate marriage" were to perpetuate the dead man's family, channel his property through the male line, and provide the widow with the support of a son in her old age.

‡ The witty intellectual sparring in this passage is similar to exchanges recorded in the Talmud. An afterlife threatens polyandry, but the lack of an afterlife means a nonsensical boast on God's part (Exodus 3:6). The first five books of the Hebrew Bible, known as the Pentateuch, are traditionally ascribed to Moses, though before the Pentateuch's narration is over, he is dead.

tioned him: "Which is the chief command among them all?" [29] And Iēsous answered: "The chief one is 'Listen, Israēl: the lord our god is one lord, [30] and you are to love the lord your god with the whole of your heart and the whole of your life, and the whole of your mind and the whole of your strength.' [31] The next most important command is this one: 'You are to love the one next to you the way you love yourself.'* There is no command greater than these two." [32] Then the scholar said to him, "That's right, teacher. It's true what you said: there is one, and no other, none except him; [33] and to love him with the whole of the heart and the whole of the understanding and the whole of the strength;† and to love the one next to you the way you love yourself—this is more than all the animals burnt to ashes as offerings, and all the other sacrifices."‡ [34] Then, seeing that [he] had answered intelligently, Iēsous said to him, "You're not far from god's kingdom." And no one dared to question him any longer.

[35] And Iēsous said in response, while he was teaching in the temple precinct, "What do the scholars mean by saying that the anointed one is David's son? [36] David himself says, inspired by the holy life-breath:

> *"'The lord said to my lord,*
> *"Sit to the right of me*
> *Until I put your enemies*
> *Under your feet.'"*

---

* Undisputed in status are the commandment to love God in the Shema (the "Hear": Deuteronomy 6:4–5) and the commandment to "love thy neighbor as thyself" (Leviticus 19:18). Parallel to the latter is the famous saying of Hillel, the most renowned of the Pharisees: "What is hateful to you, do not do it to your neighbor: that is the whole Torah."

† Notice the difference in the potentialities named in the Shema the second time. There was no fixed, authoritative text of the Bible in any language at this period.

‡ See Micah 6:6–8. A "holocaust" in ancient ritual meant that instead of all or most of the sacrificial animal's edible parts' being saved to eat, the entire carcass was burned to ashes—a rare and extreme measure.

³⁷ "David himself calls him lord, so how is he his son?"

And the large crowd heard him with pleasure.*

³⁸ And in his teaching, he said, "Watch out for the scholars, who are always ready to walk around in long robes and be greeted respectfully in the marketplaces, ³⁹ and have the seats of highest honor in the synagogues, and the couches of highest honor at banquets. ⁴⁰ They wolf down the homes of widows and say long prayers as a pretext. They're going to get a heavier verdict given on *them* than they ever gave!"†

⁴¹ Then when he was sitting in front of the treasury, he watched how the crowd was putting copper coins into the treasury, and many rich people put in a lot. ⁴² But a destitute widow came and put in two lepta, worth a quadrans.‡ ⁴³ And he called his students over and said to them, "*Amēn* I tell you: this destitute widow has put in more than all the others who put money into the treasury. ⁴⁴ They all of course put in out of their excess, but she did it out of her shortfall, putting in everything she had, the whole of what she was living on."

CHAPTER 13

¹ Then when he was making his way out of the temple precinct, one of his students said to him: "Teacher, look at how magnificent the stones are, and how magnificent the buildings are!"

---

* This quotation is from the beginning of Psalm 110. It is likely that the poem's speaker, a court musician, represents the divinity addressing the king, but Jesus' view apparently is that the communication is between David and the Messiah.

† The wording in Greek suggests that they acted regularly, and harshly, as judges.

‡ The rich are contributing handfuls of change, but the widow's coins are fantastically low in value. Women left without breadwinners could earn from indoor crafts such as spinning and weaving, but they competed with unpaid female slaves and servants.

² But Iēsous said to him, "You see these huge buildings? There won't be a stone left on top of another here: they will all be torn down."*

³ Then as he was sitting on the mountain with the olive trees, opposite the temple, Petros and Iakōbos and Iōannēs and Andreas questioned him privately: ⁴ "Tell us, when will these things happen, and what the sign will be when all these things are about to be fulfilled?" ⁵ And Iēsous proceeded to tell them, "Watch out, so that no one leads you astray. ⁶ Many will come in my name, saying, 'It's me,' and they'll lead many people astray. ⁷ When you hear about wars, and hear rumors of wars, don't be alarmed. It's necessary that these things happen, but that won't yet be the end. ⁸ One nation will rise up against another, and one kingdom against another, there will be earthquakes in various places, there will be famines: these things will be the beginning of the labor pains.†

⁹ "Watch out for yourselves. They'll hand you over to the governing councils,‡ and in the synagogues you'll be beaten within an inch of your lives, and you'll stand before governors and kings because of me, to give testimony to them. ¹⁰ But it's necessary, first of all, for the good news to be proclaimed to all nations. ¹¹ And when they hand you over and bring you in, don't worry beforehand about what to say: instead, whatever is given to you at that time, say it; it won't in fact be you speaking, but the holy life-breath. ¹² And one brother will hand over another to death, and a father will hand over his child, and children will rebel against their parents and have them put to death. ¹³ And you'll be

---

* The Second Temple, renovated by Herod the Great, was in fact mostly razed by the Romans in 70 c.e. as they put down a Jewish rebellion. Today, only the Wailing Wall remains standing.

† These images also suggest the First Jewish–Roman War of 66–73 c.e., including the siege of Jerusalem, but also the motifs of apocalyptic literature going back for several centuries, and the writings of Jewish prophets as early as the eighth century.

‡ The local versions of the Sanhedrin.

hated by everyone because of my name. But whoever holds out to the end will be rescued.*

[14] "But when you see 'the annihilating abomination' set up where it shouldn't be—the reader has to realize what that means†—then those in Ioudaia had better run to the hills, [15] and whoever's on the roof had better not come down or go into his house to get anything, [16] and no one in the field should go back to get his cloak. [17] Pity the women who have children in their wombs, and the women who are nursing, in those days!

[18] "Pray that this doesn't happen in the winter. [19] Those days will be a shattering such as there hasn't been since the beginning, when the world's foundations were founded by god, until this moment, and never will be again. [20] And if the lord didn't cut short the days, no mortal being would be rescued. But because of the chosen ones, whom he chose, he has cut short the days.

[21] "But at that time, if someone says to you, 'Look, here's the anointed one' or 'Look, he's right there,' don't believe him. [22] False anointed ones and false prophets will emerge, and they'll perform 'signs' and 'marvels' to lead the chosen astray, if that were possible. [23] But you, watch out. I've told you all this beforehand.

[24] "But during those days, after that shattering,

> *The sun will be shadowed over,*
> *and the moon won't give off her luster,*
> [25] *And the stars will be falling from the sky,*
> *and the powers in the skies will be shaken.*‡

---

* The imagery now reflects the persecution of Jesus' followers by both Jewish and Roman authorities. However, major persecutions did not begin until Nero lashed out at the Christians in Rome in the year 64.

† Daniel 9:27, 11:31, and 12:11. The Gospel author may be referring to an attempt to install a statue of the emperor Caligula there in or around 40 C.E. But there were many desecrations in 70 C.E., when the conquering general actually entered the Holy of Holies.

‡ See Isaiah 13:10.

²⁶ "And then they'll see the son of mankind coming on clouds, with great power and glory. ²⁷ And then he'll send out his messengers and gather [his] chosen ones from the sources of the four winds, from the end of the earth to the end of the sky.*

²⁸ "But from the fig tree, learn the analogy. As soon as her branch becomes tender and sprouts leaves, you know that summer's near. ²⁹ It's the same for you too: when you see that these things are happening, you must know that he's near, right at the gates.

³⁰ "*Amēn* I'm telling you: this generation won't by any means pass away until all these things have happened. ³¹ The sky and the earth will pass away, but the things I'm telling you will never pass away.

³² "But about that day or the hour, no one knows; not even the messengers in the sky know, and not the son, but the father only.

³³ "Watch out, stay awake, as you don't know when the crisis will come. ³⁴ It's like a man going abroad, who leaves his home and puts his slaves in charge, each with his own work, and orders the doorkeeper to be on the alert— ³⁵ so, all of you, be on the alert. You don't know when the master of the house is coming, whether in the evening or in the middle of the night, or when the rooster crows,† or at dawn. ³⁶ Make sure that he doesn't come suddenly and find you sleeping. ³⁷ But what I say to you, I say to everyone: Be on the alert."‡

---

* Again, this is language typical of apocalyptic literature.

† This might be as early as 3:00 A.M.

‡ Jesus' followers associated the apocalypse with his Second Coming, which they expected in short order, like his appearances after the crucifixion. The indefinite delay contributed to provisos of uncertainty in the Gospels.

CHAPTER 14

¹ It was two days before the *pascha* and the festival of bread made without yeast, and the high priests and the scholars were seeking a way to seize him by stealth and kill him. ² In fact, they said, "Not at the festival, so that there won't be an uproar from the people."*

³ And when he was in Bēthania,† in the house of Simōn (who had a skin disease‡), he was reclining at the table when there came a woman with an alabaster jar of perfume, which was genuine, extremely costly nard. She broke open the jar and poured its contents over his head. ⁴ But some of the people present were complaining to each other: "What was the point of wasting the perfume? ⁵ This perfume could have been sold for more than three hundred denarii,§ and the money could have been given to the destitute." And they snarled at her. ⁶ But Iēsous said, "Leave her alone. Why are you making trouble for her? She's done me a good service. ⁷ You'll have the destitute among you forever, and whenever you want you can do good for them. But you're *not* going to have me forever. ⁸ What she had in her power to do, she did. She acted in advance to perfume my body for burial. ⁹ *Amēn*

---

* This was the greatest of the three Jewish pilgrimage festivals; the Torah command to appear "before God," with sacrifices on each occasion, meant that Jews from all over the world visited the Temple. The Passover of the Angel of Death, who spared the Jewish firstborn but slew the Egyptian ones, was celebrated with feasting to commemorate the miraculous liberation of the Hebrew people from Egyptian slavery. It is not clear why the officials do not follow through on their own plan and wait until the crowds from the festival are dispersed.

† See the note at Verse 11:1 concerning the likely identity and location of this town.

‡ This was probably not leprosy or another severe condition showing on the skin, which would not allow him normal social interactions (Leviticus 13–14).

§ Around the yearly wages of a laborer in good times.

I tell you, wherever in the whole world the good news is spread, what she did will be spoken of as part of it, so that she'll be remembered."*

[10] Then Ioudas Iskariōth, one of the twelve, went to the high priests, meaning to hand him over to them. [11] And when they heard him, they were thrilled, and they promised to pay him in silver. So he was seeking to hand him over at the right moment.

[12] Then on the first day of the festival of bread made without yeast, when people used to sacrifice the *pascha*,† his students said to him, "Where do you want us to go, where we can prepare for you to eat the *pascha*?" [13] And he sent two of his students, telling them, "Get moving and go to the city, and a person carrying a water jar will come face to face with you. Follow him, [14] and wherever he goes in,‡ say to the head of the house that the teacher asks, 'Where's my accommodation, where I can eat the *pascha* with my students?' [15] And he'll show you an upstairs room, a large one, comfortably furnished and ready. Then you need to make ready for us there." [16] And the students went out, and came to the city, and they found that it was just as he'd told them, and they prepared the *pascha*.

---

* Nard, or spikenard, is a resin peculiar to a Himalayan plant. Perfumes were not only for preparing corpses for interment—traditionally women's work—but were also offered as sacrifices. But *kingly* or *messianic* anointing was another matter; the verb used here for rubbing on oil or ointment is different from the verb—from which "Christ" derives—for anointing a king.

† *Pascha* is the slaughtered animal, a lamb for each household, as well as the Passover festival itself. The lambs were slaughtered in the Temple courtyard. The past tense of the verb here strongly suggests that the Temple, along with its sacrifices, no longer existed when the Gospel of Mark was written. The complex was destroyed in 70 C.E.

‡ Men were not the usual carriers of water in the ancient world. This water carrier is given the technically masculine but in effect vague designation as "a person," probably because it would be unseemly if the men were pictured following a woman in the street, a circumstance with sordid overtones.

¹⁷ And when it was evening, he came with the twelve. ¹⁸ Then while they were reclining and eating,* Iēsous said, "*Amēn* I tell you that one among you, eating with me, is going to hand me over." ¹⁹ They grew distressed, saying one by one, "It can't be me, can it?" ²⁰ But he said to them, "It's one of the twelve, who's dipping into the bowl along with me.† ²¹ This is because the son of mankind is going on his way—just as it's been written about him‡—but he has it coming, that specimen of mankind through whom the son of mankind is handed over. It would be better for *that* specimen of mankind if he hadn't been born."§

²² Then while they were eating, he took a loaf of bread, blessed it, and broke it into pieces and gave it to them, saying, "Take it: this is my body." ²³ Then, taking the cup, he gave thanks for it and gave it to them,¶ and they all drank from it.** ²⁴ And he said to them, "This is my blood of the dispensation,†† the blood poured out for the sake of many people.‡‡ ²⁵ *Amēn* I tell you, I'll never again drink any of what the vine yields until that day when I drink it new in god's kingdom."

²⁶ Then once they had sung a song of praise, they went out onto the mountain with the olive trees. ²⁷ And Iēsous said to them, "You'll all fall away, because it's been written,

---

* This is the manner familiar from Classical culture.

† Here, bread is dipped into a common bowl to pick up portions of prepared food.

‡ The scriptural reference is uncertain.

§ This could be self-conscious wordplay on the developing terminology of Jesus' identity. (See pp. xxix–xxxi of the Introduction on "Son of Man.")

¶ These prayers are *kiddush,* "sanctification," prescribed in the Oral Torah that was supplementary to scripture.

** This was the usual way for men to drink at a festive gathering, from the same cup, each taking a turn.

†† See "covenant" in the Glossary.

‡‡ Reminiscent of sacrificial blood spurting from an artery and ritually caught in cups, as in the ceremony of slaughtering the Passover lambs. But consuming blood was forbidden to Jews.

'I'll strike the shepherd down,
*And the sheep will be scattered in all directions.'**

²⁸ "But after I'm awakened, I'll go ahead of you into Galilaia."
²⁹ But Petros said to him, "Even if all the others fall away, I won't."
³⁰ But Iēsous said to him, "*Amēn* I'm telling you: before tomorrow, during this actual night, before the rooster crows twice, you'll deny three times that you know me." ³¹ But Petros spoke passionately: "Even if I have to die along with you, I'll never deny you." And all the others said likewise.

³² Then they came to the place whose name is Gethsēmani,† and he said to his students, "Sit here while I pray." ³³ And he took with him Petros and Iakōbos and Iōannēs. And as horror and anguish started to come over him, ³⁴ he said to them, "The life within me is in terrible pain, to the point of death. Stay with me and keep awake." ³⁵ And going ahead a little, he fell on the ground in supplication and asked that, if it were possible, the appointed time might pass by him. ³⁶ And he said, "*Abba*—father—everything is possible for you. Take away this cup from me. But still it has to be what you want, not what I want." ³⁷ Then he came and found them sleeping, and he said to Petros, "Simōn, are you sleeping? Didn't you have the strength to stay awake for a single hour? ³⁸ Keep awake and pray, so that you don't come to be tested. The life-breath is eager, but the mere body is feeble." ³⁹ And he went away again and prayed, saying the same thing. ⁴⁰ Then he came back again and found them sleeping, since their eyes were weighed down, and they didn't know how to answer him. ⁴¹ Then he came a third time and said to them, "Are you still sleeping and taking it easy? Enough! The time has come. Look, the son of mankind is being handed over to wrongdoers. ⁴² Get up, let's go! Look, the one handing me over is almost here."

---

* Zechariah 13:7.

† "Place of the Oil Press." This is capitalized in the Greek text, unlike the words for what is traditionally called the Mount of Olives in English.

⁴³ And right away, while he was still speaking, Ioudas arrived, one of the twelve, and along with him a mob, armed with swords and clubs, who came from the high priests and scholars and elders.* ⁴⁴ The one handing Iēsous over had told them a signal to act on, saying, "Whoever I kiss, it's him. Get hold of him and take him away under guard." ⁴⁵ So right when he arrived, Ioudas approached him and said, *"Rabbí!"* and gave him the kiss of respect.† ⁴⁶ And they laid hold and took control of him. ⁴⁷ And a certain one of the bystanders drew a sword and struck the chief priest's slave, taking off his ear.

⁴⁸ And Iēsous' response to them was to say, "You've come out with swords and clubs to seize me, as if I were a bandit?‡ ⁴⁹ Day after day I was with you in the temple precinct teaching, and you didn't take hold of me. But this is the way the writings can be fulfilled." ⁵⁰ And everyone ran off, leaving him behind.§ ⁵¹ But there was a certain young man accompanying him, wearing only a linen cloth over his bare body, and they took hold of him. ⁵² But he left the linen cloth behind and ran off naked.¶

⁵³ And they led Iēsous away to the chief priest, and all the high priests and elders and scholars came together, ⁵⁴ and Petros followed him at a distance clear into the chief priest's courtyard, where he sat with the retainers and warmed himself by the fire.

---

* It seems extremely unlikely that the Jewish hierarchy—normally anxious to help keep the peace—effected the arrest, much less in this provocative manner. Would the Roman regime ever have authorized such a move, and would Jews have undertaken it on the night of their most important festival, against fellow celebrants?

† See "kiss" in the Glossary.

‡ See "thief" in the Glossary.

§ See Verse 27 above.

¶ This mysterious and haunting incident is recounted only in Mark. The "young man" (a rare word in the Gospels, probably connoting distinction) is lightly dressed in linen, which was above average in cost and showiness; lower-class Jews dressed in wool. I concur with those scholars who think that the streaker is an important person, known but deliberately not named. A common force of the Greek pronoun *tis,* used here, is "a certain someone."

⁵⁵ And the high priests and the whole of the high council* were looking for testimony against Iēsous to justify putting him to death, but they couldn't find any. ⁵⁶ Many people in fact gave false testimony against him, but all the testimony didn't match. ⁵⁷ And certain people stood up and gave false testimony against him, saying, ⁵⁸ "We heard him saying, 'I'll destroy this shrine that was built with human hands, and in the course of three days† I'll build another one without the aid of anyone's hands.'"‡ ⁵⁹ But even on this point, their testimony didn't match. ⁶⁰ And the chief priest stood up among them and questioned Iēsous, saying, "Don't you have any answer? What are these people accusing you of in their testimony?" ⁶¹ But he was silent and gave no answer. Again the chief priest questioned him, now saying to him, "Are *you* the anointed one, the son of the blessed one?"§ ⁶² And Iēsous said, "I am, and you'll see the son of mankind sitting to the right of the power and coming with the clouds of the sky."¶ ⁶³ Then the chief priest tore his tunic** and said, "Why do we need any more witnesses? ⁶⁴ You've heard the blasphemy. What's your decision?" And they all condemned him as deserving death.††

* The Sanhedrin.

† Again, by inclusive reckoning, the "three days" of the text is a generous calculation for a period including only one full day.

‡ The claim appears elsewhere in the Gospels (John 2:19), but it is not worded this way. In any event, Jesus would be foretelling his death and resurrection. See "T/temple" in the Glossary.

§ I do not think the chief priest identifies the Messiah as God's literal son. (See p. xxxi of the Introduction.) Though "son of God" is an epithet of the Messiah in the Dead Sea Scrolls, descent from David is emphasized, and Hebrew Bible passages are quoted that cannot be understood in a genetic sense: for example, in 2 Samuel 7:14, God declares to David, who is well into his existence and whose human paternity is undoubted, "I will be a father to him, and he will be a son to me."

¶ See Psalms 110:1 and Daniel 7:13.

** See Leviticus 10:6; tearing clothing could be a mere rhetorical gesture for pagans, but it was forbidden to Jewish priests.

†† This religious body does not have the authority to condemn a man to

⁶⁵ Then some began to spit on him and wrap up his head to hide his face,* and to punch him and say to him, "Give us a prophecy!" And the retainers took him and slapped him around.

⁶⁶ And while Petros was below in the courtyard, one of the chief priest's slave girls came, ⁶⁷ and, seeing him warming himself at the fire, she stared at him and said, "You too, you were with the Nazarēnos Iēsous." ⁶⁸ And he denied it, saying, "I don't know *or* understand what you're talking about." And he went out into the forecourt. [Then the rooster crowed.]

⁶⁹ But the slave girl, looking at him, began saying again to the bystanders, "He's one of them." ⁷⁰ And he denied it again. Then after a little while the bystanders in turn said to Petros, "It's true, you're one of them—in fact, you're a Galilaian." ⁷¹ And he began to curse, and to swear, "I don't know this guy you're talking about."† ⁷² And right after he'd spoken the rooster crowed a second time. And Petros remembered what Iēsous had told him: "Before the rooster crows twice, you'll deny three times that you know me." And he broke down and cried.

CHAPTER 15

──────

¹ And right at dawn, the high priests had a consultation with the elders and the scholars and the whole of the high council. Then they tied Iēsous up, led him away, and handed him over to Pilatos.‡

² And Pilatos questioned him, saying, "Are you the king of the

──────────

death independently for a political crime, which is the reason he is passed on to Pilate.

* The soldiers literally "veil him around," possibly a gendered insult.

† See "curse" and "swear" in the Glossary.

‡ This is the Roman governor of Judea. A contemporary inscription concerning his tenure provides tangible evidence that the crucifixion story is factual.

Ioudaioi?"* And he answered by saying, "*You* say so." ³ And the high priests made many accusations against him. ⁴ But Pilatos questioned him again, saying, "Don't you have any answer? Look how many things they're accusing you of!" ⁵ But Iēsous no longer gave any answer, and this surprised Pilatos.

⁶ At the festival every year he released to them one prisoner they asked for.† ⁷ Now, there was someone called Barabbas, being held in chains along with other insurrectionists who during the insurrection had committed murder.‡ ⁸ So the crowd came up and proceeded to ask Pilatos to do what he usually did for them. ⁹ But Pilatos responded to them by saying, "Do you want me to release to you 'the king of the Ioudaioi'?" ¹⁰ He in fact knew that the high priests had handed him over because of jealousy. ¹¹ But the high priests stirred up the crowd to demand the release of Barabbas to themselves instead. ¹² Then Pilatos, responding again, said to them, "So what [do you want] me to do with [the one you call] 'the king of the Ioudaioi'?" ¹³ Then they yelled back, "Hang him on the stakes!"§ ¹⁴ But Pilatos said to them, "What's he

---

* A pointed question: the Romans sometimes made use of client kings, such as Herod the Great and his heirs, but cooperative local potentates were of course the only candidates.

† There is no independent corroboration of this custom, but it might have been this governor's improvisation, or a regular practice in line with other accommodations of the Jews, such as exemption from Roman military service and from formal worship of the Roman emperor.

‡ The name means "son of the father" in Aramaic. His is a far more typical kind of troublemaking than Jesus' to come to a provincial government's notice. There are several historical accounts of religious zealotry or separatist agitation combined with banditry or assassination during these decades. (See "thief" in the Glossary.) But if Barabbas had been involved in an actual insurrection, it is unthinkable that he would be made available for release.

§ Crucifixion was a standard Roman method of execution for those without citizen rights, and was a brutal display of state power. (It was, for example, the execution method for thousands of escaped slaves after the failed Spartacus rebellion in the first century B.C.E.: their crosses were set beside a thoroughfare in southern Italy, where the rebellion had occurred.) Nails went through the wrists, not the palms, and bleeding (including from a preliminary scourging) joined ex-

in fact done wrong?" But they yelled even louder, "Hang him on the stakes!"

¹⁵ Now Pilatos, wishing to mollify the crowd, released Barabbas to them, had Iēsous flogged,* and handed him over to be hung on the stakes.

¹⁶ The soldiers led Iēsous off into the palace, meaning the provincial government's headquarters,† and they called together their whole cohort. ¹⁷ And they put a purple robe on him, and they wove a garland out of thorny branches and put it on him.‡ ¹⁸ And they began to greet him: "Joy, king of the Ioudaioi!" ¹⁹ And they struck his head with a reed, and spat on him, and they knelt down and groveled before him. ²⁰ And when they'd finished taunting him, they took off the purple robe and put his own clothes back on him.

Then they led him out to hang him on the execution stakes. ²¹ And they commandeered a man passing by, Simōn, a Kurēnaios, who was coming in from the countryside, and who was the father of Alexandros and Roufos, to carry his stake.§

²² And they took him out to the place called Golgotha, which

---

posure and other stresses until the victim was too weak to raise his head and keep his airway open. Seneca the Younger writes of ghoulish added tortures, such as impalement of the genitals. The loincloths pictured in Christian art notwithstanding, the crucified were hung up naked, which in the case of traditional Jews, brought up to observe strict modesty, would have been an acute humiliation in itself.

* The whip for punishing criminals had leather thongs with lead beads or bone fragments on the ends. Jewish law limited the number of blows to forty, but the Romans had no limit.

† A Roman-era building—identified here as the provincial governor's headquarters—excavated next to the Tower of David Museum in the Old City of Jerusalem is one of few extant sites that can with reasonable certainty be linked with the life of Jesus.

‡ Purple dye was expensive, and the color was associated with high rank. Greeks and Romans used garlands and not metal crowns as marks of civic honor.

§ This is an eerie documentary touch, identifying the man by hometown and family members, and probably referring to the regulation that allowed soldiers to enlist provincial civilians as porters for journeys of limited length. The vertical

translates as "the Place of the Skull,"* ²³ and they tried to give him wine infused with myrrh.† But he wouldn't take it. ²⁴ And they hung him on the stakes, and they divided up his clothes, throwing lots for them to decide who would get what. ²⁵ It was the third hour after dawn when they hung him on the stakes. ²⁶ And a written sign‡ had the charge against him written on it:

"The king of the Ioudaioi."

²⁷ And along with him two bandits were hung on stakes,§ one on his right and one on his side "with the blessed name."¶
²⁹ And those who passed by on the road insulted him, shaking their heads and saying, "So much for you! Destroying the shrine and building it again in three days!** ³⁰ Come down off those stakes and rescue yourself." ³¹ Similarly the high priests, along with the scholars, made fun of him among themselves, saying, "He saved other people, but he can't save himself. ³² The anointed one, the king of Israēl, needs to come down from the stakes, so that we can see and believe." And those who were hanging on stakes alongside him berated him.
³³ And when it was the sixth hour after dawn, there was darkness over the whole earth, and the darkness lasted until the ninth

---

stake could be planted in the regular place of execution, so that only the horizontal crosspiece would have to be carried there.

* By tradition the crucifixion site is the location of the Church of the Holy Sepulcher. This would have been beside a busy thoroughfare, from which travelers were meant to see what was happening.

† A narcotic combination; myrrh still retains its reputation as a painkiller.

‡ The *titulus*, regular at crucifixions.

§ See Verse 14:48 above. Verse 28 here is excised from the standard Greek text as spurious. It quotes Isaiah 53:12 and reads, "And the scripture was fulfilled that says, 'He was counted among the lawless.'"

¶ The left side, considered ill-omened, was given euphemistic or apotropaic (for warding off evil) designations.

** Again, the literal "three days" represent two by inclusive reckoning.

hour. ³⁴ And at the ninth hour Iēsous shouted in a loud voice: *"Elōi elōi, lema sabachthani?"* The translation of this is "My god, my god, why have you abandoned me?"* ³⁵ And some of those standing near heard him and said, "Look, he's calling Ēlias!" ³⁶ Then someone ran [and] filled a sponge with vinegar, stuck a reed into it, and offered him a drink,† saying, "Let it be, all of you—we should see whether Ēlias comes to take him down."‡ ³⁷ But Iēsous let out a loud cry and breathed his last.

³⁸ Then the curtain of the inner shrine split in two from top to bottom.§ ³⁹ And when the centurion, who was standing facing him, saw how he breathed his last, he said, "Truly, this man was the son of god."¶

⁴⁰ But there were also women watching from far off, among them Maria the Magdalēnē, Maria the mother of the younger Iakōbos and of Iōsēs, and Salōmē. ⁴¹ When he was in Galilaia they followed him and waited on him. And there were many other women who had come up with him to Hierosoluma.**

⁴² Soon enough, it was evening. Since it was the day of preparation, that is, before the *sabbaton,* ⁴³ Iōsēf came from Arimathaia, a prominent member of the council,†† and he himself was waiting for god's kingdom. He dared to go in to Pilatos and ask him for

---

* From Psalms 22:1, but this is an Aramaic version.

† Very probably, if ironically, the sour wine or vinegar belongs to the Roman soldiers; it was their regular refreshment on duty.

‡ The preoccupying concern at this climactic moment is with Elijah, the prophet repeatedly identified with Jesus. Elijah ends his earthly life with a visible and glorious journey into heaven (2 Kings 2:9–12).

§ The Holy of Holies in the Temple, the room considered to contain God's actual power and presence, was kept untouched and covered.

¶ The centurion, a division commander, is probably in charge of the proceedings.

** Despite Mary Magdalene's later reputation, there is no evidence of a lurid past for her. Jesus' women followers were apparently women of independent means (see Luke 8:2–3), probably widows.

†† This is perhaps the same Sanhedrin that has passed judgment on Jesus.

the body of Iēsous. ⁴⁴ But Pilatos was surprised that he was already dead. He called in the centurion and asked him if he'd been dead for some time now. ⁴⁵ And when he learned from the centurion that this was the case, he granted the corpse to Iōséf. ⁴⁶ Then Iōséf bought linen, and took Iēsous down and wrapped him in the linen and placed him in a tomb hewn out of solid rock and rolled a stone against the door of the tomb.* ⁴⁷ And Maria the Magdalēnē and Maria the mother of Iōsēs looked on and saw where he was placed.

CHAPTER 16

¹ And when the *sabbaton* had passed, Maria the Magdalēnē, and Maria the mother of Iakōbos, and Salōmē bought aromatic spices so that they could go and rub them on him. ² And very early on the first day of the *sabbata* week, they went to the tomb after the sun had risen.† ³ And they said to each other, "Who's going to roll away the stone from the door of the tomb for us?" ⁴ But when they looked up, they saw that the stone had been rolled away; yet it was very large.

⁵ And when they went into the tomb, they saw a young man sitting on the right side of it, draped in a white robe, and they were stunned. ⁶ But he said to them, "Don't be stunned. You're looking for Iēsous the Nazarēnos, who was hung on the stakes.

---

* Many sorts of work, including burial of the dead, were banned on the Sabbath. Furthermore, Deuteronomy 21:22–23 forbids corpses of the executed ever to be hung on display overnight. Does Joseph volunteer to manage this ritually delicate situation? He, and not a traditional contingent of women, initially prepares the body. This is, at any rate, a rich man's burial, in a laboriously carved-out, permanent space that Jesus appears to have all to himself.

† Perhaps Jesus was buried so quickly that there was no time to properly prepare his body, apparently the work of women exclusively at this period in Judea, as it was in Greece. Or they did not dare approach when he was buried at the behest and expense of an important man?

He's awakened; he's not here. See, this is the place where they laid him. ⁷ But be on your way, and tell his students, including Petros, that he's going ahead of you into Galilaia: there you'll see him, just as he told you."

⁸ Then they went bolting out of the tomb, convulsed and out of their minds with shock. But they said nothing to anyone, as they were terrified.

[But to those around Petros they reported in a few words what they'd been instructed to report. And afterward Iēsous himself sent out through them, from the place the sun rises clear to where it sets, the sacred proclamation that never rots away, of rescue that lasts for all time. *Amēn.*]*

[⁹ Then he rose to his feet at dawn on the first day of the *sabbaton* week, and appeared first to Maria the Magdalēnē, from whom he'd expelled seven demons.† ¹⁰ She went and brought the news to those who had been with him and were now mourning and crying. ¹¹ But when *they* heard he was alive and had been seen by her, they didn't believe it.

¹² But afterward he was seen in another form by two of them, as they were walking, on a journey to the countryside. ¹³ Then they went back and brought the news back to the others, who didn't believe them either.

¹⁴ [But] later he appeared to the eleven themselves as they were reclining at the table; and he berated them for their failure to trust and their calloused, thick-skinned hearts, because they hadn't believed those who saw him after he awakened. ¹⁵ And he said to them, "Travel to the whole world and announce the good news to all that god made. ¹⁶ Whoever trusts and is baptized will

* Early Greek manuscripts have two different endings to the Gospel of Mark, the shorter one within these brackets, and without verse numbers; and a longer one, also within brackets, which follows.

† A woman demoniac would have been differentiated sharply from other women, and this may be at the root of the persistent but unsubstantiated stories that she was a prostitute.

be rescued; but whoever doesn't trust will be condemned.* [17] And these signs will go along with those who trust: by using my name they'll expel demons; they'll speak in languages unknown to them;[†][18] [and] they'll lift up snakes [in their hands];[‡] and if they drink anything deadly, it won't hurt them at all; they'll lay their hands on the sick, who will then get well."

[19] So then the lord Iēsous, after he'd spoken to them, was taken up into the sky and sat at god's right side. [20] And they went out and made the announcement everywhere, and the lord worked with them and confirmed the message by the signs that accompanied it.]

---

* This passage is one version of the so-called Great Commission for evangelization.

† This probably looks forward to the Pentecost miracle narrated in Acts 2:1–13: Jesus' ethnically disparate followers become mutually intelligible at a mass gathering after his death.

‡ An odd miracle, unless it recalls Moses' healing bronze snake figure, lifted on a pole (Numbers 21:4–9).

THE GOOD NEWS
ACCORDING TO MATHTHAIOS

CHAPTER 1

——

[1] A roll of the line of births up to Iēsous the Anointed, the son of David, the son of Abraam.

[2] Abraam fathered Isaak, Isaak fathered Iakōb, Iakōb fathered Ioudas and his brothers, [3] Ioudas fathered Fares and Zara from Tamar, Fares fathered Esrōm, Esrōm fathered Aram, [4] Aram fathered Aminadab, Aminadab fathered Naassōn, Naassōn fathered Salmōn, [5] Salmōn fathered Boes from Rachab, Boes fathered Iōbēd from Routh, Iōbēd fathered Iessai, [6] Iessai fathered David the king.

David fathered Solomōn from the wife of Ourias, [7] Solomōn fathered Roboam, Roboam fathered Abia, Abia fathered Asaf, [8] Asaf fathered Iōsafat, Iōsafat fathered Iōram, Iōram fathered Ozias, [9] Ozias fathered Iōatham, Iōatham fathered Achaz, Achaz fathered Ezekias, [10] Ezekias fathered Manassēs, Manassēs fathered Amōs, Amōs fathered Iōsias, [11] Iōsias fathered Iechonias and his brothers at the time of the exile to Babulōn.

[12] After the exile to Babulōn, Iechonias fathered Salathiēl, Salathiēl fathered Zorobabel, [13] Zorobabel fathered Abioud, Abioud fathered Eliakim, Eliakim fathered Azōr, [14] Azōr fathered Sadōk, Sadōk fathered Achim, Achim fathered Elioud, [15] Elioud fathered Eleazar, Eleazar fathered Matthan, Matthan fathered Iakōb, [16] Iakōb fathered Iōsēf the husband of Maria, from whom Iēsous, called the Anointed, was fathered.

¹⁷ So all the generations from Abraam until David were fourteen, and from David to the exile to Babulōn fourteen, and from the exile to Babulōn to the Anointed One fourteen generations.*

¹⁸ The birth of Iēsous the Anointed One happened this way. When his mother Maria had been betrothed to Iōsēf, but before they came together, she was found to have a child in her womb through the holy life-breath. ¹⁹ Now Iōsēf her man, being decent and not wanting to make a public spectacle of her, planned to let her go discreetly.† ²⁰ But when he had thought carefully about these things, look, a messenger of the lord appeared to him in a

---

* The striking opening of this Gospel helps characterize the book as concerned with the continuity and fulfillment of the Jewish tradition. (The earliest ancient authority on the Gospels, Bishop Papias [roughly 60–130 C.E.], claims that Matthew was first written in Hebrew or Aramaic.) This long genealogy particularly echoes the one in Genesis 5, listing paternal descent from Adam to Noah's sons. But now the point is the identity of Jesus as a Messianic "shoot" (descendant) of David, according to predictions like those of Isaiah 11:1. Matthew mentions five mothers, but only because they play important narrative roles in scripture; the emphasis is very much on "fathering," or (literally, according to the Hebrew verb often translated as "beget") "causing to be born." In three neat and (nearly) equal segments (achieved by the omission of several names, and with the length of the segments perhaps calculated according to a Hebrew alphanumeric code), Jesus' lineage goes forward from Abraham, with whom God made the covenant, through a number of patriarchs; then through the kingship as descended from David; then through and past the Babylonian Exile, with names becoming obscure because the kingship no longer exists: Zerubbabel, the last man in the line whose existence is definitely attested to by the Hebrew Bible, was a provincial governor for the ruling Persians and led exiles back to Judah in the late sixth century B.C.E. The most glaring difficulty is of course the lack of a bloodline through to Jesus, as David's descendant Joseph is merely the husband of Mary, not Jesus' biological father.

† Mary is legally bound to her betrothed by an agreement between the families, which is why the same term ("let go") as for divorce is used for the impending (and inevitably awkward) split; the marriage is just not consummated, an event that waits for the whole community's witness and celebration of the union. A girl believed to have had premarital sex could have been executed according to the law of the Torah (Deuteronomy 22:20–27), but rural folkways may have been less stringent.

dream and said, "Iōsēf son of David, don't be afraid to take Maria as your wife, since what has been fathered in her is from the holy life-breath. [21] She will give birth to a son, and you are to call him by the name Iēsous; he will rescue his people from their offenses."* [22] All of this happened to fulfill what was spoken by the lord through the prophet, who said,

> [23] *"Look, a young girl will have a child in her womb and will*
>   *give birth to a son,*
> *And they will call him by the name Emmanouēl,"*

the translation of which is "with us is god."† [24] When Iōsēf awakened from sleep, he did as the lord's messenger had commanded him and took her as his wife, [25] but he did not become familiar with her‡ until she had given birth to a son. And he called him by the name Iēsous.

---

* Straying from and redemption by God is the basic Hebrew Bible understanding of history. God's chosen people stray from obedience but are put back on the right path. The name Jesus is from the root for "rescue."

† The quotation is from Isaiah 7:14, and the name Emmanuel is referred to again in Isaiah 8:8 and 8:10. The original message in context is that a young woman (the Greek word *parthenos*, and its Hebrew predecessor in scripture, *almah*, do not stipulate physical virginity; an *almah* can actually be married) is pregnant, and that the child will have a name indicating that God champions the nation; by the time the child is eating solid food, it will be the fresh curds and honey of security and prosperity, not the stored grain of wartime and siege. In Isaiah the child might be either the author's own or a prince and the heir to the throne of Judah, Hezekiah.

‡ The Hebrew Bible euphemism for sex: the "know" of the King James.

CHAPTER 2

———

¹ When Iēsous had been born in Bēthle'em in Ioudaia* in the days of Hērōdēs the king,† look, diviners from where the sun rises appeared at Hierosoluma, ² saying, "Where is the king of the Ioudaioi who has been born? We did see his star at its rising‡ and have come to prostrate ourselves before him."§ ³ But when the king Hērōdēs heard, he was agitated, and so was the whole of Hierosoluma along with him; ⁴ and he gathered together all the high priests and the people's scholars, and questioned them as to where the anointed one was supposed to be born. ⁵ They told him, "In Bēthle'em in Ioudaia: here is in fact what's been written about it by the prophet:

> ⁶ *"And you, Bēthle'em, land of Iouda,*
> *Are by no means the least among the leaders of Iouda:*
> *Out of you will come a leader*
> *Who will shepherd my people Israēl."¶*

⁷ Then Hērōdēs, on the sly, called in the diviners and found out from them at what time precisely the star had begun to shine, and ⁸ he sent them to Bēthle'em, saying, "Travel there and make

---

* "Ioudaia" here (and generally in the Gospels) means the Jewish heartland and the home of Jerusalem and the Temple, not the entire Roman multiethnic province of Judea, which went by the same name in Greek. See below at Verse 6 concerning Bethlehem.

† The Roman client-king Herod the Great died in 4 B.C.E., providing an end date for Jesus' birth according to this account.

‡ In these two verses there is neat wordplay involving the "risings [of heavenly bodies]," meaning the east, and the "rising" of this one star.

§ The appearance of a star at the birth of great leaders, and foreign embassies bringing gifts on such special occasions, are familiar from ancient legend and historiography. *Magos* is a term for a dream interpreter, astrologer, or magician, skills associated with the Near East, especially Babylon.

¶ Micah 5:2.

careful inquiries about where precisely the child is, and when you find him, bring the news back to me, so that I can go prostrate myself before him too." ⁹ Once they'd heard the king, they traveled there, and—look—the star they had seen at its rising went ahead of them until it came to stand over the place where the child was. ¹⁰ When they saw the star there, their joy was heaped on joy, in great abundance. ¹¹ And coming into the house, they saw the child with Maria its mother, and falling down they prostrated themselves before it and opened their boxes of valuables and presented it with gifts of gold and frankincense and myrrh.* ¹² Then, receiving in a dream a divine warning not to return to Hērōdēs, they withdrew by another route to their own country.

¹³ But once they had withdrawn, look, a messenger of the lord appeared in a dream to Iōsēf, saying, "Get up and take the child and its mother and escape to Aiguptos and stay there until I tell you otherwise. Hērōdēs is about to search for the child to do away with it." ¹⁴ Then he got up, took the child and its mother at night, and withdrew into Aiguptos, ¹⁵ and he stayed there until the death of Hērōdēs, for the fulfillment of what had been spoken by the lord through the prophet, who said,

> *"Out of Aiguptos I have called my son."*†

¹⁶ Then Hērōdēs, seeing that he had been tricked by the diviners, was overwhelmed by fury, and sent people to do away with all the boys in Bēthle'em and the whole surrounding district who

---

* These gifts are some of the most expensive by weight in the ancient world. Aromatic tree or shrub resins like these two, used ritually as incense in some cults, and sometimes in embalming corpses, were imports from distant, difficult terrains such as the Arabian Peninsula and Somalia.

† Hosea 11:1, which refers to the nation of Israelites as "my son," delivered from slavery in Egypt. Jewish flight *into* Egypt is historically more credible: people had probably been seeking refuge there from the immediate east—as both Abraham's and Jacob's clans are shown doing—for thousands of years.

were two years old and younger, according to the precise time he had found out from the diviners. ¹⁷ Then was fulfilled what had been spoken through Ieremias the prophet when he said,

> ¹⁸ *"A sound in Rama was heard,*
> *Of crying and loud lamenting:*
> *It was Rachēl crying for her children,*
> *And she didn't want to be comforted,*
> *Because they are gone."**

¹⁹ But after Hērōdēs met his end, look, a messenger of the lord appeared in a dream to Iōsēf in Aiguptos, ²⁰ saying, "Get up, take the child and its mother and travel to the land of Israēl: those who were seeking to take the child's life have died." ²¹ He got up, took the child and its mother, and went to the land of Israēl.†

²² But when he heard that Archelaos was king in Ioudaia in place of his father Hērōdēs, he was afraid to go there. Receiving a divine warning in a dream, he withdrew into the region of Galilaia. ²³ And arriving there, he settled in a town called Nazaret, for the fulfillment of what was spoken through the prophets, that he would be called a Nazōraios.‡

---

* Jeremiah 31:15; Rachel, the mother of Joseph and Benjamin, stands for all Jewish mothers. Jeremiah was referring to the Babylonian conquest of Judah: the exiles set out from the town of Ramah.

† The ancient name of the united nation, then of its northern kingdom.

‡ Again, "Judea" means the Jewish heartland and not the entire large multiethnic province of the Romans. Archelaus, unlike his brother Antipas, who inherited rule over Galilee, was known as a bungling tyrant. There is in fact no prophetic designation of the Messiah as coming from Nazareth, but there *were* important figures, Samson and Samuel, designated Nazarites, meaning a man set aside for God who may not cut his hair, drink wine, or have any contact with a corpse.

CHAPTER 3

¹ In those days Iōannēs the baptizer arrived, [and] in the wasteland of Ioudaia he proclaimed ² this message: "Change your purpose, because the kingdom of the skies has come near."*

³ This in fact was the man spoken of through Ēsaïas the prophet, who said,

> *"The voice of someone shouting in the wasteland:*
> *'Prepare the lord's road!*
> *Make his beaten paths straight!'"*†

⁴ Now as for himself, Iōannēs had clothing made from camel hair, and an animal-skin belt covering his groin, and his food was locusts and wild honey. ⁵ At that time, the inhabitants of Hierosoluma and all of Ioudaia and everyone who lived in the region around the Iordanēs made their way to him, ⁶ and they were baptized in the river Iordanēs by him when they acknowledged their offenses.

⁷ When he saw many of the Farisaioi and Saddoukaioi coming to where he was baptizing, he said to them: "You viper hatchlings! Who warned you to run from the anger that's coming? ⁸ So produce a harvest that's fit for a new purpose, and ⁹ don't presume to say to yourselves, "We have Abraam as our father!"—because I say to you that God can raise up offspring for Abraam from these stones. ¹⁰ Already the ax is poised at the roots of the trees: so every tree that doesn't produce good fruit will be chopped down and thrown into the fire.

¹¹ "I baptize you with water so that you can change your purpose, but the one coming after me is more powerful than I am;

---

* See the note on baptism at Mark 1:4.

† Isaiah 40:3; see the note at Mark 1:3.

I'm not fit to carry his sandals; *he*'ll baptize you with the holy life-breath, and with fire. ¹² His winnowing fork is in his hand, and he'll clean his threshing floor out completely and gather the grain together in his barn, but he'll burn the chaff in a fire that can't be put out."

¹³ Then Iēsous came from Galilaia to Iōannēs at the Iordanēs to be baptized by him. ¹⁴ But Iōannēs tried to stop him, saying, "I need to be baptized by you, but you come to me? ¹⁵ Iēsous answered by saying to him, "Let me go ahead for now, since it's fitting for us to satisfy in this way everything that rectitude requires." Then Iōannēs let him go ahead. ¹⁶ As soon as Iēsous had been baptized and come up from the water, look, the skies opened [to him] and he saw [the] life-breath [of] god coming down as if it were a dove [and] alighting on him; ¹⁷ and look, there was a voice out of the skies saying, "This is my beloved son, in whom I've taken delight."*

CHAPTER 4

―――

¹ Then Iēsous was led into the wilderness by the life-breath to be tested by the slanderer.† ² And since he didn't eat for forty days and forty nights, he was starving afterward. ³ And the one who was testing him came near and said to him, "If you're god's son, tell these stones to becomes loaves of bread." ⁴ But he answered by saying, "It's been written: a person is not to live by bread alone, but by every command that comes out of god's mouth."‡

⁵ Then the slanderer took him into the holy city and stood

---

* Compare the language used by God to Abraham during the "Binding of Isaac" (Genesis 22:2).

† See "devil" in the Glossary.

‡ This quotes Deuteronomy 8:3: the context is that during the forty years the Israelites wandered in the wilderness, they ate only the miraculous manna.

him on the pinnacle of the temple [6] and said to him, "If you're god's son, throw yourself down. It's been written, you know, that

> *"'He'll assign your care to his messengers,*
> *And in their arms they'll lift you,*
> *So that you never slam your foot against a stone.'"*

[7] Iēsous told him, "It's been written in turn: 'You are not to test the lord your god.'"*

[8] The slanderer took him to another place, a very high mountain, and showed him all the kingdoms of the world and their glory, [9] and he told him, "I'll give you all these things if you fall down and worship me." [10] Then Iēsous said to him, "Get out of here, satanas! It's in fact been written, 'You are to worship the lord your god and serve him alone in his rites.'"† [11] Then the slanderer left him, and, look, messengers came to him and tended to him.

[12] Once he heard that Iōannēs had been handed over,‡ he withdrew into Galilaia; [13] then, leaving Nazara, he went and settled in Kafarnaoum beside the sea in the region of Zaboulōn and Nefthalim, [14] for the fulfillment of what was spoken through the prophet Ēsaïas when he said,

> [15] *"Land of Zaboulōn and Nefthalim,*
> *The road beside the sea, across the Iordanēs,*
> *Galilaia of the other nations:*
> [16] *The people sitting in darkness*
> *Has seen a great light,*

---

* James the Just, the leader of the early Jesus movement in Jerusalem, was reported to have been martyred by being thrown from this same Temple pinnacle. The devil quotes from Psalms 91:11–12, Jesus from Deuteronomy 6:16 or perhaps Isaiah 7:12.

† Deuteronomy 6:13 and 10:20.

‡ This is all that appears here of the story of John's demise, which in Mark covers 6:17–29.

> *And for those sitting in death's land and shadow,*
> *Light has dawned."*

¹⁷ From then on Iēsous began to proclaim this message: "Change your purpose, since the kingdom of the skies has come near."

¹⁸ Walking by the sea of Galilaia, he saw two brothers, Simōn who was called Petros† and Andreas his brother, casting a net into the sea, as they were fishermen. ¹⁹ And he said to them, "Come, follow me, and I'll turn you into fishers for human beings." ²⁰ And right away they left their nets and followed after him. ²¹ And walking on from there, he saw two other brothers, Iakōbos the son of Zebedaios and Iōannēs his brother, in the boat with Zebedaios their father, putting their nets in order, and he called them. ²² And right away they left the boat and their father and followed him.

²³ And he traveled around the whole of Galilaia, teaching in their synagogues and proclaiming the good news of the kingdom and healing every disease and debility among the people.

²⁴ Then the news of him went out to the whole of Suria, and they brought him everyone who was unwell, suffering from all kinds of diseases and other torments, [and] those possessed by demons and the moonstruck‡ and the paralyzed, and he cured them. ²⁵ And large crowds followed him from Galilaia and the Ten Cities and Hierosoluma and Ioudaia and the region across the Iordanēs.§

---

* Isaiah 9:1–2, in the sequence of passages about Emmanuel, the new king to be born to save the nation. Zebulun and Naphtali are progenitors of two of the Twelve Tribes of Israel, giving their names to north central regions of the Jewish territory, considered to be out of the Jewish mainstream.

† See the second note at Mark 3:16.

‡ I.e., they had epilepsy, popularly attributed to supernatural causes.

§ The geographic and (perhaps) cultural range is impressive, Syria being an area north of Judea, and the Ten Cities and the Transjordan (east of the Jordan River) being overlapping regions with substantial Greco-Roman populations.

CHAPTER 5

---

¹ Seeing the crowds, Iēsous climbed up the mountain. Once he'd taken a seat there, his students came up to him, ² and he opened his mouth to speak and taught them, saying,

> ³ *"Happy are those destitute in the life-breath,"*
> *because theirs is the kingdom of the skies.*
> ⁴ *Happy are those who mourn,*
> *because they will be comforted.*†
> ⁵ *Happy are the gentle,*
> *because they will be heirs of all the earth.*
> ⁶ *Happy are those starving and parched for justice,*
> *because they will have as much as they can eat.*
> ⁷ *Happy are those who show mercy,*
> *because they will be shown mercy.*
> ⁸ *Happy are those who are pure at heart,*
> *Because they will see god.*
> ⁹ *Happy are the makers of peace,*‡
> *because they will be called 'sons of god.'*§
> ¹⁰ *Happy are those hounded for the sake of justice,*
> *because theirs is the kingdom of the skies.*

¹¹ "Happy are you when they insult you and hound you and say every kind of malicious thing about you [falsely] because of

---

* See "poor" and "spirit" in the Glossary. The best sense here seems to be "happy in life-breath," not "destitute in life-breath." In the Greek, which follows the Hebrew syntax, there is no connective verb "are" in the first segment of each Beatitude ("Blessedness" or "Happiness") until Verse ɪɪ.

† Bereavement in the ancient world could be a particularly stark crisis for women and children because of impoverishment. "Comfort" tended to mean material support as well as emotional consolation.

‡ The Greek word, *eirēnopoioi,* is actually a rare one, needing a somewhat estranging translation.

§ For "sons of God," an honorific term, see p. xxxi of the Introduction.

me. ¹² Grow giddy with joy, because your wages in the skies will be generous. This, you see, is how they hounded the prophets who came before you.

¹³ "You are the salt—not of the sea, but of the land; but if salt loses its bite and is dulled and dumbed down, what are you going to use to salt *it* with?* It's no longer good for anything but to be thrown out and stamped under people's feet.

¹⁴ "You are the light of the universe. A city lying on a hilltop can't be kept hidden! ¹⁵ People don't light a lamp and put it under a basket, but rather on a lamp-stand, and it gives light to everybody in the house. ¹⁶ In this way, let your light shine before people's faces, so that they see the good things you do and glorify your father who is in the skies.

¹⁷ "Don't set me down as having come to annihilate the law or the prophets.† I haven't come to annihilate but to fulfill. ¹⁸ *Amēn* I'm telling you: until the sky and the earth pass away, not a single dot or a single hook in the letters will pass out of the law, not until everything has been done.‡ ¹⁹ Whoever nullifies a single one of these commands, even one of the least important, and teaches other people to do the same, he'll be called the least important in the kingdom of the skies. But whoever carries out the commands and teaches them will be called great in the kingdom of the skies.§

---

* "Salt" was a common metaphor for shrewdness, good taste, and wit. The verb used here for the loss of salt's taste would normally denote stupidity. As a preservative of meat, salt may allude to immortality. (See "flesh" in the Glossary.) It was also added to sacrificial offerings.

† With "set me down" and "the law set down," I'm trying to reproduce a pun: the verb for "deem" (*nomizō*) is visibly related to the word for "law" or "custom," *nomos*. The Law and the Prophets were the two most important parts of Jewish scripture.

‡ This verges into apocalyptic language. The hierarchy's uses of scripture centered instead on the interpretation of ritual, law, and ethics for the present time, not on a future culmination of scriptural messages. The iota and the keraia (here, "dot" and "hook") were tiny elements in Hebrew and Aramaic lettering.

§ The Matthew Gospel is famously more friendly to traditional Judaism with

²⁰ "Hence I tell you that unless your lawfulness excels that of the scholars and the Farisaioi, you will never enter into the kingdom of the skies.

²¹ "You've heard what was said to the people of ancient times: 'You are not to commit murder';* whoever commits a murder will be liable to be convicted. ²² But I say to you that anyone who's angry with his brother will be liable to be convicted. And whoever says to his brother *'Raka!'*† will be liable to the high council,‡ and whoever says, 'You imbecile!' will be liable to *ge'enna* with its fires.§ ²³ So if you're presenting your offering at the altar, and there you remember that your brother has something against you, ²⁴ leave your offering there, in front of the altar, and get out. First be reconciled with your brother, and then come back and present your offering. ²⁵ Rush to be gracious toward your adversary at law, while you're with him on the way to court, or the adversary may just turn you over to the judge, and the judge to the bailiff, and you could be thrown into prison. ²⁶ *Amēn amēn* I'm telling you: you'd never get out of there until you paid every last quadrans you owe.¶

²⁷ "You've heard that it was said: 'You are not to violate marriage.' ²⁸ But I say to you that every man who looks at someone else's wife with a willful craving has already violated marriage with her in his heart.** ²⁹ If your right eye sets a trap for you, pull

---

its emphasis on the scriptural law that, construed down to the letter, governed all parts of life.

* Exodus 20:13, Deuteronomy 5:17.

† Aramaic, probably meaning something like "half-wit."

‡ The Sanhedrin.

§ See "hell" in the Glossary. There are close parallels to this passage in rabbinic literature.

¶ A quadrans is a very low denomination of Roman coinage. Rabbinic literature takes a strong interest in interpersonal peacemaking.

** Rabbinic writings carefully prescribe avoiding physical desire outside marriage, but see "lust" in the Glossary about confusion with a puritanical sort of enmity toward natural drives per se. The hypothetical woman here is very likely

it out and throw it away from you. It's better for you to lose one part of your body than for your whole body to be thrown into *ge'enna.** [30] And if your right hand sets a trap for you, cut it off and throw it away from you. It's better to lose one part of your body so that the whole of your body doesn't go to *ge'enna.*†

[31] "It was said: 'Whoever wants to let his wife go must give her a written notice of putting her away.' [32] But I say to you that any man who lets his wife go, except on the grounds that she's whoring, makes her violate marriage, and whoever marries a woman let go by her husband violates marriage.‡

[33] "Again, you've heard what was said to the people of ancient times: you are not to violate your oath: you are to fulfill your oaths to the lord. [34] But I tell you not to take oaths at all: not by the sky, since it's god's throne, [35] and not by the earth, since it's a foot-rest for his feet; and not by Hierosoluma, since it's the city of the great king;§ [36] nor should you take an oath by your own head, because *you* can't make a single one of your own hairs white or black. [37] Let the pledge you give be a repeated 'Yes,' or 'No.'¶ Anything beyond this comes from the malicious one.**

[38] "You've heard what was said: 'An eye in exchange for an eye,' and 'A tooth in exchange for a tooth.'†† [39] But I tell you not to face off against someone malicious. Instead, if anyone slaps you on

_____

a wife (see the Glossary for "woman/wife"), as adultery tended to be narrowly defined in this way.

* See "hell" in the Glossary.

† Also in line with rabbinic writings: the eyes that can generate lust and the hands that can perpetrate lustful acts must be objects of careful control.

‡ See "divorce," "adultery," and "fornication" in the Glossary.

§ David, who had reigned in the tenth century B.C.E.

¶ The Talmud similarly disapproves of taking oaths and indicates that a repeated yes or no is legally as valid as an oath.

** See "devil" in the Glossary.

†† Exodus 21:23–24, Leviticus 24:19–20, and Deuteronomy 19:21.

[your] right cheek, turn the other cheek to him as well.* [40] And if someone wants to take you to court and take your tunic, let him have your cloak as well.† [41] And if anybody commandeers you as a porter for a mile, get going with him for two.‡ [42] If someone asks you for something, give it to him, and if someone wants to borrow from you, don't turn away from him.§

[43] You have heard what was said: 'You are to love the one next to you,' and you are to hate your enemy.¶ [44] But I say to you: Love your enemies and pray for those who hound you and make cases against you, [45] so that you become sons of your father in the skies, because he causes his sun to rise over the malicious and the upstanding alike, and he sends rain to the lawful and the unlawful. [46] If you simply love those who love you, what reward will you get? Don't even the tax-collectors do the same thing?** [47] And if

---

* Striking someone's right cheek with the back of the left hand has been the emblematic insulting blow in the Middle East for millennia, not only because it is a child's punishment, but also because of superstitious ideas about right and left.

† This exuberant peacemaking would leave a man naked or partly naked in public—and in a legal forum, no less; this would be a gross violation of Jewish propriety and a great embarrassment to his opponent.

‡ Roman state functionaries could commandeer the services of provincials, but with limitations. The joke here may concern a helper who won't go away even when he's supposed to.

§ Compare Psalms 112:5. But the instruction here in Matthew to lend on request looks daunting in the face of scriptural protections of debtors. The periodic remission of debts was one measure (Deuteronomy 15:1, Nehemiah 10:31); also, interest was forbidden (Exodus 22:25, Leviticus 25:37). Workarounds had been developed, however, for the sophisticated economy of the late Second Temple period.

¶ Leviticus 19:18. The Greek is literally "the one next to you" where we see the English biblical "neighbor." In Jewish scripture there is no general prescription or allowance for hating enemies, but rather many admonitions (as at Leviticus 19:33) to treat strangers, foreigners, and even personal enemies generously and decently. It is in pagan literature, particularly in forensic rhetoric, that the persecution of enemies is cited as a duty.

** The animus against tax collectors shown in the Gospels was rooted in the system: the right to collect taxes in a province was granted in a commercial con-

you welcome only your brothers, what's extraordinary in what you're doing? Don't those in the other nations do the same thing? ⁴⁸ So be what you were meant to be, be complete, as your father in the sky is complete!"*

Chapter 6

¹ "[But] take care not to perform your righteousness in front of people, to create a spectacle for them. If you do this, you don't get any reward from your father in the skies. ² When you make a merciful gift,† don't have a trumpet blasted ahead of you, as those play-actors do in the synagogues and the streets, to cadge praise from people. *Amēn* I'm telling you: they have their full payment. ³ No, when you make a merciful gift, don't even let your "better" hand know what your right hand is doing. ⁴ That way, your gift will be made in secret, and your father, who sees in secret, will give you the payment that's due.

⁵ "And when you pray, don't be like those play-actors who love to stand in the synagogues and on the street corners to pray, on display to people. *Amēn* I tell you: they have their full payment. ⁶ When *you* pray, go into your storeroom and lock your door,‡ and pray to your father who is in secret. And your father who sees in secret will pay you in full.

⁷ "When you pray, don't burble on and on as the people of

---

tract requiring only that a given sum be turned over to the central government, so profits could be greatly increased by extortion on the ground.

* See "perfect" in the Glossary. The comparison of the human and the divine here is difficult to construe.

† A variety of charitable giving is approved in the Talmud.

‡ The secluded and secure room named here, a *tameion*, would not have been a bedroom but rather a place for storing supplies and valuables.

other nations do, who think they'll get a hearing because of the sheer amount of their talk:* ⁸ so don't be like them! Your father does know the things you need, even before you ask him.

⁹ "So this is the way for *you* to pray:

> 'Our father in the skies,
> Let your name be spoken in holiness.
> ¹⁰ Let your kingdom arrive.
> Let what you want happen
> On the earth, as in the sky.
> ¹¹ Give us today tomorrow's loaf of bread,†
> ¹² And free us from our debts,
> As we too have set our debtors free.
> ¹³ And don't bring us into the ordeal—‡
> No, rescue us from the malicious one.'§

¹⁴ "If, then, you set other people free from their blunders, your father in the sky will set you free too. ¹⁵ But if you don't set other people free, your father won't let your blunders go either.

¹⁶ "And when you fast, don't be like those play-actors with their scowling faces, who make their faces unrecognizable—so that people recognize that they're fasting.¶ *Amēn* I'm telling you:

---

* Words addressed to the gods in pagan ritual could well have seemed copious, elaborate, and repetitious to traditional Jews. Some of the *Homeric Hymns* (poems thought to reflect public performances) end with the promise of a fresh tribute to the same god, to follow immediately.

† There is no good basis for translating this adjective as "daily"; a word expressing the idea of "a future" or "tomorrow's" loaf appears the best choice among several not very satisfactory ones inherited from manuscript and interpretive traditions left very unsettled.

‡ See "temptation" in the Glossary.

§ Note that the prayer's final words, about "the kingdom, the power, and the glory" of God, words established through Protestant Bibles in much of the world's liturgy, are absent from the consensus reconstruction of the Greek text.

¶ Regular or ritual fasting is not prescribed in the Hebrew Bible, so a proud

they have their full payment. [17] When *you* fast, put oil on your head and wash your face, [18] so that people don't recognize that you're fasting; but your father who's in private will; and your father who sees in private will pay you in full.

[19] "Don't hoard up your hoards on earth, where moths and rust ruin them and robbers break in and rob you of them. [20] Hoard up your hoards in the sky, where moths and rust don't ruin anything, and where robbers don't break in and rob. [21] Where your hoard is, there your heart will be as well.*

[22] "The eye is the body's lamp. If your eye is sound, then the whole of your body will be full of light. [23] But if your eye is bad, the whole of your body will be in darkness. If, then, the light in you is the same as darkness, what a great darkness that must be![†]

[24] "No one can be a slave of two masters. Either he'll hate one and love the other, or he'll be devoted to the one and show contempt for the other.[‡] You can't be a slave to both god and *mamōnas*.[§]

[25] "Because of this, I say to you: don't worry about your life, as to what you'll have to eat [or what you'll have to drink], or about your body, as to what you'll have to clothe it. Isn't life a greater thing than food, and the body a greater thing than clothing? [26] Take a good look at the birds in the sky: they don't sow seed or reap grain or gather it into barns; but your father in the sky feeds them. Aren't you worth far more than they are? [27] Which one of

---

display of such fasting may well have seemed offensive, especially to those with no alternative to hunger.

  * This passage may be influenced by the miser in Greek and Roman thought, a person so fixated on the fear of loss—particularly through thievery—that he cannot enjoy the basic pleasures of human society, such as dining with friends, but still ends up losing his entire hoard.

  † Rabbinic writings stress the importance of what the eye sees and its influence on the mind. (See above at 5:27–30.)

  ‡ A slave could in fact be jointly owned, but the passage may allude to a much more common situation, one in which a slave's owner, the head of the household, was not the one directing the work from hour to hour, so that conflicts would naturally arise.

  § A Hebrew word meaning money or property.

you, through his worries, can add one whole cubit to his height?* ²⁸ And why do you worry about clothing? Observe and learn from the lilies in the field, and how beautifully they grow. They don't exhaust themselves spinning thread. ²⁹ But I tell you that not even Solomōn† in all his glory was dressed as well as one of these flowers.‡ ³⁰ This is the field's greenery: today it exists, and tomorrow it's tossed into the oven, but god clothes it this way. Won't he much more certainly clothe you, though you have so little trust? ³¹ So don't worry, don't ask "What are we going to eat?" or "What are we going to drink?" or "What are we going to wear?" ³² All these things are what the other nations chase after. Your father in the sky knows that you need all these things. ³³ First go after [god's] kingdom and his way of doing what is right, and all these other things will be given to you as well. ³⁴ So don't worry about tomorrow, because tomorrow will worry about itself. Today's aggravation is plenty for today."

CHAPTER 7

———

¹ "Don't pass judgment, and judgment won't be passed on you. ² The very verdict you give will be the verdict given on you, and the measure you give will be the measure you get.§ ³ Why are you looking at a speck of straw in your brother's eye, but not noticing

---

* The Roman cubit was based on the length of a man's forearm and hand.

† The successor to King David, in the tenth century B.C.E., renowned for his wealthy and magnificent court.

‡ These are probably the same large white arum lilies that still grow wild in many places around the Mediterranean today. Bleaching to a snow-white color and then keeping the garment clean required special technology and expertise; white robes meant prestige and sometimes had ceremonial significance.

§ The Greek has a capering repetition of sounds and words to emphasize the sameness of what is given out and received back. The original is *krimati krinete krithēsesthe* and *metrō metreite metrēthēsetai.*

the log in your own? ⁴ Or how are you going to say to your brother, 'Just let me take that speck out of your eye,' when, look, there's a log in your own eye? ⁵ You play-actor, first take the log out of your own eye, and then you'll be able to see clearly enough to take the speck out of your brother's eye.

⁶ "Don't give a holy thing to dogs, and don't throw down your pearls in front of pigs, in case they trample them under their trotters, turn on you, and rip you to pieces.*

⁷ "Ask, and it will be given to you, seek, and you'll find, knock on the door, and it will be opened to you. ⁸ Everyone who asks gets, and every seeker finds, and the door will be opened to whoever knocks. ⁹ Or is there anyone among you who, when his son asks him for a loaf of bread, would present him with a rock? ¹⁰ Or if the son asks for a fish to eat, would the father present him with a snake?† ¹¹ So if you all, worthless as you are, know how to give valuable gifts to your children, how much more certainly will your father in the skies give things of value to those who ask him!

¹² "So the whole sum of things you want people to do for you—that's what *you* must do for them. This is what the law and the prophets amount to.‡

¹³ "Go in through the narrow gate, because the gaping gate and the roomy road are the ones leading away to destruction, and there are plenty of people going in through that gate. ¹⁴ That's because the gate that leads into life is narrow, and the road there is full of crushing hardship,§ so there are few who find life.

¹⁵ "Be on the lookout for pretend prophets, who come to you

---

* Pearls were the premier jewels of the ancient world, sometimes fetching fabulous prices. Dogs and pigs are unclean animals. Here the dogs may actually be shown getting what is acceptable for sacrifice.

† The snake is another unclean animal, and it may be poisonous as well.

‡ Hillel the Elder (the most famous Jewish sage of the Second Temple period and the leading Pharisee of his generation, probably dying around 10 C.E.) told a Gentile challenger: "Whatever is hateful to you, don't do it to your neighbor: that is the whole Torah."

§ The Roman satirist Juvenal describes dangerous, crowding traffic (including

disguised as sheep, whereas underneath they're wolves who plunder the flock. ¹⁶ You'll find out who they are by the harvests they yield. You can't gather grapes from thornbushes or figs from thistles, can you? ¹⁷ Thus every high-quality tree produces good fruit, but a low-quality tree produces worthless fruit. ¹⁸ A high-quality tree *can't* produce worthless fruit, and a low-quality tree *can't* produce good fruit. ¹⁹ Every tree that doesn't produce good fruit is cut down and thrown into the fire. ²⁰ By the harvests they yield, then, you'll recognize who people are.

²¹ "Not everyone who says to me, 'Lord! Lord!' will come into the kingdom of the skies; no, it will only be the person who carries out the will of my father in the skies. ²² Many people will say to me on that day, 'Lord! Lord! Didn't we prophesy in your name, and expel trouble-making spirits in your name, and perform many powerful acts in your name?' ²³ And then I'll declare to them: 'I never knew you. Get away from me, because what you've been working at is criminal.'

²⁴ "Whoever hears these things I'm saying and puts them into practice can be compared to a shrewd man who built his house on solid rock. ²⁵ Then the rain came down, and the rivers in flood encroached, and the winds blew and fell violently on the house, but the house didn't fall, because it was founded on rock. ²⁶ But whoever hears these things I'm saying and doesn't put them into practice can be compared to a stupid man, who built his house on sand. ²⁷ Then the rain came down, and the rivers in flood encroached, and the winds blew and struck against that house, and it fell, and its fall was a massive one."*

²⁸ And it happened that, when Iēsous finished saying these things, the crowds were dumbfounded at his teaching. ²⁹ In teaching them, in fact, he was like someone with genuine authority, and not like their scholars.

---

wagons with immense and heavy loads) on ancient streets, which were roughly paved if at all. See "tribulation" in the Glossary.

* Survival when everything else is swept away is familiar apocalyptic teaching.

CHAPTER 8

---

[1] After he came down from the mountain, large crowds followed him. [2] And look, a leper approached him and fell at his feet, saying, "Master, if you want to, you can cleanse me." [3] And Iēsous held out his hand and touched him, saying, "I do want to. Be cleansed!" and right away his leprosy was cleansed away. [4] Then Iēsous said to him, "See that you tell no one, but get going and show yourself to the priest and make the offering Mōüsēs set out in the law, as proof for them."*

[5] When he came to Kafarnaoum, a centurion approached him and pleaded with him, [6] saying, "Sir, my boy† is lying in the house paralyzed, in terrible torment." [7] And Iēsous said to him, "I'll come in person and heal him." [8] But the centurion answered by saying, "Sir, I'm not a fit person to have you come under my roof; but only say the word, and my boy will be healed. [9] I do know this because I myself am a person deployed under other people's authority, and I have soldiers under me, and I say to this one, 'Get on the road!' and he gets on the road, and to another, 'Come here!' and he comes, and to my slave, 'Do this!' and he does it." [10] When Iēsous heard, he was amazed, and said to his followers, "*Amēn* I tell you, I haven't found this much trust in anyone in Israēl. [11] But I'm telling you that many people will come from as far as the places where the sun rises and where it sets, and they'll recline at the table with Abraam and Isaak and Iakōb in the kingdom of the skies, [12] while the kingdom's sons will be thrown out into the darkness—*far* out; in that place there'll be crying and grinding of teeth in pain." [13] And Iēsous told the centurion: "Be on your way. It's to be done for you as you trusted it would." And [his] slave boy was healed within that hour.‡

---

* See Leviticus 13–14.

† See "child" and "servant" in the Glossary.

‡ A centurion, the leader of a unit of a hundred men in the Roman army, is an

[14] And coming into Petros' home, Iēsous saw his mother-in-law lying ill with a burning fever, [15] and he grasped her hand, and the fever left her, and she got up and proceeded to wait on him.*

[16] When it was evening, they brought him many people possessed by demons, and he expelled the spirits by the spoken word, and he healed everyone who was unwell, [17] for the fulfillment of what was spoken through Ēsaïas the prophet, who said:

> *"He took on our infirmities,*
> *And shouldered our diseases."*†

[18] But Iēsous, seeing a large crowd around him, gave an order to go away to the opposite shore. [19] But a scholar approached and said to him, "Teacher, I'll follow you wherever you go." [20] But Iēsous said to him, "Foxes have dens, and the birds of the sky have shelters, but the son of mankind has nowhere to lay his head down."‡ [21] Another of [his] students said to him, "Give me permission to go back and bury my father first." [22] But Iēsous said to him, "Follow me and leave the dead to bury their dead."§

[23] Now as he boarded the boat, his students followed him.

---

emblematic outsider. He is likely not an ethnic Roman, however, since at this period the Roman army drew recruits from all over the Empire; and he would probably not be on active service in Galilee, as, unlike Judea, the territory was not occupied. He may well be a "God-fearer" or "God-worshipper," a pagan admirer of and partial participant in Jewish practices, as he respects the purity restrictions that are supposed to keep Jesus out of his dwelling.

* See the note at Mark 1:30.

† Isaiah 53:4, from an important passage about the mysterious "suffering servant."

‡ See pp. xxix–xxxi of the Introduction. This human being is, ironically, worse off than an animal in his material circumstances.

§ One way to comprehend this command, which would have been shocking in all contemporary cultures, is to recall the belief in resurrection in the flesh on the last day for the righteous: this would leave no one on earth after the general destruction to inter the dead but other dead people.

²⁴ But look, a violent storm arose on the sea, so that the boat was wrapped in waves, but he himself was sleeping. ²⁵ Then they approached and woke him, saying, "Master, rescue us, we're going under!" ²⁶ But he said to them, "Why are you such cowards, you people with hardly any trust?" Then he got up and scolded the winds and the sea, and there was a great calm. ²⁷ And the men were amazed, saying, "What kind of person is this? Even the winds and the sea obey him!"

²⁸ Then he came to the other side, to the region of the Gadarēnoi,* and two people possessed by demons came out from among the tombs and met him; they were excessively violent, to the extent that no one was strong enough to pass by on the road there. ²⁹ And look, they yelled out, saying, "What's your business with us, son of god? Have you come here to torture us before our time?" ³⁰ Now there was, far off from them, a large herd of pigs, grazing. ³¹ The demons pleaded with him, saying, "If you expel us, send us into that herd of pigs." ³² And he told them, "Get out!" And once they'd come out, they went into the pigs; but look, the entire herd barreled down the crag and died in the water. ³³ The herders ran off, and when they reached the city they gave news of everything, including what had happened to the men possessed by demons. ³⁴ And look, the whole city came out to meet Iēsous, and when they saw him they pleaded for him to leave their district.

CHAPTER 9

¹ Then, boarding a boat, he crossed over and went to his hometown.

² And look, they brought to him a paralyzed man, lying on a

---

* In Mark 5, the people are "Gerasenes" (Gerasēnoi).

stretcher. And Iēsous saw their trust and said to the paralyzed man, "Be brave, child! You're absolved from your offenses." ³ But look, some of the scholars said inwardly, "He's blaspheming."*
⁴ But Iēsous, seeing what they were brooding over in their hearts, said, "Why are you brooding over such malignant things in your hearts? ⁵ What's actually easier to say, 'You're absolved from your offenses' or 'Get up and walk around'?† ⁶ So that you know the son of mankind has the power on earth to absolve people from their offenses"—then he said to the paralyzed man: "Get up, pick up your stretcher, and go along home." ⁷ And he got up and went away to his home. ⁸ The crowds who saw it were filled with awe, and they glorified god for giving so much power to human beings.

⁹ And passing on from there, Iēsous saw a man sitting at the tax booth, and he was called Maththaios, and he said to him, "Follow me." And he got up and followed him.‡

¹⁰ And it happened that as Iēsous was reclining at the table in the house, look, many tax-collectors and other wrongdoers had come and were reclining with Iēsous and his students. ¹¹ And when the Farisaioi saw, they said to his students, "Why does your teacher eat with tax-collectors and other wrongdoers?" ¹² And Iēsous, hearing this, said to them, "People who are strong and healthy don't have any need for a doctor; no, it's those who are unwell. ¹³ Be on your way, and learn what this means: 'I want mercy and not a sacrifice.' I didn't in fact come to call people

---

* If so, he is subject to the death penalty (Leviticus 24:13–16).

† A joke that can be read into the story in Mark 2:3–12, that the shorter command is simpler and therefore better, would not work here: the "blasphemous" command is four words long in Greek, the other command three words long. The point that survives, however, is that the miracle works whether "blasphemously" worded or not.

‡ Matthew takes the place of Levi in this incident much like the one in Mark (2:13–17). This Gospel is ascribed to Matthew, and he is listed—as a tax collector—as one of the Twelve (10:3).

who are already within the law, but, instead, those who've gone wrong."*

¹⁴ Then Iōannēs' students approached him, asking, "Why do we and the Farisaioi fast [often], but your students don't fast?" ¹⁵ And Iēsous said to them, "The sons of the bridal hall can't mourn while the bridegroom is with them, can they? But the days will come when the bridegroom is taken away from them, and *then* they'll fast. ¹⁶ No one patches an old cloak with a patch made of unshrunken cloth. The reinforcement would pull away from the cloak, and an even worse tear would be made. ¹⁷ And people don't put young wine into old wineskins; otherwise, of course, the skins would burst, and the wine would spill out, and the skins would be ruined. Instead, people put young wine into new wineskins, and both are safely preserved."

¹⁸ Iēsous was still telling them these things when, look, a leader† came, prostrated himself to him, and said, "My daughter has just died; but come and lay your hand on her, and she'll live." ¹⁹ And Iēsous got up and followed him, and his students did the same.

²⁰ But look, a woman who'd had blood flowing from her for twelve years came up behind and touched the hem of his cloak, ²¹ since she said to herself, "If I just touch the hem of his cloak, I'll be cured."‡ ²² And Iēsous turned around, saw her, and said, "Daughter, be brave: your trust has cured you." And from that hour, the woman was cured.

---

* The quotation is from Hosea 6:6 (a longer version of the thought is the famous Micah 6:6–8): material gifts to God are rejected in favor of good behavior. It in fact became a central rabbinic principle that material sacrifice in the Temple—no longer possible after the building was destroyed—is to be replaced in this way.

† In Mark 5:22 he is the head of a synagogue.

‡ The woman touches the *kraspedon* ("hem" or "edge" or "border"), which could be the tassels Israelite men are commanded to wear, to remind them of the law, in Numbers 15:37–41 and Deuteronomy 22:12. But this would seem highly unlikely, as she is breaking the law by her physical contact while she has a discharge.

²³ Then when Iēsous came to the leader's house and saw the flute players, and the crowd in an uproar,* ²⁴ he said, "Out of here, all of you: the little girl isn't in fact dead, only sleeping." But they jeered at him. ²⁵ When the crowd was removed, he went in and grasped her hand, and the little girl woke up. ²⁶ Then talk of this went out to that whole land.

²⁷ Then as Iēsous passed on from there, two blind men followed [him], yelling and saying, "Have pity on us, son of David!" ²⁸ As he was going into the house, the blind men approached him, and Iēsous said to them, "Do you trust that I can do this?" They said to him, "Yes, lord." ²⁹ Then he touched their eyes, saying, "It must be done for you as you trust it will." ³⁰ And their eyes were opened, but Iēsous snapped at them in warning, saying, "See that no one finds out about this." ³¹ But they went and spread the word about him in the whole of that land.

³² After they had gone, look, people brought Iēsous a mute man possessed by a demon. ³³ And after the demon was expelled, the deaf man began to speak, and the crowds were amazed, saying, "Nothing like this has ever appeared in Israēl before." ³⁴ But the Farisaioi said, "He expels demons through the power of their leader."

³⁵ Then Iēsous made a circuit of all the towns and villages, teaching in their synagogues and announcing the good news of the kingdom and curing every disease and every infirmity.

³⁶ But when he saw the crowds, he was wrenched with pity for them, because they were harassed and beaten down, like sheep who have no shepherd.† ³⁷ At this point he said to his students, "The crop is a large one, but there aren't many workers. ³⁸ So ask the owner of the crop to send workers out into his crop."

---

* Flute players would be usual in a funeral procession, along with noisy and demonstrative mourners.

† There are many verses of the Hebrew Bible to this effect, such as Ezekiel 34:5.

CHAPTER 10

——

¹ Then, calling his twelve students to him, he gave them power over unclean spirits, so that they could expel them and cure every disease and every infirmity. ² These are the names of the twelve envoys: first Simōn, who was called Petros, and Andreas his brother, and Iakōbos the son of Zebedaios, and Iōannēs his brother, ³ Filippos and Bartholomaios, Thōmas and Maththaios the tax-collector, Iakōbos the son of Alfaios, and Thaddaios, ⁴ Simōn the Kananaios, and Ioudas the Iskariōtēs, who actually handed him over.*

⁵ Iēsous sent these twelve out, giving them orders by saying, "Don't go down the road to other nations, and don't enter any town of the Samaritai.† ⁶ Instead, travel to the lost sheep of Israēl's household. ⁷ And when you're traveling, announce this message: "The kingdom of the skies has come near." ⁸ Cure the ailing, wake up the dead, cleanse lepers, expel demons; you've taken for free, so give for free. ⁹ Don't acquire gold or silver or copper coins in your belts, ¹⁰ don't take a bag for your journey or two tunics or sandals or a staff: the worker deserves his food.‡

---

* This list of the "apostles" is different only in detail from the one in Mark 3:13–19, where my footnotes describe points of interest.

† Nowhere else in the Gospels is Jesus actually shown forbidding even these geographical contacts, which would have made travel between Jerusalem and Galilee difficult, and travel to the Ten Cities region probably impossible. The other three Gospels reflect the historical reality of energetic proselytizing of Gentiles from the time of Paul of Tarsus, who died around the middle of the 60s.

‡ Only Jesus himself is ever specifically shown raising the dead in the Gospels. See Mark 6:8–10 concerning Essene customs; in Matthew not even footwear or a staff for self-defense appears to be allowed. The traditional translation, indicating that "the workman is worthy of his hire," could be read to mean that he's worth whatever's he's paid. The concern is far more likely to be that all workers be adequately compensated, which was far from the case in the ancient world with its slavery-based economies. Fair compensation was, in fact, a Jewish ethic the Talmud came to reflect. But conflict over material support was particularly intense in early Christian communities, where new social structures were being tried

¹¹ Whichever town or village you come to, ask who in it is deserving, and stay in his house until you leave the locale. ¹² And when you go into the household, greet it kindly. ¹³ And if the household is deserving, your wish for peace will be realized for it. But if the household isn't deserving, your wish for peace will turn back and be realized for *you*.* ¹⁴ As for whoever doesn't take you in hospitably or listen to what you have to say, when you go out of that house or town, shake off the dust on your feet.† ¹⁵ *Amēn* I tell you, it will be easier for the land of Sodoma and Gomorra on the day of judgment than for that town.‡

¹⁶ "Look, I'm sending you out like sheep among wolves. Be shrewd as snakes but innocent as doves.§

¹⁷ "Watch out for people. They'll hand you over to the governing councils,¶ and they'll flog you in their synagogues. ¹⁸ And you'll be brought before governors and kings because of me to give testimony to them and to the foreign nations. ¹⁹ But when they hand you over, don't be worried about how to speak or what about. At that time, what you say will be given to you. ²⁰ You yourselves, in fact, will not be the ones speaking; instead, it will be the life-breath of the father that's speaking in you.**

---

out. In 2 Thessalonians 3:10–11 the complaint about support goes the opposite way: some followers of Jesus are layabouts and should not be fed.

  * The traditional greeting is, of course, "Shalom!," roughly "Peace!"

  † A mysterious curse, probably related to the soles as the lowest, dirtiest part of the body.

  ‡ See Genesis 19:1–26. These cities and all the surrounding land were consumed with a rain of sulfur from heaven. The inhabitants' crime was not essentially "sodomy" (though homosexual rape had been threatened) but the outraging of hospitality.

  § The command is full of irony. The Greek word for shrewdness is the same one used for the snake in the Garden of Eden (Genesis 3:1) in the Septuagint; nor is the innocence of doves a straightforward quality in the Jewish Bible: they are more often silly and flighty than angelic, resembling the recusant prophet Jonah (whose name means "Dove").

  ¶ The local Sanhedrins.

  ** Vigorous parallel Jewish-Roman persecutions would have had very little

²¹ "One brother will hand another over to death, and a father will hand over his child, and children will rebel against parents and have them put to death. ²² And you'll be hated by everyone because of my name. But whoever holds out to the end will be rescued.

²³ "When they come after you in one town run for refuge to the next, since—*amēn* I tell you—you won't reach the end of Israēl's towns until the son of mankind comes.*

²⁴ "A student isn't above the teacher, and the slave isn't above his master. ²⁵ It's enough for the student to become like his teacher and the slave like his master. If they've called the head of the house Be'elzeboul, how much more will they bad-mouth the rest of those in his household!

²⁶ "So don't be afraid of them; nothing in fact is covered over that won't be uncovered,† or hidden that won't be revealed. ²⁷ What I tell you in the darkness, say in the light, and what you hear whispered in your ear, spread the news of it from the roofs. ²⁸ And don't fear anything from those who kill the body but aren't able to kill the life within it. Be afraid, instead, of the one who can destroy both the life and the body in *ge'enna*.‡ ²⁹ Aren't two

---

scope after the destruction of the Temple in 70 C.E., when the Jewish population was decimated in its homeland and terrorized in the Diaspora. In John 14:15–26, a supernatural "advocate" is identified with the Holy Spirit.

* Around 112 C.E., Pliny the Younger, as a provincial governor in Asia Minor, wrote to the emperor Trajan about his attempts to repress Christianity and received an encouraging reply. Regular trials with defense speeches were evidently not conducted: the accused were brought before a magistrate, interrogated, and asked to demonstrate by a ritual sacrifice to the emperor that they were not Christians. (The methodology of mass political purges was in line with Roman suspicions of new foreign cults and nighttime meetings of large numbers of people.) However, a cosmopolitan missionary like Paul, claiming Roman citizenship, could by his own account defend himself and even ingratiate himself with officials he was brought before.

† Literally "veiled" and "unveiled," the latter being the image of "apocalypse."

‡ See "hell" in the Glossary.

sparrows sold for an *assarion*?* But not one of them will fall to the ground without your father's willing it. [30] But as for you, even the hairs on your head are all counted.† [31] So don't be afraid—you're worth more than a whole flock of sparrows!

[32] "Everyone who acknowledges me before human beings— I'll acknowledge him before my father who is in [the] skies. [33] But whoever denies me before human beings—I'll deny him before my father who is in [the] skies.

[34] "Don't suppose that I've come to bring peace to the earth; I've come not to bring peace, but a sword. [35] I've in fact come to divide a man from his father and a daughter from her mother and a bride from her mother-in-law; [36] and a person's enemies will be members of his own household.

[37] "Whoever loves his mother or father more than me doesn't deserve me, and whoever loves his son or daughter more than me doesn't deserve me.‡ [38] And whoever doesn't take up the stake he'll be hung on and follow after me doesn't deserve me. [39] Whoever's found his life will lose it, whoever's lost his life because of me will find it.

[40] "Whoever welcomes you all welcomes me, and whoever welcomes me welcomes the one who sent me. [41] Whoever welcomes a prophet because he's a prophet will get a prophet's reward, and whoever welcomes an upright man because he's an upright man will get a just man's reward. [42] And whoever gives only a cup of cold water to one of these little ones to drink, be-

---

* A tiny unit of Roman coinage. The sparrows would probably be for a Temple sacrifice; small birds are cited in the Torah as acceptable substitutes for the larger offerings the poor cannot afford.

† See Psalms 40:12 and 69:4.

‡ This passage may reflect the early Christian cult of celibacy—notice the direction of the relationships. Parental control over children (even as adults), including their marriages, was for all practical purposes absolute, and the refusal of children with a new religion to marry and to stay settled was a major social disruption, sometimes met with violence.

cause he's a student, *amēn* I tell you, he certainly won't lose his reward."

CHAPTER 11

---

¹ And it happened that when Iēsous had finished giving these instructions to his twelve students, he went on from there to teach and spread the word in their towns.

² Now Iōannēs, when he heard in prison about the work the Anointed One was doing, sent him a message through his students ³ to ask him, "Are you the one coming, or must we expect someone else?" ⁴ And Iēsous answered by saying to them, "Be on your way and take the news to Iōannēs of what you hear and see.

> ⁵ *The blind see again and the crippled walk,*
> *Lepers are cleansed and the deaf hear,*
> *And the dead awaken and the destitute get good news.**

⁶ So it's a happy man who isn't tripped up by me."

⁷ As these people went on their way, Iēsous began to speak to the crowds about Iōannēs: "What did you go out into the wasteland to gape at? A reed shaken by the wind? ⁸ No? Then what *did* you go out to see? A man dressed in luxurious clothes? Take a look: those who wear luxurious clothes are in kings' houses. ⁹ Then what *did* you go out to see? A prophet? Yes, I tell you, and somebody greater than a prophet. ¹⁰ This is the one about whom it's been written:

> *'Look, I'm sending my messenger ahead of you,*
> *And he'll build your road in front of you.'†*

---

* Isaiah 35:6–7.

† Isaiah 40:3.

[11] "*Amēn* I tell you, among those born from women, no one greater than Iōannēs the baptizer has arisen. But the one with the least stature in the kingdom of the skies is greater than he is. [12] From the days of Iōannēs the baptizer until now the kingdom of the skies is assaulted, and its assailants try to seize it by force. [13] All the prophets and the law up to Iōannēs in fact delivered prophecies. [14] And if you want to accept it, he's Ēlias who was to come.* [15] Whoever has ears had better hear!

[16] "Who should I say this generation is like? They're like children sitting in marketplaces and calling to each other, [17] saying,

> 'We played the flute for you—no dancing to the sound!
> We sang the mourning song—your chests you didn't pound!'†

[18] "When Iōannēs came, you know, he didn't eat or drink, so they say, 'He has a demon in him.' [19] The son of mankind came, and he eats and drinks, so they say, 'Look, this guy is an *eater* and a *drinker of wine*, a friend of tax-collectors and other wrongdoers.' But wisdom is vindicated by the actual work she carries out."‡

[20] Then he began to criticize the cities in which most of his acts of power had been done, because they had not changed their thinking. [21] "You have it coming, Chorazin, you have it coming, Bēthsaïda, because if the acts of power that were done in you had been done in Turos or Sidōn, they would have changed their way of thinking a long time ago in burlap and ashes. [22] Yet I tell

---

* That is, John is the second coming of this prophet of miracles and religious purification and restoration.

† This may have been a singsong taunt or part of a game.

‡ *Fagos* is extremely rare and literally just indicates that someone eats: it may be a virtually made-up insult here. This is even more likely for the second criticism, launched with another rare and literally descriptive word: almost no one abstained from alcohol altogether in the ancient world; wine was the default drink at meals, and much safer than the bacteria-ridden water generally available. Again, tax collectors were predatory Imperial contractors. This might be the personified Wisdom found in Proverbs and in certain noncanonical books of Jewish scripture.

you, on the day of judgment it will be easier for Turos and Sidōn than for you. ²³ And you, Kafarnaoum, you won't be raised up to the sky, will you? No, you'll go down to hades—because if the acts of power that were done in you had been done in Sodoma, the city would be there to this day. ²⁴ Yet I tell you that for the land of Sodoma the day of judgment will be easier than for you."*

²⁵ On that occasion, Iēsous responded by saying, "I give you all the credit, father, lord of the sky and the earth, because you've hidden away these things from clever and insightful people, but put them on display to babies.† ²⁶ Yes indeed, father, because this appeared as the right choice in your eyes. ²⁷ Everything was given over to me by my father, and no one recognizes the son unless it's the father, and no one recognizes the father unless it's the son— and anyone to whom the son wishes to reveal him.‡

²⁸ "Come here to me, everyone who is exhausted and loaded down, and I'll give you rest. ²⁹ Take my yoke on yourselves and learn from me, because I'm gentle and humble at heart, and you'll find rest for your lives. ³⁰ My yoke is easy on those beneath it, and the load I put on you is light."

---

* The idea of infidels who are more susceptible to the truth than God's chosen people has a long history stretching back into Hebrew scripture. See especially Jonah 3:5–9. Tyre and Sidon were Phoenician cities known for idolatry, including child sacrifice. See Genesis 19 concerning Sodom.

† Jesus sounds sarcastic here, using the jingle *ekrupsas* ("you have hidden away") and *apekalupsas* ("you have put on display").

‡ The father "recognizing" his son is suggestive: in the Greek and Roman social systems, a son's acknowledged legitimacy was key to family standing and inheritance. Newborn infants with suspect paternity were "exposed," or cast aside to die or be picked up by slave traders.

CHAPTER 12

———

¹ On that occasion, Iēsous made his way through the grainfields on the *sabbata;* and his students were hungry and began to pluck the heads of grain and eat them. ² And the Farisaioi, when they saw, said to him, "Look, your students are doing what's forbidden to do on the *sabbaton.*" ³ But he said to them, "Haven't you read what David did when he was starving—and the people with him were too— ⁴ how he went into god's house and ate the loaves of presentation? He wasn't permitted to eat them, and the people with him weren't either; nobody was, except the priests. ⁵ Or haven't you read in the law that on the *sabbata* the priests in the temple desecrate the *sabbaton* yet aren't guilty? ⁶ But I tell you that something greater than the temple is here. ⁷ But if you recognized the meaning of 'I want mercy and not a burnt offering,' you wouldn't have condemned those who aren't guilty. ⁸ The ruler of the *sabbaton* is in fact the son of mankind."*

⁹ And passing on from there, he came to their synagogue. ¹⁰ And look, there was a man with a withered hand, and they questioned him, saying, "Is it permitted to heal on the *sabbata?*" They were looking to bring a formal accusation against him. ¹¹ But he said to them, "Would there be anyone among you who, if he had a single sheep and it fell into a pit on the *sabbata,* wouldn't take hold of it and lift it out? ¹² A person is worth so much more than a sheep! That means it's permitted to do good on the *sabbata.*"† ¹³ Then he said to the man, "Stretch out your

---

* Compare Mark 2:23–28, and see the footnote. The regular and special sacrifices the priests must make on the Sabbath (Numbers 28:9–10) are of course permitted work. Hosea 6:6 is quoted here.

† Permission to do work on the Sabbath in order to save life does not extend to livestock. Notice that the hypothetical person in this example is poor and in danger of losing what may be his only capital: strict Sabbath observance was easier for the wealthy.

hand!" And he stretched it out, and it was restored to soundness and was just like the other hand. ¹⁴ But after the Farisaioi went away, they formed a plot against him to destroy him.

¹⁵ But Iēsous, realizing this, withdrew from that place. But large [crowds] followed him, and he healed them all. ¹⁶ But he sternly insisted that they must not make him a public figure, ¹⁷ so that what was spoken through Ēsaïas the prophet, when he said this, could be fulfilled:

> ¹⁸ *"Look, this is my servant, whom I chose,*
> *My beloved one in whom my life has taken delight.*
> *I will place my life-breath on him,*
> *And he will proclaim judgment to the other nations.*
> ¹⁹ *He won't squabble or yell,*
> *And no one will hear his voice in the streets.*
> ²⁰ *He won't break a reed already damaged,*
> *And he won't snuff out a smoking wick*
> *Until he brings judgment to its victory,*
> ²¹ *And the other nations will find hope in his name."**

²² Then a demon-possessed blind and mute man was brought to him, and he healed him, so that the mute man could now speak and see. ²³ And all the crowds were stunned, and they said, "This can't be the son of David, can it?"† ²⁴ But the Farisaioi, when they heard, said, "This man can only expel demons through the power of the demons' ruler, Be'elzeboul." ²⁵ Knowing what was on their minds, Iēsous said to them, "Every kingdom that's split in two and has the two pieces pitted against each other is turned into a wasteland, and every city or household that's split

---

* Isaiah 42:1–4. Most probably, this "Servant Song" (see p. xxix of the Introduction) refers to Israel itself and the example it can set despite, or because of, its own oppression. But the passage was later taken both to allude to the Messiah and to explain Jesus' obscurity in life.

† This would be the Messiah, as David was the original divinely chosen and anointed king.

in two and has the two pieces pitted against each other won't remain standing. ²⁶ And if satanas throws out satanas, he's split in two, with the two pieces of him pitted against each other. So how will his kingdom remain standing? ²⁷ And if I expel demons through the power of Be'elzeboul, through whose power do *your* sons expel them? For this reason, they'll be your judges in deciding this matter. ²⁸ But if through the power of god's life-breath I expel demons, then god's kingdom has arrived ahead of you. ²⁹ Or how can anyone come into a strong man's house and carry off his things, unless he ties up the strong man first? Only then can he plunder the house. ³⁰ Whoever's not with me is against me, and whoever isn't gathering with me is scattering.*

³¹ "For this reason I tell you, people will be pardoned from every sort of wrongdoing and blasphemy, except that they won't be pardoned from blasphemy against the life-breath. ³² Even if someone speaks against the son of mankind, he'll be pardoned, but if someone speaks against the holy life-breath, he won't be pardoned, neither in this era or in the era that's coming.†

³³ "Either assume the tree is good, and that its fruit is good too, or assume the tree is bad, and that its fruit is bad too, as the tree's known by its fruit. ³⁴ You viper hatchlings, how can you say excellent things when *you*'re useless? The mouth in fact says what overflows from the heart. ³⁵ The excellent person takes excellent things from his excellent storeroom, but the useless person takes useless things from his useless storeroom. ³⁶ I tell you that for every worthless thing people say, they'll give an account on the day of judgment; ³⁷ on the basis of the accounts you give, you'll be acquitted, or on the basis of the accounts you give you'll be condemned."

³⁸ Then some of the scholars and Farisaioi responded to him by saying, "Teacher, we want to see a sign from you." ³⁹ But he

---

* See the Glossary for "Satan," the archetypal "opponent." The "sons" in Verse 27 must refer to miracle workers favored by the religious authorities.

† See "S/spirit" in the Glossary.

answered by saying to them, "A useless, unfaithful* generation is looking for a sign! But a sign won't be given to it, unless it's the sign of Iōnas the prophet. ⁴⁰ Iōnas of course was in the belly of the sea monster for three days and three nights: in the same way, the son of mankind will be in the heart of the earth for three days and three nights.† ⁴¹ The Nineuitai men will stand up at the judgment along with this generation and give their judgment against it, because they changed their thinking to obey Iōnas' proclamation, and look, something greater than Iōnas is here!‡ ⁴² The queen of where the south wind comes from will stand at the judgment along with this generation and give her judgment against it, because she came from the boundaries of the earth to hear the wisdom of Solomōn, and look, something greater than Solomōn is here.§

⁴³ "When an unclean spirit comes out of a person, it passes through waterless places seeking a place to rest, but doesn't find any. ⁴⁴ Then it says, 'I'll return to my house again, where I came from.' But when it arrives, it finds the building unoccupied, swept out, and put in order. ⁴⁵ Then it goes on its way and brings back with it seven other spirits more terrible than itself, and they go in and take up residence there. And the final plight of that person is worse than the original one. That's what it will be like for this terrible generation."¶

---

* In standard translations, "adulterous," referring to Israel's straying from her metaphoric marriage to God.

† The most extreme expression of inclusive reckoning: Jesus is in fact interred only for two nights and one full day.

‡ Jonah survives in the sea monster, repents, and is disgorged (Jonah 1:17–2:10). The citizens of pagan Nineveh—here respectfully called *andres* (see "man" in the Glossary)—are immediately ready to convert at the prophet's proclamation (Jonah 3:1–5).

§ The wealthy pagan Queen of Sheba (1 Kings 10, 2 Chronicles 9) pays a respectful visit to Solomon.

¶ See "evil" and "S/spirit" in the Glossary.

⁴⁶ While he was still speaking to the crowds, look, his mother and his brothers were standing outside, looking to speak to him. [⁴⁷ And someone said to him, "Look, your mother and your brothers are standing outside, looking to speak to you."] ⁴⁸ But in answer he said to the one who had told him this: "Who's my mother, and who are my brothers?" ⁴⁹ Then he stretched out his hand toward his students and said, "Look: my mother and my brothers! ⁵⁰ Whoever in fact does what my father in the skies wants is my brother and sister and mother."*

CHAPTER 13

¹ On that day, Iēsous went out of the house and sat down beside the sea. ² And large crowds gathered where he was, so that he boarded a boat and sat down, and the whole crowd stood on the shore.

³ And he told them many things through analogies. He said, "Look, a sower went out to sow. ⁴ And as he sowed, it happened that some of the seed fell along the road, and the birds came and made short work of it. ⁵ And other seed fell on stony places, where it didn't have much earth, and right away it sprouted and rose up, because it didn't have any depth of earth. ⁶ But when the sun rose up, the seedings were seared, and due to their lack of roots, they withered. ⁷ And other seed fell among the thorny weeds, and these came up and strangled the seedings. ⁸ But other seeds fell onto good ground and produced a harvest, with one kernel yielding a hundred, another sixty, another thirty more. ⁹ Whoever has ears had better hear."

¹⁰ Then the students approached and said to him, "What's the

---

* Again, a key question about this strikingly untraditional attitude is whether Jesus is keeping relatives out of their own house while it is full of his followers.

reason you speak to them through analogies?" [11] As an answer, he told them, "The secrets* of the skies' kingdom have been granted to you to know, but haven't been granted to those others. [12] If in fact someone has something, more will be given to him, and he'll have more than enough. But if someone doesn't have something, even what he does have will be taken away from him. [13] This is the reason I speak to them through analogies: when they look, they don't really look, and when they hear they don't really hear, and they don't understand; [14] and in them the prophecy of Ēsaïas is fulfilled: he said,

> "'You'll certainly hear, but you'll never understand;
> You'll definitely look, but you'll never see,
> [15] Because this people's heart has turned stony,
> And its ears are slow to hear.
> They have closed their eyes,
> So that they never see with their eyes
> Or hear with their ears
> Or understand with their heart
> Or turn around and let me heal them.'†

[16] "But your eyes are fortunate because they see, and your ears because they hear. [17] *Amēn* I tell you that in fact many prophets and upright men longed to see what you've looked at, but they didn't see it; and to hear what you've heard, but they didn't hear it.

[18] "So you yourselves, listen to the analogy of the sower. [19] Whenever someone hears the true account of the kingdom but doesn't understand it, the malicious one comes and snatches what has been sown in his heart: this is the person who's sown along the road. [20] The person sown in rocky places is the one who hears the account and right away takes it in with joy. [21] Yet he

---

* See the note at Mark 4:11 on "mystery."

† Isaiah 6:9–10. Notice the wide differences from the version in Mark 4:12. The Septuagint text was highly fluid.

doesn't take root, but instead is merely of the moment, and when grinding hardship and hounding come because of the account, he falls away. ²² And the one sown among the thorny weeds: he hears the account, but the anxieties of this present life and the false appeal of wealth strangle what he heard, and it can't bear grain. ²³ But the one sown onto good ground, he's the one who hears the account and understands it: he does produce a harvest, and every kernel yields a hundred, or sixty, or thirty more."

²⁴ He offered them another analogy, saying, "The kingdom of the skies can be compared to a person sowing good seed in his field. ²⁵ But while everyone was sleeping, the enemy came and in addition sowed darnel-weed all through his wheat crop, and went away. ²⁶ And when the shoots sprouted and bore grain, then the darnel-weed appeared as well. ²⁷ Then the slaves belonging to the head of the household approached and told him, 'Master, didn't you sow good seed in your field? Then where does the darnel-weed come from?' ²⁸ But he said to them, 'Somebody who's an enemy to me did this.'* The slaves then said to him, 'So do you want us to go and gather up the weeds?' ²⁹ And he said to them, 'No, no, it's too great a risk that in gathering up the darnel, you'd uproot the wheat along with it. ³⁰ Let both of them grow up together until the harvest, and at the proper time for the harvest, I'll say to the harvesters, "First gather the darnel and bind it in bundles, so that you can burn it up, but bring the crop all together to my barn."' "

³¹ He offered them another analogy, saying, "The kingdom of the skies is like a mustard seed that a man took and sowed in his field, ³² and though it's the smallest of all seeds, once it's grown, it's bigger than all other garden plants and becomes a tree, so that the birds of the sky come and find shelter among its branches."

---

* A typical accusation in peasant societies. Livestock diseases, soured milk, and crop mildew have also historically often been blamed on malign neighbors. In reality, darnel seed is hard to tell from wheat seed (and nearly impossible to separate before the invention of special devices) and was often sown with it unwittingly.

³³ He spoke to them with another analogy. "The kingdom of the skies is like yeast that a woman took and hid in three *sata** of flour, and waited until the whole lump of dough was risen with the yeast." ³⁴ Iēsous said all these things through analogies to the crowds, and without an analogy he said nothing to them, ³⁵ so that there could be a fulfillment of what was spoken through the prophet when he said,

> *"I'll open my mouth to speak in analogies,*
> *I'll utter what's been hidden since the foundation [of the*
>   *universe]."*†

³⁶ Then he left the crowds and went into the house. And his students came to him and said, "Enlighten us about the analogy to the darnel in the field." ³⁷ And he answered them by saying, "The son of mankind is the one who sows the good seed, ³⁸ and the field is the world, and the good seed is the sons of the kingdom, while the darnel is the sons of the malicious one,‡ ³⁹ and the enemy sowing the darnel is the slanderer, and the harvest is the era come to fruition, and the harvesters are messengers. ⁴⁰ Hence the way the darnel is gathered and burned [up] in the fire is the way it will be when the era comes to fruition. ⁴¹ The son of mankind will send out his messengers, and they'll gather from his kingdom everyone who's an obstacle, and everyone who commits crimes, ⁴² and they'll throw them into the fiery oven; and there'll be crying and grinding of teeth in pain in that place. ⁴³ Then the upright people will shine out like the sun in their father's kingdom. Whoever has ears had better hear.

⁴⁴ "The kingdom of the skies is like a treasure hidden in a field. A man found it, then hid it, and now in his joy he goes and puts up for sale everything he has and buys that field.

---

* The *saton* is a dry measure of around three gallons.

† See Psalms 78:2; the Hebrew, however, refers to a "proverb" and "riddles."

‡ See "evil" in the Glossary.

⁴⁵ "Then there's this: the kingdom of the skies is like a man in mercantile trade who was looking for beautiful pearls. ⁴⁶ Having found one very valuable pearl, he went away and sold everything he had and bought it.*

⁴⁷ "Once again: the kingdom of the skies is like a dragnet that was thrown into the sea and gathered every kind of thing. ⁴⁸ Once it was full, they drew it up onto the shore, sat down, and collected the good things and put them into buckets, and threw out the bad things.† ⁴⁹ That's the way it will be when the era comes to fruition: the messengers will come out and separate the useless people from among the upright ⁵⁰ and throw them into the fiery oven. In that place there'll be crying and teeth-grinding from pain.

⁵¹ "Have you understood all these things?" They told him, "Yes." ⁵² Then he said to them, "This is the reason every scholar who's been trained for the kingdom of the skies is like a man who's head of a household, and who brings new things and old things out of his storeroom."‡

⁵³ Then it happened that, when he'd completed these analogies, he departed from that place. ⁵⁴ And he came to his hometown and taught the people in their synagogue, so that they were dumbfounded and said, "Where did he get this insight and these acts of power? ⁵⁵ Isn't this the builder's son? Don't they say that his mother's Mariam, and that his brothers are Iakōbos and Iōsēf and Simōn and Ioudas? ⁵⁶ And aren't all his sisters here with us? So where did he get all of this?" ⁵⁷ So they were tripped up by him. But Iēsous said to them, "A prophet isn't treated dishonorably except in his hometown and in his own house." ⁵⁸ And in

---

* Pearls were the most celebrated and expensive jewels of the ancient world, sometimes fetching legendary prices.

† The discards would include not only garbage but any creatures without fins and scales, forbidden food for Jews (Leviticus 11:9–12).

‡ That is, even for the learned among Jesus' followers, this new, apocalyptic knowledge must be acquired in addition to a mastery of older scripture.

that place he didn't perform many powerful acts, because of their lack of trust.*

CHAPTER 14

—

¹ At that juncture, Hērōdēs the client king heard what was to be heard about Iēsous. ² And he said to his slaves, "This is Iōannēs the baptizer: he's awakened from among the dead, and for this reason powers are at work in him."

³ Now Hērōdēs had seized Iōannēs and chained [him] up and put him in prison because of Hērōdias, the wife of his brother Filippos, ⁴ as Iōannēs had said to him, "It's not lawful for you to have her."† ⁵ And he wanted to kill him, but he feared the mass of the people, because they held him to be a prophet.

⁶ But when it was Hērōdēs' birthday, Hērōdias' daughter danced in front of everyone, and Hērōdēs was delighted with her. ⁷ Hence he promised on oath to give her whatever she asked for. ⁸ And at her mother's prompting, she said, "Give me, right here on a platter, the head of Iōannēs the baptizer." ⁹ And the king was anguished, but because of the oaths he'd sworn and the guests reclining at the table with him, he commanded it to be given to her. ¹⁰ So he sent and had Iōannēs beheaded in the prison. ¹¹ Then his head was brought on a platter and given to the little girl, and she brought it to her mother. ¹² And his students came and took the corpse and interred it, then went and brought the news to Iēsous.‡

¹³ And when Iēsous heard it, he withdrew in a boat from where he was to an uninhabited place to be by himself. But the crowds

---

* See Mark 6:1–6, and the notes.

† See the note at Mark 6:18.

‡ See the note at Mark 6:22 for some background and implications of this episode.

heard and followed him on foot from the towns. ¹⁴ And when he got out of the boat he saw a large crowd and was wrenched with pity for them and healed those who were ill.

¹⁵ When evening came, the students approached him and said, "This is a place no one lives in, and by now quite some time has passed. Send the crowds away, so that they can go into the villages and buy themselves food." ¹⁶ But [Iēsous] said to them: "They have no need to go. *You* give them something to eat." ¹⁷ But they told him, "We don't have anything here except five loaves and two fish." ¹⁸ Then he said, "Bring them here to me." ¹⁹ And he ordered the crowd to recline on the grass,* and taking the five loaves and two fish, he looked up to the sky, blessed the loaves, broke them into pieces, and gave the pieces to the students, and the students gave them to the crowds. ²⁰ And all the people ate until they were full, and they picked up twelve baskets full of leftover broken pieces. ²¹ And about five thousand grown men had eaten, besides women and children.

²² And right away, he made his students board the boat and go ahead of him to the opposite shore, while he sent the crowds away. ²³ Once he'd sent the crowds away, he climbed up a high mountain to pray on his own. And when evening came, he was alone there. ²⁴ Now, the boat was already many stades† away from land, and was being pounded by waves, as the wind was against them. ²⁵ And during the fourth watch of the night‡ he came toward them, walking on the sea. ²⁶ And when the students saw him walking on the sea, they were frantic, saying, "It's a ghost!"; and they cried out in fear. ²⁷ But right away, [Iēsous] spoke to them, saying, "Be brave—it's me; don't be afraid." ²⁸ But Petros answered him by saying, "Master, if it's you, order me to come to you on the water." ²⁹ So he said, "Come!" Then Petros got out of

* See the note at Mark 6:40 for a comparison.

† A stade is around six hundred feet—but these are not quite the same as modern feet.

‡ Since there were only four watches during the night, this must be near dawn.

the boat, walked on the water, and went toward Iēsous. ³⁰ But seeing [how powerful] the wind [was], he was frightened, and as he started to sink, he shouted the words, "Master, save me!" ³¹ And right away Iēsous stretched out his hand, took hold of him, and said to him, "You with hardly any trust! Why did you waver?" ³² And once they'd climbed up onto the boat, the wind stopped. ³³ And those on the boat prostrated themselves before him, saying, "Truly, you are god's son."

³⁴ Then they crossed over and came to land at Gennēsaret.* ³⁵ And the men of that place recognized him and sent word to the whole of that surrounding region, and they brought him everyone who was unwell. ³⁶ And they begged him just to let them touch the hem of his cloak: and everyone who touched it was completely cured.

CHAPTER 15

——

¹ Then Farisaioi and scholars came to Iēsous from Hierosoluma and said, ² "Why do your students overstep the laws the ancestors handed down? They're in fact not washing [their] hands when they eat bread." ³ But he answered by telling them, "Why do you overstep god's command through what *you* hand down? ⁴ God in fact said, 'Honor your father and your mother,' and 'Whoever insults his father or mother is to end his life and die.' ⁵ You, on the other hand, say, 'Whoever tells his father or mother "Whatever help might have come from me is an offering" ⁶ is not allowed to honor his father at all.' So you've canceled what god spoke by this handing down of yours. ⁷ You play-actors, Ēsaïas was right when he prophesied about you, saying,

* A town on the western shore of the Sea of Galilee, not far south of Capernaum.

⁸ "'This people honors me with their lips alone,
  While their heart is far away from me.
  ⁹ *Uselessly they "worship" me,*
  Teaching human injunctions as the teachings.'"*

¹⁰ And he called the crowd to him and told them, "Listen and understand. ¹¹ What comes into a person's mouth, however indiscriminately, doesn't make him dirty; no, it's what makes its way *out* of the mouth that makes a person dirty."†

¹² Then the students approached and said to him, "Do you know that the Farisaioi were tripped up and upset when they heard what you said?" ¹³ And he answered by saying, "Every plant that my father in the sky didn't plant will be rooted out. ¹⁴ Forget about them. They're blind guides [of blind people]. If one blind man guides another, both of them will fall into a pit."

¹⁵ In response Petros said to him, "Explain to us what [this] analogy means!" ¹⁶ And he said, "Even now, don't you all have any understanding either? ¹⁷ You don't realize that everything making its way into the mouth goes into the belly and then gets dropped down the latrine? ¹⁸ But the things making their way out of the mouth come out of the heart, and *these* dirty a person. ¹⁹ Out of the heart come nasty calculations, murders, violations of marriage, whoring, thefts, lying testimonies, backstabbing lies. ²⁰ These are what make a person dirty; eating with unwashed hands doesn't make a person dirty."‡

²¹ Then Iēsous set off from that place and withdrew to the region of Turos and Sidōn. ²² And look, a Chananaia woman from that district came out and began to scream the words "Have pity

---

* Isaiah 29:13. Torah, the name for the five "Books of the Law," means "teaching."

† See Mark 7:1–15 and the notes.

‡ This may seem a shockingly sweeping rejection of Jewish law and custom, but like much rabbinic writing, it stresses the importance of innocent intentions over physical purity.

on me, lord, son of David! My daughter is possessed by a very troublesome demon." ²³ But he didn't have anything to say in reply to her. Then his students approached and pressured him, saying, "Get rid of her, because she keeps screaming after us." ²⁴ But he answered by saying, "I was sent only to the lost sheep of the house of Israēl." ²⁵ Then she came and prostrated herself before him, saying, "Sir, come to my rescue!" ²⁶ But he said in answer, "It's not right to take the offspring's loaf and toss it to the little doggies." ²⁷ But she said, "Yes, master, but the little doggies do eat some of the crumbs that fall from their masters' table." ²⁸ Then Iēsous said in answer to her, "Woman, your trust is great. It must be done for you as you wish." And her daughter was healed from that hour.*

²⁹ Then Iēsous passed on from that place and went to the sea of Galilaia, and he climbed up a mountain and sat down there. ³⁰ And large crowds came to him, bringing with them the crippled, the blind, the deformed, the mute, and many others, and they put these people at his feet, and he healed them. ³¹ As a result, the crowd was amazed at seeing the mute speak, the deformed whole, the crippled walk, and the blind see. And they glorified the god of Israēl.

³² Then Iēsous, calling his students to him, said, "I'm wrenched with pity for the crowd, because they've been staying with me here for three days already, and they have nothing to eat. But I don't want to send them off hungry, in case they collapse on the road." ³³ And the students told him, "Where in this place no one lives in are we to get enough loaves to fill up such a large crowd?" ³⁴ But Iēsous said to them, "How many loaves do you have?" They said, "Seven, and a few tiny fish." ³⁵ And he ordered the crowd to recline on the ground, ³⁶ and took the seven loaves and the fish, and when he'd given thanks, he broke them into pieces

---

* Compare the version of this witty passage to its counterpart at Mark 7:24–30, and see the notes there on ethnicity, ideas of the covenant, and humorous vocabulary.

and gave them to the students, and the students gave them to the crowds. ³⁷ And they all ate until they were full. And they took up seven hampers full of leftover broken pieces. ³⁸ And those who ate were four thousand grown men, aside from the women and children.

³⁹ And he sent the crowds off, boarded a boat, and went into the district of Magadan.*

CHAPTER 16

———

¹ Now the Farisaioi and the Saddoukaioi approached and tested him, asking him to show them a sign from the sky. ² And he answered by telling them, ["When evening comes, you say, 'Fair weather, since the sky is blazing red.' ³ And at dawn: 'There'll be a storm today, because the sky is blazing red and gloomy.' You know how to discern the face of the sky, but you can't discern the signs of critical times?]† ⁴ A worthless and unfaithful generation keeps looking for a sign, but the only sign that's going to be given to it is the sign of Iōnas."‡ And he left them and went away.

⁵ But when the students had come to the opposite shore, they found they had forgotten to take any loaves. ⁶ And Iēsous said to them, "See that you're wary of the yeast of the Farisaioi and the Saddoukaioi."§ ⁷ But they tried to work it out among themselves and said, "It means we didn't take any loaves." ⁸ And perceiving this, Iēsous said to them, "Why are you trying to work it out

---

* Associated with "Magdala," possibly the hometown of Mary Magdalene, this is about halfway down the western coast of the Sea of Galilee.

† The disquisition on weather is thought to be interpolated, or added later, to the text.

‡ Jonah was visited with a terrible storm when he fled from his prophetic mission. He was thrown overboard and put in the way of the "big fish," inside which he repented.

§ Passover bread is rendered ritually impure by even tiny amounts of yeast.

among yourselves that it's because you don't have any loaves—you with so little trust? ⁹ Don't you realize yet, and don't you remember the five loaves for the five thousand people, and how many baskets you took up? ¹⁰ And don't you remember the seven loaves for the four thousand people, and how many hampers you took up? ¹¹ How can you not realize that I wasn't talking to you about loaves? Look out for the yeast of the Farisaioi and the Saddoukaioi!" ¹² Then they understood that he hadn't told them to look out for the yeast in bread, but rather for the teachings of the Farisaioi and the Saddoukaioi.*

¹³ Then, as Iēsous was coming to the region of Kaisareia of Filippos,† he questioned his students, saying, "Who do men say the son of mankind is?" ¹⁴ And they said, "Some say that you're Iōannēs the baptizer, and others that you're Ēlias, and others that you're Ieremias‡ or another one of the prophets." ¹⁵ He said to them, "Who do *you* say I am?" ¹⁶ Simōn Petros answered him and said: "You're the anointed one, the son of the living god." ¹⁷ And Iēsous answered, telling him, "You are fortunate, Simōn Bariōna,§ because flesh and blood didn't reveal that to you—no, it was my father in the skies. ¹⁸ But it's me telling you that you *are* Petros, and that on this rock I'll build my assembly hall,¶ and the gates of hades won't gain the victory over it.** ¹⁹ I'll give you the keys to the

---

* Compare the probable wit in the Mark 8:14–21 version.

† See the note at Mark 8:27.

‡ Jeremiah was a prophet known particularly for his prediction of the fall of Jerusalem in 587 B.C.E., during the Babylonian conquest of Judah, and for his denunciatory and mournful writings.

§ "Simon Son of Jonah" in Aramaic.

¶ See the second note at Mark 3:16. This is the only passage giving a clear rationale for why this disciple is called Petros, meaning "Rock." See also "church" in the Glossary.

** City gates, generally symbolic of national and royal power in the Hebrew Bible, here likely have to do with the apocalypse and a dualistic idea of heaven and hell at war.

kingdom of the skies, and whatever you chain up on earth will be chained up in the skies, and whatever you unlock on earth will be unlocked in the skies."* ²⁰ Then he stringently warned the students not to tell anyone that he was the anointed one.

²¹ From that time on, Iēsous began to point out to his students that it was necessary for him to go to Hierosoluma and endure many things at the hands of the elders and the high priests and the scholars, and to be killed, and be raised to his feet again after three days.† ²² But Petros, taking him aside, began to scold him, saying, "May you be spared, master! This must never happen to you!" ²³ But he turned around and said to Petros, "Get behind me, satanas! You're an obstacle for me, because it's not the things that belong to god you're thinking of, but instead the things that belong to human beings."

²⁴ Then Iēsous said to his students: "If someone wants to walk behind me, let him renounce all claim to himself and pick up the stake he'll be hung from and follow me. ²⁵ Whoever wants to save his life will lose it. But whoever loses his life because of me will find it. ²⁶ What kind of profit, tell me, does a person realize from the entire universe, if he loses his life? Or what would a person give in exchange for his life? ²⁷ The son of mankind is in fact about to come in the glory of his father with his messengers, and he'll give each person what he's earned by what he's done. ²⁸ *Amēn* I tell you, there are some standing here who won't taste death until they see the son of mankind coming in his kingdom."

---

* Aside from Peter's later associations with the papacy, and as simply understood as possible, the keeper of the keys controlled the household, including its slaves and servants (subject to harsh discipline) and the vital storeroom. Peter is hence pictured as the divinely authorized organizer of Jesus' followers, whose arrangements will endure through the apocalypse and into eternity.

† Literally "three days." But Jesus is buried on the evening before the Sabbath and rises on the morning after it.

CHAPTER 17

___

¹ Then after six days, Iēsous took Petros and Iakōbos, and Iōannēs the brother of Iakōbos, and brought them up onto a high mountain, on their own. ² And his form changed before their eyes, and his face shone like the sun, and his clothing became as white as light. ³ And look, Mōusēs and Ēlias were seen by them, talking with him. ⁴ Petros now responded by saying to Jesus, "Master, it's good that we're here: if you want, I'll make three shelters here, one for you and one for Mōusēs and one for Ēlias." ⁵ While he was still speaking, look, a cloud full of light overshadowed them, and look, there was a voice from the cloud saying, "This is my beloved son, in whom I've taken delight: listen to him." ⁶ And when the students heard, they fell facedown, and they were terribly frightened. ⁷ But Iēsous approached, touched them, and said, "Get up, and don't be frightened." ⁸ And when they raised their eyes they saw no one but Iēsous himself, only him.

⁹ Then as they were coming down from the mountain, Iēsous gave them a command, saying, "Don't tell anyone about the vision until the son of mankind has awakened from among the dead." ¹⁰ And his students questioned him, saying, "So what do the scholars mean when they say, 'It's necessary for Ēlias to come first'?" ¹¹ And he said to them, "Ēlias *does* come, and he will reestablish everything. ¹² But I tell you that Ēlias came already, and they didn't know him—instead, they did everything they wanted to him. In the same way, the son of mankind too is going to suffer at their hands." ¹³ Then the students understood that he'd spoken to them about Iōannēs the baptizer.*

¹⁴ Then as they came to the crowd, a man approached him and fell on his knees, ¹⁵ and he said, "Master, have pity on my son,

* Concerning Jesus' connection to Elijah through John the Baptist, see the note at Mark 9:13 on the earlier version of this passage.

since he's moonstruck and suffering terribly. Often he falls into the fire, and often into the water. ⁱ⁶ And I brought him to your students, but they didn't have the power to heal him." ⁱ⁷ And Iēsous said in answer, "You faithless generation, completely distorted! How long will I be with you? How long will I put up with you?* Bring him here to me." ⁱ⁸ And Iēsous berated the demon, and it came out of him, and the boy was healed from that hour on.

ⁱ⁹ Then Iēsous' students approached him privately and asked, "What's the reason we didn't have the power to expel it?" ²⁰ And he said to them, "The reason is that your trust is puny.† *Amēn*, I tell you, if you have trust the size of a mustard seed, you'll be able to tell this mountain, 'Move from here to there,' and it will move. And nothing will be beyond your power."‡

²² When they gathered together in Galilaia, Iēsous said to them, "The son of humankind is about to be turned over to human hands, ²³ and they'll kill him, and on the third day, he'll awaken and get up." And they were overcome with anguish.

²⁴ Then after they came into Kafarnaoum, collectors of the double drachma came to Petros and said, "Doesn't your teacher pay [the] double drachma?" ²⁵ He said, "Yes." But when he went home, Iēsous got ahead of him by asking, "What do you think, Simōn? From whom do the kings of the earth collect excise taxes or the individual tax? From their sons,§ or from strangers?" ²⁶ And when he said, "From strangers," Iēsous said to him, "Then the sons are exempt. ²⁷ But so that we don't create an obstacle for them, make your way to the sea, throw in a hook, and take up the

---

* Again, perhaps echoing a famous question of the Roman orator Cicero concerning the rebellious Catiline as well as Psalms 13:1–2.

† Note the different explanation given about the same disease, epilepsy, in the parallel passage Mark 9:14–29.

‡ Verse 21, reading "However, this one does not go out except by prayer and fasting," has been removed from the standard Greek text as spurious.

§ The phrase is in the Hebraic sense, meaning only "their own people."

first fish that rises to it, and when you open its mouth, you'll find a stater. Take that and give it to them for me and you."*

CHAPTER 18

¹On that occasion, the students approached Iēsous, saying, "Who, then, is greatest in the kingdom of the skies?" ²And he called a child to him, had it stand in the center of the gathering, ³and said, "*Amēn* I tell you, if you don't turn around and become like children, you'll never enter into the kingdom of the skies. ⁴Whoever lowers himself to be like this child, *he's* greatest in the kingdom of the skies. And whoever takes in a child like this one, he's greatest in the kingdom of the skies. ⁵And whoever takes in a child like this one in my name takes me in.†

⁶"Whoever sets a trap for one of these little ones who trust in me would be better off having a millstone—a big one drawn by a donkey—hung around his neck and being sunk in the deep sea. ⁷The world, because of its traps, has it coming! Of course it's unavoidable that traps occur, but the person who's responsible for a trap occurring has it coming! ⁸If your hand or your foot sets a trap for you, cut it off and throw it away from you. It's better for you to enter maimed or crippled into life than to have two hands or two feet and be thrown into the fire that lasts for all of time. ⁹And if your eye sets a trap for you, pull it out and throw it away

---

* The Temple tax collected from each adult Jewish male was half a shekel, equal to half a stater, or two drachmas: a drachma or a denarius was a standard daily wage for a laborer. The Temple hierarchy is purportedly taxing Jews as if they were in a subdued and occupied country, though it was of course the Romans who did this. But the Gospels' attitude toward taxpaying is always conformist.

† See "receive" in the Glossary. Children were not considered full members of society, so these strictures are unusual.

from you. It's better for you to enter into life one-eyed than to be thrown with both your eyes into *ge'enna* with its fire.*

¹⁰ "See that you don't sneer at a single one of these little ones, since I tell you that their messengers in the skies never stop looking into the face of my father in the skies.†

¹² "What do you think? If a man has a hundred sheep and one of them wanders away, won't he leave the ninety-nine on the mountains and set off to look for the wandering one? ¹³ And if he happens to find it, *amēn* I tell you, he feels more joy over it than over the ninety-nine that haven't wandered. ¹⁴ In just this way, your father in the skies is not willing for a single one of these little ones to be lost.

¹⁵ "And if your brother wrongs [you], go and prove to him what he's done, just between him and you. If he listens, then you have a brother to your credit. ¹⁶ But if he doesn't listen, take one or two others with you, so that every statement gets confirmed from the mouth of two or three witnesses.‡ ¹⁷ But if he refuses to listen to them, tell the assembly.§ And if he refuses to listen even to the assembly, let him be to you like someone belonging to another nation, or a tax-collector.¶ ¹⁸ *Amēn* I tell you, whatever you all chain up on earth will remain chained up in the skies, and whatever you unchain on earth will be unchained in the skies.**

¹⁹ "Again [*amēn*] I tell you that if two among you agree on earth about anything they ask for, it will be granted to them by my

---

* See "hell" in the Glossary.

† Verse 11, which has been translated as "The Son of Man came to save the lost," is left out of the standard edition of the Greek text.

‡ The forensic standard of the Hebrew Bible and the rabbinic writings.

§ See "church" in the Glossary.

¶ See "Gentiles" in the Glossary. This exclusion is termed as if Jesus' followers were all Jews of the Judean province, but long before the appearance of the Gospel of Matthew, this was not the case.

** See 16:17–19 above, and the notes.

father in the skies. ²⁰ In fact, where two or three gather because of my name, I'm there in the middle of that gathering."

²¹ Then Petros approached and asked him, "Master, how many times can my brother do wrong to me and still have me pardon him? As many as seven times?" ²² Iēsous told him, "I don't tell you seven times, but rather as many as seventy times seven."

²³ "That's the reason that the kingdom of the skies can be compared to a king, who wanted to settle accounts with his slaves. ²⁴ And when he began to settle them, a debtor to the amount of ten thousand talents was brought to him.* ²⁵ As he didn't have the means to pay it back, the master ordered him to be sold along with his wife and children and everything he owned, and the debt to be paid in this way.† ²⁶ Then the slave fell down and groveled at his feet, saying, 'Be patient with me, and I'll pay it all back to you.' ²⁷ And the master was wrung with pity for that slave and let him go, and remitted his loan. ²⁸ But when that slave went out, he found one of his fellow slaves, who owed him a hundred denarii,‡ and he grabbed him and choked him, saying, 'Pay what you owe!' ²⁹ His fellow slave fell down and pleaded with him, saying, 'Be patient with me, and I'll pay you back.' ³⁰ But he didn't accept that. Instead, he went and had him thrown in prison until

---

* A talent weight could be as much as a hundred and thirty pounds of silver or gold, a value unimaginable to ordinary people. (There may be some authorial confusion between minas and talents—minas figure in a parallel story at Luke 19:12–27—as local names of the currencies differed.) In any case, the size of the first debt seems fabulous for a private person; that and the initial indication of royalty (though the New Testament can be loose with that term) give the story a fairy-tale air. The monarchs of the East might refer to their managers as "slaves," but it is still hard to imagine personal loans on this scale to dependents of any kind.

† Household dissolution through "debt slavery" was possible for all those without some special status that conferred immunity. Only a tiny fraction of this debt, however, could have been satisfied in such a way; slaves were too plentiful and too cheap.

‡ Equivalent only to several months' wages for a laborer.

he paid what was owed.* ³¹ So his fellow slaves were quite outraged when they saw what had happened, and they went and reported to their master everything that had happened. ³² Then his master called him in and said to him, 'You useless slave! I remitted that whole debt of yours, since you pleaded with me. ³³ Didn't you need to have pity on your fellow slave, the way I pitied you?' ³⁴ And in a fit of rage, the master handed him over to the torturers, until he paid everything that was owed. ³⁵ That's how my father in the skies is going to treat you all, if each of you doesn't pardon his brother, and you need to have your hearts in it."

CHAPTER 19

¹ It happened that when Iēsous had finished saying these things, he left Galilaia and went to the region of Ioudaia that's across the Iordanēs.† ² And large crowds followed him, and he cured them there.

³ Then, approaching him, the Farisaioi tested him by asking whether it was lawful for a man to let his wife go for any cause. ⁴ And he answered by saying, "Haven't you read that the founder of the world from the beginning 'made them male and female,' ⁵ and that he said, 'Because of this, a man is to leave his father and mother and be fused with his wife, and the two will become one body'? ⁶ That means that they won't be two any longer, but *one body*. So what god has yoked together, a human being must not take apart." ⁷ They said to him, "So why did Mōūsēs command a

---

* Slaves had no standing in Roman law, so it would probably have puzzled those living under this law (or a provincial transplant of it) that one "slave" can enforce a debt against another.

† The Transjordan, to the east.

man to provide a written notice of putting her away, and to let [her] go?" ⁸ He said to them, "It was because your hearts were calloused and unfeeling that Mōüsēs allowed you to let your wives go. But from the beginning, it wasn't like that. ⁹ I tell you that whoever lets his wife go, except on grounds that she's whoring, and marries another woman violates marriage."*

¹⁰ [His] students said to him, "If this is the charge that a man has to bring against his wife, then it's no advantage to marry." ¹¹ But he said to them, "Not everyone accepts [this] reasoning, but only those to whom it's been granted. ¹² There are of course eunuchs who were born that way from their mothers' wombs, and there are eunuchs who become eunuchs at human hands,† and there are eunuchs who make themselves eunuchs because of the kingdom of the skies. Whoever can accept it had better accept it."‡

¹³ Then children were brought to him so that he could put his hands on them and pray. Now, the students scolded them. ¹⁴ But Iēsous said, "Leave the children alone, and don't stop them from coming to me, since the kingdom of the skies belongs to people like this."§ ¹⁵ And once he had put his hands on them, he set off from there on a journey.

¹⁶ But look, someone approached him and said, "Teacher, what excellent thing must I do to have life for all time?" ¹⁷ And he said

---

* See the notes on this passage in Mark (10:2–12). Also see "fornication" in the Glossary.

† A practice not only of Near Eastern royal courts: Roman authors report that catamites might be castrated to prolong a prepubescent appearance, and that eunuch slaves might guard wives and courtesans.

‡ Few passages show a wider gap between indigenous Palestinian culture and the ways early Christianity was quickly developing in the Roman Empire at large. There is no sign that marriage was, in any normal circumstances, optional for free Jews in their homeland; a choice to be married would not even have been discussed, only the time and the person to marry. But Christians rapidly made celibacy a cult.

§ See the note at Mark 9:37.

to him, "Why do you ask me about excellence? Only *one* is excellent.* But if you want to enter into life, guard and observe the commands." ¹⁸ He said to him, "Which ones?" And Iēsous told him, " 'You are not to commit murder,' 'You are not to violate marriage,' 'You are not to steal,' 'You are not to give lying testimony,' ¹⁹ 'Honor your father and mother,' and 'You are to love the one next to you the way you love yourself.' "† ²⁰ The young man said to him, "I've observed all of these. What's still missing for me?" ²¹ Iēsous said to him, "If you want to be as you were meant to be, then go and sell everything you have and give the money to the destitute, and you'll have a storehouseful in the skies, and come and follow me." ²² But when he heard this condition, the young man went away, stung, as he possessed a great deal.

²³ Then Iēsous said to his students, "*Amēn* I tell you that a rich man will have a hard time entering the kingdom of the skies. ²⁴ And I tell you again: It's easier for a camel to go through the eye of a needle than for a rich man to enter god's kingdom." ²⁵ But when his students heard, they were quite stunned,‡ and they said, "Then who can be rescued?" ²⁶ Looking intently at them, Iēsous said to them, "With human beings, this is impossible. But everything is possible with god."

²⁷ Then, as a response, Petros said to him, "Look, *we*'ve left behind everything and followed you. What will we have, then?" ²⁸ Iēsous said to them, "*Amēn* I tell you, at the rebirth, when the son of mankind sits on the throne of his glory, all of you as well who have followed me will sit on twelve thrones, judging the twelve tribes of Israēl. ²⁹ And everyone who's left behind houses

---

* There may be a subtle reference to the Shema at Deuteronomy 6:4 ("Hear O Israel, the Lord your God is one God …"), associated with the Ten Commandments, which are about to be cited here. In Verse 16, the man is literally "one" (I translate "someone"), a locution that does occur in the Gospels, but not often.

† See Exodus 20:12–16, Deuteronomy 5:16–20, and Leviticus 19:18.

‡ See the note at Mark 10:24.

or brothers or sisters or a father or a mother or children or fields because of my name will get a hundred times more, and will inherit life for all time.* [30] But many who are first will be last, and the last first."

CHAPTER 20

——

[1] The kingdom of the skies is like the head of a household, who went out right at dawn to hire workers for his vineyard. [2] And he agreed with the workers on a denarius a day[†] and sent them into his vineyard. [3] Then he went out around the third hour[‡] and saw others standing in the marketplace, doing nothing, [4] and he said to them, 'You too, get going to the vineyard, and whatever's right, I'll pay you.' [5] And they went, and he came out again around the sixth and the ninth hour and did the same. [6] And around the eleventh hour, he went out and found others standing around, and he said to them, 'Why have you been standing here doing nothing the whole day?' [7] They told him, 'Because no one hired us.' He told them, "You too, get going to the vineyard.' [8] And when it was evening, the owner of the vineyard said to his steward, 'Call the workers and give them their wages, starting from the last to come and ending with the first.' [9] And when those from the eleventh hour came up, they got a denarius apiece. [10] So when the earliest workers came up, they thought they would get more. But they also got a denarius apiece. [11] And once they got it, they whined to the head of the household, [12] saying, 'These peo-

* The wording is playful, but not so much as in the Mark version (10:30).

† This parable is often cited as revealing what an acceptable wage was for manual labor in first-century Palestine. But there is later evidence about the standards that may have prevailed: rabbinic literature is concerned in detail with just pay and employment conditions.

‡ The hours are measured from dawn, so the times (always approximate) depend on the season.

ple who came last put in just one hour, and now you've put them on an equal footing with us, who shouldered the whole load of the day, including the heat.' ¹³ But he answered by saying to one of them, 'I'm not treating you wrong, pal. Didn't you agree with me on a denarius? ¹⁴ Take what's yours and get out of here. I want to pay this man who's come last the same as I pay you. ¹⁵ [Or] aren't I allowed to do as I like with what belongs to me? Or is your view of me malicious because I'm good?' ¹⁶ In this way, the last will be first, and the first last."*

¹⁷ Then Iēsous, as he was going up to Hierosoluma, took aside the twelve [students] on their own on the road, and said to them, ¹⁸ "Look, we're going up to Hierosoluma, and the son of mankind will be handed over to the high priests and scholars, and they'll condemn him to death. ¹⁹ And they'll hand him over to the other nations to be taunted and flogged and hung on the stakes, but on the third day after this, he'll awaken."†

²⁰ Then the mother of Zebedaios' sons‡ approached him with her sons, and prostrated herself to ask him for something. ²¹ And he said to her, "What do you want?" She told him, "Say that these two sons of mine can sit on your right side and on your side 'with the blessed name' in your kingdom." ²² But in response, Iēsous said, "You two don't know what you're asking for. Can you drink from the drinking cup I'm about to drink from?" They told him, "We can." ²³ He said to them, "You'll drink from my drinking cup, but as for sitting on my right side and on my side 'with the blessed name,' [this] isn't mine to grant: no, those places belong to those for whom they've been prepared by my father."§

---

* Economic and religious perspectives combine here. Resources adequate to support life were literally called "life," and fate at the apocalypse was binary: eternal life or eternal death. The employer's last statement alludes to the "evil eye" of destructive envy.

† By our reckoning, only two nights and one full day.

‡ James and John.

§ See the note at Mark 10:40.

²⁴ When they heard this, the other ten were angry at the two brothers. ²⁵ But Iēsous called them over and said to them: "You know that the leaders of the other nations lord it over them, and that their great men impose top-down authority on them.* ²⁶ But it isn't to be that way among *you*. Instead, whoever among you wants to be great is to be the attendant of the rest of you, ²⁷ and whoever wants to be first among you is to be the slave of the rest of you. ²⁸ In the same way, the son of mankind didn't come to *have* attendants but to *be* an attendant, and to give his life as the price of setting many other people free."†

²⁹ Then as they were making their way out of Ierichō, a large crowd followed them. ³⁰ But look, two blind men were sitting beside the road, and once they heard that Iēsous was passing by, they yelled the words, "Have pity on us, [lord], son of David!" ³¹ The crowd scolded them and warned them to be quiet, but they only yelled the words much louder: "Have pity on us, lord, son of David!" ³² And Iēsous stopped, called them over, and said, "What do you want me to do for you?" ³³ And they said to him, "Lord, we want our eyes opened." ³⁴ And Iēsous was wrenched by pity and touched their eyes, and right away they could see again and followed him.

CHAPTER 21

¹ And when they neared Hierosoluma and came to Bēthfagē‡ at the mountain with the olive trees, then Iēsous sent off two students, ² saying to them, "Make your way to the village ahead of

---

* Two verbs with *kata* ("down") in them emphasize the arrogance of these rulers.

† See the note at Mark 10:45.

‡ A village associated with the modern village al-Eizariya, on the far side of the Mount of Olives from Jerusalem.

you, and right away you'll find a donkey tied up, and a colt with her. Untie them and bring them to me. ³ And if someone says anything to you, say, 'Their master needs them.'* And he will send them right away." ⁴ This was done to fulfill what was stated by the prophet when he said,

> ⁵ *"Tell the daughter Siōn:*
> *'Look, your king is coming to you,*
> *Humble and mounted on a donkey,*
> *And on a colt, the son of a yoked beast.'"*†

⁶ The students went on their way and did as Iēsous ordered them, ⁷ and brought the donkey and the colt and put their cloaks on them, and he mounted on top of the cloaks. ⁸ And a huge crowd spread their own cloaks on the road, while others cut branches from the trees and spread them on the road. ⁹ And the crowds that went ahead of him and behind him were chanting in piercing voices,

> "Hōsanna *for the son of David!*
> *Blessed is the one who comes in the lord's name!*
> Hōsanna, *in the highest places!"*‡

¹⁰ And when he came into Hierosoluma, the whole city was shaken, and said, "Who is this?" ¹¹ But the masses of the peo-

---

* As in Mark and Luke, there is a play on words, as *kurios* means both "master" in a general sense and "owner."

† Mount Zion in Jerusalem, site of a fortress conquered by King David, could stand by metonymy for the whole of Israel, and the "daughter(s) of Zion" (the Greek here does not reflect the "construct chain" by which Hebrew expresses possession) is (and are) repeatedly addressed in the Bible as embodying the fate of the nation. This chant apparently owes phrasing to Zechariah 2:10 and 9:9 and Zephaniah 3:14. A donkey was humbler than a horse, but ordinary people did not ride at all.

‡ See Psalms 118:25–26. *Hōsanna* means "Rescue, please" in Hebrew.

ple said, "This is the prophet Iēsous from Nazareth in Galilaia."*

¹² Then Iēsous entered the temple precinct and proceeded to throw out all the vendors and shoppers who were in the precinct, and he turned over the tables of the money-changers, and the backrest-chairs of those who were selling doves. ¹³ And he said to them, "It's been written,

> "'My house is to be called a house of prayer.'
> But you make it a cave where bandits lurk."†

¹⁴ Then blind and crippled people came to him in the temple precinct, and he cured them. ¹⁵ And when the high priests and the scholars saw the amazing things he did, and the children shouting in the precinct and saying, "*Hōsanna* to the son of David!"‡ they were angry. ¹⁶ And they said to him, "Do you hear what these people are saying?" But Iēsous said to them, "Yes. Did you never read,

> "'Out of the mouths of babies, of nursing infants, you've supplied yourself with praise?'§

¹⁷ Then he left them and went out beyond the city to Bēthania and spent the night there.

¹⁸ Then at dawn, as he was returning to the city, he found he was hungry. ¹⁹ And seeing a single fig tree by the road, he went up to her, but he found nothing on her at all but leaves, and he said

---

* At the time of the Passover pilgrimage festival, Jerusalem (whose permanent establishment is here called "the whole city") is thronged with those the leaders would call "people of the land," rustics from outside the city.

† Compare the version in Mark 11:15–17, and see the note there. The verses quoted are Isaiah 56:7 and Jeremiah 7:11.

‡ See above at Verse 9.

§ Psalms 8:2.

to her, "May there never be fruit from you again for all of time." And right then and there, the fig tree dried up.*

²⁰ And when the students saw, they were amazed, and they said, "How did the fig tree dry up then and there?" ²¹ And Iēsous responded by saying to them: "*Amēn* I tell you, if you have trust and your thinking isn't divided, not only will you do what I've done to the fig tree, but even if you say to this mountain, 'Be lifted up and thrown into the sea,' it will be done. ²² And everything that you ask for in prayer, you'll get if you have trust."

²³ Then when he'd entered the temple precinct and was teaching, the high priests and the elders of the people came to him, saying, "By what authority do you do these things—or who gave you this authority?" ²⁴ But Iēsous said to them in answer, "*I*'m going to question *you* about one matter, and if you reply, then I'll do my part and tell you by what authority I do these things. ²⁵ What was the source of the baptism John carried out? Was it heaven or human beings?" And they tried to work it out among themselves, in these terms: "If we say 'Heaven,' he'll say to us, 'Then why didn't you trust him?' ²⁶ But if we say 'Human beings,' we have the crowd to be afraid of; *they* all in fact regard Iōannēs as a prophet." ²⁷ So the answer they gave Iēsous was "We don't know." He said to them in turn: "*I*'m not telling you either by what authority I do these things.

²⁸ "But what do you think? A man had two children. And he went to the first and said, 'Child, go along today and work in the vineyard.' ²⁹ But he answered by saying, 'I don't want to'; but later he thought better of it and went. ³⁰ Going to the second son, he told him the same; and he answered by saying, '*I*'m going, sir!' But he didn't go. ³¹ Which of those two did what the father wanted?" They said, "The first." Iēsous said to them, "*Amēn* I tell you, the tax-collectors and the whores are ahead of you on the way to god's kingdom. ³² Iōannēs in fact came to you on a path of rectitude, and you didn't trust him, but the tax-collectors and

* See the note at Mark 11:14.

the whores trusted him. But even when you did see, you didn't think better afterward and trust him.

³³ "Listen to another comparative story. A man who was head of a household planted a vineyard, and put a fence around it, and hollowed out a wine press in it,* and built a watchtower, and leased it to farmers and went abroad. ³⁴ When harvest time was near, he dispatched his slaves to the farmers to get his harvest. ³⁵ But the farmers took his slaves, and one they nearly skinned alive, and one they killed, and one they stoned. ³⁶ Trying again, he sent other slaves, more than in the first group, and they treated them the same. ³⁷ But after that he sent them his own son, saying, 'They'll have respect for my son.' ³⁸ But when the farmers saw the son, they said to each other, 'This is the heir. Come on, let's kill him, so that we can have his inheritance.' ³⁹ Then they seized him and threw him out of the vineyard and killed him. ⁴⁰ When the owner of the vineyard comes, what will he do to those farmers?" ⁴¹ They said to him, "He'll put a terrible end to those terrible people, and he'll lease the vineyard out to other farmers, who'll give the harvests they owe, right at the harvest times."†

⁴² Iēsous said to them, "Have you never read this in the writings?

> "'The stone that the builders tested and rejected—
> It turned out to head up the corner:
> ¹¹ The lord made it turn out this way—
> And it's amazing in our eyes.'‡

---

* Archaeologically excavated wine presses have been found hollowed out of solid rock.

† The Jewish inheritance, their covenant, will go to Gentiles at the critical time of the apocalyptic harvest, because the Jews have abused and killed both their prophets and God's own son.

‡ Psalms 118:22–23 has, literally, "for the head of the corner." Again, this is not a coherent architectural image, but the sense is clear: one stone stabilizes a whole building.

⁴³ "For this reason, I tell you that god's kingdom will be taken away from you and given to a nation that produces the harvests of that kingdom. [⁴⁴ And whoever falls on this stone will be shattered. And whoever it falls on will be pulverized.]"

⁴⁵ When the high priests and the Farisaioi heard his stories, they recognized that he was speaking about them. ⁴⁶ And they were looking to seize him, but they were afraid of the crowds, since these considered him a prophet.

CHAPTER 22

¹ Then as a response, Iēsous again spoke in stories for comparison, and he offered them this one. ² "The kingdom of the skies can be compared to a man who was king, and gave a wedding banquet for his son. ³ And he sent his slaves to invite to the wedding those who'd been invited before, but they didn't want to go. ⁴ Again he sent slaves, other ones this time, saying, 'Tell those I've invited, "Look, I've prepared my feast,* my bulls and other animals fattened on grain are sacrificed, and everything is prepared. Come to the wedding!"' ⁵ But they didn't care and went away, one to his own farm, and another to his business. ⁶ The rest of them seized his slaves and abused them outrageously† and killed them. ⁷ Then the king was furious, and he sent his armies, wiped out those murderers, and burned their city. ⁸ Then he said to his slaves, 'Well, the wedding banquet is prepared, but those who were invited didn't deserve it. ⁹ So make your way to the roads that head out of town, and invite to the wedding banquet as many people as you can find.' ¹⁰ And those slaves went out to

---

* The feast (following a public procession), and not any ceremony with vows, was central to an ancient wedding, as the whole community was supposed to witness the union and be assured of the families' standing and means.

† "Committed outrage against them," probably meaning rape.

the roads and rounded up everyone they could find, worthless and fine people alike, and the wedding banquet was full of people reclining at the tables. [11] But when the king came in to view the people reclining at the tables, he saw one man there who wasn't outfitted in a wedding outfit. [12] And he said to him, 'How is it that you came in here without a wedding outfit, pal?' And that muzzled *him*. [13] Then the king said to the servers, 'Tie him up hand and foot and throw him out into the darkness—far out! Where he lands, there's going to be crying and grinding of teeth in pain.' [14] There are a *lot* of invited guests, but *not* a lot of the chosen best."*

[15] Then the Farisaioi went and initiated a plot to ensnare him in an argument. [16] So they sent him their own students, along with Hērōdēs' people,† to say, "Teacher, we know you're truthful, and that on the basis of truth you teach god's path and aren't influenced by anybody, as you don't look to people's outward distinctions. [17] So tell us what you think. Is it permitted to pay the individual tax to Kaisar or not?" [18] Recognizing their malice, Iēsous said: "Why are you testing me, you play-actors? [19] Show me the currency in which the individual tax is paid." And they brought him a denarius. [20] Then he said to them, "Whose image and inscription are these?" [21] They told him, "Kaisar's." Then he said to them, "So pay Kaisar what belongs to Kaisar—give it right back to him—and pay god what belongs to god." [22] And when they heard, they were amazed, and they left him and went away.‡

---

* The traditional English "Many are called, but few are chosen" ignores jingly wordplay. The Jews deliberately skip a wedding banquet—the epitome of enjoyment, here standing for the unending heavenly feast to follow the apocalypse—and insult and infuriate the host, God. The slaves stand for the prophets ignored or martyred throughout Jewish history. One of the substitute (that is, Gentile) guests does not know how to behave either, likely meaning that he offends against Jewish custom and ethics, important to the author of Matthew.

† Courtiers or officials of the Romans' client king.

‡ See the notes on the Mark version at 12:13–17.

²³ On that day Saddoukaioi came to him, people who say that there is no rising of the dead again, and they questioned him, ²⁴ saying, "Teacher, Mōūsēs said that if someone dies without having children, his brother is to marry his wife as the next of kin and raise up seed for his brother. ²⁵ There were seven brothers living among us. And the first one married and died, and since he didn't have seed, he left his wife to his brother. ²⁶ It went the same way for the second brother too, and the third, and eventually all seven. ²⁷ After all of them, the wife died. ²⁸ So when the dead rise, whose wife is she, out of those seven? They in fact all had her." ²⁹ And Iēsous said to them in answer, "You're misled, as you don't know either the writings or the power of god. ³⁰ The fact is that, when rising again, people don't take wives, and they're not given as wives; instead, they're like messengers in the sky. ³¹ As to the dead rising, haven't you read what was spoken to you by god when he said: ³² 'I am the god of Abraam and the god of Isaak and the god of Iakōb'? He's not [the] god of corpses but of living people!" ³³ And when the crowds heard, they were dumbfounded by his teaching.*

³⁴ When the Farisaioi heard that he'd put a muzzle on the Saddoukaioi, they gathered at the same place. ³⁵ And one of them[, an expert in the law,] asked a question, testing him. ³⁶ "Teacher, what is the greatest command in the law?" ³⁷ And he told him: " 'You are to love the lord your god with the whole of your heart and the whole of your life and the whole of your mind.' ³⁸ This is the greatest and the chief command. ³⁹ The next most important is similar to it: 'You are to love the one next to you the way you love yourself.' ⁴⁰ On these two commands hang the whole of the law and the prophets."†

⁴¹ Once the Farisaioi had gathered together, Iēsous questioned them, ⁴² saying, "What do you all think about the anointed one? Whose son is he?" They said to him, "David's." ⁴³ He said to them,

---

* See the notes on the Mark version at 12:18–27.

† See the notes on the earlier version of the passage at Mark 12:28–34.

"Then what does David, inspired by the life-breath, mean by calling him 'lord' when he says,

> ⁴⁴ "'*The lord said to my lord,*
> "*Sit to the right of me*
> *Until I put your enemies*
> *Under your feet*'"?

⁴⁵ "So if David calls him lord, how is he his son?"* ⁴⁶ And no one was able to find any argument with which to answer him; and from that day on, no one even dared to question him any longer.

CHAPTER 23

____

¹ Then Iēsous spoke to the crowds and his students, ² saying, "The scholars and the Farisaioi have taken their seat on Mōüsēs' seat of authority. ³ So everything they tell you, do it and keep watch over it, but don't do according to their behavior, because they say but don't do. ⁴ They tie up heavy [and hard-to-carry] loads and put them on people's shoulders, but they themselves don't want to lift a finger to help move the things.† ⁵ All of their behavior is just a spectacle for people. They actually make their protection-boxes extra wide, and their tassels extra long.‡ ⁶ They love the

---

* This is the opening of Psalm 110: in the original sense, it likely concerns not David and the Messiah, but David and God, as related by a court musician.

† Taxes, pilgrimages, sacrifices, and burdensome purity laws were among the demands made by the Temple hierarchy and its surrogates, most prominently by the learned teachers.

‡ "Protection-boxes" refers to phylacteries, boxes containing important scripture verses, worn on the forehead and arm in obedience to Deuteronomy 6:8 and Exodus 13:9. Tassels must be worn by all Israelite males according to Numbers 15:38.

couch of highest honor at banquets, and the seats of highest honor in the synagogues,* [7] and respectful greetings in the marketplaces, and being called *rabbi* by people.

[8] "But you shouldn't be called *rabbi,* as you have one teacher, and you're all brothers.[†] [9] And don't call anyone on earth your father, because you have only one father, who's in the sky. [10] And you shouldn't be called instructors,[‡] as you have only one instructor, the Anointed One. [11] And the greatest one of you will be the attendant of the rest of you. [12] Whoever raises himself will be lowered, and whoever lowers himself will be raised.

[13] "You have it coming, scholars and Farisaioi, play-actors! You lock up the kingdom of the skies in front of people's faces. You yourselves don't in fact enter, and those who are trying to enter you keep from entering.[§]

[15] "You have it coming, scholars and Farisaioi, play-actors! You cross the sea and the dry land to gain a single convert,[¶] and when you have one, you make him twice as much a son of *ge'enna*** as you are.

[16] "You have it coming, blind guides, who say, 'If someone swears by the temple's inner shrine, it doesn't mean anything; but if someone swears by the gold of the shrine, he's bound by his oath.' [17] You morons and blind men! Which is greater, the

---

* Couch assignment at dinner parties was strictly by social rank.

† See "rabbi" and "teacher" in the Glossary.

‡ This was a word the early Christians used for the initiators of candidates for baptism.

§ Verse 14 has been excised by scholars as spurious; a standard translation is "Woe to you, scribes and Pharisees, you hypocrites! You defraud widows of their houses, and for a show make lengthy prayers. Therefore you will receive greater condemnation."

¶ Full converts to Judaism were few, largely because circumcision—which the Greeks and Romans considered a mutilation—was required, and meals with unconverted friends and relatives would no longer be permitted.

** See "hell" in the Glossary.

gold, or the shrine that makes the gold holy? [18] And you say, 'If someone swears by the altar, it means nothing; but if someone swears by the offering on it, he's bound by the oath.' [19] You blind men! Which is greater, the gift, or the altar that makes the offering holy? [20] So whoever swears by the altar swears by it and by everything on it. [21] Whoever swears by the shrine swears by it and by the one who lives in it. [22] And whoever swears by the sky swears by god's throne and by the one who sits on it.*

[23] "You have it coming, scholars and Farisaioi, play-actors! You pay your ten percent of mint, dill, and cumin,† but you've abandoned the weightier matters of the law: just verdicts, and mercy, and trust. [But] you should have put the latter into practice, without neglecting the former. [24] You blind guides! You strain out a gnat but gulp down a camel.‡

[25] "You have it coming, scholars and Farisaioi, play-actors! You clean the outside of the cup and the plate, but inside they're brimming with greed and self-indulgence. [26] Blind Farisaios! First clean the inside of the cup, so that the outside can become clean too.

[27] "You have it coming, scholars and Farisaioi, play-actors! You're like whitewashed tombs, which on the outside look attractive, but on the inside are brimming with corpses' bones and every kind of filth. [28] In the same way, on the outside you look upright to other people, but on the inside you're full of play-acting and lawlessness.

[29] "You have it coming, scholars and Farisaioi, play-actors! You build tombs for the prophets and decorate the monuments of

---

* See "T/temple" in the Glossary. The great rabbis were in fact deeply concerned about oath taking; on the evidence, Jesus is moving in the direction they and their predecessors moved, toward a more moralistic, less ritually technical and materialistic mindset.

† The tithing requirement was for ten percent of everything.

‡ Neither would be scripturally permitted for Jews to eat (Leviticus 11:4 and 23).

upright people, [30] and you say, 'If we'd lived in the days of our ancestors, we wouldn't have joined them in shedding the prophets' blood.' [31] So you testify against yourselves, admitting you're the descendants of those who murdered the prophets!* [32] So take the container in which your fathers' offenses were measured, and fill it up yourselves. [33] You snakes, viper hatchlings! How can you escape being sentenced to *ge'enna*?

[34] Because of this, look, I keep sending you prophets and men of understanding and scholars. Some of them you'll kill and hang on stakes, and others you'll flog in your synagogues and pursue from town to town[†] [35] So it's coming down on you, all the righteous blood poured out on the earth, from the blood of righteous Abel to the blood of Zacharias son of Barachias, whom you murdered between the shrine and the altar.[‡] [36] *Amēn* I tell you, all these things will come down on this generation.

[37] "Oh, Ierousalēm, Ierousalēm, who kills the prophets and stones those sent to her, how often I've wanted to gather your offspring together, the way a hen gathers her chicks under her wings, but you all didn't want that! [38] Look, your house is left desolate for you. [39] I do in fact tell you that you'll never see me again until you say,

"'Blessed is the one who comes in the name of the lord.'"[§]

---

* The number of prophets actually killed by their own people or their own regimes is very small, at least according to the Hebrew Bible.

† Floggings as a punishment meted out through synagogues are well documented, and anger over religious nonconformity could lead to mob violence, but there is a reason Jesus was sent to the Romans for a hearing and execution: critical law enforcement powers, i.e., capital punishment for public order offenses, belonged to provincial Imperial regimes.

‡ Abel is humankind's first murder victim (Genesis 4:1–16). The other victim named has not been definitely identified, but is a recent victim if length of time is in fact the point.

§ Psalms 118:26.

CHAPTER 24

———

¹ When Jesus had left the temple precinct and was walking away, his students came up to point out the temple's buildings to him. ² He responded by saying to them "Don't you see all these things? *Amēn* I tell you, not a stone will be left on another here: they will all be torn down."*

³ While Iēsous was sitting on the mountain with the olive trees, the students came to him privately, saying "Tell us, when will these things happen, and what will be the sign of your presence to come, and the era come to fruition?"

⁴ Jesus answered by telling them, "See to it that you're not led astray. ⁵ Many people will come in my name, saying, 'I'm the anointed one,' and they'll lead many astray. ⁶ You're going to hear of wars and rumors of wars; see to it that you don't panic. These things do have to happen, but it won't be the end yet. ⁷ One nation will rise up against another, and one kingdom against another. There'll be famines and earthquakes in various places. ⁸ All these things are the beginning of birth pains.

⁹ "At that time they'll hand you over to be ground down and killed, and you'll be hated by all nations because of my name. ¹⁰ And at that time, many people will fall away and hand over and hate each other, ¹¹ and many false prophets will rise up and lead many people astray. ¹² Because lawlessness will be rife, many people's love will grow cold. ¹³ Whoever endures to the end will be rescued. ¹⁴ And this good news of the kingdom will be heralded throughout the world as a testimony to all nations, and then the end will arrive.

¹⁵ "So when you see 'the annihilating abomination,' spoken of by the prophet Daniēl, set up in a holy place (the reader needs to realize what this means),† ¹⁶ then those in Ioudaia had better

---

* The Temple was devastated in 70 C.E.

† Daniel 9:27, 11:31, and 12:11. See the note at Mark 13:14.

run to the hills. ¹⁷ And nobody on a housetop had better come down to get things from his house. ¹⁸ And no one in the field had better come back to get his cloak. ¹⁹ Pity the ones with children in their wombs and the ones nursing in those days.

²⁰ "Pray that you won't have to run for it in the winter or on the *sabbaton*.* ²¹ At that time, you see, there'll be a great shattering, such as there never was from the beginning of the universe until this moment, and never will be again. ²² And if those days weren't cut short, no mortal life would be rescued. But for the sake of the chosen ones, those days will be cut short.

²³ "At that time, if anyone says to you, 'Look, here's the anointed one!' or 'Here he is!' don't believe it. ²⁴ False anointed ones and false prophets will arise and present great 'signs' and 'marvels' that would lead even the chosen ones astray, if that were possible. ²⁵ See, I've told you ahead of time. ²⁶ So if they tell you, 'Look, he's in the wilderness,' don't go out there; or if it's 'Look, he's in the storerooms,' don't believe it.† ²⁷ Just as the lightning comes from the place the sun rises and flashes clear to where it sets, so it's going to be when the son of mankind is with you again. ²⁸ Wherever the carcass is, there the eagles will gather.‡

²⁹ "But right after that shattering in those days,

> "'The sun will be shadowed over,
> And the moon won't give off her luster;
> And the stars will fall from the sky,
> And the powers of the skies will be shaken.'§

* A refugee's exertions would violate the Sabbath restrictions on work, as well as preempt worship.

† Likely sarcastic. Access to any provisions was strictly limited and their storage places (whether public or private) locked up. Connections to corruption or banditry may be suggested.

‡ The equivalent of the English adage "Where there's smoke, there's fire." The signs of the end will be obvious.

§ Isaiah 13:10.

[30] "And then the sign of the human being's son will appear in the sky, and then all the tribes of the earth will beat their breasts, and they'll see* the son of mankind coming on the sky's clouds, with power and great glory. [31] And he'll send out his messengers with a loud trumpet call, and they'll gather his chosen ones from the sources of the four winds, and from one end of the sky to the other.†

[32] "But from the fig tree, learn the analogy: As soon as its branch becomes tender and sprouts leaves, you know that summer is near. [33] It's the same for you too: when you see all these things, you'll know that he's near, right at the gates. [34] *Amēn* I tell you, this generation won't by any means pass away until all these things have happened. [35] The sky and the earth will pass away, but the things I tell you will never pass away.

[36] "About that day and hour no one knows, not even the messengers of the skies, and not the son: no one except the Father, him alone.

[37] As in the days of Nōe, you see, that's what it will be like when the son of mankind is with you again. [38] Just as in [those] days before the flood, you see, people were eating and drinking, marrying and being given in marriage, up to the day Nōe entered the ark, [39] and they didn't know, until the flood came and did away with all of them: that's what it will [also] be like when the son of mankind is with you again. [40] At that time, two men will be in the field: one will be taken along and one left behind. [41] Two women will be grinding at the mill: one will be taken along and one left behind.

[42] "So stay on the alert, because you don't know on what day your master is coming. [43] But this you do need to know: if the

---

* Some of the jingles of the Gospels are simply beyond the bounds of modern taste, as well as beyond the ingenuity in English of this translator. Here "they will beat" and "they will see" are exact rhymes: *kopsontai* and *opsontai*.

† See Daniel 7:13–14.

head of the house had known in which watch* the thief was coming, he would have been on the alert and not have let his house be broken into. ⁴⁴ For this reason, you, too, be ready, because the son of mankind will come at a time you don't expect.†

⁴⁵ "So who's the trusty and shrewd slave, the one the master's put in charge of his household, so that he could give the others their food at the right time? ⁴⁶ That slave's a happy one if his master finds him doing that when he comes back. ⁴⁷ *Amēn* I tell you, he'll put him in charge of all his property. ⁴⁸ But if it's a bad slave, and he says in his heart, 'My master's taking his time,' ⁴⁹ and he starts beating his fellow slaves, and eats and drinks with drunks, ⁵⁰ that slave's master will come on a day he doesn't anticipate and at an hour he doesn't have in mind. ⁵¹ Then he'll cut him practically in two and put him where the play-actors go: there'll be crying and grinding of teeth in pain there."‡

CHAPTER 25

———

¹ "Next, the kingdom of the skies can be compared to ten unmarried girls, who took their lamps and went out to meet a bridegroom. ² Now, five of them were silly, and five were sensible. ³ The silly ones, though they took their lamps, didn't take any olive oil along with them. ⁴ But the sensible ones took olive oil in jars along with their lamps. ⁵ While the bridegroom took his time, they all nodded off and soon were sleeping. ⁶ But in the

---

* The four watches of the night were the ordinary system by which nocturnal time was counted.

† Again, the reappearance of Jesus at the apocalypse was expected in short order, and the indefinite delay required explanation.

‡ "Cutting to pieces" was a Roman term for flogging, and persistently delinquent slaves were sent to special prisons for punishment. See "hypocrite" in the Glossary.

middle of the night, a shout arose: "Look, the bridegroom! Come out to meet [him]!" ⁷ Then all those girls woke up and put their lamps in order. ⁸ But the silly ones said to the sensible ones, 'Give us some of your olive oil, because our lamps are going out.' ⁹ But the sensible ones answered by saying, 'There couldn't possibly be enough for us and you both. Find your way instead to the merchants and buy some for yourselves.' ¹⁰ But while they were going away to buy it, the bridegroom came, and the girls who were ready went in with him to the wedding banquet, and the door was shut. ¹¹ But later the rest of the girls came too, saying, 'Sir, sir, open up for us.' ¹² But he said in answer, '*Amēn* I tell you, I don't know you.'* ¹³ Stay on the alert, then, because you don't know the day or the hour.

¹⁴ "That's just the way it was when a man about to go abroad called his own slaves and handed over to them everything that belonged to him. ¹⁵ And he gave five talents to one,† and two to another, and one to another, each according to his abilities, and went abroad. Right away, ¹⁶ the one who'd gotten the five talents went and put them to work and made a further five talents in profit. ¹⁷ In the same way, the one with two made a profit of a further two. ¹⁸ But the one who'd gotten a single talent went away and dug a hole in the ground and hid his master's silver.

¹⁹ "After a long time, the master of those slaves came back and reckoned up the accounts with them. ²⁰ And the one who'd gotten five talents approached, bringing a further five talents and saying, 'Master, you handed five talents over to me: look, I made a further five talents in profit.' ²¹ His master said to him: 'Well done, you excellent and trustworthy slave! You've been trustworthy in a few things, so I'll put you in charge of many things.

---

* The girls are waiting for the important wedding procession to arrive, but it is unclear why they would wait alone outdoors for so long at night, vulnerable and wasting lamp oil.

† A talent was standard weight of silver or gold, and though the weight might vary according to the locale, the value was at least quite substantial and more commonly enormous.

Enter into the joy of your master.' [22] [But] then the one with two talents approached and said, 'Master, you handed two talents over to me: look, I made a further two talents in profit.' [23] His master said to him: 'Well done, you excellent and trustworthy slave! You've been trustworthy in a few things, so I'll put you in charge of many things. Enter into the joy of your master.' [24] But then the one who'd gotten a single talent approached and said, 'Master, I knew you're a hard man, harvesting where you didn't sow and gathering in where you didn't scatter anything out, [25] so because I was afraid I went and hid your talent in the ground. Look, you've got what's yours.' [26] But his master responded by saying to him, 'You worthless, work-shy slave! You knew that I harvest where I didn't sow, and gather in where I didn't scatter anything out. [27] So you needed to put my silver on the bankers' tables, and when I returned I could have gotten back what's mine along with its "offspring." [28] So you all, take the talent from him and give it to the one has ten talents. [29] To everyone who has something, you see, more will be given, and he'll have more than enough, but if someone doesn't have something, even what he does have will be taken away from him. [30] Now throw out the useless slave into the darkness—far out. In that place there'll be crying and teeth ground in pain.'

[31] "But when the son of mankind comes in his glory, and all the messengers along with him, then he will sit on the throne of his glory. [32] And all the nations will be gathered before him, and he'll separate them from each other the way a shepherd separates the sheep from the goats, [33] and he'll make the sheep stand at his right, and the goats at the side 'with the blessed name.' [34] Then the king will say to those on his right: 'Come, you who are blessed by my father, inherit the kingdom prepared for you since the foundations of the universe were laid. [35] I was starving, you see, and you gave me something to eat, I was parched, and you gave me something to drink, I was a foreigner and you took me in. [36] I was naked and you put clothes on me, ailing and you looked in on me, in prison and you came to me.' [37] Then the upright people

will respond to him by saying, 'Lord, when did we see you starving and fed you, or parched and gave you something to drink? ³⁸ When did we see you, a foreigner, and take you in, or naked and put clothes on you? ³⁹ When did we see you ailing or in prison and came to you?' ⁴⁰ Then in answer the king will say to them, '*Amēn* I tell you, as far as you did it for a single one of my brothers here, who are of no importance at all, you did for to me.' ⁴¹ Then he'll say to those on the side 'with the blessed name,' 'Take the road away from me, you cursed people, into the fire that lasts for all time and has been prepared for the slanderer and his messengers. ⁴² I was starving, you see, but you didn't give me anything to eat, I was parched and you didn't give me anything to drink, ⁴³ I was a foreigner and you didn't take me in, naked and you didn't put clothes on me, ailing and in prison and you didn't look in on me.' ⁴⁴ Then they also will answer by saying, 'Lord, when did we see you starving or parched or a foreigner or naked or ailing or in prison, and didn't attend to you?' ⁴⁵ Then he'll answer them by saying, '*Amēn* I tell you, as far as you didn't do it for a single one of these people here, who are of no importance at all, you didn't do it for me either.' ⁴⁶ And they'll go to punishment for all time, but the upright will go to life for all time."

Chapter 26

——

¹ Then it happened that, when Iēsous had finished saying all these things, he told his students, ² "You know that the *pascha* takes place in two days, and the son of mankind is going to be handed over to be hung on the stakes."

³ Then the high priests and the elders of the people gathered at the court of the chief priest, who was called Kaïafas.* ⁴ And they were plotting together to seize Iēsous by stealth and kill

---

* His tenure during this time is confirmed by the historian Josephus.

him. ⁵ But they said, "Not at the festival, in case there's an uproar among the people."*

⁶ And when Iēsous was in Bēthania at the house of Simōn the leper,† ⁷ a woman approached him with an alabaster jar of extremely costly perfume‡ and poured its contents over his head as he was reclining at the table. ⁸ And when the students saw, they complained, saying, "What was the point of this waste? ⁹ This could have been sold for a lot of money, to give to the destitute." ¹⁰ But Iēsous, aware of their reaction, said, "Why do you make trouble for the woman? The service she's done me is in fact a good one. ¹¹ You'll have the destitute among you forever, but you're *not* going to have me forever. ¹² She actually put this perfume on my body to prepare me for burial. ¹³ *Amen,* I tell you, wherever in the whole world this good news is proclaimed, what she did will be spoken of, so that she'll be remembered."

¹⁴ At this point the one called Ioudas Iskariōtēs, one of the twelve, made his way to the high priests ¹⁵ and said, "What are you willing to pay me, if I hand him over to you myself?" And they counted out thirty silver coins and paid him.§ ¹⁶ And from then on, he sought to hand him over at the right moment.

¹⁷ And on the first day of the festival of bread made without yeast, the students approached Iēsous and said to him, "Where do you want us to prepare for you to eat the *pascha?*" ¹⁸ And he said, "Get moving and go to the city, to such and such a person,¶ and tell him, 'The teacher says, "My time is near; I'm going to observe the *pascha* at your place with my students."'" ¹⁹ And they did as Iēsous directed, then prepared the *pascha.*

---

* Why, then, do the officials not wait until the Passover pilgrims have returned home?

† Probably not leprosy, as the disease rendered a person untouchable.

‡ See the note at Mark 14:9.

§ These are likely "shekels of Tyre," acceptable in the Temple and worth four denarii each, a denarius representing a standard day's wage.

¶ This suggests that the home from which Jesus was arrested was (at least at some point) known but not mentioned, presumably for the sake of discretion.

²⁰ And when it was evening, he reclined at the table with the twelve. ²¹ And while they were eating, he said, "*Amēn* I tell you that one of you will hand me over." ²² Then they grew very distressed, and began saying to him one by one, "It can't be me, can it, master?" ²³ But he answered by saying, "It's the one who, along with me, has dipped his hand into the bowl—he'll hand me over. ²⁴ The son of mankind is going on his way—just as it's written about him. But he has it coming, that specimen of mankind by whom the son of mankind is handed over. It would be better for *that* specimen of mankind if he hadn't been born."* ²⁵ Responding, Ioudas—the one handing him over—said, "It's not me, is it, *rabbí*?" He told him, "You're the one who said it."

²⁶ Then while they were eating, Iēsous took a loaf of bread and blessed it, broke it in pieces, and gave it to his students, saying, "Take it and eat it: this is my body." ²⁷ And taking the cup, he gave thanks for it and gave it to them, saying, "Drink from it, all of you. ²⁸ This is my blood of the dispensation, the blood poured out for the sake of many people for pardon from their offenses. ²⁹ I tell you, from now on I won't ever drink any of this, which the grapevine yields, until the day I drink it new in my father's kingdom with you." ³⁰ Then, once they'd sung a song of praise, they went out onto the mountain with the olive trees.

³¹ And Iēsous said to them, "You'll all fall away tonight because of me, as it's been written,

> "'I'll strike the shepherd down,
> And the sheep of the flock will be scattered in all directions.'†

³² "But after my awakening, I'll go ahead of you into Galilaia."

³³ But Petros responded to him by saying, "Even if all the others fall away because of you, I'll never fall away." ³⁴ Iēsous said to him, "*Amēn* I'm telling you: during this actual night, before the

---

* See the Introduction, pp. xxix–xxxi, concerning "Son of Man."

† Zechariah 13:7.

rooster crows, you'll deny three times that you know me." [35] Petros said to him, "Even if I have to die with you, I absolutely won't deny you." And all the other students said the same.

[36] Then Iēsous came with them to the place called Gethsēmani,* and he said to his students, "Sit here while I go over there and pray." [37] And he took with him Petros and the two sons of Zebedaios,† and pain and anguish began to come over him. [38] Then he said to them, "The life within me is in terrible pain, to the point of death. Stay here and keep awake with me." [39] And going ahead a little, he fell facedown, saying in prayer, "My father, if it's possible, let this cup pass by me—but even so, it has to be what you want, not what I want." [40] Then he came to the students and found them sleeping, and he said to Petros, "What's this? Didn't you have the strength to stay awake with me for a single hour? [41] Stay awake and pray, so that you don't come to be tested. The life-breath is eager, but the mere body is feeble." [42] Then again, a second time, he went away and prayed, saying, "My father, if this can't pass by me unless I drink it, then what you want must happen." [43] Then he came back again and found them sleeping, since their eyes were weighed down. [44] Then he left them again and went away and prayed a third time, saying the same thing once more. [45] Then he came to his students and said to them, "Are you *still* sleeping and taking it easy? Look, the time has come, and the son of mankind is going to be handed over to wrongdoers. [46] Get up, let's go! Look, the one handing me over is almost here."

[47] And while he was still speaking, look, Ioudas came, one of the twelve, and along with him was a large mob, armed with swords and clubs, who were from the high priests and the elders of the people.‡ [48] The man handing him over had told them a signal to act on, saying, "Whoever I kiss, it's him: get hold of

* "The Place of the Olive Press."

† James and John.

‡ See the note at Mark 14:43.

him." ⁴⁹ So right away he approached Iēsous and said, "Joy, *rabbí*!" and gave him a demonstrative kiss. ⁵⁰ But Iēsous said to him, "Do what you came for, pal."* Then they came up to Iēsous, laid hands on him, and took hold of him. ⁵¹ But look, one of the people with Iēsous stretched out his hand and drew his sword, with which he struck the chief priest's slave and took off his ear.† ⁵² Then Iēsous said to him, "Put your sword back where it belongs. All those who take up the sword are destroyed by the sword. ⁵³ Or do you think I can't call on my father to put more than twelve legions of messengers at my disposal right now?‡ ⁵⁴ But if I did that, how would the writings be fulfilled that say it has to happen this way?"§ ⁵⁵ At that time Iēsous said to the mobs, "You've come out to seize me with swords and clubs, as if I were a bandit? Day after day I was sitting in the temple precinct teaching, and you didn't take hold of me. ⁵⁶ All of this has happened so that the prophets' writings could be fulfilled."¶ Then all the students left him and ran off.

⁵⁷ So they took hold of Iēsous and led him away to Kaïafas the chief priest, where the scholars and the elders were gathered.** ⁵⁸ But Petros followed him at a distance up to the chief priest's courtyard and went in and sat down with the retainers to see how it would end.

* The word is not the important term *filos* ("close friend": see "love" in the Glossary), but the ironic and condescending *hetairos* (see Matthew 20:13 and 22:12).

† Compare the (textually vexed) account in Mark 14:47, and see pp. xxv–xxvi of the Introduction. Here, one of Jesus' actual followers—not of course a person permitted to be heavily armed in occupied Judea—draws "his" sword; but the verb I render literally as "stretching out his hand" represents a movement out of the proper sequence. As I try to reconstruct plausible versions of the historical scene, I think it's possible that someone grabbed a soldier's or bodyguard's sword in the fray.

‡ That is, as many as 72,000 troops.

§ Reference(s) uncertain.

¶ It is uncertain what the citation(s) would be.

** The high priest chairs the Sanhedrin, the highest Jewish governing body; but this body is answerable to the Roman occupation.

⁵⁹ Now the high priests and the whole high council were seeking false testimony against Iēsous so that they could put him to death. ⁶⁰ But they couldn't find any, even though a lot of false witnesses came forward. At last, two came forward ⁶¹ and stated, "This man said, 'I have the power to destroy god's shrine and rebuild it in the course of three days.' "* ⁶² Then the chief priest stood up and asked him, "Don't you have any answer to what they accuse you of in their testimony?" ⁶³ But Jesus was silent. Then the chief priest said to him, "I put you under oath to the living god, to make you tell us if you're the anointed one, god's son."† ⁶⁴ Iēsous said to him, "*You* said it. Still, I tell you all: soon you'll see the son of mankind sitting to the right of the power, and coming on the sky's clouds."‡

⁶⁵ Then the chief priest tore his clothes,§ saying, "He's blasphemed. Why do we need any more witnesses? Look, now you've heard the blasphemy. ⁶⁶ What's your decision?" They said in answer, "He's guilty; he deserves death." ⁶⁷ Then they spat in his face and punched him, and others slapped him around, ⁶⁸ saying, "You, anointed one, give us a prophecy: who's the one who hit you?"

⁶⁹ But meanwhile Petros was sitting outside in the courtyard, and a slave girl came up to him and said, "You too, you were with Iēsous the Galilaios." ⁷⁰ But he denied it in front of all of them, saying, "I don't know what you're talking about." ⁷¹ After Petros went out to the gateway, another slave girl saw him and said to the people there, "He was with Iēsous the Nazōraios." ⁷² And once more, he denied it, swearing, "I don't know the guy." ⁷³ After a little while, those standing there came up and said to Petros,

---

* The Temple stands for Jesus' body; the claim *is* made, but only in John 2:19. Again, inclusive reckoning counts all units of time fully, even the unit at the end or beginning of which something takes place.

† See the note at Mark 14:61.

‡ Psalms 110:1 and Daniel 7:13.

§ The tearing of clothes was forbidden to him (Leviticus 10:6 and 21:10).

"It's true, you're one of them too: in fact, your dialect gives you away." [74] At this point he started to curse himself, and to swear,* "I don't know the guy!" And right away, a rooster crowed.

[75] Then Petros remembered what Jesus had told him: "Before the rooster crows, you'll deny three times that you know me." And he went outside and cried bitterly.

CHAPTER 27

[1] When dawn had broken, all the high priests and the elders of the people came up with a plot against Iēsous so that they could kill him, [2] and they tied him up and led him away and turned him over to Pilatos the governor.[†]

[3] Then Ioudas, the one who turned him over, saw that he was condemned, and was full of remorse. He returned the thirty silver coins to the high priests and the elders, [4] saying, "I did wrong, handing someone over for his innocent blood to be shed." But they said, "What's that to us? It's going to be your lookout." [5] Then he threw the silver coins down in the shrine and withdrew, and he went and hanged himself. [6] Then the high priests took the silver coins and said: "It isn't lawful to put these in the treasury, since they're the price of blood." [7] So they came up with a plan and spent the coins on a potter's field, to be used for burying foreigners.[‡] [8] Hence that field is called "the field of blood" up to this day. [9] Then what was stated by Ieremias the prophet was fulfilled: he said: "And they took the thirty silver coins, that

---

* See "swear" and "curse" in the Glossary.

† As confirmed by a contemporary inscription, this was the Roman governor at the time.

‡ This field is associated with a place called Akeldama in Jerusalem. Where fertile land was at a premium, a plot with pitted, clayey soil was an ideal one for cheap burials. Here is the first firmly identified "potter's field."

princely price that the sons of Israēl placed on me, ¹⁰ and they used them to pay for the potter's field, as the lord commanded me."*

¹¹ Now Iēsous stood in front of the governor. And the governor questioned him, saying, "Are you the king of the Ioudaioi?" And Iēsous said, "*You* say so."† ¹² But when he was accused by the high priests and the elders, he gave no answer. ¹³ Then Pilatos said to him, "Don't you hear all their testimony against you?" ¹⁴ But Iēsous gave him no answer, not even to a single charge, and this disturbed the governor deeply.

¹⁵ At every festival, the governor had made a habit of releasing to the crowd the one prisoner they wanted. ¹⁶ At that time, they were holding a notorious prisoner called [Iēsous] Barabbas.‡ ¹⁷ So when they were assembled, Pilatos said to them, "Who do you want me to release to you, [Iēsous] Barabbas or Iēsous who's called the anointed one?" ¹⁸ He knew, you see, that they'd turned him over out of jealousy.

¹⁹ As he was sitting on the platform, his wife sent a message to him, saying, "You have no business with that upright man; today, in a dream, I suffer terribly because of him."

²⁰ But the high priests and the elders persuaded the crowds to ask for Barabbas, and to destroy Iēsous. ²¹ But the governor responded by saying to them, "Which of the two do you want me to release to you?" and they said, "Barabbas!" ²² Pilatos said to them, "So what should I do with Iēsous, who's called the anointed one?" They all said, "He's got to be hung on the stakes!"§ ²³ But he said, "What has he actually done wrong?" But they just screamed even louder, saying, "He's got to be hung on the stakes!"

²⁴ Seeing that it was no use, but that, on the contrary, the situation was turning into a riot, Pilatos took water and washed his

---

* Zechariah 11:13. The context is an insulting underpayment for work.

† See the note at Mark 15:2.

‡ See the note at Mark 15:6.

§ See the note at Mark 15:13.

hands in front of the crowd, saying, "I don't bear any responsibility for this man's blood. It'll be *your* lookout."* ²⁵ Then the whole of the people answered him by saying, "His blood can be on us, and on our children." ²⁶ Then he released Barabbas to them, had Iēsous flogged† and turned him over to be hung on the stakes.

²⁷ Then the governor's soldiers took Iēsous with them to the governor's headquarters and brought down on him their whole division. ²⁸ They stripped him and draped him in a scarlet military cloak. ²⁹ And they wove a garland from thorny branches and put it on his head, and they put a reed in his right hand,‡ and fell on their knees in front of him, taunting him by saying, "Joy to you, king of the Ioudaioi!" ³⁰ And they spat on him, and took the reed and beat his head with it. ³¹ Then, when they'd finished taunting him, they took the cloak off him and put his own clothes back on him, and led him away to be hung on the stakes.

³² When they came out, they found a man, a Kurēnaios by the name of Simōn, and they commandeered him to carry Iēsous' stake.§

³³ And they came to the place called Golgotha, which means the Place of the Skull.¶ ³⁴ They gave him wine mixed with gall to drink; but when he tasted it, he refused to drink.** ³⁵ And once

---

* See Deuteronomy 21:1–9 for the ritual involving handwashing, performed by Jewish officials when a murderer is unknown. It is not likely that Pilate would even have known about the ritual, or would have wished to renounce responsibility publicly.

† That is, with a whip studded with small sharp objects for cutting flesh.

‡ Scarlet came from an expensive dye. This is a high military officer's cloak, such as the emperor himself could wear in his capacity as commander in chief, or merely in propaganda images. But the scepter is a Near Eastern symbol of royalty.

§ Acquiring temporary porters by force was a right of Roman soldiers. The horizontal crosspiece alone could be deemed an adequate load.

¶ By tradition, the site of the Church of the Holy Sepulcher. Even in antiquity, a thoroughfare passed by it.

** Probably an extension of the mocking torments; the gall (sometimes used on nipples to wean babies) would make the wine undrinkable.

they had hung him on the stakes, they shared out his clothes, throwing lots for the pieces. [36] Then, sitting down there, they kept watch over him. [37] And they put above his head a sign that had the charge against him written on it:*

"This is Iēsous, the king of the Ioudaioi."

[38] At that time, two bandits† were hanging on stakes along with him, one on the right, and one on the side "with the blessed name." [39] And those who passed by on the road insulted him, shaking their heads [40] and saying, "You, destroying the shrine and building it again in three days!‡ Save yourself [and] climb down from that cross, if you're god's son!" [41] Similarly the high priests too, along with the scholars and the elders, ridiculed him, saying, [42] "He saved other people, but he can't save himself. He's the king of Israēl—he needs to climb down from that stake now, and then we'll believe in him. [43] He trusted in god—let god come to his rescue now, if he wants him." He had said, in fact, "I am god's son."§ [44] And the bandits hanging on the other stakes beside him jeered at him in the same way.

[45] But from the sixth hour after dawn until the ninth, darkness came over the whole earth, [46] and around the ninth hour, Iēsous shouted in a loud voice the words

"Eli eli, lema sabachthani?"

This means, "My god, my god, why have you abandoned me?"¶ [47] Some of those standing there, when they heard this, said,

---

* The *titulus,* a regular element of crucifixions.

† See "thief" in the Glossary.

‡ Again, the literal "three days" represent two by inclusive reckoning.

§ The onlookers' insult contains wording about rescue familiar from the Psalms but may also hint at the exposure of unwanted infants in Greco-Roman culture, a compelling cause for which decision (which, within a family, belonged to the husband alone) was the belief that the child had been fathered by someone else.

¶ From Psalms 22:1, but this is an Aramaic version.

"He's calling out to Ēlias!" ⁴⁸ Then right away, one of them ran and got a sponge, filled it with vinegar, stuck it on a reed, and offered it to him to drink from.* ⁴⁹ But the others said, "Let it be—we should see whether Ēlias comes to save him."† ⁵⁰ But once again Iēsous cried out with a loud voice and gave up his life-breath.

⁵¹ And look, the curtain of the inner shrine split in two from top to bottom.‡ And the earth shook, and rocks split. ⁵² And tombs opened, and many bodies of holy ones who had gone to sleep awakened. ⁵³ They came out of the tombs after his awakening, and came into the holy city and appeared to many people.

⁵⁴ And the centurion and those with him who were keeping watch over Iēsous saw the earthquake and everything else that happened, and they were terrified, saying, "Truly, this was god's son."§

⁵⁵ Now many women were there, watching from far off, who had followed Iēsous from Galilaia to wait on him.¶ ⁵⁶ Among them were Maria the Magdalēnē, Maria the mother of Iakōbos and Iōsēf, and the mother of Zebedaios' sons.**

⁵⁷ When evening fell, a wealthy man came from Arimathaia,†† and his name was Iōsēf; he himself had been a student of Iēsous. ⁵⁸ He approached Pilatos and asked for Iēsous' body. Then Pilatos ordered it to be given to him. ⁵⁹ And Iōsēf took the body,

---

* The vinegar or sour wine is probably part of the soldiers' rations.

† The persecuted Elijah, with his visible journey into heaven (2 Kings 2), seems a natural rescuer at this moment; he has already been associated with Jesus repeatedly.

‡ The Holy of Holies in the Temple, the space considered to contain God's actual power and presence, was kept separated, untouched, and covered.

§ The centurion, a division commander, is probably in charge of the proceedings.

¶ Probably women of independent means, as indicated in Luke 8:1–3.

** John and the other James.

†† A home of uncertain location.

wrapped it [in] clean linen, [60] and placed it in his own new tomb, which he had hewn out of solid rock, and he rolled a stone against the door of the tomb and went away.* [61] But Mariam the Magdalēnē was there, and the other Maria: they were sitting across from the burial site.

[62] On the next day, which is after the day of preparation,† the high priests and the Farisaioi gathered before Pilatos, [63] saying, "Sir, we remember now what that hustler claimed when he was still alive: 'After three days, I will wake up.' [64] So order the burial site to be secured until the third day,‡ so that his students don't have the chance to come and steal him and tell the people, 'He's woken up from among the dead.' In that case, the last hustle would be worse than the first." [65] Pilatos said to them, "Take a detachment of guards. Get going and secure the place as you see fit." [66] And they went on their way and secured the burial site, sealing the stone in place with the help of the guards.

CHAPTER 28

[1] After the *sabbata,* when the first day of the *sabbata* week had dawned, Mariam the Magdalēnē and the other Maria went to see the burial site. [2] And look, there was a great earthquake. And

---

* He may act as a mediator between the Jewish hierarchy and the Roman governor concerning the tricky matter of burial on the eve of the Sabbath: the necessary work may not take place after sundown. Deuteronomy 21:22–23 forbids corpses of the executed ever to be hung on display overnight. Perhaps these are the reasons he prepares the corpse himself, even though this is conventionally a women's task. He is, in any event, a wealthy man, with a prestigious new tomb at his disposal.

† The officials appear to be conducting this dishonest business with a foreigner on the Sabbath, a triple outrage against Jewish law and ethics.

‡ In modern terms, from Friday through Sunday.

a messenger of the lord, coming down from the sky and approaching, rolled away the stone and sat on top of it. ³ And his appearance was like lightning, and his clothing white as snow. ⁴ And those who were keeping guard shook with fear of him, and they became like corpses. ⁵ But in response, the messenger said to the women, "*You* must not be afraid, because I know that you're looking for Iēsous, who was hung on the stakes. ⁶ He isn't here: in fact, he's awakened, just as he said. Come look at the place where he was lying. ⁷ Now be on your way quickly and tell his students that he's risen from among the dead, and look, he's going ahead of you into Galilaia—there you'll see him. Look, I've told you."

⁸ And quickly leaving the tomb with fear and great joy, they ran to bring the news to his students. ⁹ But look, Iēsous met them, saying, "Joy to you!" They approached him and seized his feet and prostrated themselves before him. ¹⁰ Then Iēsous said to them, "Don't be afraid. Get moving, take word to my brothers that they should leave for Galilaia, and there they'll see me."

¹¹ But while they were on their way, look, some of the guards went into the city and reported to the high priests everything that had happened. ¹² And after the high priests had gotten together with the elders and come up with a scheme, they gave the soldiers a substantial sum in silver, ¹³ telling them, "Say, 'His students came during the night and stole him away while we were sleeping.' ¹⁴ And if the governor comes to hear of this, we'll talk [him] around and make sure you don't have to worry about it."* ¹⁵ Then the soldiers took the silver coins and did as they were instructed. And this story has been spread by the Ioudaioi up to this [very] day.

¹⁶ Then the eleven students made a journey to Galilaia, to the mountain where Iēsous had directed them. ¹⁷ And when they saw him they prostrated themselves, but some wavered. ¹⁸ Then Iēsous came near and spoke to them, saying, "All the authority in the sky and on [the] earth has been given to me. ¹⁹ So set off on

---

* Dereliction of guard duty carried the death penalty.

your journeys and make all nations students, baptizing the people in the name of the father and the son and the holy life-breath, [20] and teaching them to observe everything I have commanded you;* and look, I myself am with you through all the days until the era comes to fruition."

---

* The most famous version of the Great Commission.

THE GOOD NEWS
ACCORDING TO LOUKAS

CHAPTER 1

¹ Inasmuch as many have put their hand to the task of drawing up a narrative of the things brought to fulfillment among us, ² according to the way those who were the original eye-witnesses and servants of the story have passed it on to us; ³ I also have deemed it right that, precisely following everything from the onset, I write it down in the proper order for you, Theofilos, your excellency, ⁴ so that you can ascertain, in this reliable form, the stories in which you have been instructed.*

⁵ In the days of Hērōdēs king of Ioudaia, there happened to be a priest by the name of Zacharias, in the Abia division of daily duties, and his wife was one of the descendants of Aarōn, and her name was Elisabet.† ⁶ They were both lawful before god's eyes,

---

* This introduction is stylistically very different from the three other Gospels, and substantially different from the rest of this one. Here are judiciously angled compound words and harmonious pleonasms. It is all a single elaborate opening sentence, four verses long. The matter as well as the manner is different. Like a Classical author, Luke—probably an associate of Paul of Tarsus—has a patron to attend to before anything else. This passage resembles, besides a conventional dedication, the opening of a forensic speech. Theophilos is presumably a convert under instruction, but he is also rhetorically characterized as a judge or a jury member being presented with a story that must be logical and convincing in detail.

† The mention of Herod the Great (73–4 B.C.E.), who though Jewish was of Idumean and Nabatean stock, and a client ruler for the Romans, contrasts sharply

making their way blamelessly in the commands and the other lawful requirements of the lord. [7] But they had no child, because Elisabet was unable to bear any, and both of them were far along in their days.

[8] But it happened that, while he was serving before god as a priest in the successive order of his division, [9] he was chosen by lot, according to the custom of the priesthood, to go into the lord's shrine and offer incense.* [10] And the whole of the people prayed outside during the hour of the incense offering. [11] Then there appeared to him a messenger of the lord, standing to the right of the altar for incense. [12] And Zacharias was thunderstruck when he saw this, and fear overcame him. [13] But the messenger said to him,

> *"Don't be afraid, Zacharias,*
> *Because your entreaty has been heard,*
> *And your wife Elisabet will give birth to a son for you,*
> *And you will call his name Iōannēs.*
> [14] *And you will have joy and delight.*
> *And many will find joy in his birth,*
> [15] *Since he will be great in the eyes of [the] lord—*
> *And wine and liquor he must never drink—*
> *And he will be filled with the holy life-breath*
> *When he is still in his mother's womb,*
> [16] *And he will turn many of the sons of Israēl*
> *To the lord their god;*
> [17] *And he will go ahead, before him,*
> *With the life-breath and power of Ēlias,*

---

with this couple of ancient and distinguished Jewish lineage. The priests held hereditary office traced back to the time of Moses, and their organization in divisions to carry out the daily sacrifices and blessings dated back to the reign of David. Elizabeth herself is descended from Moses' high priest Aaron.

* There were twenty-four divisions of the Jewish priesthood, and each division would minister at the Temple for a week at a time. Drawing or casting lots was a widespread practice in the ancient world for discerning the divine will.

To turn the hearts of fathers to their children,
And the disobedient to the insight of the lawful,
To make ready for the lord a people prepared."*

¹⁸ But Zacharias said to the messenger: "On what evidence can I be sure of this? I'm an old man, you see, and my wife is far along in her days." ¹⁹ And the messenger answered by saying to him, "I am Gabriēl, and I stand in god's presence, before his face,† and I have been sent here to speak to you and to give you this good news. ²⁰ But look: you will be silent and unable to speak until the day these things happen: this is the price of not believing the things I've told you, which will be fulfilled in their proper time."

²¹ But the people were waiting for Zacharias, and they were surprised that he was staying such a long time in the shrine. ²² And when he came out, he wasn't able to speak to them, and they recognized that he had seen a vision in the shrine; and he kept making signs to them, but he remained mute. ²³ Then it came about that the days of his service were completed, and he went away to his home.

²⁴ After these days, his wife Elisabet conceived and kept herself in seclusion for five months, saying, ²⁵ "This is what the lord has done for me in the days when he looked on me, to take away my shame among humankind."‡ ²⁶ But in the sixth month, the

---

* The prophecy has many elements in common with praise and prophetic songs in the Hebrew Bible. Like Isaac (Genesis 18:1–15, 21:1–7), John will assure the future of his people by his miraculous birth to a previously barren woman. Like Samson (Judges 13:5) and Samuel (1 Samuel 1:11), he will be a Nazarite, with ascetic abstentions attached to him. Like a number of the prophets, he will restore the covenant by bringing the wayward people back to God and the nation's laws. Elijah, the prophet taken up into the sky at the end of his earthly life (2 Kings 2:3–12), was of particular interest around the time of Jesus' life, a time of apocalyptic expectation and dispute over the existence and nature of the afterlife.

† See Daniel 8:15–26, 9:21–27.

‡ When marriage was nearly universal among free people, and when children were considered essential, infertility was a great humiliation. The verb "look on" in Greek is a narrow rendering of *pagad* in Hebrew, which means something more

messenger Gabriēl was sent by god to the town of Galilaia with the name Nazareth,* ²⁷ to a young girl who was betrothed to a man with the name Iōsēf, from the house of David,† and the name of the young girl was Mariam.‡ ²⁸ And entering her home and approaching her, Gabriēl said, "Joy to you, who are given such a joyful favor!§ The lord is with you." ²⁹ Now, she was thoroughly confused at the speech, and was trying to work out what this greeting could mean. ³⁰ But the messenger said to her:

> *"Don't be afraid, Mariam: you've found favor with god.*
> ³¹ *And look, you'll conceive in your womb and give birth to a*
> *son,*
> *And you are to call him by the name Iēsous.*¶
> ³² *He will be great and will be called the son of the highest one.*
> *And the lord god will give him the throne of David his ances-*
> *tor.*
> ³³ *And he will be king over the house of Iakōb for endless ages,*
> *And for his kingdom there will be no end."*

---

like "treat with special favor"—God's characteristic treatment of deserving infertile women.

* Matthew 2:23 records the prophecy "He will be called a Nazarene," but there is no such statement in the Hebrew Bible. See the note there, and also Verse 15 above, concerning the possible confusion between the word for Nazarene (indicating geographical origin) and the word for Nazarite (a religious designation).

† Matthew 1:1–17 and Luke 3:23–38 both trace Jesus' genealogy through the male line back to King David, as a qualification for the status of Messiah, or God's anointed ruler. The connection in Matthew and Luke depends (despite the lack of a blood tie) on Joseph's origin in Bethlehem, David's native town, which according to Micah 5:2 will be the origin of another great ruler.

‡ Virginity was assumed in unmarried girls. Technically, the Greek word *parthenos* does not refer to lack of sexual experience, but merely to the unmarried state. Luke does not allude to any legal or social consequences of an extramarital pregnancy, as Matthew does in 1:18–25; see the note at Verse 19.

§ The greeting plays on the similarity of the verbs *chairō* and *charitoō.*

¶ Greek for Yeshua (our "Joshua"), who led the Hebrew conquest of Canaan. The root is the verb for "save." It was a common name at this place and time.

[34] But Mariam said to the messenger, "How will this happen, since I'm not familiar with a man?"* [35] Then the messenger said to her:

> "The holy life-breath will come over you,
> And the power of the highest one will send a shadow over you:†
> Therefore, also, the holy one who is born will be called the son
>   of god.

[36] "And look, Elisabet your relative has conceived a son herself in her old age, and now this is the sixth month for the woman they said could not bear children: [37] because nothing god decrees will prove impossible." [38] And Mariam said, "Look, the lord's slave! Let it be as you've decreed." And the messenger went away from her.

[39] Then, during the following days, Mariam set off and traveled with eager haste to the hill country, to a town of Iouda.‡ [40] And she came into Zacharias' house and greeted Elisabet. [41] And it happened that when Elisabet heard Mariam's greeting, the baby capered in her womb, and Elisabet was filled with the holy life-breath, [42] and she raised her voice and said with a loud cry,

> "You, among all women, are blessed,
> And the harvest of your womb is blessed.

[43] "But why is it that my lord's mother comes to me? [44] Look, as soon as your call of greeting came and entered my ears, the baby

---

* The same euphemism, usually translated as "to know," is used in the Hebrew Bible.

† A shadow or shade is a Hebrew Bible image of protection.

‡ The town of Mary's destination in the Jewish heartland is not identified, but her journey could be well over a hundred miles. The custom of married women's visits to each other is witnessed even in the very restricted context of Classical Athens, but I'm unaware that young unmarried women anywhere enjoyed any such privilege.

in my womb capered with delight. ⁴⁵ Happy, then, is the one who trusted in the fulfillment of the things spoken to her by the lord."

⁴⁶ And Mariam said:

> *"All my being exalts the lord,*
> ⁴⁷ *And my life-breath has delighted in god my rescuer,*
> ⁴⁸ *For he's looked on his slave's lowliness.*
> *So look, from now on, all generations will call me happy,*
> ⁴⁹ *Because the one with power has done great things for me;*
> *And his name is holy;*
> ⁵⁰ *And his mercy lasts from generation to generation*
> *Of those who hold him in awe.*
> ⁵¹ *He's shown strength with his arm.*
> *He's scattered those with an arrogant spirit in their hearts.*
> ⁵² *He's taken the rulers down from their thrones,*
> *And lifted up the lowly.*
> ⁵³ *He's filled the hungry with good things*
> *And sent the rich away empty.*
> ⁵⁴ *He's come to the aid of Israël his servant,*
> *Keeping mercy in his mind,*
> ⁵⁵ *Just as he promised to our fathers,*
> *To Abraam and his seed for an endless age."* *

⁵⁶ And Mariam stayed with her about three months, then returned to her own home.

⁵⁷ But for Elisabet the time was ripe for her to have her child, and she gave birth to a son. ⁵⁸ And those who lived around her and her relatives heard that for her the lord had exalted his mercy, and they shared her joy. ⁵⁹ And it came about that on the

---

* This passage, known by the Latin translation of its first word as the Magnificat ("Exalts"/"Glorifies"/"Enlarges"), follows fairly closely the thanksgiving of Hannah, the mother of Samuel, for her pregnancy in 1 Samuel 2:1–10 and shows the same extraordinary reach, linking one woman's fertility to God's comprehensive and eternal protection of his chosen people, especially the distressed and humble among them. The song also has language in common with the "Messianic Apocalypse" among the Dead Sea Scrolls.

eighth day they came to circumcise the child, and they were going to call him by his father's name Zacharias.* ⁶⁰ But the child's mother answered back, saying, "No, certainly not: he will be called Iōannēs."† ⁶¹ And they said to her, "But there's no one in your family who's called by that name." ⁶² And they kept signaling to the child's father to let them know what he wanted the child called. ⁶³ And he had them give him a tablet, and he wrote these words: "Iōannēs is his name." And they were all amazed. ⁶⁴ And his mouth was opened then and there and his tongue freed, and he spoke, blessing god. ⁶⁵ And awe came over all of those who lived around them, and in the whole of the hill country of Ioudaia talk of all of these things spread around. ⁶⁶ And everyone who heard stored it in their hearts, saying, "So what will this child turn out to be? Certainly the hand of the lord was with him."

⁶⁷ And Zacharias his father was filled with the holy life-breath and prophesied, saying,

> ⁶⁸ *"Blessed is the lord the god of Israēl,*
> *Because he looked on his people and made good their ransom,‡*
> ⁶⁹ *And he has tossed up his horn that is our rescue§*
> *In the house of his servant David,*
> ⁷⁰ *As he spoke to us through the mouths of his holy prophets in*
>   *ages past*

---

* Circumcision of male infants (Genesis 17:9–14)—decreed in preparation for the birth of Isaac, the first child given in fulfillment of God's covenant with Abraham—is essential to Jewish identity.

† The Hebrew means "God is gracious." Special circumstances could justify a name with no precedent in the family.

‡ Wholesale "freeing" normally takes place only immediately after wars, when the captured, threatened with permanent enslavement, can be ransomed back if their families or states make it worth the captors' while. It was a common metaphor for the Jews to use of their whole nation, which was comparatively poor and perpetually defeated.

§ The image is of a strong young bull tossing his horns in preparation for combat.

> [71] *About rescue from our enemies and from the hands of all who*
> *hate us,*
> [72] *To show mercy to our fathers*
> *And to be mindful of his holy dispensation,*
> [73] *The oath he swore to Abraam our father,**
> *To let us,* [74] *once we were rescued from the hands of our ene-*
> *mies,*
> *Serve him without fear,* [75] *in piety and lawfulness*
> *Before his eyes throughout our days.*
> [76] *But you, child, will be called the prophet of the highest one;*
> *Since you will go ahead of the lord, to prepare his pathways,*
> [77] *To give knowledge of rescue to his people*
> *By pardon from their offenses*
> [78] *Through mercy from god's inmost self,*
> *Causing dawn to look on us from the heights,*
> [79] *To shine on those sitting in darkness and the shadow of*
> *death,*
> *And to guide our feet the right way, on the path of peace."†*

[80] And the child grew and gained strength in the life-breath, and was in the wilderness until the day of his presentation to Israēl.‡

---

* These promises, repeated from Genesis 12 onward, mainly concern land and descendants.

† Zacharias' outpouring contains phrasing found in Genesis, Psalms, Isaiah, and other scriptural books. The meanings are clear enough in their essentials, but the presentation here is unusually difficult, with trailing clauses and concatenations of verbs, some of these in the infinitive form, which makes their functions rather vague: Greek grammar and syntax differ widely from those of Hebrew, and the Septuagint was plainly not a sophisticated model for translation. As often in the Gospels, the most important imagery is that of Isaiah.

‡ Jews at this period had no coming-of-age ceremony, and the Greek word *anadexis* is normally used for royal or official investiture or the display of a god's image.

CHAPTER 2

¹ It happened in those days that a decree came out from Kaisar Augoustos* that the entire inhabited world must be registered. ² This registration first happened when Kurēnios was governor of Suria.† ³ And everyone traveled to be registered, each one to his own town. ⁴ And Iōsēf too went up from Galilaia, from the town of Nazareth, to Ioudaia and the town of David that is called Bēthle'em—because he was from the house and lineage of David—⁵ to be registered, along with Mariam, who was betrothed to him, and who was pregnant.‡ ⁶ And it happened that while they were there, the days reached their full sum for her to give birth, ⁷ and she gave birth to a son, her firstborn, and she wrapped him in bands of cloth and laid him down in a feeding trough, because there was no other place for them where they were staying.§

* Augustus Caesar, the first Roman emperor, was the adoptive son and heir of the civil warrior and dictator Julius Caesar.

† In the manner of a Classical historiographer, Luke indicates the year by naming the head of government. The Latin name of this Roman governor was Publius Sulpicius Quirinius, and according to the historian Josephus he was not in office before 6 C.E., when Roman rule by occupation began. Herod the Great, however, who appears later in this story, died in 4 B.C.E.

‡ No worldwide or Roman Empire–wide registration is reported elsewhere, though particular regions (Syria and Judea had joint administration of the census) had their inhabitants counted for assessment of a "head tax" of individuals. But the requirement for heads of households to report to ancestral homes sounds needless and disruptive and is not attested elsewhere. If the decree did obtain, hardly "everyone" would have had to travel: most clans were geographically deeply rooted. Luke tells of the journey to show that Jesus, though known as a Nazarene, was actually the great ruler from Bethlehem who fulfilled the prophecy in Micah 5:2.

§ *Kataluma* is not the usual word for a commercial inn, but rather simply for a place to stay. It is probably an ordinary Judean house, which means that animals slept indoors on the ground floor at night and were removed at daybreak; humans slept in a loft with limited space and privacy. The empty feeding trough along one wall (I avoid "manger," which suggests the magazine-stand-like object in a

⁸ And there were shepherds in that district, camping out in the field, on guard to safeguard their flock throughout the night. ⁹ Now a messenger from the lord stood before them, and the lord's glory shone all around them, and they were fearful on a fearsome scale.* ¹⁰ And the messenger said to them, "Don't be afraid, since, look, I'm bringing you good news, of a great joy that will be shared with the whole people: ¹¹ today a rescuer has been born for you in the town of David, and he is the lord, the anointed one. ¹² And here is the sign for you to recognize him: you'll find the infant wrapped in cloth bands and lying in a feeding trough." ¹³ And instantly there appeared, together with the messenger, a massive assembly of the sky's army,† praising god and speaking these words:

> ¹⁴ *"Glory is god's in the highest places,*
> *and on earth, among human beings,*
> *peace is for those who have found favor with him."*

¹⁵ And it happened that, when the messengers had gone away from them into the sky, the shepherds said to each other, "We *have* to go across to Bēthle'em and see this thing that's happened, which the lord has revealed to us." ¹⁶ And they went in a hurry and searched, and found Mariam and Iōsēf, and the infant lying in the feeding trough. ¹⁷ And once they'd seen, they revealed what had been said to them about this child. ¹⁸ And everyone who heard was amazed at the things the shepherds told them. ¹⁹ And

---

Christmas crèche) could have provided a satisfactory bed for a baby. Swaddling or tight wrapping was traditional baby care.

* These men are probably staying with the flock all night to look after ewes and their offspring during lambing season. But mock-military language, including pleonastic flourishes parallel to the Hebrew infinitive absolute, is applied to them: literally, they "guarded guard-duties" and "feared a great fear."

† The "heavenly host" is the army, numerous as the stars, that the Hebrew Bible's God is pictured leading across the sky.

Mariam kept all these things safe in her memory, considering in her heart what they might mean. ²⁰ And the shepherds returned, glorifying and praising god for all they had heard and seen, in just the way it had been told to them.

²¹ And when the eight days before his circumcision were completed, he was called by the name Iēsous, as he was called by the messenger before he was conceived in the womb.

²² And when the days were completed before their purification according to the law of Mōüsēs, they took him up to Hierosoluma to dedicate him to the lord, ²³ as it has been written in the lord's law: "Every male offspring that opens the womb of its mother for the first time will be designated as set aside for the lord"; ²⁴ and a sacrifice must be offered, as it's stated in the lord's law: "a pair of turtledoves or two pigeon chicks."*

²⁵ And look, there was a man in Ierousalēm by the name of Sumeōn, and he was a lawful and reverent man, awaiting the consolation of Israēl, and the holy life-breath was with him. ²⁶ And it had been revealed to him by the holy life-breath that he would not see death before he saw the lord's anointed one. ²⁷ And under the guidance of the life-breath he came into the temple precinct. When the parents brought the child in to carry out for it what was customary according to the law, ²⁸ Sumeōn took the child in his arms and blessed god and said,

²⁹ *"Now, master, you're letting your slave go*
In peace, according to your promise,

---

* See the note at Verse 1:59 concerning circumcision. Leviticus 12 decrees that a woman (but not her husband or baby) be purified after childbirth through isolation and animal sacrifice, in parallel to her purification after menstruation. Exodus 13:1–16 (Verse 2 is quoted here) has as a context the Hebrews' liberation from Egypt: all firstborn creatures are to be "set aside" (see the Glossary for "holy") and sacrificed, but animal sacrifices "buy back" or redeem firstborn human male offspring, given that Hebrew children were spared from the tenth plague, the death of the firstborn.

³⁰ *Since my eyes have seen the rescue you bring,*
³¹ *Which you have prepared before the eyes of all peoples,*
³² *As a light for revelation to other nations,*
And glory for your people Israēl."*

³³ And there were the child's mother and father, astonished over the things said about the child. ³⁴ And Sumeōn blessed them, and he said to Mariam the child's mother, "Look, he is destined for the falling and the rising again of many in Israēl, and for a sign that will be contradicted— ³⁵ [but] a sword will pierce your own life, too—so that the motives in many hearts will be unveiled."†

³⁶ And there was Anna, a prophetess, a daughter of Fanouēl, from the tribe of Asēr. She was advanced in age, with many days behind her; she had lived with her husband for seven years after being a young, unmarried girl, ³⁷ and then as a widow to the age of eighty-four. She never left the temple precinct but served there with fasts and entreaties all night and all day.‡ ³⁸ And at this moment she came near and gave thanks to god and spoke about the child to everyone awaiting the ransoming of Ierousalēm.

---

* This resembles the other thankful poetic and prophetic outpourings so far in Luke, and has similar quasi-Hebraic syntax.

† Simeon turns now to the oracular mode, with its familiar riddling manner. The "falling" may allude (but probably not exclusively) to the military disasters to come for Judea. "Rising again" is the term for resurrection of the dead. Jesus' mission or fate is a "sign" fraught in many ways; just two are the long-prevailing secrecy about his identity, and the contrast between the shameful death and the glorious return to life. The mother's grief is foretold, perhaps even with an allusion to a scene at the cross: in John 19:34, Jesus' side is pierced by a spear. The end of the speech points to apocalyptic ideas: "unveiling" is literally what the Greek for "apocalypse" means. (My translation in Verse 32 above is "revelation.")

‡ It may not have been an unusual fate to be widowed so young and never to remarry. Girls normally married around the time of menarche, and mature women were far less eligible as spouses than older and previously married men were. And across the ancient world, it was considered virtuous for a widow not to remarry. Prophecy was not a calling restricted to men: Miriam, Deborah, Huldah, and Noadiah were women prophets of the Hebrew Bible.

³⁹ Then when they had completed everything according to the lord's law, they returned to Galilaia and their own town, Nazareth. ⁴⁰ And the child grew and became strong; he was full of understanding, and the favor of god was on him.

⁴¹ And every year his parents traveled to Ierousalēm for the festival of the *pascha.* ⁴² And when he was twelve years old, they went up as usual for the festival. ⁴³ When the days of the festival were over, they turned back toward home, but the boy Iēsous stayed back in Ierousalēm, and his parents didn't know. ⁴⁴ Assuming he was in the group of travelers, they traveled for a day and then proceeded to search for him among their relatives and other people they knew.* ⁴⁵ And when they didn't find him, they turned back to Ierousalēm to search for him. ⁴⁶ And it transpired that after three days they found him in the temple precinct, sitting among the teachers and listening to them and asking them questions. ⁴⁷ Everyone who listened was transported by his understanding and his responses. ⁴⁸ But when his parents saw him, they were shattered. And his mother said to him, "Child, why have you treated us this way? Look, your father and I were searching for you frantically all this time." ⁴⁹ But he said to them, "Why were you searching for me? Didn't you know that I had to be busy with my father's concerns?"† ⁵⁰ But they didn't understand what he said to them. ⁵¹ And he came down with them and went to Nazareth and minded them, but his mother kept all these things safe in her heart. ⁵² And Iēsous advanced [in] understanding as he advanced [in] age, and [in] the favor he found in the eyes of god and humankind.

* The heedlessness of the parents about their only son may seem strange, but the normal assumption in a clan or tribe is that a child is never alone and will not go far.

† The noncanonical Infancy Gospel of Thomas goes far in this direction, with adults (in their ignorance of Jesus' identity and power) horrified at the boy's behavior.

CHAPTER 3

———

¹ And in the fifteenth year of the reign of Tiberias Kaisar, when Pontios Pilatos was governor of Ioudaia, and Hērōdēs was the client king of Galilaia, and Filippos his brother was client king of the region of Itouraia and Trachōnitis, and Lusanias was client king of Abilēnē, ² and when Annas and Kaïafas were chief priests,* a call of the lord came to Iōannēs the son of Zacharias in the wasteland. ³ And he went through [the] whole region around the Iordanēs, proclaiming baptism for a new purpose and pardon from offenses,† ⁴ as it's been written in the book of Ēsaïas the prophet's sayings:

> *"The voice of someone shouting in the wasteland:*
> *'Prepare the lord's road,*
> *Make his beaten paths straight.*
> ⁵ *Every ravine will be filled,*
> *And every mountain and hillock will be lowered,*
> *And crooked things will be made straight,*
> *And the rough roads made into smooth ones,*
> ⁶ *And all mortal beings will see the rescue god brings.'"‡*

⁷ So he said to the crowds who traveled out to be baptized by him, "You viper hatchlings! Who warned you to run from the anger that's coming? ⁸ So produce harvests that are fit for people who've changed their purpose, and don't start to say to your-

---

* Again, such scene-setting is in the tradition of Roman historiography, with the year identified by officeholders. Tiberius is Augustus' successor as Roman emperor. These client kings are Herod the Great's sons. Annas and Caiphas do not actually seem to have held the Jewish high priesthood at the same time, but rather the former was deposed by the Romans in favor of the latter, his son-in-law.

† See the note at Mark 1:4 concerning baptism.

‡ Isaiah 40:3–5. See the note at Mark 1:3.

selves, 'We have Abraam as our father.' I tell you in fact that god can raise offspring for Abraam from these stones. ⁹ Already the ax is poised at the roots of the trees. So every tree that doesn't produce a good harvest is going to be cut down and thrown into the fire."

¹⁰ Then the crowds questioned him, saying, "So what should we do?" ¹¹ And he answered by telling them, "Whoever has two tunics* needs to share with someone who doesn't have any, and whoever has food should do the same." ¹² Even tax-collectors came to be baptized, and they said to him, "Teacher, what should we do?" ¹³ And he said to them, "Don't collect more than you were assigned to."† ¹⁴ And those on military service asked him, "And us—what should we do?" And he told them, "Don't shake down anyone, or blackmail anyone with a threat of false charges, and be content with your pay."‡

¹⁵ The people were looking toward the future, and they were all trying to work it out in their hearts about Iōannēs, as to whether he might possibly be the anointed one, ¹⁶ but Iōannēs responded to them all by saying, "I baptize you with water, but someone more powerful than me is coming; I'm not fit to untie a thong on his sandals.§ He'll baptize you with the holy life-breath, and with fire. ¹⁷ His winnowing fork is in his hand to clean his threshing floor out thoroughly and gather the grain into his barn, and he'll burn the chaff with a fire that can't be put out."

---

* Such a person would be moderately well off, since the production, processing, and weaving of wool were labor-intensive enough to make even basic clothing scarce.

† The Roman Imperial regime outsourced tax collection to private contractors and did not normally concern itself with the extortion by which the collectors' profits could be increased.

‡ Imperial soldiers were in practice as free to commit abuses as Imperial tax collectors were. Jews were formally exempt from service in the Roman army, but some enlisted anyway.

§ Care of feet was among the dirtiest and smelliest of slaves' and servants' regular tasks.

¹⁸ So then he was proclaiming the good news to the people, urging many other things besides these. ¹⁹ But Hērōdēs the client king, who was condemned by him because of Hērōdias his brother's wife, and because of all the other crimes Hērōdēs had committed, ²⁰ added this on top of everything: he locked Iōannēs away in prison.*

²¹ But first it happened that when all the people had been baptized, and when Iēsous had been baptized and was praying, the sky opened, ²² and the holy life-breath came down to alight on him in a form with a body, appearing as a dove,† and a voice came from the sky: "You are my beloved son; I've taken delight in you."‡

²³ And for him, Iēsous was about thirty years old when he started, and he was the son, it was supposed, of Iōsēf, the son of Ēli, ²⁴ the son of Maththat, the son of Leui, the son of Melchi, the son of Iannai, the son of Iōsēf, ²⁵ the son of Mattathias, the son of Amōs, the son of Naoum, the son of Esli, the son of Naggai, ²⁶ the son of Maath, the son of Mattathias, the son of Semeïn, the son of Iōsēch, the son of Iōda, ²⁷ the son of Iōanan, the son of Rēsa, the son of Zorobabel, the son of Salathiēl, the son of Nēri, ²⁸ the son of Melchi, the son of Addi, the son of Kōsam, the son of El-madam, the son of Ēr, ²⁹ the son of Iēsous, the son of Eliezer, the son of Iōrim, the son of Maththat, the son of Leui, ³⁰ the son of Sumeōn, the son of Ioudas, the son of Iōsēf, the son of Iōnam, the son of Eliakim, ³¹ the son of Melea, the son of Menna, the son of Mattatha, the son of Natham, the son of David, ³² the son of Iessai, the son of Iōbēd, the son of Bo'os, the son of Sala, the son of Naassōn, ³³ the son of Aminadab, the son of Admin, the son of Arni, the son of Hesrōm, the son of Fares, the son of Ioudas, ³⁴ the son of Iakōb, the son of Isaak, the son of Abraam, the son of

---

* See Mark 6:14–29.

† See "S/spirit" in the Glossary.

‡ Similar language is used by God to Abraham concerning his son Isaac, in the command to sacrifice the boy (Genesis 22:2).

Thara, the son of Nachōr, [35] the son of Serouch, the son of Ragau, the son of Falek, the son of Eber, the son of Sala, [36] the son of Kaïnam, the son of Arfaxad, the son of Sēm, the son of Nōe, the son of Lamech, [37] the son of Mathousala, the son of Enōch, the son of Iaret, the son of Maleleēl, the son of Kaïnam, [38] the son of Enōs, the son of Sēth, the son of Adam, the son of god.*

CHAPTER 4

———

[1] Then Iēsous, full of the holy life-breath, returned from the Iordanēs and was led by the life-breath to the wasteland, [2] and for forty days he was tested by the slanderer,† and he ate nothing at all during those days, and when they came to an end, he was starving. [3] Then the slanderer said to him, "If you're god's son, tell this stone to become a loaf of bread." [4] But Iēsous gave him this answer: "It has been written: 'A human being is not to live through bread alone.'"‡ [5] Then he took him to a high place and showed him all the kingdoms of the world in an instant of time, [6] and the slanderer said to him, "I'll give you all this power and their glory, because it's been handed over to me, and I can give it to whoever I want. [7] So if you prostrate yourself in front of me, it will all be yours." [8] But Iēsous answered by saying to him, "It's been written: 'You are to prostrate yourself to worship the lord your god and serve him alone in his rites.'"§ [9] Then he took him

---

* Contrast this list with that of Matthew 1:1–17. Some differences will leap to the eye: this list runs from Jesus back to creation; Matthew's runs in the other direction, and only from Abraham down to Jesus. The names, the style, and even the number of generations in the overlapping period vary markedly.

† See "devil" in the Glossary.

‡ Deuteronomy 8:3. During the forty years the Israelites wandered in the wilderness after the escape from slavery in Egypt, they ate not bread but the mysterious and miraculous manna.

§ Deuteronomy 6:13 and 10:20.

into Ierousalēm and stood him on the pinnacle of the temple and said to him, "If you're god's son, throw yourself down from here. ¹⁰ It's been written, you know, that

> "'He'll assign your care to his messengers,
> And they'll guard you carefully,'

¹¹ "And that

> "'In their arms they'll lift you,
> So that you don't slam your foot against a stone.'"

¹² But Iēsous told him in response, "It's been said: 'You are not to test the lord your god.'"* ¹³ Then the slanderer, having done all he could with every test, left him until the right moment.

¹⁴ Then, in the power of the life-breath, Iēsous returned to Galilaia, and word of him went out to the whole surrounding region. ¹⁵ And he taught in their synagogues and was praised by everybody.

¹⁶ Then he came to Nazara, where he had been brought up, and he went into the synagogue on the day of the *sabbata*, as he was used to doing, and he stood up to read out loud. ¹⁷ And he was given the scroll of the prophet Ēsaïas, and when he unrolled the scroll, he found the passage where it's been written:

> ¹⁸ "*The life-breath of the lord is on me,*
> *Because he anointed me*
> *To bring good news to the destitute;*
> *He has sent me*
> *To announce to captives their freedom*
> *And to the blind the return of their sight,*

---

* The devil quotes from Psalms 91:11–12, Jesus from Deuteronomy 6:16 and perhaps Isaiah 7:12. One version of the death of James the Just, the leader of the early Jesus movement in Jerusalem, has him being thrown from this same pinnacle.

To send the oppressed off in freedom,
¹⁹ *To proclaim a welcome year of the lord.*"*

²⁰ Then he rolled up the scroll, handed it off to the attendant, and sat down; and all the people in the synagogue had their eyes fixed on him. ²¹ And he spoke up to tell them, "Today this writing has been fulfilled in your hearing."

²² And they all spoke approvingly of him, and they were greatly impressed by the words of goodwill that came out of his mouth, but they said, "Isn't this Iōséf's son?" ²³ But he said to them, "By all means, you're going to quote me that saying: 'Doctor, heal yourself! All the things we've heard were done in Kafarnaoum—do them here in your hometown too!'" ²⁴ But he added, "*Amēn* I tell you that no prophet is welcome in his hometown. ²⁵ In truth I tell you, there were plenty of widows in Israēl in the days of Ēlias, when the sky was locked up for three years and six months and there was a terrible famine in the whole land, ²⁶ but Ēlias wasn't sent to a single one of them, only to a widow woman at Sarepta in Sidōnia.† ²⁷ And there were plenty of lepers in Israēl at the time of Elisaios the prophet, but no one was cleansed of the disease but Naiman the Suros."‡ ²⁸ But having heard that, everyone in the synagogue was filled with rage, ²⁹ and they got to their feet and threw him out of the town, and took him to the brow of the hill on which their town was built, to try to hurl him off a cliff. ³⁰ But he went right through the middle of the crowd and continued on his way.

³¹ Then he went down to the town of Kafarnaoum in Galilaia,§

---

* Isaiah 61:1 and 58:6. According to the Hebrew Bible, every fiftieth year was to be a "Jubilee," requiring remission of debts and freeing of slaves.

† 1 Kings 17.

‡ 2 Kings 5.

§ Here the "going down" seems merely physical, as Capernaum is on the coast of the Sea of Galilee, whereas Nazareth is in the uplands.

and he was teaching them on the *sabbata*. ³² And they were amazed at his teaching, because what he said was full of authority.

³³ And in the synagogue was a man who had the spirit of an unclean demon in him, and he screamed in a very loud voice, ³⁴ "No! What's your business with us, Iēsous the Nazarēnos! Have you come to destroy us? I know who you are: god's holy one." ³⁵ And Iēsous took him to task, saying, "Put a muzzle on it and come out of him!" And the demon threw him down among them and came out of him without hurting him at all. ³⁶ And they were all overcome with awe, and were talking with each other and saying, "What kind of speech is this? With authority and power he commands the unclean spirits, and they come out!" ³⁷ And news of him went out to every locale in the surrounding region.

³⁸ Then he got up and left the synagogue and entered the house of Simōn. But Simōn's mother-in-law was suffering from a high fever, and they asked him about her. ³⁹ And standing over her, he took the fever to task, and it left her. And then and there she stood up and started waiting on them.

⁴⁰ When the sun was setting, everyone who had people who were debilitated by all kinds of diseases brought them to him, and he placed his hands on each one of them and healed them. ⁴¹ Demons came out of many of them, screaming and saying, "You're god's son!" But he berated them and wouldn't let them speak, because they knew he was the anointed one.

⁴² When day came, he left and traveled to a deserted place. But the crowds were looking for him, and they caught up with him and tried to stop him from traveling away from them. ⁴³ But he said to them, "I need to bring the good news of god's kingdom to other towns too, because this is the purpose for which I was sent." ⁴⁴ And he kept on announcing the news in the synagogues of Ioudaia.

CHAPTER 5

———

¹ Now it happened that, with the crowd shoving up against him and listening to god's words while he was standing by the lake Gennēsaret,* ² he saw two boats standing by the lake; the fishermen had climbed out of them and were washing the nets. ³ He boarded one of the boats, which belonged to Simōn, and he asked him to put out a little way from the shore. Then he sat and taught the crowds from the boat.

⁴ And when he'd finished speaking, he said to Simōn, "Put out to the deep water, and let down your nets for a catch." ⁵ But Simōn answered by saying, "Boss, we worked hard the entire night but took in nothing. But I'll take your word for it and let down the nets." ⁶ And once they did this, they closed them around a huge mass of fish, and their nets were starting to rip. ⁷ So they gestured to their companions in the other boat to come help them; and they came, and they filled both boats until they began to sink. ⁸ And when he saw this, Simōn Petros fell down at Iēsous' knees, saying, "Get away from me, because I'm a wrongdoer, master!" ⁹ He and all the others with him were naturally overcome with awe because of the fish they'd caught and taken in, ¹⁰ and so were Iakōbos and Iōannēs, the sons of Zebedaios, who were partners with Simōn. Then Iēsous said to Simōn, "Don't be afraid! From now on, you'll be capturing human beings—so that they *don't* die!"† ¹¹ And they brought the boats ashore, left everything behind, and followed him.

¹² And it happened that he was in one of the towns, and look, there was a man covered with leprosy, and once he saw Iēsous, he fell facedown and begged him, saying, "Master, if you want

———

* The region of Gennesaret was the populous coastal plain between Magdala and Capernaum, and the Sea of Galilee was sometimes called after it.

† The joke is based on the verb for capturing animals alive.

to, you can cleanse me!" [13] And he stretched out his hand and touched him, saying, "I do want to. Be cleansed!" and right away the leprosy left him. [14] And he ordered him to tell nobody, but to "go and show yourself to the priest and make the offering for your cleansing that Mōüsēs set out in the law, as proof for them."* [15] But now the news about him was spreading even farther, and large crowds were gathering to listen to him and to be cured of their infirmities. [16] But he kept withdrawing into the wasteland and praying.

[17] And it happened on one of these days that he was teaching, and sitting there were Farisaioi and teachers of the law, who had come out of every village of Galilaia and Ioudaia, and out of Ierousalēm; and the power of the lord was with him to heal. [18] And look, men were carrying on a stretcher a man who was paralyzed, and they were trying to bring him indoors and put [him] down in front of him. [19] But they couldn't find a way to bring him in, because of the crowd, so they climbed up onto the roof and lowered him down through the tiles, little stretcher and all, right into the middle of the crowd and in front of Iēsous. [20] And when he saw the trust they had, he said, "You there! You're pardoned from your offenses." [21] And the scholars and the Farisaioi started to work through it, saying, "Who is this who's uttering blasphemies? Who can pardon people from their offenses, unless it's god alone?" [22] But Iēsous, perceiving that they were working through it, responded by saying to them, "Why are you working through this in your hearts? [23] What's easier, to say, 'You're pardoned from your offenses,' or to say, 'Get up and walk'?† [24] But so that you know that the son of mankind has the authority on earth to pardon people from their offenses"—he

---

* See Leviticus 13–14.

† The specific joke about the relative length of the expressions that may be operative in Mark (see the note at 2:9 there) would not be operative here, because the statement of forgiveness is longer.

said to the paralyzed man, "I tell you, get up, pick up that little stretcher of yours, and make your way home." [25] And then and there, in front of them, he picked up the thing he'd been lying on and went home, glorifying god. [26] And they were all beside themselves, and they glorified god, and they were filled with reverent fear and said, "Today we've seen what we never expected to."

[27] And after these things he went out and observed a tax-collector by the name of Leui, sitting at the tax booth, and he said to him, "Follow me." [28] And he got up, left everything, and followed him. [29] Then Leui prepared a great banquet for him in his house, and there was a large crowd of tax-collectors and others who were reclining at the table with them. [30] And the Farisaioi and the scholars attached to them were griping to his disciples, saying, "What's the reason you're all eating and drinking with tax-collectors and other wrongdoers?"* [31] And Iēsous answered by telling them, "Healthy people have no need of a doctor, but those who are unwell do! [32] I haven't come to call on upright people to change their purpose, but rather on wrongdoers."

[33] But they said to him, "The students of Iōannēs often fast and offer prayers to god for what they need, and so do the students of the Farisaioi, but yours just eat and drink." [34] And Iēsous said to them, "You can't make the sons of the bridal hall fast while the bridegroom is with them, can you? [35] But the days will come when the bridegroom is taken away from them, and then, in those days, they'll fast."

[36] Then he told them, by way of analogy, "No one rips a patch from a new cloak and patches an old cloak. Otherwise, he'll rip the new one, and the patch from the new one will clash with the old one. [37] And no one puts young wine into old wineskins. Otherwise, the young wine will break the skins, and it will run out,

---

* Tax collection did function like a legal mafia, so the objections here are understandable.

and the skins will be ruined. [38] Instead, young wine is for putting into new wineskins. [39] [But] no one who's drinking the old wants the young; of course he says, "The old kind is good."*

CHAPTER 6

———

[1] And it happened that on the *sabbaton* he was making his way through fields of grain, and his students were plucking off the heads of grain and eating them, rubbing away the husks with their hands. [2] Then some of the Farisaioi said, "Why are you all doing what's not allowed on the *sabbata*?" [3] And Iēsous answered them, saying "Haven't you even read what David did when he was starving, and those [who were] with him were too? [4] [How] he entered the house of god, and took the loaves of presentation and ate them, and gave some to those with him, even though no one but the priests is allowed to eat them?" [5] And he said to them, "The ruler of the *sabbaton* is the son of mankind."

[6] And it happened that on another *sabbaton* he had entered a synagogue and was teaching, and a man was there whose right hand was withered. [7] And the scholars and the Farisaioi were watching him closely to see whether he would heal people on the *sabbaton*, so that they could come up with a charge to lay against him. [8] But he knew how they were calculating, and he said to the man with the withered hand: "Get up and stand in the center." And he stood up and stood there. [9] And Iēsous said to them, "I'm asking you if it's permitted to do good on the *sabbaton* or to do evil, to save a life or destroy it?"† [10] And he looked around at all of them and said to the man, "Stretch out your hand." And

---

* This verse is likely a later interpolation, influenced by Greek or Roman culture. The Romans in particular had connoisseur tastes in wines.

† The unanimous principle in the rabbinic writings is that saving a human life takes priority.

he did, and his hand was cured. ¹¹ And they were filled with fury and discussed with each other what they could do to Iēsous.

¹² It happened that during those days he went out onto a mountain to pray, and he stayed up all night as he prayed to god. ¹³ And when it was day, he called his students to him, and he chose twelve from among them, whom he named "envoys." ¹⁴ There was Simōn, whom he named Petros,* and Andreas his brother, and Iakōbos and Iōannēs and Filippos and Bartholomaios, ¹⁵ and Maththaios and Thōmas and Iakōbos the son of Alfaios, and Simōn who was called "zealot" ¹⁶ and Ioudas the son of Iakōbos, and Ioudas Iskariōth, who turned out to be a traitor.†

¹⁷ And he climbed down with them and stood on a level spot, and a large crowd of his students was there too, as well as a great mass of people from the whole of Ioudaia and Ierousalēm and the coast of Turos and Sidōn,‡ ¹⁸ who had come to hear him and be cured of their illnesses. And those who were troubled by crowds of unclean spirits were cured, ¹⁹ and the whole crowd§ was trying to touch him, because power went out of him and healed everybody.

²⁰ Then he raised his eyes to his students and said,

> *"Happy are you, the destitute,*
> *Because god's kingdom is yours.*
> ²¹ *Happy are you who are starving now,*
> *Because you'll have as much as you can eat.*

* See the second note at Mark 3:16.

† Compare the other lists in the Gospels, and see the note at Mark 3:19. Perhaps the most interesting development here is that someone "called a zealot" is listed among Jesus' followers. *Kananaios* (see Mark 3:18 and Matthew 10:4) does also mean a Zealot, but that word would have been easy to confuse with an adjective meaning "from Cana."

‡ I.e., both the Jewish heartland and the Phoenician coast.

§ See "crowd" in the Glossary. Across the two verses the author uses wordplay to compare the eager mass of people to the riotous mobs of demons within some of them.

> *Happy are you who are crying now,*
> *Because you'll laugh.*

[22] "Happy are you when people hate you, and when they shut you out, and revile and reject your name as evil because of the son of mankind. [23] Be joyful on that day, and dance with glee, because, look, your wages in the sky will be generous, because their ancestors treated the prophets the same way.

> [24] *"But you have it coming, you rich people,*
> *Because you've had all the comfort you're going to get.*
> [25] *You have it coming, all you who couldn't eat more now,*
> *Because you're going to starve.*
> *You have it coming, all you who are laughing now,*
> *Because you'll mourn and cry.*

[26] "You have it coming when everyone speaks well of you, because their ancestors treated the false prophets the same way.

[27] "On the contrary, I tell all those who are listening: love your enemies, treat well those who hate you, [28] bless those who curse you, [28] pray for those who mistreat you. [29] If someone hits you on the cheek, offer him the other one, and if someone takes away your cloak, don't keep back your tunic. [30] If anybody asks for something, give it to him, and if someone takes from you what's yours, don't ask for it back."*

[31] "And however you want people to treat you, treat them the same way. [32] If you love only those who love you, what credit is that to you?† Even criminals love those who love them! [33] If you [in fact] treat well only those who treat you well, what credit is that to you? Even criminals do the same. [34] And if you lend only to those from whom you hope to get the loan back, what kind of

---

* Compare Matthew 5:38–42. This version has the more specific—and more wittily presented—Jewish context stripped out.

† See "grace" in the Glossary.

credit [is] it to you? Even criminals lend to other criminals, meaning to get back an equal amount.* ³⁵ No, love your enemies and be helpful and lend without the hope of getting anything back. Then your payment will be generous, and you'll be sons of the highest one, because he's gracious to the ungrateful and to those full of mischief.

³⁶ "Be compassionate, as your father is compassionate [as well]. ³⁷ And don't give verdicts, and you'll never have verdicts given on you; and don't give guilty verdicts, and guilty verdicts will never be given on you. Pardon, and you'll be pardoned. ³⁸ Give, and things will be given to you. They'll measure out a good amount, pressed down, shaken together, and overflowing, and put it into the front of your tunic for you to take away. Your own means of measurement will in fact be used to measure for you in turn."†

³⁹ Then he gave them an analogy as well: "Is there any way a blind man can guide another blind man? Won't both of them fall into a pit? ⁴⁰ A student isn't above the teacher. But when fully prepared, every one will be like his teacher.

⁴¹ "Why are you looking at a speck of straw in your brother's eye, but not noticing a log in your own eye? ⁴² How can you say to your brother, 'Brother, just let me take out that speck that's in your eye,' when you yourself don't see the log in your own eye? You play-actor, first take the log out of your own eye, and then you'll be able to see clearly enough to take out the speck that's in your brother's eye.

⁴³ "There's no such thing as a good tree that produces low-quality fruit; neither, on the other hand, is there a low-quality tree that produces good fruit. ⁴⁴ Each tree is of course known by

---

* This does not acknowledge interest, which was part of the Jewish financial system too in this era.

† The good-natured and canny merchant crams as much as possible into the standard measuring container. A fold of the clothing at the chest was used to carry items of moderate size such as daily groceries. The repetitious wording at the end of the verse suggests witty commercial patter.

its own fruit. People don't gather figs from acanthus plants, or pick grapes from thornbushes. ⁴⁵ An excellent person brings out what's excellent from the excellent storehouse of his heart, but a useless person brings out from his useless one what's useless. His mouth speaks what overflows from his heart.

⁴⁶ "Why do you call me 'master' time after time, but don't do what I say? ⁴⁷ Everyone who comes to me and hears what I'm saying and acts accordingly—I'll show you what he's like. ⁴⁸ He's like a man building a house, who dug down and hollowed out and put the foundation on solid rock. And there was a flood, and the river crashed against that house but didn't have the power to shake it, because it had been built so well. ⁴⁹ But whoever hears me but doesn't act accordingly is like a man who built his house straight on the ground, without a foundation; and the river crashed against it, and right away it fell to pieces, and the crash of that house was a massive one."

CHAPTER 7

¹ Once he had finished saying these things for the people to hear, he went to Kafarnaoum.

² A certain centurion's slave, greatly valued by him, was unwell and about to die. ³ Having heard about Iēsous, the centurion sent elders of the Ioudaioi to him, asking him to come and bring his slave safely through the illness. ⁴ When they reached Iēsous, they urged him earnestly, saying, "He deserves this favor from you. ⁵ He loves our nation, in fact, and he personally built a synagogue for us." ⁶ And Iēsous made the journey back with them. When he was not far from the house, the centurion sent friends to say to him, "Sir, don't take the trouble: I'm really not a fit person to have you come under my roof. ⁷ That's why I didn't consider myself worthy to come to you either. But just say the word, and let my boy be healed. ⁸ I understand, because I myself, in

fact, am a person deployed under other people's authority, and I have soldiers under me, and I say to this one, 'Get on the road,' and he gets on the road, and to another one, 'Come here,' and he comes, and to my slave, 'Do this,' and he does it." ⁹ When he heard these things, Iēsous was amazed at him, and turned to the crowd following him and said, "I tell you, even in Israēl, I haven't found so much trust." ¹⁰ And when those who had been sent returned to the house, they found the slave healthy.*

¹¹ And it happened soon afterward that he was traveling to a town called Naïn,† and his students were traveling with him, along with a large crowd. ¹² And when they came near the town gates, look, a dead man was being carried out for burial—his mother's only son, and she was a widow, and a sizable crowd from the city was with her. ¹³ And seeing her, the master was wrenched with pity for her,‡ and he said to her, "Don't cry," ¹⁴ and he went up and touched the bier, while those who were carrying it stood still, and he said, "Young man, I tell you, rise!" ¹⁵ And the body sat up and began to speak, and Iēsous presented him to his mother. ¹⁶ But everyone there was overcome by reverent fear, and glorified god, saying, "A great prophet has risen among us," and "God has looked with favor on his people." ¹⁷ And this story about him went out to the whole of Ioudaia and to all the surrounding region.§

¹⁸ Then the students of Iōannēs reported to him about all

---

* The centurion, in charge of a hundred soldiers, was the essential officer of the Roman army. This one appears to be a "God-fearer" or "God-worshipper," a pagan with a friendly interest in Judaism. There is inscriptional evidence that a pagan patron could in fact donate a synagogue building.

† Probably the modern Nein, in Galilee.

‡ For a widow to lose her grown-up only son meant not just emotional trauma. She now has no one to support her and is likely past the age of bearing further children. (See Ruth 1:11–13.) Surviving personal correspondence reveals how thoroughly a widow could be cheated.

§ Even if "Judea" in this instance is only the Jewish heartland, the verse suggests that word spread into some areas where Jews were minorities.

these things, and Iōannēs called a certain pair of his students in
¹⁹ and sent them to the master with instructions to say, "Are you
the one who is coming, or should we wait for someone else?"
²⁰ When the two men reached him, they said, "Iōannēs the baptizer sent us to you to say: Are you the one who is coming, or
should we wait for someone else?" ²¹ On that occasion, Iēsous had
cured many people of diseases and other scourges and freed
them from troublesome spirits, and had given sight to many
blind people. ²² So in answer, he said to them, "Be on your way,
and report back to Iōannēs what you've seen and heard:

> "*The blind see again, the crippled walk,*
> *Lepers are cleansed and the deaf hear,*
> *The dead awaken, the destitute get good news.*'*

²³ "And it's a happy person who isn't tripped up by me."

²⁴ Once the messengers of Iōannēs had gone away, he started
to speak to the crowds about Iōannēs: "What did you go out to
the wasteland to gape at? A reed shaking in the wind? ²⁵ No?
Then what *did* you go out there to see? A man dressed in luxurious clothes? Take a look: people in splendid apparel, living cod-
dled lives, are in palaces. ²⁶ So then what *did* you go out to see? A
prophet? Yes, I tell you, and somebody greater than a prophet.
²⁷ This is the one about whom it's been written:

> "*Look, I'm sending my messenger ahead of you,*
> *And he'll build your road in front of you.*'†

²⁸ "I tell you, among all the people who are born from women,
there's no one greater than Iōannēs. But the person with the least
stature in god's kingdom is greater than him."

²⁹ And all the people listening, including the tax-collectors,

---

* These are mainly phrases found in Isaiah.

† Isaiah 40:3.

agreed that god was right because they had been baptized the way Iōannēs baptized. ³⁰ But the Farisaioi and the experts in the law rejected god's plan for them, because they hadn't been baptized by him.*

³¹ "To whom should I compare the people of this generation, and who are they like? ³² They're like children sitting in the marketplace and calling to each other and saying:

> "*We played the flute for you—no dancing to the sound!*
> *We sang the mourning song—your chests you didn't pound!*"†

³³ "Iōannēs the baptizer, you know, has come without eating a loaf of bread or drinking wine, and you all say, 'He has a demon in him.' ³⁴ The son of mankind has come eating and drinking, and you all say, 'Look, that guy's an *eater*—and a *drinker of wine*! He's a friend of tax-collectors and other wrongdoers.' ³⁵ But wisdom is vindicated by all her children."‡

³⁶ A certain one of the Farisaioi asked him to eat with him, and he came into the house of the Farisaios and reclined at the table. ³⁷ And look, a woman who was a wrongdoer in the city: she had found out that Iēsous was reclining at the table in the house of the Farisaios, and had brought an alabaster jar of perfume; ³⁸ now she stood behind him at his feet, crying, and she began to rain tears on his feet, which she wiped dry with the actual hair on her head, all the time kissing his feet and rubbing the perfume on them.§

---

* John's baptism could arguably have special functions and meanings, because it was distinct from ordinary cleansing by immersion: it was administered by one person in a single, hard-to-reach place, and it was in running water.

† Perhaps a singsong taunt or part of a game.

‡ This could be the personified Wisdom of scripture, and legal representation of widows by adult sons might be suggested.

§ This is a repeated scene in the Gospels, but here it is climactically lurid, containing female tears, quite intimate and unseemly physical contact, and a euphemistically designated prostitute, as well as the Jewish euphemism for "penis"

³⁹ And when the Farisaios who had invited him there saw this, he said to himself, "If this man were a prophet, he'd know who this woman is who's touching him, and what kind of woman she is: he'd know that she's a wrongdoer." ⁴⁰ But in response, Iēsous said to him, "Simōn, I have something to say to you." "Say it, teacher," he replied. ⁴¹ "A certain moneylender had two debtors. The one owed five hundred denarii, and the other fifty.* ⁴² As neither of them was able to pay him back, he let the loans go as a favor. Now which of them is going to love him more?" ⁴³ Simōn responded by saying, "I assume that it's the one for whom he did the bigger favor." And he told him, "You judged that right." ⁴⁴ And turning to the woman, he spoke to Simōn: "Do you see this woman? I came into your house, but you didn't even give me water for my feet. She rained tears on my feet and wiped them dry with her hair. ⁴⁵ You didn't give me a kiss. Ever since she came in, she hasn't stopped kissing my feet. ⁴⁶ You didn't rub olive oil on my head; she rubbed perfume on my feet. ⁴⁷ So I tell you, she's absolved from her offenses, as many as they are, which is why she's shown great love. But whoever's absolved from just a little loves only a little." ⁴⁸ Then he said to her, "You're absolved from your offenses." ⁴⁹ Then those who were reclining at the table with him said among themselves, "Who is this, who actually absolves people from their offenses?" ⁵⁰ But he said to the woman, "Your trust has rescued you. Go in peace."

("feet"). Only with the usual ancient dining posture and furniture can the scene work: she can approach a backless dining couch and gain access to his feet while still standing on her own feet. To access the feet of a man sitting at a table, she would have to crawl under it and minister unseen to his lower body—not a good look in these circumstances.

* A denarius was a standard daily wage for a menial worker.

CHAPTER 8

———

¹ And it happened that right afterward he traveled on from one town to another and from one village to another, bringing word and announcing the good news of god's kingdom, and the twelve went with him. ² And there were certain women who had been treated for troublesome spirits in them, or for debilities. There was Maria who was called Magdalēnē,* from whom seven demons had gone out; ³ and there was Iōanna the wife of Chouzas, Hērōdēs' steward, and Sousanna, and many others who looked after them, using their financial means.

⁴ Now when a large crowd came together, with people traveling to him from one town after another, he addressed them through an analogy: ⁵ "A sower went out to sow his seed. And as he sowed, some fell along the road and was trampled down, and the birds of the sky made short work of it. ⁶ And other seed fell on stone, and once it started to grow, it withered, as it didn't have any moisture. ⁷ And other seed fell in the middle of the thorny weeds, and as the thorny weeds grew up with it, they strangled it. ⁸ But other seed fell onto good ground, and when it grew, every kernel yielded a hundred more." And as he said these things, he cried, "Whoever has ears for hearing had better hear!"

⁹ His students asked him what the analogy was about. ¹⁰ And he said, "The secrets of god's kingdom have been granted to you to know;† but to everyone else, it happens through analogies, so that,

---

* This context particularly, the company of respectable women—one even connected to the client ruler's court—makes it unlikely that she had ever been unchaste, as later legend depicts her. Perhaps her background as a female demoniac contributed to the legend. The best scholarly guess about her name is that she is from a village named Magdala, but that she is "called" so is not a normal way of citing geographical origin.

† The wording about knowledge and (literally) "mysteries" (as in pagan cults

> *"'Though looking, they don't look,*
> *And though hearing, they don't have any understanding.'**

[11] "This is the comparison. The seed is god's true account. [12] The people along the road are those who hear it, but then comes the slanderer, and he takes the account out of their hearts, so that they can't trust and be rescued. [13] As for those landing on stone, when they hear the account, they take it in with joy, but they don't take root: they trust for the time being, but at the time of testing, they pull out. [14] The seed that falls into the thorny weeds is the people who do hear, but as they continue on their way, they're strangled by anxieties or wealth or life's pleasures, and they bring no grain to ripeness. [15] But the seed on good ground is the people who hear the account and hold it firmly in their good and worthy hearts and produce a harvest through endurance.

[16] "Nobody lights a lamp and then hides it in a container or puts it under a bed, but instead puts it on a lamp-stand, so that the people who find their way in see the light. [17] Nothing's hidden, you see, that won't become clear as light, and nothing's hidden away that won't be known and come into the clear light.

[18] "So keep an eye on how you listen! If somebody has something, more will be given to him; but if somebody doesn't have anything, even what he seems to have will be taken away from him."

[19] Then his mother and brothers arrived where he was, but they couldn't reach him because of the crowd. [20] But a message was sent to him: "Your mother and your brothers are standing outside, wanting to see you." [21] But he answered by saying to

---

accessible only to the initiated) suggests influence from the Gnostic ("Knowing") branch of Christianity.

* Isaiah 6:9.

them: "My mother and my brothers are these, who hear the true account and put it into practice."*

²² Now it happened that on one of those days he boarded a boat along with his students, and said to them, "Let's cross over to the other side of the lake,"† and they set off. ²³ And as they were sailing along, he fell asleep. Then a squall fell on the lake, and they were being swamped and were in danger of sinking. ²⁴ So they came to him and woke him up, saying, "Boss, boss, we're going under!" But when he woke up, he simply scolded the wind and the rough water, and they stopped, and there was calm. ²⁵ Then he said to them, "Where's your trust?" But they were awed and astounded and said to each other, "Who is this, then? He commands the winds and the water, and they submit."

²⁶ Then they sailed to the region of the Gerasēnoi, which is on the shore opposite Galilaia.‡ ²⁷ As he got out of the boat and stepped onto dry land, a certain man from the city met him. He had demons in him, and for a considerable time now he wouldn't wear clothing or stay in a house, but instead lived among the tombs. ²⁸ But when he saw Iēsous, he screamed and fell down in front of him, and said in a loud voice, "What's your business with me, Iēsous the son of god who's above everything? I beg you, don't torture me"— ²⁹ Iēsous had in fact ordered the unclean spirit to come out of the man. Many times, in fact, it had seized him violently, and he was confined in chains and shackles and kept under guard, but he would break his restraints and be driven by the demon into the wilderness. ³⁰ But now Iēsous asked him, "What's your name?" And he said "Legion," since so many demons had gone into him.§ ³¹ Then they pleaded with Iēsous fer-

---

* The tone of this depends a great deal on whether he has circled back and is in his relatives' home again at this point.

† This would very likely be the Sea of Galilee.

‡ The location is uncertain, but would likely be in the Greco-Roman "Ten Cities" region.

§ A Roman legion numbered around five thousand.

vently not to command them to go back into the abyss.* ³² Now, there was a substantial herd of pigs grazing on the mountain, so the demons begged him for permission to go into them; and he gave them permission. ³³ Then the demons went out of the human being and went into the pigs, and the herd barreled down the crag into the lake and drowned.

³⁴ When the herders saw what had happened, they ran for it and brought the news to the city and the farms. ³⁵ Then the people came out to see what had happened, and they came to Iēsous and found the man the demons had gone out of: he was sitting there, clothed and in his right mind, at Iēsous' feet—and they were terrified. ³⁶ Those who had seen it told them how the demon-possessed man had been cured. ³⁷ Then the whole mass of people from the surrounding district of the Gerasēnoi asked Iēsous to leave them, because they were overcome with terrible fear. And he boarded the boat and returned to where he'd come from. ³⁸ But the man the demons had gone out of begged to be allowed to go with him. But he sent him away, telling him, ³⁹ "Return home and tell the story of everything god has done for you." Then he went and spread the word through the city about everything Iēsous had done for him.

⁴⁰ Now when Iēsous returned, the crowd welcomed him: they had all been waiting for him. ⁴¹ And look, there came a man whose name was Iaïros, who was the leader of a synagogue, and he fell at Iēsous' feet and pleaded with him to come to his house: ⁴² he had an only daughter who was about twelve years old, and she was dying. But as Iēsous went to her, the crowd was nearly crushing the life out of him. ⁴³ Now there was a woman who'd been afflicted with a flow of blood for twelve years. [She'd spent on doctors all the money she had to live on,] yet she couldn't manage to be healed by anyone. ⁴⁴ Coming up behind Iēsous, she

---

* From the time of the Psalms, an image of both the terrors of seafaring and a metaphor for any kind of annihilation from which God could provide a rescue.

touched the hem of his cloak, and then and there, the flow of her blood stood still. [45] But Iēsous said, "Who was it who touched me?" When everybody denied it, Petros said, "Boss, the crowds around you are pushing in hard enough to crush the life out of you!" [46] But Iēsous said, "Somebody *touched* me, because I sensed that power had gone out of me." [47] Now the woman, seeing she hadn't gone unnoticed, came up trembling and fell down in front of him, and told him, with all the people looking on, the reason she'd touched him, and how she was healed on the spot. [48] And he said to her, "Daughter, your trust has healed you: go on your way in peace." [49] While he was still speaking, someone came from the home of the synagogue's leader and said, "Your daughter has died. Don't bother the teacher any longer." [50] But Iēsous heard and responded to him: "Don't be afraid; only trust, and she'll be saved." [51] But when he came to the house, he wouldn't allow anyone to go in with him except Petros and Iōannēs and Iakōbos and the girl's father and her mother. [52] Everyone was crying and beating their breasts for her. But he said, "Don't cry! She didn't die: she's just sleeping." [53] But they jeered at him, as they knew she was dead. [54] But he took hold of her hand and called out, saying, "Wake up, little girl!" [55] Her breath returned, and then and there she stood up, and he told them to give her something to eat.* [56] And her parents were absolutely stunned. But he ordered them to tell nobody what had happened.†

---

* Eating will be proof that she is not a ghost.

† Compare the story in Mark 5:21–43 and Matthew 9:18–26. This later version has one element that may be distinctly Greco-Roman in character (which would be suitable to Luke), the special concern the parents have for their "only daughter." There *was* usually only one cherished daughter even in a wealthy Greek or Roman household, as the rest would have been abandoned outdoors immediately after birth. (Infant exposure was not a Jewish practice; note at Matthew 6:3, for example, that Jesus has more than one sister.)

CHAPTER 9

¹ Then he called the twelve together and gave them power and authority over all the demons, and the ability to treat diseases, ² and he sent them out to announce god's kingdom and cure [debilities]. ³ And he said to them, "Don't take anything on the road with you, not even a staff or a bag or a loaf of bread or silver coins or two tunics [each].* ⁴ And whatever house you go into, stay there, and leave from there when you leave the locale. ⁵ And if any people don't take you in hospitably, when you go out of that town shake the dust off your feet as testimony against them."† ⁶ And they went out and went to village after village, spreading the good news and treating illness everywhere.

⁷ Now Hērōdēs the client ruler‡ heard all that had happened, and he was at a loss in dealing with it, since it was said by some people that Iōannēs had awaked from among the dead, ⁸ and by some that Ēlias had appeared, and by still others that someone else among the ancient prophets had risen again. ⁹ And Hērōdēs said, "I beheaded Iōannēs. Who is it I'm hearing things like this about?" And he was seeking to see him.

¹⁰ Then the envoys returned and went through for Iēsous what they'd done. And he withdrew and took them along with him privately to the town that's called Bēthsaïda.§ ¹¹ But the crowds found out about it and followed him. And he welcomed them and spoke about god's kingdom, and he healed those who needed treatment.

---

* Echoing the rules of the Essene sect for traveling in reliance on their fellow sectarians' hospitality; Jesus' followers, however, are not even allowed a staff for self-defense.

† A mysterious curse, but probably related to the lowliness and dirtiness of feet.

‡ This would be Herod Antipas, a son of Herod the Great and ruler of Galilee and Perea.

§ A town near the northern shore of the Sea of Galilee.

¹² Then night began to fall, and the twelve approached and said to him, "Let the crowd go so that they can make their way to the surrounding villages and farms, get lodgings, and find some provisions, because right here we're in a place no one lived in." ¹³ But he said to them, "*You* give them something to eat." But they replied, "We haven't got anything other than five loaves and two fish; unless—but of course we couldn't—we were to get on the road ourselves and buy food for this entire gathering." ¹⁴ There were in fact around five thousand grown men. But he said to his students, "Have them recline to dine in groups of [around] fifty."* ¹⁵ The students did as they were told and had them all recline. ¹⁶ Then he took the five loaves and two fish and, looking up to the sky, he blessed them and broke them into pieces and gave them to his students to set in front of the crowd. ¹⁷ And they all ate until they were full, and the excess that was gathered up afterward came to twelve baskets full of broken pieces.

¹⁸ And it happened what while he was praying on his own, and only his students were with him, he questioned them, saying, "Who do the crowds say I am?" ¹⁹ And they answered by saying, "Iōannēs the baptizer—but other people say you're Ēlias, and still others that one of the ancient prophets is on his feet again." ²⁰ But he said to them, "Who do *you* say I am?" Petros said in answer, "God's anointed one." ²¹ Then he spoke sternly to them, ordering them to tell no one about this, ²² and saying that it was necessary for the son of mankind to endure many things and be tested and rejected by the elders and the high priests and the scholars, and to be killed, but to awaken on the third day.

²³ And he said to everyone, "If someone wants to come along behind me, he needs to renounce all claim to himself and lift up day by day the stake he'll be hung on and follow me. ²⁴ Whoever wants to save his life is going to lose it, and whoever loses his life

---

* Likely a spoof on formal dining. The word for *dining* groups is used. See the more elaborate wordplay at Mark 6:40. The men assume the more casual posture, and the women and children probably eat separately.

because of me—he'll save it. ²⁵ What kind of profit, tell me, does a person realize from the entire universe, if he loses or forfeits himself? ²⁶ Whoever, in fact, is ashamed of me and the things I've said, the son of mankind, when he comes in glory—his own, and his father's, and that of the holy messengers—will be ashamed of him. ²⁷ I tell you truly, there are some of you standing here who definitely won't taste death before they see god's kingdom."*

²⁸ It happened that about eight days after he said these things, he climbed up onto a mountain to pray, taking Petros and Iōannēs and Iakōbos along. ²⁹ And it happened that while he was praying, the appearance of his face changed, and his apparel turned a flashing, lightning white.† ³⁰ And look, two men were talking with him, and they were Mōūsēs and Ēlias. ³¹ And they appeared in glory, speaking of his departure, which he was about to accomplish in Ierousalēm.‡ ³² Now Petros and those with him were weighed down by drowsiness. But once they were fully awake, they saw his glory, and the two men standing together with him. ³³ And it happened that, as those were withdrawing from him, Petros said to Iēsous, "Boss, it's good that we're here: Let's make three shelters, one for you and one for Mōūsēs and one for Ēlias"—but he didn't know what he was saying.§ ³⁴ But once he said these things, a cloud came and overshadowed them, and they were terrified while they went into the cloud. ³⁵ And a

---

* A highly problematic promise, especially given that the Gospel of Luke appeared around sixty years after Jesus' death.

† The striking metaphor shows how unusual pure white objects were; they might more often be seen in nature than as prestigious, expensive, thoroughly bleached clothing.

‡ In this context, Moses and Elijah are the perfect interlocutors. Moses led the exodus (from the Greek for, literally, the "road out"; "departure" is the word I use here) of the Hebrews from slavery in Egypt, and Elijah made his exit from earth on a heavenly chariot. Also, Moses and Elijah sum up the main authority of scripture, "the law and the prophets": Moses was said to have written the Pentateuch, and Elijah was an exemplary prophet.

§ Conventionally, he is right: deities were thought to need physical shelters where they manifested.

voice came out of the cloud, saying, "This is my son, my chosen one: listen to him." ³⁶ And after the voice had come, Iēsous alone was found there. But they were silent, and in those days they reported to no one anything of what they'd seen.

³⁷ Now it happened that, on the next day, when they had come down from the mountain, a large crowd met him. ³⁸ And look, a man in the crowd shouted, saying, "Teacher, I need you to give some attention to my son, because he's the only one born to me, ³⁹ and look, a spirit seizes him, and immediately he screams, and it throws him into convulsions and makes him foam at the mouth, and it hardly backs off him but practically pounds him to pieces. ⁴⁰ I did beg your students to expel it, but they couldn't." ⁴¹ And Iēsous answered by saying, "Oh, this faithless generation, completely distorted! How long will I be with you and put up with you?* Bring your son here." ⁴² And while the boy was still only approaching, the demon slammed him to the ground and sent him into terrible convulsions. But Iēsous berated the unclean spirit and healed the boy and gave him back to his father. ⁴³ And everyone was stunned at the magnificent power of god.

While everyone was marveling over everything he was doing, he said to his students, ⁴⁴ "Store up what I'm going to say in your ears: the son of humankind is going to be turned over to human hands." ⁴⁵ But they didn't realize what this statement meant, and its meaning was disguised and hidden away from them, so that they couldn't understand it, and they were afraid to ask him about this statement.

⁴⁶ Now a dispute found its way in among them, as to who was greatest. ⁴⁷ But Iēsous perceived the dispute that was in their hearts, so he took a child and stood it next to himself ⁴⁸ and said to them, 'Whoever takes in this child in my name, takes me in, and whoever takes me in, takes in the one who sent me. Whoever's smallest among all of you, in fact, *he*'s the great one."

⁴⁹ But Iōannēs responded by saying, "Boss, we saw someone

---

* Again, this resembles a famous Ciceronian rhetorical flourish.

expelling demons in your name, and we tried to stop him, because he's not following with us." ⁵⁰ But Iēsous said to him, "Don't stop someone like that, as whoever isn't against you is for you."

⁵¹ Now it happened that as the days before he was to be taken up were attaining their full number, he fixed his intent on traveling to Ierousalēm. ⁵² And he sent messengers ahead of him, and their journey brought them into a village of the Samaritai to make ready for him. ⁵³ But those people didn't take him in, because he intended to travel to Ierousalēm.* ⁵⁴ When they saw this, his students Iakōbos and Iōannēs asked, "Master, do you want us to call fire to come down from the sky and do away with them?"† ⁵⁵ But he turned and took them to task. ⁵⁶ And they made their way to another village.

⁵⁷ And as they were traveling on the road, someone said to him, "I'll follow you wherever you go." And Iēsous replied to him, ⁵⁸ "Foxes have dens, and the birds of the sky have shelters, but the son of mankind has no place to lay his head down." ⁵⁹ Then he said to someone else, "Follow me!" But he said, "[Master,] let me go back first to bury my father." ⁶⁰ But he said to him, "Leave corpses to bury corpses—who belong to them‡—but you come and spread the news of god's kingdom." ⁶¹ And someone else said to him, "I'll follow you, master, but first let me say goodbye to those in my home." ⁶² But Iēsous said [to him], "No one who puts his hand to the plow and then looks behind him is fit for god's kingdom."§

---

* Jewish pilgrims from the north would normally take a roundabout route to avoid hostile Samaria.

† Elijah invokes God to rain fire in the presence of the priests of Baal, decisively winning a miracle contest with them (1 Kings 18).

‡ A shocking precept, but the earthbound—either living or dead—will be of no concern to those saved in the apocalypse.

§ See the story of Elisha's calling at 1 Kings 19.

CHAPTER 10

———

¹ After this, the master appointed seventy[-two] others and dispatched them two [by two] ahead of him to every town and other locale where he was about to go himself. ² And he told them, "The crop is a large one, but there aren't many workers, so beg the crop's owner to send workers out to harvest it for him. ³ Get going! Look, sending you is like sending lambs out into a pack of wolves. ⁴ Don't carry a wallet or a bag or sandals, and don't greet anyone on the road. ⁵ Whatever house you enter, first say, 'Peace to this house!' ⁶ And if anyone there is a son of peace, your peace will settle on him; if not, it will turn back and be realized for *you*. ⁷ And stay in that same house and eat and drink what they give you, since a worker deserves his pay. Don't move around from house to house. ⁸ Whenever you go into a town and the people take you in as guests, eat what's put in front of you, ⁹ and treat the infirm in that town, and tell them, 'God's kingdom has come right up to you.' ¹⁰ But if any town you enter doesn't take you in hospitably, go out into its streets and say, 'We're wiping off even the dust of your town that sticks to our feet, as a response to you. ¹¹ Even so, you should know this: god's kingdom has come right up close to you.' ¹² I tell you that it's going be easier for Sodoma on that day than for that town.*

¹³ "You have it coming, Chorazin, you have it coming, Bēthsaïda! If the acts of power performed in you had been performed in Turos and Sidōn, those people would have changed their way of thinking a long time ago and sat in burlap and ashes.†
¹⁴ Yet at the judgment it will be easier for Turos and Sidōn than

———

* See Mark 6:7–13 and the notes concerning the Essene rules for traveling, and other principles for dealing with the people in strange cities. The great outrages that the people of Sodom committed were not essentially sexual, but were crimes against hospitality (Genesis 18–19).

† That is, the Jews' historically emblematic pagan opponents, other Canaanite

for you. [15] And you, Kafarnaoum, you're not going to be raised up to heaven, are you? No, you'll go down to hades.

[16] "Whoever listens to you listens to me, and whoever rejects you rejects me; and whoever rejects me rejects the one who sent me."

[17] Now the seventy[-two] returned with joy, saying, "Master, even the demons submit to us when we say your name!" [18] But he told them, "I was watching as satanas fell from the sky like a bolt of lightning.* [19] Look, I've given you the authority to trample on snakes and scorpions, and authority over all the power of the enemy, and nothing will ever harm you. [20] Still, don't be glad that the spirits submit to you; be glad instead that your names have been written in the skies."†

[21] On that same occasion, he delighted [in] the holy life-breath and said, "I give you all the credit, father, lord of the sky and the earth, because you've hidden away these things from clever and insightful people, but put them on display to babies. Yes, father, since this is the way that found favor in your eyes.‡ [22] Everything's given over to me by my father, and nobody, unless it's the father, knows who the son is,§ and nobody knows who the father is, unless it's the son—or anyone to whom the son wishes to reveal him."

[23] Then he turned to the students in private and told them,

---

peoples, would adopt the characteristic Jewish mode of penitence if they had seen the miracles that Jewish towns have seen.

* Perhaps due in part to dualistic Zoroastrian influences and Greek and Roman stories of the first generations of the gods, stories circulated among Jews about cosmic rebellion against God. The apocalyptic, noncanonical Book of Enoch contains an account of the contesting realms of good and evil.

† The sky as a scroll, and the "book of life" in which the names of the righteous are recorded, are traditional images that may be reflected here.

‡ Jesus sounds sarcastic here, using the jingle *ekrupsas* ("hidden away") and *apekalupsas* ("put on display").

§ This might allude to the ancient preoccupation with paternity, or even to the right of Greek and Roman husbands to get rid of a baby they suspected of being illegitimate rather than raise it.

"Those eyes are fortunate that see what you're seeing. ²⁴ I say to you in fact that many prophets and kings longed to see what you're seeing, but they didn't see it, and they longed to hear what you're hearing, but they didn't hear it."

²⁵ But look, a certain expert in the law stood up and put him to the test by saying, "Teacher, what do I need to do before I can inherit a life for all time?" ²⁶ So he said to him, "What's been written in the law? What do you read there?" ²⁷ He then answered by saying, " 'You are to love the lord your god with the whole of your heart and the whole of your life and the whole of your strength and the whole of your mind'; 'and the one next to you the way you love yourself.' "* ²⁸ So Jesus said to him, "That's the right answer. Do this, and you'll live." ²⁹ But because the man wanted to show that he was in the right, he asked, "So who's the one next to me?"

³⁰ As a rejoinder, Iēsous said, "A certain man went down from Ierousalēm to Ierichō† and stumbled onto some bandits, who stripped him and beat him and went away leaving him half dead. ³¹ By chance a certain priest was going down on that road, and he saw him but passed by on the other side. ³² In the same way, a Leuitēs also [happened to] come to the place, saw him, and went by on the other side.‡ ³³ But a certain Samaritēs on a journey§ came to where he was and, seeing him, was wrenched with pity. ³⁴ And he went up to him and bandaged his wounds, first pouring

---

* Deuteronomy 6:5 and Leviticus 19:18. See the Glossary for "neighbor."

† A busy major route. See the note at Mark 10:33 for the symbolism of "going down" from Jerusalem.

‡ Possibly because touching a corpse would ritually defile them. Priests and Levites formed the two most important contingents for service in the Temple.

§ The division between Jews and Samaritans dated back many centuries. The Samaritans had had their own temple on Mount Gerizim, near Samaria, the capital of the Northern Kingdom, and had long contested Jerusalem and the Southern Kingdom's claim to be the inheritor of God's covenant. This man is thus not only despised by Jews, but he is outside Samaritan territory and thus vulnerable himself.

on olive oil and wine,* and put him on his own mount and took him to an inn and took care of him. ³⁵ And the next day he took out two denarii† and gave them to the innkeeper and said, 'Take care of him, and whatever you spend above this, I'll reimburse you for it when I come back this way.'‡ ³⁶ Out of these three, who do you think turned out to be 'next to' the man who ran into the bandits?" ³⁷ And he said, "The one who had mercy on him." And Iēsous said to him, "Even *you* need to be on your way and do something like that!"

³⁸ While they were traveling, he came to a certain village, and a certain woman named Martha took him in as a guest. ³⁹ And she had a sister called Mariam, who was sitting at the master's feet and listening to what he was saying. ⁴⁰ Now Martha was bustling about with the extensive work of hospitality—but then she stood in front of him and said, "Master, don't you mind that my sister's left me to do all this work alone? Then tell her to come help me!"§ ⁴¹ But the master answered by telling her, "Martha, Martha, you're worried and agitated over so many things, ⁴² but only one's necessary. Mariam, you see, has chosen the excellent part of all this, and it's not going to be taken away from her."

CHAPTER 11

———

¹ And it happened that Iēsous was in a certain place praying. Once he finished, one of his students said to him, "Master, teach us how to pray, the way John taught his students." ² And he said to them, "When you pray, say,

---

* Which, respectively, soothe and disinfect.

† That is, a laborer's wages for two days.

‡ Innkeepers were notorious for swindles, so this act of trust is extraordinary.

§ The sisters are apparently without a servant, so the tasks of entertaining would be onerous for one person.

'Father, let your name be spoken in holiness. Let your kingdom
   arrive.
³ *Give us day by day tomorrow's loaf of bread,*
⁴ *And set us free from our offenses,*
Since we ourselves have set free everyone bound to us likewise.
And do not bring us into the ordeal.'"*

⁵ Then Iēsous said to them, "Let's say one of you has a friend and comes to him in the middle of the night and says to him, 'My friend, lend me three loaves, ⁶ since a friend of mine has dropped in on me after a journey, and I don't have anything to put on the table for him.' ⁷ So the other answers from inside by saying, 'Don't bother me! My door's locked already, and my children are in bed with me. I can't get up and give you anything.' ⁸ I tell you, even though he won't get up and give him anything because he's friends with him, because of the sheer shamelessness of the man outside, the man inside will get up and give him everything he needs. ⁹ So I'm telling you, ask, and it will be given to you, search, and you'll find, knock and the door will be opened to you. ¹⁰ Everyone, in fact, who asks gets, and whoever searches finds, and the door [will be] opened to whoever's knocking. ¹¹ What father among you, if his son asks for a fish, would give him a snake instead? ¹² Or if he asks for an egg, would give him a scorpion?† ¹³ So if all of you, worthless as you are, know how to give valuable gifts to your children, how much more will the father in the sky give the holy life-breath to those who ask him for it."

¹⁴ Then he was expelling a demon, [and it was] mute. And it happened that once the demon came out, the mute man spoke, and crowds were amazed. ¹⁵ But some of them said, "It's through the power of Be'elzeboul, the ruler of demons, that he expels demons." ¹⁶ And others put him to the test by asking him for a

---

* See the notes on Matthew 6:9–13, which represent the prayer commonly used in liturgy.

† Both snakes and scorpions are unclean, and they may both be poisonous.

sign from the sky. [17] Perceiving their thoughts, though, he said to them, "Every kingdom that's split in two and has the two pieces pitted against each other is going to be turned into a wasteland, and a house pitted against itself is going to fall. [18] And if Satan is split in two and pitted against himself, how will his kingdom remain standing? You say I expel demons through the power of Be'elzeboul. [19] But if I expel demons through the power of Be'elzeboul, through whose power do your sons expel them? For that reason, they're going to be your judges in deciding this matter. [20] But if [I] expel demons by the finger of god, then the kingdom of god has arrived ahead of you. [21] When a strong man, heavily armed and armored from head to toe, guards his own palace, his possessions are left in peace. [22] But when somebody stronger attacks him and wins the fight against him, he takes away the full set of arms and armor on which the other relied, and he divides his plunder.* [23] Whoever's not with me is against me, and whoever isn't gathering with me is scattering.

[24] "When an unclean spirit comes out of a person, it passes through waterless places seeking a place to rest, but doesn't find any. [Then] it says, 'I'll return to my house, where I came from.' [25] But when it comes, it finds the building swept out and put in order. [26] Then it goes on its way and brings back with it seven other spirits more terrible than itself, and they go in and take up residence there. And the final plight of that person is worse than the original one."

[27] While Iēsous was saying these things, a woman in the crowd raised her voice and said to him, "Happy is the womb that carried you, and happy are the breasts that nursed you." [28] But he

---

* This is a farcical set of images in the circumstances. Outside the gladiatorial arena, the fully armed man of the time—a virtual human tank—was the Roman soldier equipped for action. The private homeowner thus equipped is stripped of his armor by the victor, as if he were a Vergilian or Homeric warrior defeated in single combat.

said, "As a matter of fact, happy are those who hear what god says and observe it in practice."

²⁹ As the crowds grew more numerous, he spoke up: "This generation is a useless generation. It demands a sign, but no sign will be given to it except the sign of Iōnas. ³⁰ The son of mankind will be the kind of sign to this generation that Iōnas was to the Nineuitai. ³¹ The queen of where the south wind comes from will rise up at the judgment along with the men of this generation and give her judgment against them, because she came from the boundaries of the earth to hear Solomon's wisdom, but look, someone greater than Solomon is here. ³² The Nineuitai citizens will stand up at the judgment along with this generation and give their judgment against it, because they changed their thinking in response to Iōnas' proclamation, but look, someone greater than Iōnas is here.*

³³ "Nobody lights a lamp and puts it in a cellar [or under a basket]. Instead, he sets it on a lamp-stand, so those who come in see the light.

³⁴ "Your eye is your body's lamp. When your eye is sound, your whole body is full of light too. But when your eye is bad, your body's in darkness too. ³⁵ So look out that the light in *you* isn't the same as darkness. ³⁶ So if your whole body is lit up, with no part of it in darkness, it will be wholly lit up, as when a lamp sheds light on you with a ray like lightning."

³⁷ While he was speaking, a Farisaios invited him to a meal at his home; and he went in and reclined at the table. ³⁸ But the Farisaios was shocked to see that he didn't wash by immersion before the meal.† ³⁹ But the master said to him, "Now, you Farisaioi clean the outside of the cup and the dish, but inside you're

---

* See 1 Kings 10 and 2 Chronicles 9 on the Queen of Sheba, and Jonah 3. Conscientious heathens may stand in judgment of God's chosen people.

† This was not scripturally required, but was apparently a common practice during the late Second Temple period.

brimming with greed and malice. ⁴⁰ Idiots, didn't the same one make the outside and the inside? ⁴¹ Instead, give as a gift of mercy the things inside, and, look, everything will be clean for you.*

⁴² "But no, you have it coming, Farisaioi! You pay your ten percent of mint and rue and every kind of garden plant,† but you bypass justice and the love of god. You should have put the latter into practice, without bypassing the former.

⁴³ "You have it coming, Farisaioi! What *you* love is the seat of honor in the synagogues, and respectful greetings in the market-places.

⁴⁴ "You have it coming, Farisaioi! You're like unmarked tombs, with people walking over you who don't realize it."

⁴⁵ In answer, somebody from among the experts in the law said to him, "Teacher, you commit an outrage against us too by saying these things."

⁴⁶ But he said, "And you too, the legal experts, you have it coming! You load people with loads that are hard to carry, but you don't lift a finger to help with those loads.‡

⁴⁷ "You have it coming! You build tombs for the prophets, though your ancestors killed them. ⁴⁸ That makes you witnesses, and you endorse the things your ancestors did, because they killed the men, and you build the buildings. ⁴⁹ That's why god's wisdom as well has said, 'I'll send prophets and envoys, and they'll kill some, and hound others,'§ ⁵⁰ so that this generation can be charged with the blood of all the prophets that's been poured out since the foundations of the universe were laid, ⁵¹ from the blood of Abel to the blood of Zacharias, who was

---

* Jewish learning developed a veritable science of charitable donations, which are scriptural in foundation.

† The tithing requirement was ten percent of everything.

‡ Likely the Temple tax and the ritual requirements that were time-consuming and expensive for ordinary Jews.

§ Jeremiah 7:25–26—but there the prophets are only ignored.

killed between the altar and the sanctuary.* Yes, I tell you, this generation will be charged with it.

⁵² "You have it coming, experts in the law. You've taken away the key of knowledge. You haven't gone in yourselves, and you've stopped those who were trying to go in."

⁵³ Once he'd gone out of there, the scholars and the Farisaioi began to hold a terrible grudge against him, and to drill him by word of mouth about a number of things, ⁵⁴ lying in ambush to pounce on some statement emerging from his mouth.

CHAPTER 12

¹ Meanwhile, tens of thousands of people gathered in a crowd, so many that they were trampling each other. Iēsous began to speak to his students first of all: "Be wary of the yeast of the Farisaioi, which is play-acting.†

² "But nothing's covered over that won't be uncovered,‡ or hidden that won't be revealed. ³ Because of that, what you've said in the dark will be heard in the light of day, and what you've whispered in someone's ear in the storage rooms§ will be announced from the roofs.

⁴ "I tell you, my dear friends, don't fear those who kill the body, and after that have nothing more they can do. ⁵ I'll point

---

* For the death of Abel, see Genesis 4:1–16. This Zechariah has not been identified with certainty but is probably a recent martyr, as length of time seems to be the point here. The Hebrew Bible certainly does not provide a long list of prophets murdered by their own people, though some were persecuted by them.

† A tiny amount of yeast can pollute the Passover bread, which must be completely unleavened. See "hypocrite" in the Glossary.

‡ The two verbs play on the imagery of *apocalypsis*, literally "unveiling"; the first verb is an intensive form of the Greek for "to veil."

§ Virtually the only private places in the hypersocial ancient world.

out to you who you should fear: fear the one who, after that killing, has the power to throw you into *ge'enna*.* Yes, I tell you, you need to fear him. ⁶ Aren't five sparrows sold for two assaria? But not one of them is forgotten by god.† ⁷ No, even the hairs on your heads are all counted. Don't be afraid: you're worth more than a whole flock of sparrows!

⁸ "But I tell you, if anyone acknowledges me before human beings, the son of mankind will acknowledge him before god's messengers; ⁹ but if anyone denies knowing me when he's before human beings, he'll be denied before god's messengers.

¹⁰ "And anyone who makes a statement against the son of mankind will be absolved from it, but whoever blasphemes against the holy life-breath won't be absolved.

¹¹ "When they bring you up before the synagogues, the rulers, and the authorities, don't worry what your defense should be, or how to make it, or what you should say at all. ¹² The holy life-breath will certainly instruct you at the time as to what you need to say."‡

¹³ Someone in the crowd said to him, "Teacher, tell my brother to divide the inheritance with me."§ ¹⁴ But he said to him, "Hey, you—who appointed me judge or executor for the two of you?" ¹⁵ And he said to them, "Look out and keep on guard against every kind of greed, because when someone has more than he needs, his life doesn't depend on his possessions."

¹⁶ Then he told them a story to illustrate, saying, "A certain rich man owned very productive land. ¹⁷ And he calculated inwardly, saying, 'What will I do? I don't have anywhere to store

* See "hell" in the Glossary.

† The assarion was a copper coin worth one-sixteenth of the daily wage the Gospels depict as standard. God is shown as mindful of the lives of his own low-cost Temple offerings.

‡ See the note at Matthew 10:20.

§ It must be a younger brother speaking. The Jews seem to have practiced a species of primogeniture from the earliest times.

my crops.' ¹⁸ Then he said, 'Here's what I'll do: I'll tear down my barns and build bigger ones, and I'll store there all my grain and other good things. ¹⁹ And I'll say to the life within me,* "Life, you have many good things laid away for many years to come. Rest, eat, drink, have a good time!"' ²⁰ But god said to him, 'You idiot: on this actual night, they're demanding your life back from you. All of your provisions—who are they going to belong to?' ²¹ That's how it goes for anyone who fills storehouses for himself but isn't rich for god."

²² He said to [his] students, "Because of this, I say to you: don't worry about your life, as to what you'll have to eat, or about your body, as to what you'll have to clothe it. ²³ Life is a greater thing than food, and the body is a greater thing than clothing. ²⁴ Consider the crows: they don't sow or reap grain, and they don't have a storeroom or a barn, but god feeds them. You're worth so much more than birds! ²⁵ Which of you, by worrying, can add a whole cubit† to his height? ²⁶ So if you can't do even the most trivial thing, why worry about everything else? ²⁷ Consider the lilies, and how beautifully they grow. They don't exhaust themselves spinning thread. But I tell you, not even Solomōn in all his glory was dressed as beautifully as one of these flowers. ²⁸ This is the field's greenery, which exists today but tomorrow is thrown into the oven, so if god clothes it this way, how much more certainly will he dress you, though you have so little trust! ²⁹ So don't look out for what you're going to eat or what you're going to drink, and don't go bouncing off the walls about it. ³⁰ These are all of course the things that the other nations in the world chase after, but your father knows that you need these things. ³¹ No, go after his kingdom, and these other things will be given to you as well. ³² Don't be afraid, little flock, because your father has resolved to give you the kingdom.

* See "soul" in the Glossary.

† The Roman unit was the length from the elbow to the tip of the middle finger.

³³ "Sell your possessions and give them away as gifts of mercy. Provide yourselves with wallets that won't get worn out, and a storehouse in the skies that will never rob you of your expectations, where a robber* won't come near or a moth destroy anything. ³⁴ Where your storehouse is, there your heart will be too.

³⁵ "Keep your clothes belted up high, and keep the lamps burning.† ³⁶ Then you'll be like people who're waiting for their master to get back from a wedding, so that when he comes and knocks, they can open the door right away for him. ³⁷ Those are happy slaves, when the master comes and finds them on the alert. *Amēn* I tell you, he'll belt up his own clothes for them and have them recline at the table, and he'll come and wait on them. ³⁸ Even if he comes during the second or third watch of the night‡ and finds it like that, those will be happy people. ³⁹ But be aware of this: If the head of the house had known what time the thief was coming, he wouldn't have let his house be broken into. ⁴⁰ You too have to be ready, because the son of mankind is coming at a time you don't expect."§

⁴¹ Then Petros said, "Master, are you making this comparison just for us, or for everybody?" ⁴² And the master said, "Now, who's the trusty, shrewd manager, whom the master will put in charge of his contingent of slaves, to give them [their] measure of grain at the right time? ⁴³ That's a happy slave, if the master, when he comes, finds him behaving this way. ⁴⁴ I tell you that he'll put him in charge of all his property. ⁴⁵ But if that slave says in his heart, 'My master's taking his time coming,' and he starts to beat the slave boys and girls, and to eat and drink and get drunk, ⁴⁶ that

---

* I have tried to reproduce the play on sound between *anekleipton* ("never falling short") and *kleptēs* ("thief").

† Belting up kept the legs unimpeded for work, and lamps could prolong the working day.

‡ There were four watches of the night, so these would be toward midnight and in the small hours.

§ Again, the Gospels, circulating decades after Jesus' return was expected, were concerned to address the resulting doubts and anxieties.

slave's master will arrive on a day when the slave doesn't anticipate it, and at a time he doesn't have in mind, and he'll practically cut him in two and put him where those who aren't to be trusted go.*

⁴⁷ "The slave who knew what his master wanted but didn't get ready or carry out what he wanted will get a lengthy beating. ⁴⁸ But the one who didn't know, though he did things to earn some blows, will get just a brief beating. From everyone who's been given a lot, a lot will be required; and from the one who's been entrusted with a lot, they will demand even more.

⁴⁹ "It's fire I've come to bring to the earth, and how I wish it were already kindled! ⁵⁰ But I need to be baptized beyond baptism, and I'm seized with anguish until it's completed. ⁵¹ Do you think I've appeared here to bring peace to the earth? No, I tell you, it was to bring division. ⁵² From now on, five in one house will be divided, three against two and two against three. ⁵³ They'll be divided, father against son and son against father, mother against daughter and daughter against mother, mother-in-law against her son's bride and the bride against the mother-in-law."†

⁵⁴ Jesus said to the crowds, "As soon as you see [the] cloud rising from the place the sun sets, straight off you say, 'A rainstorm's coming,' and that's what happens. ⁵⁵ And when you see the south wind blowing, you say, 'It'll be burning hot,' and it is. ⁵⁶ You playactors! You know how to interpret the face of the earth and sky. Why don't you know how to interpret this critical time?

⁵⁷ "And why don't you also judge for yourselves what's lawful and right? ⁵⁸ So make it your business to reconcile with your adversary at law while you're on the road with him, heading off to

---

* I.e., the tortures and imprisonment of a misbehaving slave are compared to those of punishment in the afterlife. See "faith" in the Glossary.

† This may refer to the cult of celibacy and virginity that arose among the early Christians. Biographies of early saints emphasize young Christians' resistance to marriage and the trouble this caused across generations.

the magistrate. Otherwise, he may drag you off to the judge, and the judge will hand you over to the bailiff, and the bailiff will throw you into prison. ⁵⁹ I tell you, you'll never get out of there until you've paid the very last lepton you owe."*

CHAPTER 13

——

¹ At that actual juncture, some people there reported to him about the Galilaioi whose blood Pilatos had mixed with that of their sacrifices. ² And in response he said to them, "Do you think these Galilaioi were wrongdoers, beyond all the other Galilaioi, because these things have been inflicted on them?† ³ No, I tell you; on the contrary, if you don't change your thinking, you're all going to be destroyed, as they were. ⁴ Or those eighteen that the tower at Silōam fell on, killing them‡—do you think they were answerable for that, more than all the other people who were living in Ierousalēm? ⁵ No, I tell you: on the contrary, if you don't change your way of thinking, you're all going to be destroyed, as they were."

⁶ Now he told this story by way of illustration: "Somebody had a fig tree, which was planted in his vineyard, and he came looking for fruit on it but couldn't find any. ⁷ And he said to his vineyard-keeper, "Look, for three years now I've come looking for fruit on this fig tree but haven't found any. [So] cut her

* This is one of the smallest coins in circulation, a tiny copper one worth a tiny fraction of a Roman as, which itself has often been called a "penny."

† The incident is not otherwise known. It probably involved the sacrifice of Passover lambs by pilgrims in the Jerusalem Temple courtyard—an eclectic, crowded place vulnerable to trouble and surveilled from on high by armed members of the Roman garrison. A sacrificial animal's blood was unclean: it was passed ritually away from the slaughtered lambs in special cups.

‡ A spring of the same name was near the inner wall of Jerusalem, but nothing is known from any other source about this accident.

down—what's the reason for her wasting ground?" ⁸ But the vineyard-keeper answered by saying, 'Master, leave her alone for one more year, until I dig around her and put on some manure, ⁹ and if she produces fruit next year, then fine; if she doesn't, you can cut her down."*

¹⁰ Now, he was teaching in one of the synagogues on the *sabbata*. ¹¹ And look, there was a woman who for eighteen years had had a spirit of debility in her and was bent double and completely unable to unbend and stand upright. ¹² When he saw her, Iēsous called her over and said to her: "Woman, you're set free from your debility," ¹³ and he placed his hands on her. And, then and there, she straightened herself up and started to glorify god. ¹⁴ But in response, the head of the synagogue was angry that Iēsous had performed a healing on the *sabbaton*, and he said to the crowd, "There are six days on which it's necessary to work. So on these, you can all come and be healed, but not on the day of the *sabbaton*." ¹⁵ But the master answered him by saying, "You play-actors! Doesn't each one of you, on the *sabbaton*, untie his ox or donkey from the feeding trough and lead it away to water it?† ¹⁶ But this woman is a daughter of Abraam, and, look, satanas had chained her up for eighteen years—and she didn't need to be set free from this chain on the day of the *sabbaton*?" ¹⁷ And while he said these things, all those opposing him were humiliated, whereas the whole crowd was happy at the glorious things that were being done by him.

¹⁸ Hence he said, "To what is the kingdom of god comparable, and what shall I compare it to? ¹⁹ It's comparable to the seed of a mustard plant: a man took the seed and tossed it into his garden, and it grew and became a tree, and the birds of the sky found shelter among its branches."

---

* See the note at Mark 11:14.

† Routine and essential care of animals was of course provided for by Sabbath regulations—in this case, a beast actually needs to be removed from the ground floor of the house so that the human residents can use the space.

²⁰ And he spoke once again: "What am I going to compare to the kingdom of god? ²¹ It's comparable to yeast. A woman took it and hid it in three *sata** of flour, and waited until the whole lump of dough was risen with the yeast."

²² Then he went on his way through towns and villages one by one, teaching and making his journey to Hierosoluma.

²³ And someone said to him, "Master, will only a few people be rescued?" But he said to them, ²⁴ "All of you, exert yourselves to come in through the narrow gate, because many people—I'm telling you—try to come in, but they're not strong enough. ²⁵ Once the head of the house has gotten up and locked the gate, you'll proceed to stand outside and bang at the gate and say, "Sir, open up for us!" but he'll say to you in answer, "I don't know where you're from." ²⁶ Then you'll proceed to say, "We ate and drank right across from you, and you taught in our streets." ²⁷ And he'll speak to you like this: "I don't know [you] where you're from. Keep away from me, all of you who work at nothing but outrage!" ²⁸ There's going to be crying and grinding of teeth in pain in *that* place, when you'll see Abraam and Isaak and Iakōb and all the prophets in the kingdom of god, while you're thrown out! ²⁹ Then they'll arrive from where the sun rises and from where it sets, and from where the north and the south winds come, and they'll recline on dining couches in god's kingdom. ³⁰ And look, some who are in the lowest positions now will be in the highest then, and some who are in the highest ones will be in the lowest."

³¹ At that exact hour, certain Farisaioi approached, saying to him, "Leave here and be on your way, because Hērōdēs wants to kill you." ³² But he said to them, "You be on your way and tell that fox for me, 'Look, I'll be expelling demons and carrying out healings today and tomorrow, but on the third day, I'll be finished. ³³ Still, today and tomorrow and on the day after, I need to

---

* One *saton* was about one and a half pecks.

be on my way, because it's impossible for a prophet to be destroyed outside Ierousalēm.*

³⁴ "Ierousalēm, Ierousalēm, who kills prophets and stones those sent to her! How often I've wanted to gather your children together as a bird gathers her brood under her wings—but you didn't want that.† ³⁵ Look, your house is abandoned. [But] I tell you all: You will never see me until [the time comes] when you say,

"'Blessed is the one coming in the name of the lord.'"‡

CHAPTER 14

¹ Then it happened that when he came into the house of a certain leading Farisaios on the *sabbaton* to eat bread, they were watching him closely.

² And look, there was a certain man in front of him, who had dropsy. ³ And Iēsous reacted by speaking to the experts in the law§ and the Farisaioi in these terms: "Is it permitted to treat diseases on the *sabbaton* or not?" ⁴ They held their peace, and he took hold of him, healed him, and sent him away. ⁵ Then he said to them, "Which of you has a son or an ox who's fallen into a pit, and doesn't pull him out right away, even though it's the day of the *sabbaton*?" ⁶ And they weren't able to answer him back about these things.¶

---

* A deeply sarcastic response. In fact, however "prophet" is defined, extremely few were killed by the Jerusalem regime.

† The images of the sly, predatory fox and the protective hen suggest animal fables. The work on two days and the rest on the third allude to the passion and the resurrection.

‡ Psalms 118:26.

§ See "scribe" in the Glossary.

¶ In rabbinic teaching, the suspension of Sabbath rules to save life on the Sabbath does not apply to animals, but it certainly applies to sons.

⁷ Then, noticing how the other guests chose the couches of honor for themselves, he gave them a comparative lesson, telling them, ⁸ "When you've been invited by somebody to a wedding banquet, don't lie down on the first couch, in case somebody more distinguished than you has also been invited by him. ⁹ Then the one who's invited both you and him might just come and say to you, 'Give your place to him'—and then, in humiliation, you'll proceed to take the lowest place. ¹⁰ Instead, when you're an invited guest, make your way to the lowest place and recline there, so that when the man who's invited you comes, he'll say to you, 'My friend, move up higher.' Then you'll make an excellent showing before all those who are reclining with you: ¹¹ because everyone who raises himself will be lowered, and whoever lowers himself will be raised."*

¹² Then he turned and said to the man who'd invited him: "When you're giving a luncheon or dinner, don't summon your friends or brothers or your other relatives, or your rich neighbors; they'd just invite you back themselves later on, and you'd be repaid. ¹³ Instead, when giving a banquet, invite beggars, mutilated people, the crippled, the blind. ¹⁴ And you'll be happy and blessed, because they don't have the means to pay you back, but you'll in fact be repaid when good people are awakened for a new life."

¹⁵ Someone who was reclining at the table with him heard these things and said to him, "Whoever eats a loaf of bread in god's kingdom will be happy and blessed."

¹⁶ But he said to him, "A certain man was putting on a great feast, and he invited many people. ¹⁷ Then he sent out his slave at the time of the feast to tell those he'd invited, 'Come, because it's already prepared.' ¹⁸ But they all began to make excuses in the

---

* Etiquette around hierarchical dining couches is depicted in detail in contemporary Classical sources; the segmentation of the guests apparently made it easier for Roman hosts to serve food and drink of sharply different quality according to the guests' importance.

same sort of way. The first one told him, 'I've bought a field, and I have no choice but to go out and see it. Please, accept my excuse.' ¹⁹ And the second said, 'I've bought five pair of oxen and I'm on my way to try them out. Please, accept my excuse.' ²⁰ And the third said, 'I've married a woman, and this is the reason I can't come.' ²¹ And the slave, arriving back at home, reported these things to his master. Then the head of the house was furious, and said to his slave, 'Go out quickly to the streets and the alleys of the city and find the beggars and the mutilated and the blind and the crippled, and bring them in here.' ²² But the slave said, 'Master, what you ordered has been done, but there's still room.' ²³ Then the master said to the slave, 'Go out to the country roads and paths and *force* them to come in,* so that the house will be full to bursting.' ²⁴ I'm telling all of you that not one of those gentlemen who were invited will taste my banquet."

²⁵ Large crowds were traveling with him, and he turned and said to them, ²⁶ "If anyone comes to me and doesn't hate his own father and mother and his children and brothers and sisters and even his own life besides, he can't be my student. ²⁷ Whoever doesn't carry his own execution stake and come after me can't be my student.

²⁸ "Which of you who wants to build a tower doesn't first sit down and figure out how much it's going to cost, to see if he has enough resources to complete it? ²⁹ Otherwise, when he's laid the foundation but doesn't have means to finish, everybody who's looking on is going to start ridiculing him, ³⁰ saying, 'This guy started to build but didn't have the means to finish.' ³¹ Or what king goes against another king to wage war with him but doesn't first sit down and plan whether, with a force of ten thousand, he has the means to meet the king with twenty thousand who's coming against him? ³² If he doesn't have the means, while the other's still far away he sends off an embassy and asks for peace

---

* That is, go from the urban beggars to notoriously poor rural laborers.

terms. ³³ In the same way, then, every one of you who doesn't part with everything he possesses can't be my student.

³⁴ "So salt is a fine thing; but if salt actually loses its bite and is dulled and dumbed down, what are you going to use to flavor *it*? ³⁵ It's not even suitable for the soil or the manure pile: people simply throw it out of bounds.* Whoever has ears had better hear!"

Chapter 15

¹ Now all the tax-collectors and other wrongdoers came near him to listen to him. ² And the Farisaioi and the scholars both were griping loudly, saying, "He welcomes wrongdoers and eats with them."

³ But he spoke and addressed this analogy to them: ⁴ "What man among you, who has a hundred sheep and loses one, doesn't leave the ninety-nine behind in the wilderness and go after the lost one until he finds it? ⁵ And when he finds it, he joyfully puts it on his shoulders, ⁶ and when he goes back home, he calls together his friends and neighbors, saying to them, 'Share this joy with me, because I've found my lost sheep.'† ⁷ I tell you that, in the same way, there'll be more joy in the sky over one wrongdoer who changes his purpose than over ninety-nine upstanding people who don't need to change their purpose.

---

* See the note at Matthew 5:13. Spoiled salt (common in the ancient world, because of unstable salt-based mixtures) is in fact a special waste product, which will poison either soil or fertilizer and can safely be disposed of only in a barren place.

† As in Matthew 18:12–13, the scenario is doubtful. A single lost animal— unlikely to be recovered—is not worth leaving a large herd in the open; at most, a child or servant would be sent to search. But Luke adds improbability. Finding the animal would hardly be a cause of community celebration, which for a man of substance would necessitate slaughtering at least one animal: he would not even come out ahead.

⁸ "Or what woman, who has ten drachmas and loses one, doesn't light a lamp and sweep her house and search carefully until she finds it? ⁹ And when she finds it, she calls together her women friends and neighbors, saying, 'Share this joy with me, because I've found the drachma I lost.'* ¹⁰ So, I tell you, that's the kind of joy among god's messengers when one wrongdoer changes his purpose."

¹¹ Then he said, "A certain man had two sons. ¹² And the younger of them said to the father, 'Father, give me the share of the property that will fall to me.' So he divided between them what the family lived off. ¹³ Then after a few days, the younger son got together everything that belonged to him and went abroad into a distant country, and there he threw his property around, living with reckless abandon. ¹⁴ After he'd spent everything he had, there came a severe famine throughout that country, and he started to fall short of essentials. ¹⁵ Then he went and hired himself out to one of that country's citizens, and this man sent him into his fields to graze pigs. ¹⁶ And he longed to fill himself up with some of the carob pods the pigs were eating, but nobody would let him have him any.† ¹⁷ Then, coming to himself, he said, 'How many of my father's hired workers have more loaves than they can eat, while I'm dying of hunger here? ¹⁸ I'll set off and travel to my father, and I'll say to him, "Father, I've done wrong toward heaven and before your face; ¹⁹ I no longer deserve to be called your son: treat me like one of your hired workers."' ²⁰ Then he set off and came to his father. But while he was still at a distance, his father saw him and felt a wrenching pity: he ran to him, threw his arms around his neck, and kissed him warmly. ²¹ But the son said to him, 'Father, I've done wrong toward heaven and before your face; I no longer deserve to be called your son.'

---

* The woman's whole savings amounts to about ten days' male wages. The lexicon indicates that she may just be seeking congratulations.

† In a comical degree of misery, he's not allowed the forage or slops of these unclean animals in a pagan district.

²² But the father said to his slaves: 'Quick, bring out a robe, the best one there is, and put it on him, and put a ring on his finger and sandals on his feet, ²³ and bring the calf that's been fed on grain, sacrifice it, and let's eat and celebrate, ²⁴ because my son here was a corpse, but he's come back to life; he was lost but now he's been found.' Then they began to celebrate. ²⁵ Now his older son was in the field, and as he was coming back and nearing the house, he heard music and dancing. ²⁶ He called one of the slave boys to him and asked what was going on here. ²⁷ And he told him, 'Your brother's come back, and your father sacrificed the grain-fed calf* for him, because he got your brother back safe and sound.' ²⁸ And he was furious and didn't want to go in, so his father came out and appealed to him. ²⁹ By way of an answer, he told his father, 'Look, for all these years I've been slaving away for you, and I never once ignored any order from you, but you never once gave me a young goat so that I could celebrate with my friends. ³⁰ But now that this son of yours has come back, after he wolfed down, in the company of whores, the property that was your livelihood, you've sacrificed the grain-fed calf for him.' ³¹ But he said to him, 'Child, you're always with me, and everything I have is yours. ³² But there was no choice but to celebrate and be joyful, because your brother here was a corpse, but now he's come to life, and he was lost, but he's now been found.'"

* The weaned calf kept in a stall and fed on grain—human food—so that its meat would be particularly rich and tender, and butchered while it was still relatively small, was a great luxury.

CHAPTER 16

¹ Then he also said to his students, "There was a certain rich man who had a manager,* and a complaint got around to the rich man that the manager was throwing around the rich man's property. ² So he summoned him and said to him, 'What's this I hear about you? Give me an account of your management, because you can't be manager any longer.' ³ Then the manager said to himself, 'What am I going to do? My master's taking away my job as manager. I'm not strong enough to dig in the earth, but I'm ashamed to beg. ⁴ I know what I'll do, so that when I'm out of my job as manager, people will welcome me into their homes.' ⁵ So he called in, one by one, each of his master's debtors. He said to the first, 'How much do you owe my master?' ⁶ And he said, 'A hundred baths of olive oil.'† So he said to him, 'Take your document, sit down quickly, and write "fifty."' ⁷ Next he said to the second one, 'Okay, you: how much do you owe?' And he said, 'A hundred cors of grain.'‡ And he said to him, 'Take your document and write "eighty."' ⁸ Then the master praised the manager with his lawless mismanagement, because he'd behaved shrewdly, given that the sons of this age are shrewder in dealing with their own generation than the sons of light are.§ ⁹ So *I* say to you: make friends for yourselves using the *mamōnas*¶ of that mismanage-

---

* In the ancient world, owners of substantial property almost never supervised its operations in detail. The manager in this story is an *oikonomos* (from the Greek words for "house" and "law"—notice the play on "law" in Verses 8 and 9), which yielded the English word "economy."

† A "bath" is around six gallons.

‡ A "cor" is about six and a half bushels.

§ See Paul of Tarsus in 1 Thessalonians 5:5 for more of this apocalyptic terminology.

¶ Hebrew for material possessions, usually in a bad sense.

ment, so that when it's used up, they welcome you into the shelters that last for all time.*

¹⁰ "The trustworthy person is trustworthy in the smallest matter as well as in a great one; and an unlawful person is unlawful in the smallest matter as well as in a great one. ¹¹ If, therefore, you all haven't proven trustworthy in unlawful *mamōnas*, who's going to trust you with true *mamōnas*? ¹² If you haven't proven trustworthy in what belongs to someone else, who's going to give you anything for your own?

¹³ "No household slave can serve two masters. Either he'll hate the one and love the other, or he'll be loyal to one and have contempt for the other. You people can't be slaves to god and to *mamōnas* too."

¹⁴ The Farisaioi, who love money, heard all these things and turned up their noses at him with a decided sneer. ¹⁵ So he said to them, "You're the ones who justify yourselves in the sight of human beings, but god knows your hearts; because whatever is exalted and proud among humans is an abomination in god's eyes.

¹⁶ "The law and the prophets lasted until Iōannēs; since then, the kingdom of god is proclaimed as the good news, and everyone tries to get into it by violence. ¹⁷ But it's easier for the sky and the earth to pass away than for a single hook on a letter of the written law to be dropped.†

¹⁸ "Everyone who lets his wife go and marries another woman is violating marriage, and whoever marries a woman who's been let go by her husband violates marriage.

---

* No sane man would, in the first place, dismiss a manager without taking back the seal that gives him the authority to act for his employer (or owner). The ethical point of this far-fetched story must be the eternal rewards of charity and the impossibility of cheating God, through generosity toward fellow human beings, of what belongs to him. The *nomos* or law (see the note at Verse 1) must allude to the Jewish scriptural law as outdated.

† The two isolated-looking verses entail a curious acknowledgment of the disorder and conflict caused by Christians' rejection of the Jewish law. A keraia is the hooked stroke in some Hebrew and Aramaic letters.

¹⁹ "There was a certain rich man, and he habitually dressed in purple and linen, enjoying himself splendidly every day. ²⁰ And a certain beggar by the name of Lazaros used to lie at his gate, covered with sores ²¹ and longing to fill himself with things that fell from the rich man's table; but instead the dogs actually came and licked his sores.* ²² Then it happened that the beggar died and was taken up by the messengers to Abraam's embrace.† Then the rich man also died and was interred. ²³ And in hades he lifted up his eyes while he was being tortured and saw Abraam far away, with Lazaros in his embrace. ²⁴ And he called out and said, 'Father Abraam, have pity on me and send Lazaros: he could dip his fingertip in water and cool down my tongue, because I'm in agony in these flames.' ²⁵ But Abraam said, 'Child, keep in mind that you got your good things during your life, while Lazaros got only bad things during his. But now he's being consoled here, and you're in agony. ²⁶ And besides all this, between us and all of you a huge, rock-solid chasm has been built, so that those who might want to step across to you couldn't, and those where you are couldn't cross over from there to us either.' ²⁷ But he said, 'Then I beg you, father, to send him to my father's house, ²⁸ as I have five brothers. I want him to warn them, which could keep them from coming into this place of torture." ²⁹ But Abraam said, 'They have Mōüsēs and the prophets:‡ they'd better listen to them.' ³⁰ But he said, 'They won't, father Abraam, but if someone makes his way to them from among the dead, they'll change their thinking.' ³¹ But he told him, 'If they don't listen to Mōüsēs and the prophets, even if someone rises from among the dead, they won't be persuaded.'"

---

* These are the only creatures more miserable than he is, the dogs Jews considered unclean and untouchable.

† Probably lying in front of him as his partner on a dining couch.

‡ That is, the Torah, or first five books of the Hebrew Bible, purportedly written by Moses, and the Hebrew Bible's prophetic books.

CHAPTER 17

¹ Then he said to his students, "For traps not to occur is something that can't be had—but the person who makes them occur has it coming. ² It would be more to his advantage if a stone big enough to grind grain with were hung around his neck and he were thrown into the sea, than if he set a trap for one of these little people.* ³ Watch out for yourselves!

"If your brother commits an offense, take him to task, and if he changes his purpose, let him off. ⁴ Even if he commits seven offenses a day against you but then turns back to you seven times, saying, 'I've changed my purpose,' you're to let him off."

⁵ Then the envoys said to the master, "Strengthen our trust!" ⁶ But the master said, "If your trust were only as big as a mustard seed, you could say to [this] mulberry tree, 'Uproot yourself, and plant yourself in the sea!'—and it would obey you.†

⁷ "Which of you has a slave who plows or grazes a flock? When he comes in from the field, would you tell him, 'Come here right away and recline at the table!'? ⁸ Wouldn't you tell him the opposite: 'Get something ready for my dinner, put a cloth around your waist, and serve me while I eat and drink, and after that you can eat and drink'? ⁹ You don't thank the slave, do you, for doing what he was ordered to? ¹⁰ It's the same for you: when you've done everything you were ordered to, say, 'We're worthless slaves: we've only done what we were obliged to.'‡

---

* Unclear, because there is no context, whether this means children, as in Matthew 18:1–10, or simple or poor people.

† The seeds of this shrub were notoriously tiny, whereas mulberry trees can grow very large and put down deep roots.

‡ Masters might in fact eat with their slaves when there was no formal company, and Roman masters waited on their slaves at the Saturnalia festival. The master conceived of here, not distinguishing between a farm laborer and a house slave and making one man do double duty while he himself dines alone—a re-

¹¹ And it happened that during the journey to Ierousalēm, he passed along the border between Samareia and Galilaia.*

¹² And as he was entering a certain village, ten men with leprosy came to meet [him], and they stood far off. ¹³ Then they raised their voices, saying, "Iēsous, boss, have pity on us." ¹⁴ And when he saw, he said to them, "Be on your way and show yourselves to the priests." And it happened that as they were still heading there, they were cleansed.† ¹⁵ And one of them, seeing that he was cured, turned back and glorified god with a loud voice; ¹⁶ and he fell facedown at Iēsous' feet, thanking him; but he was a Samaritēs.‡ ¹⁷ And Iēsous said in response, ¹⁸ "Weren't there ten who were cleansed? Where are the other nine? There's no evidence they turned back to give the glory to god? It's only this foreigner?" ¹⁹ And he told him, "Stand up and be on your way. Your trust has rescued you."

²⁰ Interrogated by the Farisaioi as to when god's kingdom was coming, he answered them by saying, "God's kingdom doesn't arrive under scrutiny. ²¹ And they're not going to say, 'Look, it's here,' or 'It's there'—since, look, god's kingdom is inside you all."§

²² But he said to his students: "The days will come when you long to see just one of the days of mankind's son, but you won't see it. ²³ And they'll say to you, 'Look, he's there,' [or] 'Look, he's

---

viled practice in the ancient world—would in reality be alienating someone whose loyalty he needs.

* Apparently going east to avoid Samaria, as Jewish pilgrims from Galilee tended to do.

† Jesus and the sufferers both follow the Levitical prescriptions for isolation and for clearance under priestly authority: notice that Jesus does not approach or touch them.

‡ Thus, both foreign to Jews and particularly despised by them.

§ The end date of secular history concerned Jesus' followers more and more urgently as the first century progressed; they had expected this event soon after the resurrection. There have been efforts to construe *entos* (my "inside") as "among," or "at your disposal," or "in your possession," but these seem strained: *entos* usually means "within."

here.' But don't go and run after them. ²⁴ Just like a lightning flash, flashing to light up the sky from one end to another—that's what the son of mankind will be like [in his day]. ²⁵ But first he'll have to suffer many things and be tested and rejected by this generation. ²⁶ And as it happened in Nōe's days, that's how it will be in the days of mankind's son. ²⁷ They were eating, they were drinking, they were marrying, they were being given in marriage until the day Nōe entered the ark and the flood came and destroyed them all.* ²⁸ That's exactly the way it happened in the days of Lōt: they ate, they drank, they bought, they sold, they planted, they built. ²⁹ But on the day Lōt went out of Sodoma, fire and sulfur rained from the sky and destroyed them all.† ³⁰ That's how it will be on the day when the son of mankind is revealed.‡ ³¹ On that day, whoever's on the roof, while his things are inside the house, had better not go down and get them, and likewise whoever's out in the field had likewise better not turn back for what's left behind. ³² Remember Lōt's wife!§ ³³ Whoever looks to secure his life for himself will lose it, but whoever loses it will bring it to life again. ³⁴ I tell you, on that night there will be two on one bed, and the one will be taken along but the other left behind. ³⁵ Two women will be grinding grain in the same place, and the one will be taken along while the other's left behind."¶ ³⁷ And in response they said to him, "Where, master?" And he said to them, "Where the dead body is, there the eagles will gather."**

---

* Genesis 6:11–7:23.

† Genesis 19.

‡ Literally "unveiled," the imagery of the Greek word for apocalypse.

§ Genesis 19:26: she is turned into solid salt through only a backward look at her home while fleeing.

¶ Verse 36, translated as "Two will be in the field; one will be taken, the other left behind," has been excised as spurious.

** Similar to our saying "Where there's smoke, there's fire": the events will be self-evident.

CHAPTER 18

¹ Now he told them a story for comparison, to show that it's essential to pray at all times and not get discouraged. ² He told them, "There was a certain judge in a certain town who didn't fear god or feel any compunction toward mankind. ³ There was a widow in that town, and she kept coming to him, saying, 'Give me lawful vindication against my opponent at law!' ⁴ For some time, he was unwilling. But later on, he said to himself, 'Even though I don't fear god or feel any compunction toward mankind, still, as this widow is giving me so much trouble, I'll give her vindication, ⁵ so that she doesn't keep coming and beat me down in the end and leave me with a black eye.'" ⁶ And the master said, "Listen to what the judge who doesn't care about the law says. ⁷ Won't god vindicate those he's chosen, who shout for him day and night? Is he going to wait patiently where they're concerned? ⁸ I tell you that he'll give them vindication in a hurry. Be that as it may, will the son of mankind find trust on earth when he comes?"

⁹ And he told this comparative story to certain people who had confidence in their own justice and lawfulness and treated everyone else as if they didn't exist. ¹⁰ "Two people walked up into the temple precinct to pray. The one was a Farisaios, and the other was a tax-collector. ¹¹ The Farisaios stood by himself and prayed in this way: 'God, I'm thankful to you that I'm not like the rest of mankind—looters, criminals, violators of marriage—or even like this tax-collector. ¹² I fast twice between one *sabbaton* and the next, and I give ten percent of all I take in.' ¹³ The tax-collector, on the other hand, stood far away and couldn't even bring himself to raise his eyes to the sky, but instead beat his chest, saying, 'God, have mercy on me, a criminal.'* ¹⁴ I tell you,

---

* The temptations of unaudited tax collection under the auspices of the Roman Empire were so great that the profession itself was a brand of shame. The

he's the one who'd been put in the right when he went back down to his house, and not the other, because everyone who raises himself will be lowered, but whoever lowers himself will be raised."

¹⁵ They were even bringing him babies so that he could touch them. And when the students saw, they scolded the parents. ¹⁶ But Iēsous called for the babies to be brought to him, saying, "Let the children come to me, and don't stop them, because god's kingdom belongs to people like these. ¹⁷ *Amēn*, I tell you, whoever doesn't welcome god's kingdom the way a child would can never enter it."*

¹⁸ Then a certain leader questioned him, saying, "Excellent teacher, what do I have to do to inherit life for all time?" ¹⁹ Iēsous said to him, "Why do you call me excellent? Nobody is excellent except god alone. ²⁰ You know the commands: 'You must not violate marriage, you must not commit murder, you must not steal, you must not lie in your testimony, honor your father and your mother.'"† ²¹ And he said, "I've observed all these since my youth." ²² Having heard this, Iēsous said to him, "There's still one thing left for you to do: sell everything you have and share it out among the destitute, and you'll have a storehouseful in [the] skies, and come follow me." ²³ But when he heard this, he was heartbroken, as he was very wealthy.

²⁴ Looking at him [who was now so heartbroken], Iēsous said, "How hard a time those with property have as they try to make their way into god's kingdom. ²⁵ It's in fact easier for a camel to go through the eye of a needle than for a rich man to enter into

---

Pharisee boasts of tithing—an indigenous religious tax amounting to ten percent of income, mandated by the Torah—as well as keeping fasts that are not scripturally mandated.

  * It would in fact be shocking, according to ancient mores, for parents to ask for a leader's attention for their young children, let alone for babies.

  † From the Ten Commandments, at Exodus 20:1–17 and Deuteronomy 5:6–21.

god's kingdom." ²⁶ But those who heard him said, "Then who can be rescued?"* ²⁷ And he said, "The things that are impossible for human beings are possible for god."

²⁸ But Petros said, "Look, we left behind what was ours and followed you." ²⁹ And he said to them, "*Amēn* I tell you that there's nobody who left a house or a wife or brothers or parents or children because of god's kingdom ³⁰ who won't get them [back] many times over right now, in the present, as well as life throughout the ages in the age that's coming."†

³¹ Now Iēsous took the twelve aside and said to them, "Look, we're going up to Ierousalēm, and everything that's been written by the prophets will be fulfilled for the son of mankind. ³² He'll in fact be handed over to the foreign nations, and taunted and treated outrageously and spat on, ³³ and they'll flog him and kill him, but three days later‡ he'll awaken." ³⁴ But they understood nothing of these things, and this message was hidden from them, and they didn't realize what was being said.

³⁵ Now it happened that when he was approaching Ierichō, a certain blind man was sitting beside the road, begging. ³⁶ When he heard the crowd making its way past, he asked what was happening there. ³⁷ They gave him the news that Iēsous the Nazōraios was going by. ³⁸ Then he shouted the words "Iēsous, son of David, have pity on me!" ³⁹ And those walking ahead of Iēsous scolded the man, telling him to be quiet, but he only yelled much louder, "Son of David, have pity on me!" ⁴⁰ Stopping, Iēsous ordered the man to be brought to him and when he came near, he asked him, ⁴¹ "What do you want me to do for you?" And he said, "Lord, I want to see again." ⁴² And Iēsous said to him, "See again! Your

---

* Wealth had normally been considered good in itself, and the means to carry out religious and charitable duties.

† A witty promise: a home and loved ones are most worth having—but not when extravagantly multiplied.

‡ Again, reckoned from only two nights and one full day.

trust has healed you." ⁴³ And there and then he regained his sight, and he followed Iēsous, glorifying god. And the whole of the people, when they saw this, gave praise to god.

CHAPTER 19

¹ Then he entered Ierichō and was passing through it. ² But look, there was a man who was called by the name Zakchaios, and he was the chief tax-collector, and was personally wealthy;* ³ and he was trying to see which one Iēsous was, but due to the crowd he couldn't, because he hadn't grown to a normal height, and was still small. ⁴ So he ran ahead and climbed up a sycamore tree to see Iēsous, as he was about to pass through by that route. ⁵ And when Iēsous came to the spot, he looked up and said to him, "Zakchaios, hurry up and climb down, because I need to stay at your house today." ⁶ And he hurried and climbed down, and welcomed him with joy. ⁷ And when they saw, everyone complained loudly, saying, "He's gone in to relax as the guest of a man who's a criminal." ⁸ But Zakchaios stood fast and said to the master: "Look, master, I'm giving away half of my property to the destitute, and if I've extorted anyone, I'm paying him back four times as much."† ⁹ And Iēsous said to him, "A rescue has come to this house, seeing that he's a son of Abraam too;‡ ¹⁰ the son of mankind has in fact come to seek out and rescue what was lost."

¹¹ While they were listening to these things, he went on to tell them a story for the sake of comparison, because he was near

---

* An Imperial provincial tax collection contracting business was in practice allowed to operate privately for profit maximization.

† Both Jewish and Roman law prescribed awards of multiple damages, so it might look as if this man is passing judgment on himself, his victims not being in a position to bring a lawsuit.

‡ He has a Jewish name; tax collectors appear to have been ostracized from the mainstream of local communities in the Judean province.

Ierousalēm and they thought that god's kingdom was about to appear then and there;* ¹² so he said: "A certain man from a noble family made a journey to a distant country to claim a kingship for himself and then return home.† ¹³ But before he left he called ten of his slaves, gave them ten minas,‡ and said to them, 'Do some business until I come back.' ¹⁴ But the citizens of his country hated him, and they sent a follow-up delegation saying, 'We don't want him to be king over us.' ¹⁵ And it happened that when he came back, having received the kingship, he had those slaves to whom he'd given the silver called to him, so that he could find out what kind of profit they'd made. ¹⁶ Now, the first one appeared before him, saying, 'Master, your mina has earned ten minas more!' ¹⁷ And he said to him, 'Good for you, excellent slave! Since you were trustworthy in this very small matter, take power over ten cities.' ¹⁸ Then the second one came, saying, 'Your mina, master, has made five minas!' ¹⁹ And he said to this one in his turn: 'You too—take over five cities.' ²⁰ Then the third one came and said, 'Master, look, it's your mina, which I kept stored away in a handkerchief; ²¹ I was afraid of you, you see, because you're a hard man: you take for yourself what you haven't left in safekeeping and harvest what you haven't sown.'§ ²² He said to him, 'I'll judge you by the words from your own mouth, useless slave. You knew I'm a hard man, taking for myself what I haven't left in

---

* The events in the Gospels present a fundamental interpretive problem articulated here: If Jesus was so important, why did this not manifest quickly and unmistakably in history?

† In the Roman Imperial system, selected members of the indigenous ruling class might be given the title of ruler and limited power to run local affairs. This man probably travels a long way for his investiture by the Romans.

‡ A mina (*mna*) was worth a hundred Greek drachmae, and a drachma was almost exactly equivalent to a denarius, a standard day's wage.

§ The Roman laws on "deposit," or the safekeeping of goods in the owners' absence, were stringent, and were an underpinning of sophisticated Imperial finance; and property rights related to agriculture—now a massive international industry—were the ancient basis for the Roman legal system. God is depicted here as a sharp dealer, even in contrast to Empire-wide materialistic legal norms.

safekeeping, and harvesting what I haven't sown? ²³ So what was the reason you didn't deposit my silver on a banker's table? Then I could have collected it, along with its "offspring," when I came back.'* ²⁴ Then he said to those at hand, 'Take the mina from him and give it to the one who has ten minas.' ²⁵ But they said to him, 'Master, he *has* ten minas.' ²⁶ 'I tell you that everyone who has something will be given more, while if someone doesn't have something, even what he does have will be taken away. ²⁷ And another thing: those enemies of mine who didn't want me to be king over them—bring them here and slaughter them in front of me.' "

²⁸ And once he'd said these things, he continued ahead on his way, going up toward Hierosoluma.

²⁹ And it happened that when he approached Bēthfagē and Bēthania near the place named the Mountain of Olives,† he sent off two of his students, ³⁰ saying, "Get moving and go to the village ahead, and as soon as you enter it you'll find a colt‡ tied up, which no one has ever ridden; then untie him and bring him here. ³¹ And if someone asks you, 'What's the reason you're untying him?' simply say, 'His master needs him.' " ³² The ones he sent went away and found things were just as he had told them. ³³ As they were untying the colt, his masters said to them, "Why are you untying that colt?" ³⁴ And they answered, "Because his master needs him."§ ³⁵ And they brought him to Iēsous and threw

* Jews were scripturally forbidden to lend money for interest, but lending to and through non-Jews were workarounds.

† The villages are associated with the modern village al-Eizariya, on the far side of the Mount of Olives from Jerusalem. Here the mountain has, unusually, a formal, capitalized name.

‡ A young horse, donkey, or mule; the tradition indicates a donkey.

§ The play on words that may exist in Mark and Matthew—it is unclear in the Greek whether "of him" (or "of them," the dam and her colt) goes with "master" (which can mean "owner") or with the noun "need"—is made quite explicit here, as the colt's legal "masters/owners" actually show up to object, but seem to cede to the witty assertion that Jesus is the true "master/owner."

their cloaks over the colt, and they mounted Iēsous on him.
³⁶ And as he made his journey, they spread their cloaks down on
the road.* ³⁷ And when he drew near the path down the mountain with the olive trees, the whole crowd of his students, in their
joy, began to praise god with loud shouts for all the acts of power
that they had seen, ³⁸ and their words were:

> *"Blessed is the one who's coming,*
> *The king, in the name of the lord;*
> *Peace is in the sky,*
> *And glory in the highest places!"*†

³⁹ Then some of the Farisaioi in the crowd said to him,
"Teacher, take your students to task." ⁴⁰ But he answered by saying, "I tell you, if they fall silent, the stones will cry out."

⁴¹ And when he drew near and saw the city, he cried over her,
⁴² saying, "If only you too had known, on this day, what would
bring peace—! As things are, that's hidden from your eyes. ⁴³ But
surely the days will find you when your enemies set up a barri-
cade against you and encircle you all around, and close in on you
on every side. ⁴⁴ And they'll bring you, and your children inside
you, level with the ground, and they won't leave one stone in you
on top of another, to pay you back for not recognizing the time
when god was here, watching over you."‡

---

* See Esther 6:6–9 concerning the splendor and power implied by ceremoni-
ous riding.

† See Psalms 118:26. This last sentence in the chant is likely a statement of fact
and not a wish or a plea.

‡ This describes the siege and destruction of Jerusalem by the Romans in
70 C.E., and it suggests a Roman viewpoint. There is perhaps even an allusion to
the signature Roman circumvallation, or siege enclosure, barring both the escape
of anyone in the city and the arrival of relief forces or supplies from elsewhere.
The "pacification" of a polity is also one way Romans termed its reduction and
decimation. But at the end of the passage, the idea often translated as "visitation"
(in Greek, literally "looking-on," though the Hebrew word is the less pointed
pagad), or the gracious attention of God, brings home that Jews in particular are

⁴⁵ Then, once he came into the temple precinct, he began to throw out the vendors, saying to them, ⁴⁶ "It's been written,

> "'And my house will be a house of prayer,'
> but you made it a cave where bandits lurk.'"*

⁴⁷ And there he was, teaching in the temple precinct day after day. And the high priests and the scholars and the leading men among the people were seeking to destroy him, ⁴⁸ but they couldn't find a way to do it, as the whole of the people were glued to him, listening.

CHAPTER 20

———

¹ And it happened that, on one of the days when he was teaching the people in the temple precinct and giving the good news, the high priests and the scholars, along with the elders, loomed near ² and spoke, addressing him: "Tell us, by what authority do you do these things, or who is it who gave you this authority?" ³ In answer, he said to them, "I'm going to question you myself about a matter, and you must answer me. ⁴ Did the baptism Iōannēs carried out come from heaven or from human beings?" ⁵ And they tried to work it out among themselves, in these terms: "If we say 'From heaven,' he'll say, 'Then why didn't you trust him?' ⁶ But if we say 'From human beings,' the people as a whole are going to stone us, as they've come to believe that Iōannēs was a prophet." ⁷ So they answered that they didn't know where it had

---

being punished, and for the reason often adduced: they disregarded God's favor and tried his patience too long. The passage has been used to date the Gospel of Luke as definitely after the year 70.

* See the note at Mark 11:17. The verses quoted are Isaiah 56:7 and Jeremiah 7:11.

come from. ⁸ And Iēsous said to them: "*I*'m not telling you either by what authority I do these things."

⁹ And he undertook to tell the people this story for the sake of comparison: "A [certain] man planted a vineyard, then leased it to farmers and went abroad for a considerable time. ¹⁰ And at the proper time he dispatched his slave to the farmers so that they could give him a share of the vineyard's harvest. But the farmers nearly skinned him alive, and sent him away empty-handed. ¹¹ Then the owner tried again, sending another slave, but they nearly skinned him alive too, and treated him shamefully,* and sent him away empty-handed. ¹² Then he tried again, sending a third slave, and on this one they inflicted some serious wounds and threw him out. ¹³ Then the owner of the vineyard said, 'What am I going to do? I'll send my son, whom I love. Perhaps they'll have respect for him.' ¹⁴ But when they saw him, the farmers worked it out with each other and said, 'This is the heir. Let's kill him, so that the inheritance will be ours.' ¹⁵ And they threw him out of the vineyard and killed him. So what will the owner of the vineyard do to them? ¹⁶ He'll come and destroy those farmers and give the vineyard to others."†

Those who heard this said, "May that never happen!" ¹⁷ But he gave them a penetrating look and told them, "Then what's this mean, that's been written?

"'*The stone that the builders tested and rejected—*
It turned out to head up the corner.'‡

¹⁸ "Everybody who falls over that stone will be shattered, and anyone on whom it falls will be pulverized."

---

* Probably meaning that they raped him.

† I.e., the Jewish inheritance, their covenant, will go to Gentiles.

‡ Psalms 118:22: "for the head of the corner" is an architecturally vague image of one stone stabilizing a building.

¹⁹ And at that very time, the scholars and the high priests were trying to get their hands on him, but they were afraid of the crowd, since they knew that they themselves were the target of this story he'd told.

²⁰ Then they watched closely and sent spies, who were acting the part of upright people, so that they could use what he said against him, which would provide a chance to turn him over to the control and authority of the governor.* ²¹ And they questioned him, saying, "Teacher, we know that what you say and teach is straightforwardly correct, and that you don't judge with favoritism, but rather on the basis of truth you teach god's path. ²² Is it permitted for us to pay tax to Kaisar or not?" ²³ But detecting their malice, he said to them, ²⁴ "Show me a denarius. Whose image and inscription does it have on it?" They said, "Kaisar's." ²⁵ He told them, "In that case, pay Kaisar what belongs to Kaisar—give it right back to him—and pay god what belongs to god."† ²⁶ And they weren't able to use against him what he said in front of the people, so they fell silent, amazed at his answer.

²⁷ And certain Saddoukaioi came to him, people who say [in contradiction] that there is no rising of the dead again;‡ and they questioned him, ²⁸ saying, "Teacher, Mōusēs wrote down for us that if someone's brother dies when he has a wife but is childless, his brother has to take the wife and raise up seed for his brother.§ ²⁹ So there were seven brothers. And the first one took a wife but died childless. ³⁰ Then the second ³¹ and then the third took her, and it actually went the same way with all seven, who died without leaving children. ³² Finally, the wife died too. ³³ So when the

* Though the Jewish authorities rule in religious matters, they are wary of impinging on Roman law-enforcement prerogatives.

† See the notes on the Mark passage at 12:13–17.

‡ As characterized by the Jewish-Roman historian Josephus, the Sadducees were an elite sect overlapping with the priesthood.

§ Levirate marriage, as described in Genesis 38:8 and Deuteronomy 25:5–6.

dead rise, whose wife will the woman be? All seven in fact had her as a wife."

³⁴ But Iēsous said to them, "The children of this world of time* take wives and are given as wives, ³⁵ but those who are judged worthy to partake in that other world of unending time and in the rising from among the dead don't take wives, and aren't given as wives either. ³⁶ They also in fact can no longer die, as they're equals of the messengers, and they're children of god, being children of rising again. ³⁷ That the dead rise Mōüsēs himself showed in the passage about the bush, when he spoke of the lord as 'the god of Abraam and the god of Isaak and the god of Iakōb.' ³⁸ God isn't a god of corpses but of living people, because through him they are all alive."†

³⁹ In response, some of the scholars said, "Teacher, that was the right thing to say!" ⁴⁰ They in fact no longer dared to ask him anything.

⁴¹ Then he said to them, "What do they mean by saying that the anointed one is David's son? ⁴² In fact, David himself says, in the book of praise songs:‡

> "*'The lord said to my lord:*
> *"Sit to the right of me*
> ⁴³ *Until I put your enemies*
> *Under your feet."'*

⁴⁴ "David thus calls him lord, so how is he his son?"§

⁴⁵ With the whole of the people hearing, he said to [his] stu-

---

* Literally "of this age," but tricky to translate with the full meaning. See "time" in the Glossary.

† See the notes on the Mark version of the passage at 12:18–27.

‡ This is the literal meaning of "psalms," our English word for which is based on the Greek and Hebrew title for this biblical book.

§ The quotation is from the beginning of Psalm 110 but is construed here as David addressing the Messiah, not (which is probable) as a court musician representing God addressing David.

dents, ⁴⁶"Be on your guard against the scholars, who're always ready to walk around in long robes and love to be greeted respectfully in the marketplaces, and to have the seats of highest honor in the synagogues, and the couches of highest honor at banquets.* ⁴⁷They wolf down the homes of widows and say long prayers as a pretext. They're going to get a heavier verdict given on *them* than they ever gave!"†

CHAPTER 21

¹Looking up, he saw the wealthy putting their offerings into the treasury, ²but then he saw a certain needy widow there putting in two lepta,‡ ³and he said, "I tell you truly that this destitute widow put in more than everybody else did; ⁴they all of course put in offerings out of their excess, but she did it out of her shortfall, putting in the whole of what she had to live on."

⁵While some were speaking about the temple, and the beautiful stones and votive offerings that decorated it,§ he said, ⁶"These things that you're all gazing at—there will come days when there won't be one stone left on top of another: every one of them will be torn down."¶

---

* Literally, they sit in the "first chairs" (our word "cathedral" comes from a Christian bishop's claim to such a seat) and lie on the "first couches."

† In their (for us not well defined) capacity as experts in jurisprudence or as magistrates in practice.

‡ A vanishingly small currency.

§ There was scriptural allowance for freewill, votive, and other supplementary offerings (Deuteronomy 12:5–6 and 11), which could take the form of implements and decorations. Openly personal and specific votive offerings—images of healed body parts, for example—to pay for divine help were usual in pagan temples, but a *do ut des* ("I give so that you give") attitude toward divinity was not characteristic of Jews.

¶ The magnificent renovated Second Temple was destroyed by the Romans in 70 C.E.

⁷ Then they questioned him, saying, "Teacher, so when will these things take place, and what will be the sign for when they're about to happen?" ⁸ And he said, "See to it that you're not led astray. A lot of people will come in my name, saying, 'It's me,' and 'The time is close now.' Don't set out following at their backs. ⁹ When you hear about wars and insurrections, don't panic. It's necessary that these things happen first, but the end won't be right away."

¹⁰ Then he said to them, "One nation will rise up against another, and one kingdom against another; ¹¹ there'll be great earthquakes, and there'll be starvation and contagion* in various places, and there will be both terrifying portents and powerful signs from the sky.

¹² "But before all these things, they'll lay hold of you and prosecute you, turning you over to the synagogues and prisons, and you'll be brought before kings and governors because of my name. ¹³ This will result in your testifying. ¹⁴ So resolve in your hearts not to prepare in advance for your defense. ¹⁵ I myself will put clever words in your mouth, which all those who're opposed to you won't be able to withstand or contradict.† ¹⁶ And you'll be handed over even by parents and brothers and other relatives, and by close friends, and they'll put some of you to death. ¹⁷ And you'll be hated by everybody because of my name. ¹⁸ But not a hair on your head will ever be destroyed. ¹⁹ By holding out, you'll be put in secure possession of your lives.‡

²⁰ "But when you see Ierousalēm surrounded by armies, then you'll know that her desolation is close at hand.§ ²¹ Then those in

---

* The wordplay here is intense and not really within the scope of English usage: I render only "starvation and contagion" for the near-twins *limoi* and *loimoi*.

† Especially in Luke, with its style that is on average closer to formal oratory, the advice not to bother preparing a speech in defense of one's life must have sounded strange. The prevailing Greek and Roman education systems aimed above all at rhetorical excellence.

‡ See the note at Matthew 10:23.

§ Events of 70 C.E.

Ioudaia had better run to the mountains, and those in the city had better clear out, and those in the villages had better not come into the city, ²² since these are the days of retribution, for fulfilling everything that has been written. ²³ Pity the women who have children in their wombs, and the women who are nursing, in those days. There will be great distress in the land, and rage toward this people. ²⁴ And they'll fall to the sword's devouring mouth, and they'll be taken as captives to every nation, and Ierousalēm will be trampled by foreign nations, until the crises of those nations are brought to completion.

²⁵ "And there will be signs in the sun and moon and stars, and on earth anguish in nations that are helpless before the crashing, surging sea. ²⁶ People will be half dead from terror, and from dread of the things on the move against all the inhabited world, since the powers of the skies will be shaken; ²⁷ but then they'll see the son of mankind coming on a cloud with power and great glory.* ²⁸ When these things begin to happen, stand up straight from where you're crouching and raise your heads, because your liberation is close at hand."

²⁹ And he gave them an analogy: "You see the fig tree and all the other trees. ³⁰ As soon as they sprout leaves, you can see for yourself and be sure that summer is already near. ³¹ In the same way, when you see these things I've spoken of happening, be sure that god's kingdom is near. ³² *Amēn* I tell you that this generation absolutely won't pass away until everything happens. ³³ The sky and the earth will pass away, but the things I'm saying will absolutely not pass away.

³⁴ "Look out for yourselves, so that your hearts aren't weighed down by wild, drunken parties and the cares of ordinary life:†

---

* Daniel 7:13.

† These two sets of distractions sound incongruous, but fairly exuberant nightly socializing was considered normal and respectable for Greek and Roman men.

then that day won't spring on you suddenly, without warning, [35] like a snare. It will rush in, in fact, on everyone living on the face of the whole earth. [36] So stay awake and on the watch at every juncture, begging to have enough strength to escape all these things that are going to happen, and to stand before the son of mankind."

[37] During the days he was in the temple precinct teaching, but as for the nights, he went out and spent them in the place they call the Mountain of Olives. [38] And the entire people got up early in the morning to come listen to him in the temple precinct.

CHAPTER 22

—

[1] Now the festival of the bread made without yeast, called the *pascha,* was approaching, [2] and the high priests and the scholars were looking for a way to destroy him, as they were afraid of the people.

[3] Then satanas entered into Ioudas, who was called Iskariōtēs, and who counted among the twelve. [4] And he went away and spoke with the high priests and the commanders of the temple guards* about a way to hand him over. [5] And they were thrilled and promised to pay him in silver. [6] And he agreed and was looking for the right moment to hand him over to them, when the crowd wasn't there.

[7] Then came the day of bread made without yeast, [on] which sacrificing the *pascha* was required. [8] And he sent off Petros and Iōannēs, saying, "Be on your way and prepare the *pascha* for us so

---

* Literally, the "generals"; the Jews were allowed a contingent of their own to keep order in the Temple and to deal with internal religious enforcement. These may be the same people the Gospels elsewhere call the Temple hierarchy's "retainers." Police forces in the modern sense did not exist in the ancient world, and law enforcement, such as it was, often depended on leaders' bodyguards.

that we can eat it." ⁹ But they asked him, "Where do you want us to prepare it?" ¹⁰ He said to them, "Look, once you've gone into the city, a person carrying a jar of water will come face to face with you. Follow him into the house he makes his way back to,* ¹¹ and say to the head of that household, 'The teacher asks you, "Where's the accommodation where I can eat the *pascha* along with my students?"' ¹² And that person will show you an upstairs room, large and comfortably furnished: make preparations there." ¹³ And they went away and found it just as he had told them, and they got the *pascha* ready.

¹⁴ And when the time came, he reclined at the table, and his envoys joined him. ¹⁵ And he said to them, "I'm eager beyond eagerness to eat this *pascha* with you before my suffering. ¹⁶ But I tell you, in fact, that I absolutely won't eat it until its purpose is fulfilled in god's kingdom." ¹⁷ Then when he was handed a cup, he gave thanks for it and said, "Take this and share it out among yourselves.† ¹⁸ I tell you, in fact, [that] from now on, I will certainly not drink any of this, which the grapevine yields, until god's kingdom comes." ¹⁹ Then, taking a loaf, he gave thanks for it, broke it into pieces, and gave it to them, saying, "This is my body, given for the sake of you all. Do this to keep me in your minds." ²⁰ And in the same way, he took the cup after they had feasted, saying, "This cup is the new dispensation, through my blood that has been poured out for your sake.‡

²¹ "But look, the hand of the one who's giving me up is with me, on the table,§ ²² because the son of mankind is going on his way, as it's been decreed—but he has it coming, that specimen of

---

* See the note at Mark 14:14.

† The shared cup was customary.

‡ Jesus' abstention from meat and wine on this festival dedicated to their enjoyment is shocking, as (again) is the idea of eating human flesh, and of drinking sacrificial blood like wine, as if the vessels in which it was caught for disposal had been hijacked. Note that in Luke the "dispensation" or covenant is a new one.

§ A "hand" stands for a person's power and willed activity.

mankind by whom he's handed over." ²³ And they began to argue among themselves as to which of them, in that case, was about to do this.

²⁴ But then there also arose a squabble among them as to which of them could be regarded as the greatest. ²⁵ But he said to them, "The kings of the foreign nations act as their masters, and those who have power over them are called 'benefactors.'* ²⁶ But that's not the case for you—it's the opposite: the greatest one among you has to become like the youngest, and whoever's leading has to become like the one serving. ²⁷ Who, after all, is greater, the one reclining at the table or the one serving? Isn't it the one reclining? But I myself, surrounded by you all, am like the one who's serving.

²⁸ "But you're the ones who've endured with me in my ordeals. ²⁹ Hence I make over the kingdom to you, just as my father made it over to me, ³⁰ so that you can eat and drink at my table in my kingdom, and so that you can sit on chairs of state judging the twelve tribes of Israel.

³¹ "Simōn, Simōn, look, satanas has claimed the whole group of you for himself, to sift like grain. ³² But I've pleaded on your behalf, so that your own loyalty won't fall short. But once *you*'ve turned back, give your brothers some backbone." ³³ But Petros said to him, "With you, master, I'm ready to take the path even to prison, and even to death." ³⁴ But he said, "I tell you, Petros, today the rooster won't crow until you deny three times that you know me."

³⁵ And he said to them, "When I sent you out without a wallet or a bag or sandals, did anyone miss anything?" And they said, "No, not a thing." ³⁶ Then he said to them, "Now it's the opposite: whoever has a wallet must take it, and the same for a bag, and

---

* A "benefactor" might be, for example, the person named in an inscription on a building he has donated. The larger situation Jesus suggests is that "good deeds" among the pagans are acknowledged networks of control, whereas for Jews they are supposed to be religious duties.

whoever doesn't have a sword needs to sell his cloak and buy one. ³⁷ I tell you in fact that this, that's been written, must be fulfilled in me: 'And he was counted among the lawless.' And in fact what concerns me has its fulfillment." ³⁸ Then they said, "Master, look, here are two swords." And he said to them, "It's enough."*

³⁹ Then he went out and made his way, according to his habit, to the mountain with the olive trees, and his students followed him as well. ⁴⁰ And once he reached the place, he said to them: "Pray that you don't come to be tested." ⁴¹ But he himself withdrew from them to the distance of a stone's throw, and, falling on his knees, he prayed, ⁴² saying, "Father, if you're willing, take away this cup from me. But even so, what you want must happen, not what I want." ⁴³ [And there appeared to him a messenger from the sky, strengthening him. ⁴⁴ And in his anguish he prayed more strenuously, and his sweat became like clots of blood falling on the ground.] ⁴⁵ Then, standing up after his prayer, he went to his students and found them lying asleep, worn out from their distress. ⁴⁶ And he said to them, "Why are you sleeping? Stand up and pray, so that you don't come to be tested!"

⁴⁷ While he was still speaking, look, a mob came. And the man called Ioudas, one of the twelve, was at the head of it, and he came up to Iēsous to kiss him. ⁴⁸ But Iēsous said to him, "Ioudas, it's with a kiss that you're handing the son of mankind over?" ⁴⁹ But those with him saw what was going to happen, and they said, "Master, what if we strike with a sword?" ⁵⁰ And one of them—someone—struck the chief priest's slave and took off his right ear. ⁵¹ But Iēsous responded by saying, "That's enough of this!" and touching his ear, he healed him.

⁵² Then Iēsous said to those who'd come against him, the high

* Other Gospel prescriptions for traveling gear, including defensive weapons, are largely explainable in terms of Essene rules, but these swords are anomalous: they cannot be hidden by clothes (as could the daggers of the "dagger-men" assassins), and carrying them defies the Roman occupiers and the Jewish authorities as well. Probably this account is distorted to accommodate the expanding tradition of the slave's hacked-off ear; see below at Verses 49–51.

priests and the commanders of the temple guards, and the elders:* "You've come out against me with swords and clubs, as if I were a bandit?† ⁵³ Day after day I was with you in the temple precinct, and you didn't raise your hands against me. But this is your time, and the reign of darkness."

⁵⁴ Taking hold of him, they led him away, and led him into the house of the chief priest, and Petros followed at a distance. ⁵⁵ After they had lit a fire in the center of the courtyard and sat down together, Petros sat down among them. ⁵⁶ But some slave girl, seeing him sitting with his face to the light, glared at him and said, "Him too—he was with him." ⁵⁷ But he denied it, saying, "I don't know him, woman." ⁵⁸ But after a little while, someone else saw him and said, "You too, you're one of them." But Petros said, "It's not me, man." ⁵⁹ Then after about one hour, somebody else insisted, saying, "It's the truth: he was with him too; and he's even a Galilaios." ⁶⁰ But Petros said, "I don't know what you're talking about, man." And then and there, while he was still speaking, the rooster crowed. ⁶¹ And the master turned and gave Petros a penetrating look, and Petros recalled the master's words: he'd said to him, "Before the rooster crows today, you'll deny three times that you know me." ⁶² And he went out and cried bitterly.

⁶³ And the men who had hold of him started to taunt him, beating him savagely ⁶⁴ and wrapping up his head to hide his face,‡ then asking him again and again, "Give a prophecy! Who's the one who hit you?" ⁶⁵ And they aimed many other insults at him.

⁶⁶ Then when the day broke, the people's council of elders gathered, both the high priests and the scholars, and they took him into their council chamber ⁶⁷ and said, "If you're the anointed

---

* See the note at Mark 14:43.

† "Bandits" were groups who had strongholds in the wilderness and could function as insurrectionists.

‡ They "veil him around," possibly an insult with gender overtones.

one, tell us." But he said to them, "If I told you, there's no way you'd believe me. ⁶⁸ And if I asked, there's no way you'd answer. ⁶⁹ But from now on, the son of mankind will be seated to the right of god's power." ⁷⁰ Then they all said, "That means *you*'re god's son?"* But he addressed them: "*You* say I am." ⁷¹ Then they said, "What further testimony do we need? We've heard it ourselves, from his own mouth."

CHAPTER 23

¹ Then their entire assembly got up and took him to Pilatos.

² There they began to accuse him, saying, "We've found him to be leading our nation astray and stopping the people from paying taxes to Kaisar, and saying that he himself is the anointed king."

³ But Pilatos questioned him, saying, "Are you the king of the Ioudaioi?" And in answer, he told him, "*You* say so." ⁴ But Pilatos said to the high priests and the crowds, "I don't find any guilt in this man." ⁵ But they persisted, saying, "With his teaching, he rattles the people throughout Ioudaia, starting from Galilaia and clear to here."

⁶ When he heard this, Pilatos asked whether the man was a Galilaios, ⁷ and when he found out that he was from the jurisdiction of Hērōdēs, he sent him to Hērōdēs,† who was in Hierosoluma himself during those days.

⁸ And when Hērōdēs saw Iēsous, he was overjoyed, because for quite a long time he'd been wanting to see him, since he'd

---

* See the note at Mark 14:61 on how unusual the literal claim would be in this religious context.

† Herod Antipas, a son of Herod the Great, who was client king of Galilee and Perea.

heard about him, and he was hoping to see some sign performed by him. ⁹ So he asked him quite a few questions, but Iēsous gave no answer to him. ¹⁰ But the high priests and the scholars stood there fiercely accusing him. ¹¹ Hērōdēs [too], along with his soldiers, treated him with utter contempt, taunting him and putting splendid apparel on him. Then he sent him back to Pilatos.¹² And Hērōdēs and Pilatos became friends with each other on that exact day; before this, they had been each other's enemies.

¹³ Now Pilatos called together the high priests and the leaders and the people ¹⁴ and said to them, "You brought me this man on the grounds that he was misleading the people, but look, before your eyes I examined him, and I didn't find this man guilty of any of the things you accuse him of. ¹⁵ Neither did Hērōdēs; in fact, he sent him back to us, and look, nothing deserving death has been done by him. ¹⁶ So once I've punished him, I'm going to let him go."*

¹⁸ Then the whole mass of them screamed the words, "Get rid of him, and release Barabbas to us instead!" ¹⁹ Now, *he* had been thrown into prison because of a certain insurrection that had taken place in the city, and murder.† ²⁰ Once again Pilatos called on them, wanting to release Iēsous. ²¹ But they only called out in opposition, saying, "Hang him on the stakes! Hang him on the stakes!"‡ ²² Then he said to them a third time, "What has he in fact done wrong? I've found no guilt in him that's worthy of death. So I'm going to punish him and let him go." ²³ But they pressed hard, demanding with loud voices that he be hung on the stakes, and their voices won out.

²⁴ Then Pilatos gave a verdict to meet their demand. ²⁵ He released the one who'd been thrown into prison for sedition and

---

* Verse 17 has been deleted as spurious. It reads: "He was compelled to release one person to them at every festival." See the note at Mark 15:6.

† See the note at Mark 15:7.

‡ See the note at Mark 15:13.

murder, whom they'd demanded, and he handed over Iēsous to do with as they wished.*

²⁶ And as they led him away, they laid hold of Simōn, a certain Kurēnaios, who was coming from the countryside, and they put the stake on him to carry behind Iēsous.†

²⁷ A great mass of the people followed him, including women who beat their breasts and lamented for him.‡ ²⁸ Turning toward them, Iēsous said, "Daughters of Ierousalēm, don't cry for me. Instead, cry for yourselves and your children, ²⁹ because, look, the days are coming when they'll say, 'The fortunate ones are the women who could have no children, and the wombs that haven't given birth, and the breasts that haven't nursed.' ³⁰ At that time, they'll start to say to the mountains, 'Fall on us!' and to the hills, 'Cover and hide us!' ³¹ Because if they can do these things with wet wood, what's going to happen with dry wood?"§

³² Two others besides, ordinary criminals, were led along with him to be executed.

³³ Then when they came to the place called the Skull,¶ they hung him and the criminals on stakes there, one on his right and one on the "better" side. ³⁴ [But Iēsous said, "Father, pardon them, since they don't know what they're doing."]** And they divided his clothes, throwing lots for them.

---

* An anti-Semitic authorial dodge; of course Jesus remains in Roman custody and is executed by the Romans.

† Creating porters by impression was a (purportedly regulated) right of Roman soldiers. It was normal for the condemned to carry only the horizontal crosspiece.

‡ Women played special roles in mourning, as in burial.

§ Verse 30 quotes Hosea 10:8. These predictions seem to refer to the First Jewish–Roman War (66–73 C.E.), during which the Temple was destroyed and Judea brutally reduced. The wet and dry wood probably mean the relatively mild unrest at the time of Jesus' execution versus the full-scale rebellion that ended Roman patience with the province.

¶ By tradition, the site of the Church of the Holy Sepulcher. Even in antiquity, a busy thoroughfare passed by it.

** This quotation is thought to be an early insertion in the textual tradition.

³⁵ And the people stood there, looking on. But the leaders turned up their noses and sneered at him, saying, "He rescued other people; he'd better rescue himself now, if he's god's anointed, the chosen one." ³⁶ And the soldiers taunted him as they came up to him, offering him vinegar* ³⁷ and saying, "If you're the king of the Ioudaioi, rescue yourself!" ³⁸ And there was also a notice written above him:

"This is the king of the Ioudaioi."†

³⁹ And one of the criminals hanging there insulted him, saying, "Aren't you the anointed one? Rescue yourself and us." ⁴⁰ But the other responded by scolding him, saying, "Don't you even fear god, just because you're subject to the same verdict? ⁴¹ And for us, it was the right one, since we're only getting what we deserve for what we did. But he didn't do any harm." ⁴² And he said, "Iēsous, think of me when you come into your kingdom." ⁴³ And he said to him, "*Amēn* I tell you, today you will be with me in paradise."

⁴⁴ And by this time it was about the sixth hour after dawn, but darkness fell on the whole earth until the ninth hour, ⁴⁵ the sun's light failed, and the curtain of the temple's inner shrine split in half. ⁴⁶ And Iēsous cried out, and these were the words of that loud cry: "Father, into your hands I give over my life's breath," and when he'd said this, he breathed his last.

⁴⁷ And the centurion, seeing what had happened, glorified god, saying, "Really, this man was in the right." ⁴⁸ And all the crowds that had come together there to watch this spectacle returned home beating their breasts, having watched what happened.

⁴⁹ But all those he knew, including the women who had fol-

---

* Their own standard drink when on duty.

† A *titulus* explaining the offense was customarily posted over the head of the crucified.

lowed along with him from Galilaia, stood at a distance, seeing these things.

⁵⁰ But look, there was a man by the name of Iōsēf, who was a councilor, [and] an excellent and upright man. ⁵¹ He had not consented to their counsel in taking this action;* he was from Arimathaia, a city of the Ioudaioi,† and he was waiting for god's kingdom. ⁵² He approached Pilatos and asked him for Iēsous' body, ⁵³ and he took it down and wrapped it in linen, and placed it in a tomb cut out of solid rock, where no one had been laid yet.‡ ⁵⁴ And it was the day of preparation, but the dawn of the *sabbata* was breaking.§

⁵⁵ Following along, the women who had come with him from Galilaia observed the tomb and how his body was placed in it. ⁵⁶ And they returned and prepared aromatic spices and perfumes. But over the *sabbaton,* they rested, according to the command.¶

CHAPTER 24

¹ On the first day of the *sabbata* week, in the deep dark of dawn, they went to the tomb, carrying the aromatic spices that they had prepared, ² but they found the stone rolled away from the

---

* Joseph is a member of the Sanhedrin or Jewish governing council. There is wordplay here between *bouleutēs* (councilor) and *boulē* (counsel or plan).

† Since it has to be identified in such a basic way, it was probably no more familiar to contemporary readers than it is to us.

‡ The double luxury of the gift is stressed: tombs made out of solid rock were expensive and special, and archaeology shows that they were often abundantly shared. Jesus has a brand-new one all to himself.

§ The Sabbath with its prohibition of many activities would presumably start at nightfall, as in postantique times, so Jesus' body would have needed to be taken down and buried before then. Also, Deuteronomy 21:22–23 forbids corpses of the executed ever to be hung on display overnight.

¶ One of the Ten Commandments: see Exodus 20:8–11 and Deuteronomy 5:12–15.

tomb. ³ Going inside, they didn't find the body of the master Iēsous. ⁴ While they were at a loss about this, look, two men stood near them in garments shining like lightning. ⁵ They were terrified and bowed down their faces to the ground, and the men said to them: "Why are you looking among the dead for someone who's alive? ⁶ He isn't here. No, he's awakened. Do you remember how he spoke to you when he was still in Galilaia, ⁷ telling you that the son of humankind had to be handed over to human wrongdoers, and be hung on the stakes, and awaken on the third day?" ⁸ Then they remembered the things he'd said.

⁹ Then when they'd returned from the tomb, they brought news of all these things to the eleven, and to all the others. ¹⁰ The women were the Magdalēnē Maria and Iōanna and Maria the mother of Iakōbos and the others who were with them, and they told the envoys these things. ¹¹ But in their eyes, these statements seemed like nonsense, and they didn't believe the women. ¹² But Petros got up and ran to the tomb, and when he bent down, he saw only the linen wrapping-cloths, and he went back to where he was staying, baffled at what had happened.

¹³ But look, on that same day, two of them were traveling to a village that was sixty stades from Ierousalēm, and the village's name was Emmaous,* ¹⁴ and they were conversing with each other about all these things that had transpired. ¹⁵ And it happened that as they were conversing and having their discussion, Iēsous himself came near and joined them on their journey. ¹⁶ But their eyes were overpowered, so that they couldn't recognize him.† ¹⁷ And he said to them, "What are these things you're talking back and forth about while walking along?" And they stopped and stood there, with gloomy expressions. ¹⁸ And one of them,

---

* By this measure about eleven and a half kilometers or seven miles from Jerusalem, the village has not been firmly identified and may no longer exist.

† A traveler in the Near East might not necessarily be recognizable anyway, as his cloak would be worn over his head during any long journey, to prevent sunstroke.

whose name was Kleopas, said to him by way of an answer, "Are you the only one staying in Ierousalēm who doesn't know the things that happened in the city during these recent days?" ¹⁹ And he said to them, "What kind of things?" And they said to him, "Things to do with Iēsous the Nazarēnos, who became a significant man, a prophet*—powerful in actions and speech in the eyes of god and all the people; ²⁰ and how our high priests and other leaders handed him over to be condemned to death, and they hung him on the stakes. ²¹ But we hoped that he was the one to set Israēl free. But it's just the opposite: besides everything we just told you, the third day's passing since these things happened. ²² On the other hand, some women who belong to our group shocked us out of our senses: they were at the tomb at dawn, ²³ and when they didn't find his body, they came and told us that they'd actually seen a vision of messengers who said that he was alive. ²⁴ Then some of those who were with us went to the tomb and found that it was just like the women had said—but they didn't see him." ²⁵ And he said to them, "Oh, mindless people, and so slow in your hearts to trust in everything the prophets said! ²⁶ Wasn't it necessary for the anointed one to endure these things before entering into his glory?" ²⁷ And starting from Mōüsēs and all the prophets, he explained to them what concerned himself in all the writings.†

²⁸ And they neared the village to which they were traveling, but he acted as if he were traveling farther. ²⁹ Then they put hospitable pressure on him, saying, "Stay with us, because it's almost evening, and already the day is drawing to a close." And he went in to stay with them. ³⁰ Then it happened that when he lay down at the table with them, and took the loaf and blessed it and broke

---

* Literally, the speaker calls Jesus a "man prophet," using the respectful term for "man." (See the Glossary.) He is perhaps shown groping for the right way to describe Jesus.

† Moses was said to be the author of the Torah, or first five books of the Hebrew Bible, which along with the prophetic books were the core of Jewish scripture.

it into pieces and gave it to them, ³¹ their eyes were opened, and they recognized him. But then he disappeared from their sight. ³² And they said to one another, "Weren't our hearts on fire [inside us], when he spoke to us on the road, and when he opened up to us what the writings mean?"

³³ So within the hour, they got up and returned to Ierousalēm, and found the eleven and those who were with them all gathered together ³⁴ and saying, "Really, the master has awakened, and he was seen by Simōn." ³⁵ Then the two took them through what had happened on the road and how he'd been recognized by them through the act of breaking the loaf.

³⁶ But while they were still saying these things, he himself stood among them, and said to them, "Peace to you!" ³⁷ They were stunned and terrified, thinking they were seeing a spirit. ³⁸ But he said to them, "Why are you so disturbed, and what's the reason these doubts are coming up in your hearts? ³⁹ Look at my hands and my feet, and you'll know it's me, in person. Feel me over and see, because a spirit doesn't have flesh and bones, as you can observe that I have." ⁴⁰ And having said this, he showed them his hands and feet. ⁴¹ But when sheer joy and astonishment still kept them from believing, he said to them, "Do you have anything here that's fit to eat?"* ⁴² So they gave him a piece of broiled fish. ⁴³ And he took it and ate it in front of them.

⁴⁴ Then he said to them, "These are the things I've spoken, which I said to you when I was still with you: that it is necessary for all the things that have been written in the law of Mōüsēs and in the prophets and in the songs of praise to be fulfilled concerning me."† ⁴⁵ Then he opened their minds so that they could understand the writings. ⁴⁶ And he said to them, "It's been written in just this way: the anointed one would suffer but then rise from among the dead on the third day; ⁴⁷ and a new purpose for par-

---

* A rare term, likely ironic and meaning just what I have rendered.

† The Psalms are poems that had musical settings; they were associated with King David and were performed in the Temple by a Levite choir.

don from offenses would be announced in his name to all nations, starting from Ierousalēm. [48] You yourselves are witnesses to these things. [49] And [look,] I'm going to send what my father promised to alight on you; so keep living in the city until you've been clothed with power from on high."*

[50] Now he led them [out] as far as Bēthania, and he raised his hands and blessed them. [51] Then it happened that, while still blessing them, he was separated from them and carried up into the sky.

[52] And they prostrated themselves to him, then returned to Ierousalēm with great joy, [53] and they were in the temple precinct at all times, blessing god.

---

* See Joel 2:28. This verse has also been connected to promises of the Holy Spirit in the Gospels texts, as at John 14:26. The preposition *epi* echoes scenes of Jesus' baptism in which the Spirit "alights" or "settles" on him like a dove.

The Good News
According to Iōannēs

Chapter 1

¹ At the inauguration was the true account, and this true account was with god, and god was the true account. ² He was, at the inauguration, with god. ³ Everything came into being through him, and apart from him not even a single thing came into being. What came into being ⁴ in him was life, and that life was the light of humankind. ⁵ And the light appears, radiant in the darkness, and the darkness did not take hold of it.*

⁶ There arose a man, sent by god, and his name was Iōannēs. ⁷ He came to give testimony, to testify about the light, so that everyone could believe through him. ⁸ But he was not the light; instead, he came to testify about the light.

⁹ It was the true light, which, as it comes into the universe, gives light to every human being.† ¹⁰ And he was in the universe, and the universe arose through him, but the universe didn't rec-

---

* John's opening reflects both the first verses of the Genesis creation story and Greek philosophical language. See "W/word" (or *logos*) and "beginning" in the Glossary. I render *logos* here as "true account." The pronoun used in translation for this term could be either "it" or "he" (I opt for the masculine), a thematic ambiguity: the abstraction and the person merge.

† The Greek does not leave it certain whether the light or every human being is "coming into the universe." "The coming one" is a messianic designation.

ognize him.* [11] He came into what belonged to him, but the people who belonged to him didn't accept him for themselves. [12] But to all those who accepted him, he gave the power to become, to be born, children of god, if they trusted in his name.† [13] These are the people who have been engendered not in a blood relationship, and not from what the body wants, and not from what a husband wants, but from god.‡

[14] And the spoken word, the true account, became flesh and blood, and built a shelter and sojourned§ among us, and we gazed on his splendor, a splendor that a father's only son has, full of joyful favor and truth.¶ [15] Iōannēs testified about him and shouted these words: "This was the one I spoke of: 'The one coming after me arose *before* me, because he was first, at the head of me.' [16] Out of what fills him to the full, we have all been given a share, joyful favor in exchange for joyful favor.** [17] The law was given through Mōüsēs,†† but favor and truth came into being through Iēsous, the Anointed One. [18] No one has ever seen god. But the only-

---

* The "light" of Verse 9, a neuter noun, yields a masculine pronoun in Verse 10, so the symbolic thing seems to merge into a person.

† Name is the essence of identity, and correct naming the basis of a correct relationship. Deities must always be called on by their correct names.

‡ See "birth, give/be born" in the Glossary. *Ginomai* is used once in Verse 12, *gennaō* once in Verse 13.

§ The verb reflects the Jewish patriarchs' nomadic life. The verb is also connected to the "tabernacle," the holy tent in which the Israelites are said to have worshipped before the Temple's existence.

¶ Jewish tradition included very favorable inheritance conditions for the firstborn son. Ideally for avoiding conflict and disappointment, a Jewish family would have a single thriving son, a "favor/delight/free gift" (see "grace" in the Glossary) and a vessel of "truth" because his mother is virtuous and his paternity undoubted.

** Attached to words of giving or receiving, the Greek preposition *anti* normally means "in exchange for." Its meaning in this verse likely refers to a two-sided (though of course unequal) relationship with the deity.

†† Moses is traditionally called the author of the first five books of the Bible, the Torah or Teaching, which contain both fundamental and detailed Jewish law.

born god, who is in the father's lap,* made the father understandable."

¹⁹ And this was the testimony of Iōannēs, when the Ioudaioi† dispatched priests and Leuitai‡ out of Hierosoluma [to him] to ask him, "Who are you?" ²⁰ And he admitted who he wasn't, without any denial: he admitted, "I am not the anointed one." ²¹ So they asked him, "What, then? Are you Ēlias?" And he said, "I am not." "The prophet—is that who you are?"§ And he answered, "No." ²² So they said to him, "Who are you? Allow us to give an answer to the people who sent us. What do you say about yourself?" ²³ He said,

> *"I'm the voice of someone shouting in the wasteland,*
> *'Make the lord's road straight!'*

as Ēsaïas the prophet said."¶

²⁴ Now, they had been sent from the Farisaioi,** ²⁵ and they

---

* Cleopatra had popularized an image of herself holding her infant son against her chest (*kolpos*), a propagandistic reflection of the goddess Isis with her son Horus. This influenced eventual Christian pictorial images of the divine child: he is always held by his mother and not by his father, as here.

† The Gospel of John can be particularly odd-sounding in its references to "the Jews" as if they were a separate people from Jesus and his adherents.

‡ The hereditary priesthood (concerned with Temple sacrifice) and the Levites (also a hereditary class, representing one of the Twelve Tribes of Israel, with other important religious duties) concentrate Jerusalem's traditional authority.

§ Elijah was a very important pagan-slaughtering, miracle-working, worship-purifying, tyrant-persecuting prophet. The next question may allude to Moses, a "prophet" of liberation from foreign bondage as well as a channel of the law; see Deuteronomy 18:15 and 18.

¶ Isaiah 40:3; see the note at Mark 1:3.

** When the Gospel of John appeared, at least a generation after the loss of the Temple and its rituals in 70 c.e., proponents of rabbinic Judaism—which was the new dispensation the Pharisees propagated—were rising in influence, while Christianity continued to spread.

questioned him, saying to him, "So why do you baptize,* if you're not the anointed one, and not Ēlias, and not the prophet?" [26] Iōannēs answered them with these words: "I baptize with water. Among you stands someone you don't know, [27] who is coming after me, and whose sandal thong I [myself] don't deserve to untie."† [28] These things happened in Bēthania, across the Iordanēs,‡ where Iōannēs was baptizing.

[29] The next day, he saw Iēsous coming toward him, and he said, "Look, it's god's lamb, who takes away the world's wrong-doing.§ [30] This is the one I told you about when I said, 'The man coming after me arose *before* me, because he was first, at the head of me.' [31] And I myself didn't know him then, but the purpose for which I came, baptizing in water, was for him to be revealed to Israēl." [32] Iōannēs also testified by saying, "I've watched the life-breath coming down out of the sky, appearing as a dove, and it settled on him. [33] But I myself didn't know him; no, the one who sent me to baptize in water—he told me, 'On whomever you see the life-breath coming down and settling, this is the one who baptizes people in the holy life-breath.' [34] So I've seen and testi-fied that this is god's son."¶

[35] The next day, Iōannēs was again standing with two of his students, [36] and when he saw Iēsous walking around, he said, "Look, it's god's lamb." [37] And his two students heard him speak-ing and followed Iēsous. [38] Now, Iēsous turned around and gazed at them following him, and he said to them, "What are you look-

---

* See the note at Mark 1:4 concerning baptism.

† The comparison rests, as usual, on a menial and dirty task of slaves and servants.

‡ The town of Bethany was close to Jerusalem, to the east, and on the west side of the Jordan.

§ Here the Temple sacrifices made as "sin offerings" are probably conflated with the sacrifice of a Passover lamb, one for each household, for the festival of the unleavened bread that marked the freeing of the Israelites from Egyptian slavery.

¶ See the note at Mark 1:10.

ing for?" And they said to him, *"Rabbi"*—which means, when translated, "teacher"*—"where are you staying?" ³⁹ He said to them, "Come and see." So they went and saw where he was staying and stayed with him the rest of that day; it was about the tenth hour after dawn.

⁴⁰ Andreas the brother of Simōn Petros was one of the two men who heard what Iōannēs said and followed Iēsous. ⁴¹ The first thing he did was to find his own brother Simōn and say to him, "We've found the Messias," which is translated as "anointed."†
⁴² Andreas took him to Iēsous. Iēsous looked closely at him and said, "You're Simōn the son of Iōannēs: you're going to be called Kēfas," which translates as Petros or "Stone."‡

⁴³ The next day, he wanted to set out for Galilaia,§ so he found Filippos. And Iēsous said to him, "Follow me." ⁴⁴ Now, Filippos was from Bēthsaïda,¶ the same town Andreas and Petros were from. ⁴⁵ Filippos found Nathanaēl and said to him, "The one Mōüsēs wrote about in the book of the law, and the one the prophets wrote about—we've found him. He's Iēsous the son of Iōsēf from Nazaret." ⁴⁶ But Nathanaēl said to him, "Can anything worthwhile come out of Nazaret?" Filippos told him, "Come and see!" ⁴⁷ Iēsous saw Nathanaēl coming toward him, and spoke about him: "Look, this is truly an Israēlitēs—nothing underhand in *him!*" ⁴⁸ And Nathanaēl said to him, "How is it you know me?" Iēsous answered by telling him, "Before Filippos called you, I saw you under the fig tree." ⁴⁹ Nathanaēl replied to him, *"Rabbí,* you're god's son, you're the king of Israēl." ⁵⁰ Iēsous answered by

---

* Not quite: See "rabbi" and "teacher" in the Glossary.

† See "Christ" in the Glossary.

‡ See the second note at Mark 3:16.

§ Again, Jesus' own home, the town of Nazareth, was in this hilly, more sparsely settled, and independent-spirited region, at the time ruled by the Romans' client king Herod Antipas, a son of Herod the Great.

¶ The town of Bethsaida was near the northern shore of the Sea of Galilee, and the resources of fishing and navigation would have made it a more important town than Nazareth.

telling him, "Just because I told you I saw you underneath the fig tree, you believe? You're going to see greater things than this!" ⁵¹ Then he said to him, "*Amēn amēn* I say to you all: you'll see the sky opened and the messengers of god going up and coming down in the presence of mankind's son."*

CHAPTER 2

¹ On the third day after this, there was a wedding in Kana in Galilaia,† and Iēsous' mother was there. ² And Iēsous as well, along with his students, was invited to the wedding. ³ And when the wine fell short, Iēsous' mother said to him, "They don't have any more wine."‡ ⁴ [Then] Iēsous said to her, "What business could you have with me, woman? My time hasn't come yet." ⁵ His mother said to the servers, "Whatever he tells you, do it." ⁶ In that place there were, lying on the floor, six water jars, such as the Ioudaioi use for cleansing themselves, and each of the jars was big enough for two or three measures of liquid.§ ⁷ Iēsous told the people, "Fill the jars with water," and they filled them to the top. ⁸ Then he said to them, "Now draw out some of what's inside and take it to the man presiding over the dining room." They took it to him. ⁹ When the man presiding tasted the water, now

---

* The word Jesus uses for Nathanael's nationality harks back to a much earlier and more powerful stage of Jewish history. The fig tree is a symbol of national peace and prosperity (1 Kings 4:25, Micah 4:4). Jacob (also called Israel) in his youthful exile had a dream of angels going up and down on "Jacob's Ladder," a dream related to his dynasty's God-given destiny (Genesis 28:10–17).

† The location of this town has not been identified.

‡ This is a disaster, as the community feast, and not any religious ceremony, was the heart of an ancient wedding.

§ Cleansing before meals was prescribed in the Jewish law. Each jar would contain somewhere between twenty and thirty gallons.

turned into wine, he didn't know where it had come from—but the servers who had drawn the water knew. The man presiding called the bridegroom aside [10] and said to him: "Everybody serves the good wine first, and then when they're drunk, the wine that's not so good. *You*'ve kept back the good wine until now." [11] In Kana, which is in Galilaia, Iēsous performed this as the first of his signs, and he made his glory bright and clear, and his students trusted in him.

[12] After this, he went down to Kafarnaoum*—himself and his mother and [his] brothers and his students, and there he stayed a few days.

[13] And the *pascha*† of the Ioudaioi was near, and Iēsous went up to Hierosoluma.

[14] And in the temple precinct he found people selling cattle and sheep and doves, and the coin-changers sitting there, [15] and he made a small whip out of small cords and threw them all out of the precinct along with the sheep and cattle, and he poured out the coins of the money-changers on the ground, and he turned the tables upside down. [16] And to those selling doves he said, "Get these things out of here! Don't make my father's house a house for hawking." [17] His students remembered that it had been written: "Zeal for your house will consume me."‡

[18] So the Ioudaioi responded and said to him, "What sign are you showing us, for doing these things?" [19] Iēsous responded by telling them: "Destroy this shrine, and in three days I'll raise it again."§ [20] So the Ioudaioi said, "For forty-six years, they've been

---

* Capernaum is another fishing town on the northern shore of the Sea of Galilee.

† Again, the greatest of the Jerusalem pilgrimage festivals, celebrating the release of the Hebrews from slavery in Egypt.

‡ Psalms 69:9. Also see the note at Mark 11:17.

§ Again, the resurrection took far from three twenty-four-hour days, as every unit of time is reckoned as a full one.

building this shrine, but *you*'ll raise it in three days?" [21] But he had been speaking of the shrine that was his body.* [22] So when he was raised from among the dead, his students remembered that he had said this, and they trusted in the writing and in what Iēsous had said.

[23] But when he was in Hierosoluma at the festival of the *pascha,* many trusted in his name, as they were watching the signs he performed. [24] But for his part Iēsous didn't trust himself to them, given that he knew all people, [25] and so had no need for anyone to give him testimony about humankind. He certainly knew what was in the human mind.

CHAPTER 3

———

[1] There was a man belonging to the Farisaioi,† and his name was Nikodēmos; he was a leader of the Ioudaioi.‡ [2] Nikodēmos came to him during the night, and said to him, "*Rabbí,* we know you've come from god as a teacher. Certainly no one can perform these signs you perform, unless god is with him." [3] Iēsous answered by saying to him, "*Amēn amēn* I tell you: unless someone is born anew—taking it from the top—he can't see the kingdom of god."§ [4] Nikodēmos said to him, "How can a person be born when he's old? He can hardly go into his mother's womb a second time and then be born again, can he?" [5] Iēsous answered, "*Amēn amēn*

---

* Begun by Herod the Great around 20 B.C.E., the Temple renovation was not completely finished until the sixties C.E., pathetically close to the year 70, when it was destroyed.

† See the note at Mark 2:16.

‡ This probably means that he belonged to the Jewish high council or Sanhedrin.

§ Jesus makes clever use of a verbal ambiguity: *anōthen* means both "once again" and "from above." See "heaven" in the Glossary.

I'm telling you: unless someone is born out of water* and wind, breath, spirit,† he can't enter the kingdom of god. ⁶ What's born out of flesh and blood is flesh and blood, but what's born out of the life-breath is the life-breath. ⁷ Don't be bewildered that I say to you: all of you people must be born anew, taking it straight from the top. ⁸ The wind winds, the breath breathes‡ wherever it wants to, and you hear its sound, its voice,§ but you don't know where it comes from or where it's headed. That's the way everyone is who's born out of the life-breath."¶ ⁹ Nikodēmos answered by saying to him, "How can the things you speak of come into birth—into being?"** ¹⁰ Iēsous answered by saying to him, "You're the teacher of all Israēl, and you don't know these things? ¹¹ *Amēn amēn* I tell you: what we know, we say, and we testify to what we've seen—but you people don't accept our testimony. ¹² If I've spoken to you about the things that are on this earth, yet you don't believe me, how will you believe if I speak to you about the things that are in the sky?

¹³ "But no one has gone up to the sky unless he came down from the sky before, as the son of mankind. ¹⁴ And just as Mōusēs lifted up the snake in the wilderness, so must the son of mankind

* I.e., baptism, for a long early period the only essential rite for Jesus' followers. See the note at Mark 1:4.

† See "S/spirit" in the Glossary. Jesus continues to play with verbal ambiguities.

‡ *Pneuma pnei*, a euphonious and playful expression, implying "a *pneuma* is something that does the *pneuma* thing."

§ The word *fōnē* is (here, indistinguishably) either an animate or an inanimate sound.

¶ "Born of the Spirit," the traditional translation, does not reflect the wordplay in the Greek. The word is the same *pneuma* ordinarily translated as "wind" in the earlier part of this same verse.

** Up to this verse, the verb used for "to be born" normally refers only to actual birth or begetting; now the ambiguous word is used. See "birth, give/be born" in the Glossary. Nicodemus is in effect answering his own question by a slippage of speech: there is more than one way to come into being.

be lifted up,* [15] so that whoever trusts in him can have life for all time. [16] This is in fact how much god loved the world: he gave the only son born to him, so that everyone who trusted in him wouldn't be annihilated, but would have life for all time. [17] God, you see, didn't send the son into the world to judge the world, but so the world could be rescued through him. [18] Whoever trusts him isn't judged; but whoever doesn't trust in him has been judged already, because he didn't trust in the name of the only son born to god. [19] The judgment is this: the light came into the world, but people loved darkness rather than light, as the things they did were contemptible. [20] Everyone who does despicable things hates the light and doesn't come near the light, for fear that it's going to find him guilty of what he's done. [21] But whoever acts on the truth comes to the light, so that the things he's done show brightly and clearly that they were done through the power of god."

[22] After these things, Iēsous and his students went into the countryside of Ioudaia, and there he spent time with them and was baptizing.

[23] Meanwhile, Iōannēs was baptizing at Ainōn near Saleim, because there was a lot of water there, and people were showing up there and were baptized. [24] Iōannēs had of course not been thrown into prison yet.†

[25] Now a controversy arose between Iōannēs' students and a Ioudaios concerning cleansing. [26] And they came to Iōannēs and said to him, "*Rabbí,* the one who was with you on the other side

---

* In Numbers 21:6–9, the Israelites wandering in the wilderness are attacked by poisonous snakes as a punishment from God for complaining. Once the people repent and Moses intercedes with God for them, God instructs him to make a bronze snake and set it on the end of a pole: the mere sight of it cures snakebite. The "lifting up" wordplay will become usual in John for crucifixion (lifting up on the cross), resurrection, and ascension to heaven.

† The location of these baptisms is uncertain. See Mark 6:14–20, Matthew 14:3–5, and Luke 3:19–20 about John the Baptist's imprisonment, to which this Gospel author only alludes.

of the Iordanēs, to whom you testified—look, he's baptizing, and everyone's coming to him." ²⁷ Ioannēs responded by saying, "No one can receive a single thing unless it's given to him from the sky. ²⁸ You yourselves can testify on my behalf [that] I said, 'I'm not the anointed one; instead, I'm sent ahead of him.' ²⁹ It's the bridegroom who gets the bride; the friend of the bridegroom is the one who stands and listens to him and has joy on top of joy at the voice of the bridegroom. So this joy of mine had been made complete. ³⁰ He has to increase, and I have to decrease.*

³¹ "The one who comes from above is above everyone. But whoever's *from* the earth is *of* the earth and speaks *of* the earth. The one coming from the sky [is above everyone]. ³² What he's seen and heard, this he testifies to, but no one accepts his testimony. ³³ Whoever's accepted his testimony has placed a seal on god's truthfulness.† ³⁴ The one god sent says the things god has spoken, as he gives more of the life-breath than anyone can measure. ³⁵ The father loves the son and gives everything into his hands.‡ ³⁶ Whoever trusts in the son has life for all time; whoever disobeys the son won't see life: no, the anger of god against him remains."

CHAPTER 4

———

¹ So when Iēsous found out that the Farisaioi had heard he was recruiting and baptizing more students than Ioannēs did— ² but

---

* The point of marriage in the ancient world was fertility: the married blessing of "increase" is a traditional wish in many cultures.

† Two modes of legal certainty are combined symbolically in this verse: verbal testimony that must be true, under stringent penalties (Deuteronomy 19:15–21), and the seal that conveys its owner's authority and protects his important documents from tampering.

‡ In the ancient world well-to-do fathers did not tend to preside over day-to-day business affairs into middle age, but let sons or other trusted people do it.

as a matter of fact Iēsous himself wasn't baptizing them: his students were— ³ he left Ioudaia and went back to Galilaia.

⁴ But he had to go through Samareia.* ⁵ Thus he came to a town of Samareia called Suchar, near the plot of land that Iakōb gave to Iōsēf his son. ⁶ In that place was Iakōb's spring.† So Iēsous, worn out from his journey, was just sitting by the spring. It was about the sixth hour after sunrise. ⁷ There came a woman, a native of Samareia, to draw water. Iēsous said to her, "Give me a drink." ⁸ His students, you see, had gone away into the city to buy provisions. ⁹ The Samaritis naturally said to him, "How is it that you, a Ioudaios, ask me for a drink, though I'm a Samaritis? The Ioudaioi certainly don't have anything to do with the Samaritai."‡ ¹⁰ Iēsous answered and said to her, "If you knew the gift god can give, and who it is who's saying to you, 'Give me a drink,' you would have asked *him,* and he would have given *you* living water." ¹¹ [The woman] said to him, "Sir, you don't even have a bucket, and the well is deep. So how do you come to have this living water?§ ¹² Surely you're not greater than our forefather Iakōb, who gave us this well and drank out of it himself—and so did his sons and his flocks?" ¹³ Iēsous answered and said to her, "Everyone drinking any of this water will be thirsty again. ¹⁴ But whoever drinks any of the water *I* give him will, for all of time, not be thirsty; no, the water I give him will become in him a spring of water leaping up into life for all time." ¹⁵ The woman said to him,

---

* Not so: there was an alternate route, popular with Jews, through the Transjordan.

† See Luke 10:25–37, and the note on Samaritans. Given the two groups' competing claims, these are hard-hitting references to Jacob (also called Israel), the progenitor of the Twelve Tribes, and to his most famous son, Joseph.

‡ The Jews treat the Samaritans as they would any pagans, as untouchable.

§ The word for "living" in Greek was applied to inanimate things that had power and motion, such as a blazing fire, a bubbling spring, or a flowing river. A deep well's water, probably only seeping up through the sand at the bottom, does not seem to fit well into this category. Proto-Christian baptism such as John practiced was done in *running* water, which was associated with divine power, purity, and eternal life.

"Sir, give me this water, so that I won't get thirsty and keep coming all the way here to draw water."* ¹⁶ He said to her, "Go and call your man, and come back here." ¹⁷ The woman answered by telling him, "I don't have a man." Iēsous told her, "It's good that you said, 'I don't have a man.' ¹⁸ You've had five men, and the man you have now isn't lawfully yours.† That was the truth you spoke." ¹⁹ The woman said to him, "Sir, I see you're a prophet. ²⁰ Our forefathers fell down to worship on this mountain;‡ but you people say that Hierosoluma is the place where it's necessary to worship." ²¹ Iēsous said to her, "Woman, believe me that the hour is coming when you'll worship the father neither on this mountain nor in Hierosoluma. ²² You people worship what you don't know. *We* worship what we *do* know, because rescue comes from the Ioudaioi. ²³ But the time is coming, and it's here, now, when the true worshippers will worship the father in the life-breath and in truth. The father is in fact searching for people like this, to worship him. ²⁴ God is a wind, a breath, a spirit, and those worshipping him must worship in the life-breath and in truth."§ ²⁵ The woman said to him, "I know the Messias is coming, who's called 'the anointed one.'¶ When he comes, he'll bring us word of everything." ²⁶ Iēsous said to her, "It's me, the one who's talking to you."

²⁷ At this point, his students came, and they were shocked that

* In the Near East, water shortages have always fallen most heavily on women, who may spend hours a day hauling water for basic household uses from distant wells.

† See "husband" in the Glossary: the word used for her household partner can be ambiguous. Bereavement, abandonment, and poverty were the commonest circumstances to push a woman into an arrangement outside the law.

‡ The Mount Gerizim location of the Samaritan temple, which was now destroyed.

§ See "S/spirit" in the Glossary.

¶ The Israelite community was not divided around the time of David, God's anointed king, so all its descendants share the Hebrew scripture references to this kingly rescuer and guardian of his people.

he was talking with a woman. However, no one said, "What are you trying to do?" or "Why are you talking with her?"* ²⁸ The woman then left her water jar behind† and went away into the town and told the people, ²⁹ "Come see the man who told me everything I've done. He couldn't be the anointed one, could he?" ³⁰ The people went out of the town and came to him.

³¹ In the meantime, the students appealed to him, saying, "*Rabbí*, eat!" ³² But he said to them, "I have food to eat that you don't know about." ³³ So the students said to one another, "What? Someone's brought him something to eat?" ³⁴ Iēsous said to them, "My food is to do what the one who sent me wants, and to complete his work. ³⁵ Don't you yourselves say, 'Four months more, and the harvest will be here'? Look, I tell you, lift up your eyes and see the fields, which are pale and ready for reaping. ³⁶ The reaper gets his pay already and gathers in the grain for life without end, so that the sower and the reaper together are full of joy. ³⁷ In this case, in fact, the byword is true: 'One man is the sower, and another the reaper.' ³⁸ I've sent you out to reap what you didn't work to grow. Others worked, and you've come for what their work achieved."‡

³⁹ Many of the Samaritai from that town trusted in him because of the account the woman gave when she testified, "He told me everything I've done." ⁴⁰ So when the Samaritai came to him, they asked him to stay with them, and he stayed for two days.§ ⁴¹ And many more of them had trust because of his own

---

* As a woman, a stranger, and a member of a despised group, she is normally to be avoided on triple grounds.

† A large, watertight jar was no trivial part of a household's equipment; nor will water fail to be missed at home; the woman is treating this encounter as a piece of urgent news.

‡ Apocalyptic imagery. The previous workers are probably the scriptural prophets.

§ Accepting the Samaritans' hospitality and eating their food, Jesus must commit prolonged violations of the Jewish purity laws, as well as outraging national prejudice.

account. [42] To the woman they said, "We no longer believe because of what you said, as we've now heard it for ourselves, and we know this is truly the rescuer of the world."

[43] After those two days he left that place and went to Galilaia. [44] Iēsous himself in fact testified that a prophet doesn't have honor in his own fatherland. [45] So when he went to Galilaia, the Galilaioi received him hospitably, having seen all that he did in Hierosoluma during the festival, as they themselves had gone to the festival.*

[46] So he went back to Kana in Galilaia, where he'd made wine out of water.

And in Kafarnaoum there was a royal official† whose son was ailing. [47] When this man heard that Iēsous had arrived in Galilaia from Ioudaia, he went to meet him and asked him to come down with him and heal his son, as he was about to die. [48] So Iēsous said to him, "If you people don't see signs and wonders, you never believe." [49] The official said to him, "Sir, come down before my child dies." [50] Iēsous told him, "Be on your way! Your son is going to live." This man believed what Iēsous told him, and went on his way. [51] Even before he reached home, his slaves met him, saying his boy was going to live. [52] So he asked them what time he had gotten better. They then told him, "Yesterday, at the seventh hour after dawn, the fever left him." [53] So the father realized that this was the time when Iēsous had said to him, "Your son is going to live"; then he came to have trust, and so did his entire household. [54] [But] this was the second sign that Iēsous performed after he went from Ioudaia to Galilaia.‡

---

* In the other Gospels (Mark 6:4, Matthew 13:57, and Luke 4:24), Jesus' remark about honor is made understandably in the course of insulting treatment by his hometown neighbors. Here the remark is at odds with the narrative.

† Literally a "kingly man," this is probably a functionary from the court of Herod Antipas, who was then king of Galilee and a client of the Romans.

‡ The first was turning water into wine at the wedding at Cana (2:1–11 above).

CHAPTER 5

———

¹ After these things, there was a festival of the Ioudaioi,* and Iēsous went up to Hierosoluma. ² Now in Hierosoluma, by the sheep gate, there is a pool called in Hebrew Bēthzatha, with five porticoes around it.† ³ In these there lay a mass of debilitated people: the blind, the lame, the paralyzed. ⁵ In that place was a man who'd been debilitated for thirty-eight years. ⁶ When Iēsous saw him lying there and realized that he'd been waiting quite a long time, he said to him, "Do you want to be made well?" ⁷ The debilitated man answered him, "Sir, I don't have anyone who could put me into the pool when the water's disturbed. Whenever I'm going there, someone else steps down ahead of me."‡ ⁸ Iēsous said to him, "Get up, pick up your stretcher, and walk." ⁹ And right away the man was made well, and picked up his stretcher and walked.

But that day was the *sabbaton.* ¹⁰ So the Ioudaioi said to the man who'd been cured, "It's the *sabbaton,* and it's not permitted that you pick up your stretcher." ¹¹ But he answered them, "The man who made me well told me, 'Pick up your stretcher and walk.'" ¹² They asked him, "Who's the man who told you, 'Pick it up and walk'?" ¹³ But the man who'd been healed didn't know who he was, as Iēsous had slipped away through the crowd in that place. ¹⁴ Afterward Iēsous found him in the temple precinct and said to him, "Look, you're well now: don't do wrong any more, and that

———

* This could be any of the three pilgrimage festivals.

† This is the area northeast of the Temple. The gate was very likely for the animals being brought in for sacrifice.

‡ An explanation added into some versions of this passage later (in the excised Verse 4) is that an angel was thought to stir the water, after which the first person entering it would be cured. The man has no servant or family member to bring him there in time.

will keep anything worse from happening to you."* ¹⁵ The man went away and reported back to the Ioudaioi that Iēsous was the one who'd made him well. ¹⁶ And this was the reason the Ioudaioi proceeded to hound Iēsous: he was doing these things on the *sabbaton.*

¹⁷ [Iēsous] had this response for them: "My father's been working this whole time, and I'm working too." ¹⁸ So because of this, the Ioudaioi tried even harder to kill him: not only did he break the *sabbaton,* but he also called god his own father, making himself out to be god.

¹⁹ So Iēsous responded by telling them: "*Amēn amēn* I tell you, the son can't do anything on his own, but only what he sees the father doing: whatever he does, the son does likewise. ²⁰ The father loves the son specially and shows him everything he himself does, and will show him even greater work than this, so that you'll all be amazed. ²¹ In fact, just as the father awakens the dead and brings them back to life, the son as well brings back to life whoever he wants to. ²² And the father, in fact, doesn't judge anyone, but has granted all judgment to the son, ²³ so that all people honor the son as they honor the father. Whoever doesn't honor the son doesn't honor the father who sent him.†

²⁴ "*Amēn amēn* I tell you, the one hearing what I say and trusting in the one who sent me has life for all time and doesn't come under judgment, but instead has crossed over from death to life. ²⁵ *Amēn amēn* I tell you, the time is coming, and it's here now, when the dead will hear the voice of god's son, and those who've heard it will live. ²⁶ Just as the father possesses life in himself, in fact, so he's granted his son as well life to possess in himself.

---

* In Greek or Roman literature, these words would be the insulting menace of a beating.

† See below in Chapters 13–17 for more analogies to the traditional father-son relationship. In Verse 20 here, the verb *fileō* is used for the father's love of the son, suggesting a bond more special and purposeful than an ordinary paternal one. See "love" in the Glossary.

²⁷ And he gave him the authority to pass judgment, because he's mankind's son.* ²⁸ Don't be amazed at this, because the time is coming when all those in the tombs will hear his voice ²⁹ and make their way out: those who've done excellent things will be raised to their feet to live, and those who have done unworthy things will be raised to their feet to be judged.

³⁰ "I can't do anything on my own. As I hear, I judge, and my judgment is lawful, because I'm not looking to do what I want, but rather what the one who sent me wants.

³¹ "If I give testimony about myself, my testimony isn't true. ³² There's someone else who testifies about me, and I know the testimony he gives about me *is* true. ³³ You sent messengers to Iōannēs, and he has testified to the truth. ³⁴ But I myself don't accept testimony from a human being; instead, I say these things so that *you* all can be rescued. ³⁵ He was a lamp, burning and shining, and you were willing to be delighted for a while by his light.

³⁶ "But I have testimony that's greater than that of Iōannēs. The work my father gave me to complete, the work itself that I do testifies on my behalf that the father sent me. ³⁷ And the father who sent me—*he's* testified on my behalf. You've never heard his voice or seen his form, ³⁸ and you don't have what he's spoken remaining within you, because the one he sent is the one you don't trust. ³⁹ You search the writings, because you think you possess in them life for all time; but it's these that testify on my behalf. ⁴⁰ But you don't want to come to me to have life.

⁴¹ "I don't accept glory from human beings; ⁴² no, I know you all, and that you don't have the love of god in you. ⁴³ I've come in the name of my father, but you don't accept me; if someone else comes in his own name, you'll accept him. ⁴⁴ How can you trust when you accept glory from each other but don't look for the glory that comes from the one god?

⁴⁵ "Don't think I'm going to indict you before the father. The

---

* See p. xxix of the Introduction. This use of "son of mankind" here is particularly puzzling.

one who's indicting you is Mōŭsēs, on whom you've placed your hopes. ⁴⁶ If you trusted Mōŭsēs, you would trust me: he in fact wrote about me. If you don't trust what he wrote, how will you believe what I'm speaking about?"*

CHAPTER 6

¹ After these things, Iēsous went away to the other side of the Sea of Galilaia or Tiberias.† ² A large crowd followed him, because they were observing the signs he performed to heal debilitated people. ³ But Iēsous went away up the mountain and sat there with his students. ⁴ It was near the time of the *pascha*, the festival of the Ioudaioi.

⁵ So, lifting his eyes and noticing that a large crowd was coming toward him, he said to Filippos, "Where can we buy loaves so that these people can eat?" ⁶ He said this to test him: he himself knew what he was about to do. ⁷ Filippos answered him: "Two hundred denarii worth of loaves aren't enough for each of these people to get a tiny [share]."‡ ⁸ One of the students, Andreas the brother of Simōn Petros, said to him, ⁹ "There's a little kid here who has five barley loaves and two little cooked fish. But what are these good for, when there are so many to feed?" ¹⁰ Iēsous said, "Have the people recline for a meal." There was a lot of grass in

---

* This passage contrasts sharply with the Hebrew scriptures, the Mishnah, and other sources concerning the rules of forensic evidence, insisting on the validity of testimony that is not only from a blood relative, and not only hearsay, but also invisible and inaudible to everyone but the person it favors. More generally, the claim of the exclusive right to interpret scripture, let alone in connection to a critical matter, outrages tradition. But apocalyptic literature does vividly posit final, divine judgment of large categories of people.

† The Greek reads "of Galilaia of Tiberias." Tiberias was a new town on the Sea of Galilee's western shore, named for the Roman emperor Tiberius; the name Tiberias was sometimes applied to the sea as well.

‡ Matthew 20:2 shows a single denarius as a worker's daily wage.

the place. So the men reclined; they numbered about five thousand.* ¹¹ So Iēsous took the loaves, gave thanks for them, and shared them out to those reclining there, and the same for the fish, as much as they wanted. ¹² And when they were full, he said to his students, "Gather together the leftover pieces, so that nothing's wasted." ¹³ So they gathered them together and filled twelve baskets with the pieces of the five barley loaves that were left over by those who had eaten. ¹⁴ So the people who saw the sign he performed said, "This is truly the prophet coming into the world." ¹⁵ Then Iēsous, knowing that they were about to come and drag him away to make him king, withdrew again onto the mountain, all by himself.

¹⁶ When it was evening, his students went down to the sea, ¹⁷ boarded a boat, and went over the sea to Kafarnaoum. But it was already dark, and Iēsous hadn't yet come to them. ¹⁸ Then a great wind started to blow, and the sea was violently agitated. ¹⁹ Now they'd come about twenty-five or thirty stades† when they caught sight of Iēsous walking on the sea and getting near the boat, and they were frightened. ²⁰ But he said to them, "It's me. Don't be frightened." ²¹ They wanted to take him onto the boat, but right away the boat got to the shore where they were heading.

²² The next day, the crowd that had stayed on the other side of the sea realized that there had been only the one small boat there, and that Iēsous hadn't boarded it along with his students; instead, his students had sailed away alone. ²³ Other [small] boats came from Tiberias and approached the spot where they'd eaten the bread, once the lord had given thanks. ²⁴ So when the crowd saw that neither Iēsous nor his students were there, they them-

---

* Greco-Roman mores resisted women's assuming the same relaxed dining posture as men. Women also might literally not count in the reckoning of the size of groups.

† The stade is a variant measurement, but they appear to be near the middle of the lake.

selves boarded the small boats and sailed to Kafarnaoum looking for Iēsous. ²⁵ And when they found him on the other side of the sea, they said to him, "*Rabbí,* when did you get here?"

²⁶ Iēsous answered them by saying, "*Amēn amēn* I tell you, you're looking for me not because you've seen signs, but because you ate some of the loaves and were stuffed full. ²⁷ Don't work for food that gets used up, but for food that lasts for a life without end, which the son of mankind will give you, as it's on him that god the father has put his seal."* ²⁸ Then they said to him, "What should we do to work at god's work?" ²⁹ Iēsous answered by telling them, "This is god's work, that you trust in the one he sent."

³⁰ Then they said to him, "So what sign are you going to give that we can see, and that will make us trust you? What work are you going to carry out? ³¹ Our fathers ate *manna* in the wilderness, as it's been written: 'He gave them bread from the sky to eat.' "† ³² Iēsous said to them, "*Amēn amēn* I tell you, it wasn't Mōüsēs who gave you bread from the sky; no, it is my father who gives you the true bread from the sky. ³³ God's bread is in fact the one coming down from the sky and giving life to the world." ³⁴ So they said to him, "Master, give us this bread forever!" ³⁵ Iēsous told them, "*I*'m the bread of life. Whoever comes to me will never starve, and whoever trusts in me will never be parched.

³⁶ "But I told you that, even though you've seen [me], you don't believe. ³⁷ Whatever the father grants me will reach me, and whoever comes to me, I won't throw out, ³⁸ because I came down from the sky not to do what *I* want, but what the one who sent me wants. ³⁹ And this is what the one who sent me wants: that

---

* The seal functioned as a modern signature does, creating a unique image that carried personal legal authority.

† The manna (Hebrew for "What is it?") was a special food God sent to be collected morning and evening, so that the Israelites wandering in the wilderness after their escape from Egyptian slavery would not starve before they could reach the Promised Land of Canaan. The quotation is from Psalms 78:24.

out of everything he gave me, I let nothing be destroyed, but instead set it on its feet [on] the last day.* [40] This is in fact what my father wants: that everyone looking at the son and trusting in him will have life for all time; and I'll put him on his feet [on] the last day."

[41] Then the Ioudaioi were muttering about him because he said, "I'm the bread that came down from the sky," [42] and they said, "Isn't this Iēsous the son of Iōsēf, the Iēsous whose father and mother we know? Then what does he mean by 'I came down from the sky'?" [43] Iēsous, reacting, said to them, "Don't mutter among yourselves! [44] No one can come to me unless the father, who sent me, draws him along, but *I*'ll set him on his feet on the last day. [45] It's been written in the prophets, 'And they'll all be taught by god':† everyone who's listened to and learned from the father is coming to me. [46] Not that anyone has seen the father— only the one who's from god: *he*'s seen the father. [47] *Amēn amēn* I tell you, whoever believes has life for all time. [48] I am the bread of life. [49] Your fathers ate the *manna* in the wilderness,‡ but they died. [50] This is the bread that comes down from the sky, so that anyone can eat some of it and not die. [51] I'm the living bread that came down from the sky. If anyone eats any of this bread I give him, he'll live for all time, and the bread I'll give him is my mortal body,§ given for the life of the world."

[52] Then the Ioudaioi were fighting among themselves, saying, "How can this man give us [his] body to eat?" [53] Iēsous said to them, "*Amēn amēn* I tell you, if you don't eat the body of mankind's son, and drink his blood, you won't have life in you.

---

* Jesus' language reflects that of filial obedience and inheritance throughout ancient literature. The "last day" is the end of ordinary history, as depicted in apocalyptic literature; resurrection of the body was a belief of the Pharisees.

† Quoted loosely from Isaiah 54:13.

‡ See the note at Verse 31 above.

§ See "flesh" in the Glossary.

⁵⁴ Whoever eats my body and drinks my blood has life for all of time, and I'll raise him to his feet on the last day. ⁵⁵ My body, you see, is the true food, and my blood is the true drink. ⁵⁶ Whoever eats my body and drinks my blood remains and lives in me, and I in him.* ⁵⁷ Just as the living father sent me and I live through the father, whoever eats me will live because of me. ⁵⁸ This is the bread that's come down from the sky, not like what our fathers ate—and they still died. Whoever eats this bread will live for all of time."

⁵⁹ He said these things when he taught in the synagogue in Kafarnaoum.

⁶⁰ Many of his students who'd listened said, "This is rough talk. Who can stand to listen to it?" ⁶¹ But Iēsous, sensing inwardly that his students were muttering about this, said to them, "Does *this* trip you up? ⁶² Then what if you were to watch the son of mankind climbing up to where he was before? ⁶³ The breath is what creates life; the body alone is good for nothing.† The things I've said to you are breath and life. ⁶⁴ But there are some of you who don't believe." Iēsous of course knew from the beginning which ones didn't believe, and which one would hand him over. ⁶⁵ And he told them, "This is why I've told you that no one can come to me unless it's granted to him by the father."

⁶⁶ Because of this, many [of] his students turned back and no longer walked with him. ⁶⁷ So Iēsous said to the twelve, "You don't also want to move on?" ⁶⁸ Simōn Petros answered him: "Master, to whom would we go? *You* have the words of life that last for all of time.‡ ⁶⁹ And we've come to believe and to recognize that you are god's holy one." ⁷⁰ Iēsous answered them: "Didn't I choose the twelve of you myself? But among you, one is a

---

* The repeated, emphatic prescription here of drinking blood is particularly shattering. Jewish law forbade the consumption of blood from sacrifices.

† See "S/spirit" and "flesh" in the Glossary.

‡ I reluctantly translate *rēmata* as "words"; see "W/word" in the Glossary.

slanderer."* ⁷¹ He meant Ioudas the son of Simōn Iskariōtēs,† as he—even though he was one of the twelve—was going to hand Iēsous over.

CHAPTER 7

¹ And after this, Iēsous traveled around by foot in Galilaia, as he didn't want to travel around in Ioudaia, because the Ioudaioi were looking to kill him.‡ ² Near at hand was a festival of the Ioudaioi, "the pitching of tents."§ ³ And his brothers said to him, "Leave here and move on to Ioudaia, so that your students also can see the work you're doing, ⁴ as no one acts in secret and at the same time seeks to be in the public eye. As long as you're doing these things, show yourself clearly to the world." ⁵ Not even his brothers, in fact, trusted in him. ⁶ So Iēsous said to them: "The critical time for me isn't here yet, but for you that time is always at hand. ⁷ The world can't hate you, but it hates me, because I testify against it, saying the things it does are malicious. ⁸ You all go up to the festival. I'm not going up to this festival, because for me the time hasn't come to fruition." ⁹ This is what he said, and he stayed in Galilaia.

---

* See "devil" in the Glossary.

† That Judas' second name is shown as inherited argues against the claim that the name marks him as an insurgent.

‡ Again, there is no difference in Greek between Judeans and Jews: Judea means either the Jewish heartland and home of the Temple, or the whole Roman province, including the remote and restive Galilee. If Jesus' alienation from Ioudaioi in the Gospel of John is at least in part geographical, it makes more sense.

§ This is the festival of Booths or Tabernacles, or Sukkot, an autumn harvest celebration, named for the huts made for holding it outdoors, huts that also commemorate the wandering of the Israelites in the desert after the escape from Egypt.

¹⁰ But once his brothers had gone up to the festival, then he also went up, not openly but [as if] in secret. ¹¹ Now, the Ioudaioi were looking for him at the festival, and asking, "Where is he?" ¹² And there was a lot of muttering about him in the crowds. Some people were saying, "He's an excellent man," [while] others said, "No, not at all: he leads the crowd astray." ¹³ No one, however, was speaking openly about him, out of fear of the Ioudaioi.*

¹⁴ The festival was already half over when Iēsous went up into the temple precinct and began to teach. ¹⁵ The Ioudaioi were naturally amazed, saying, "How did this man come to be literate, when he never studied?" ¹⁶ Iēsous then responded by saying to them, "My teaching isn't mine; it belongs to the one who sent me. ¹⁷ But if someone's willing to do what *he* wills, he'll know about the teaching, whether it comes from god or whether I'm speaking for myself. ¹⁸ Whoever speaks for himself is looking for his own glory, but whoever's looking for the glory of the one who sent him—he's truthful, and there's no lawlessness in him.

¹⁹ "Didn't Mōüsēs give you the law? But none of you carries out the law! Why are you trying to kill me?" ²⁰ The crowd responded, "You've got a demon in you. Who's trying to kill you?" ²¹ In response Iēsous said to them, "I performed a single work, and you're all amazed. ²² Because Mōüsēs granted you circumcision—it's not from Mōüsēs, though, but from the patriarchs—you circumcise someone even on the *sabbaton*.† ²³ Even though someone gets circumcised on the *sabbaton* so that the law of Mōüsēs isn't broken, you're angry at me because I made the whole of someone healthy on the *sabbaton*? ²⁴ Don't ren-

---

* Whether the distinction between the crowds and those they feared, if historically valid, would be due to geography, class, or rank, is unknown; in any case, the phrasing sounds strange.

† The whole of the Torah is the "Law of Moses," but the divine decree of circumcision was given to the original patriarch, Abraham, generations before Moses (Genesis 17:10–14).

der a verdict merely by what first meets your eye; instead, render a *lawful* verdict."*

²⁵ So some of the Hierosolumitai were saying, "Isn't he the one they're trying to kill? ²⁶ But look, he's speaking openly, and they say nothing to him. Perhaps the leaders truly know that this is the anointed one? ²⁷ On the other hand, we know where he's from. When the anointed one comes, nobody's going to know where he's from."† ²⁸ A shout then rose from Iēsous as he said, while teaching in the temple precinct, "You *do* know both me and where I'm from! And I didn't come at my own instigation—no, the one who sent me is full of truth—though you don't know him. ²⁹ I *know* him, because I'm *from* him, and *he* sent me." ³⁰ Then they tried to seize him, but no one laid a hand on him, because his time hadn't yet come.

³¹ But in that crowd, many believed in him, and they said, "When the anointed one comes, he's not going to perform more signs than this man has!" ³² The Farisaioi heard the crowd murmuring these things about him, and the high priests and the Farisaioi sent their retainers to seize him.‡ ³³ Then Iēsous said, "I'll be with you a little while longer, but then I'm heading off to the one who sent me. ³⁴ You'll look for me, but you won't find [me], and where I'll be, you can't go." ³⁵ So the Ioudaioi said to each other, "Where's he about to travel, where we won't find him? Surely he's not going to travel to the scattering of the Greeks, and teach the Greeks? ³⁶ What's the meaning of what he said?§ 'You'll look for me, but you won't find [me], and where I'll be, you can't go'?"

* Circumcision is prescribed for the eighth day of a Jewish male infant's life, so the Sabbath regulations against work yield to the ritual.

† The idea of the "hidden Messiah" is witnessed, for example, in the Apocryphal work 2 Esdras (13:51–52).

‡ The Romans allowed the Temple hierarchy policing powers within the religious sphere.

§ "Greeks" could signal Gentiles generally, or assimilated Jews of the Diaspora ("scattering").

[37] On the last day of the festival, the most important day, Iēsous took a stand and shouted these words: "If anyone's thirsty, he needs to come to me and drink. [38] If someone trusts in me, then, as the writing has said, from his belly rivers of living water are going to run." [39] But he said this about the life-breath, which those who trusted in him would receive; but there wasn't any life-breath yet, because Iēsous wasn't yet glorified.*

[40] So some of the crowd, after hearing his statements, said, "This is truly the prophet." [41] Others said, "This is the anointed one." And still others said, "The anointed one can't come from Galilaia, can he? [42] Hasn't the writing said that the anointed one will come from the seed of David, and from the town of Bēthle'em, where David lived?"† [43] So there was a split in the crowd because of him. [44] Some of them wanted to seize him, but no one laid hands on him.

[45] Then the retainers went to the high priests and the Farisaioi, who said to them, "Why didn't you bring him in?" [46] The retainers answered, "Nobody's ever spoken that way before." [47] Then the Farisaioi answered them, "Don't tell us: You've been led astray too? [48] Have any of the leaders come to trust in him? Or any of the Farisaioi? [49] But this crowd doesn't know anything about the law—they're cursed."‡ [50] Nikodēmos—who'd come to him in [the] past§—said to them, as he was one of them: [51] "Surely our law wouldn't let us condemn someone without first hearing from him in person and finding out what he's doing?" [52] They answered by saying to him, "You're not from Galilaia

---

* The wordplay and symbolism involve the running or "living" water of baptism, and possibly also the fluid that runs (here, literally) "from his abdominal cavity" from the spear puncture at the crucifixion (John 19:34). There are several Hebrew Bible passages echoed here.

† The prophecy of birth at Bethlehem is at Micah 5:2. The very geographical problem that the nativity stories of Matthew and Luke seek to solve is cited here.

‡ See "curse" in the Glossary.

§ See above at 3:1–21.

too, are you? Look it up and see: no prophet originates from Galilaia."*

⁵³ Then each one made his way back to his home.

CHAPTER 8

¹ Now Iēsous made his way onto the mountain with the olive trees. ² But in the early morning he made another appearance in the temple precinct, and the whole people came to him, and he sat and taught them. ³ But the scholars and the Farisaioi brought a woman who had been caught violating her marriage, and once they had made her stand in the middle of the crowd, ⁴ they said to him: "Teacher, this woman was caught in the act of violating her marriage. ⁵ Now in the law Mōüsēs commanded us to stone such women. So what do *you* say?"† ⁶ They said this to put him to the test, so that they would have grounds to bring him down with an indictment. But Iēsous bent down, and he wrote down a formal summons with his finger on the ground. ⁷ When they kept on asking him, he straightened up and said to them, "Whichever of you never did anything wrong had better be the first to throw a stone at her." ⁸ And he bent down again and kept writing on the ground. ⁹ And when they heard him, one by one, clear down the line, starting from the elders, they went out, and then it was down to Iēsous alone, and the woman in the middle of the open space. ¹⁰ And Iēsous straightened up and said to her, "Where are

---

* It is actually not clear how many prophets came from Galilee, other than the buffoonish Jonah.

† The relevant statutes are found at Leviticus 20:10 and Deuteronomy 22:22, where the offense named is only sex between *any* man and someone else's wife. The moral lopsidedness seems extended to this present scene. Where is the woman's partner in crime? Why is she so conveniently available as an object lesson? Why is Jesus suddenly appointed judge?

they, woman? Has nobody brought you down with his judgment?" [11] And she said, "Nobody, master." Then Iēsous said to her, "I'm not bringing you down either. Be on your way, [and] from now on don't do anything wrong."*

[12] Then Iēsous said to them again, "I'm the light of the universe: the one following after me doesn't walk around in darkness, but will have the light of life."† [13] The Farisaioi then said to him, "Are you testifying on your own behalf? Then your testimony isn't true." [14] Iēsous responded by telling them, "Even if I testify on my own behalf, my testimony *is* true, because I know where I come from and where I'm headed, but you *don't* know where I come from and where I'm headed. [15] You make your judgment according to the body that dies, but I don't judge anyone. [16] Even if I do judge, my judgment is true, because it's not me alone, but rather me and the father who sent me. [17] But in your law it's written that the testimony of two people is true. [18] I'm the one testifying about myself, *and* my father who sent me testifies about me." [19] So they said to him, "Where *is* your father?"‡ Iēsous answered, "You don't know either me or my father. If you knew

---

* This story occurs only in John, and a number of the earliest extant manuscripts leave the passage out. The wordplay is heavy-handed. The word for what the leaders wish to do to Jesus is *katagoreō*, literally "make a speech [in the marketplace] down." The prepositional prefix *kata* adds emphasis, so that the verb means a formal prosecution. Jesus then stoops "downward"—*katō*, an adverb—and "writes a summons"—the verb is *katagraphō*, for formal legal writing, including summoning by written order. Play on *kata-* continues in verses 8, 9, 10, and 11, and I have reproduced it in English as best I could there too.

† The symbolic and religious purport of light in John has a practical angle: you can't go out in the thick darkness of the ancient world at night if you don't have a light with you.

‡ The Jewish establishment claimed that Jesus was born out of wedlock and falsely propagated a story of divine parentage. Such a story would have been far less offensive outside pious circles in Judea. The Roman emperors, among others, portrayed themselves as descended from divinity; and when a god mated with a mortal in mythology, the first generation was nearly always illegitimate.

me, you would know my father too."* ²⁰ He made these statements at the treasury while he was teaching in the temple
precinct. But no one seized him, because his time hadn't come
yet.

²¹ Then he spoke to them again: "I'm headed off, and you'll
look for me, but in your wrongdoing you'll die. Where I'm
headed, you're not able to go."† ²² Then the Ioudaioi said, "Surely
he's not going to kill himself? He did say, 'Where I'm headed,
you're not able to go.'" ²³ But he said to them, "You belong to the
things below, but I belong to the things above. You belong to this
world, but I don't belong to this world. ²⁴ So I said to you that
you'll die in the things you've done wrong. If in fact you don't
believe that *I am,* you'll die in the things you've done wrong."
²⁵ Then they said to him, "Who *are* you?" Iēsous said to them,
"What have I been telling you from the start? ²⁶ I have many
things I could say about you, and many judgments I could make,
but the one who sent me is truthful, and the things I've heard
from him I say to the world." ²⁷ They didn't realize that he was
talking to them about the father. ²⁸ So Iēsous said [to them],
"When you lift up the son of mankind, then you'll realize that *I
am,*‡ but in my own right I do nothing: on the contrary, I say these
things as my father taught me to. ²⁹ And the one who sent me is

* Jesus' is a sophistic take on the Jewish law at best. (Compare 5:30–46 above.)
For example, though Deuteronomy 19:15 requires two witnesses to establish the
truth of testimony, a person's own testimony on behalf of himself plainly does
not count. John seems in these passages to play to a widespread and long-standing
admiration of the Jewish legal system, but his use of it is an outsider's.

† The Jews and the pagans differed markedly in their attitudes toward suicide.
The Jews developed a prohibition, though there is no explicit scriptural basis.
Some Roman Stoics staged elaborate suicides in line with their position on virtu-
ous independence of mind.

‡ Given the poor state of the text, it's far from definite that Jesus makes (for
the second time in five verses) such an extreme claim of divinity as to refer to "I
AM THAT I AM," God's pun on his cult name Yahweh in Exodus 3:14. "Lifting
up" as wordplay for crucifixion is a repeated gambit in John.

with me. He hasn't left me alone, because at all times I do what's agreeable to him."

³⁰ When he said these things, many trusted in him. ³¹ So Iēsous said to the Ioudaioi who had come to trust him: "If you remain and live in what I've spoken, you're truly my students, ³² and you'll realize the truth, and the truth will set you free." ³³ They answered him: "We're the seed of Abraam, and we've never been anyone's slaves. What do you mean when you say we'll be made free?" ³⁴ Iēsous answered them: "*Amēn amēn* I tell you: everyone who does something wrong is a slave to wrongdoing. ³⁵ But the slave doesn't stay in the house for all time, whereas the son does stay for all time. ³⁶ If the son, then, sets you free, you'll really be free.*

³⁷ "I *know* that you're the seed of Abraam—nevertheless, you seek to kill me, because what I say doesn't make any headway among you. ³⁸ I tell about what I've seen in the father's presence. So *you*, then, must do what you've heard from the father." ³⁹ They answered and said to him, "Our father is Abraam." Iēsous said to them, "If you're offspring of Abraam, you'd do the work of Abraam. ⁴⁰ But as it is, you seek to kill me, a person who's told you the truth that I heard from god. Abraam didn't do this! ⁴¹ You're doing the work of *your* father."† [So] they said to him, "We weren't born from whoring. We have a single father, and that's god." ⁴² Iēsous said to them, "If god were your father, you would love me, as I've come from god, and I've arrived here. I

---

* If these Jews are speaking about slavery in terms of their scriptural tradition, they are of course mistaken: not only is Egyptian slavery remembered as a defining trial for Abraham's descendants, but the divided kingdoms were conquered repeatedly during the historical period, and enslavement was a normal consequence of defeat. If they mean, on the other hand, that absolute chattel slavery, in which a person could be treated as an object, was not part of their inherited law or culture, they are correct. In any event, Jesus' remarks have one obvious force: the son is the heir; it will be *his* house. He can then free slaves or servants at will.

† I.e., the devil, on whom see the Glossary.

haven't come on my own! No, he sent me. ⁴³ Why don't you understand my language? ⁴³ It's because you can't hear what I'm
telling you! ⁴⁴ You belong to your father the slanderer, and you
want to carry out your father's desires. He was a murderer from
the start, and he hasn't taken a stand in the truth, because there
is no truth in him. When he tells a lie, he speaks his own language, because he's a liar and the father of lying. ⁴⁵ But because *I*
speak the truth, you don't believe me. ⁴⁶ Which of you proves me
guilty of any wrongdoing? If I'm speaking the truth, why don't
you believe me? ⁴⁷ The one who's from god listens to the things
god says. That means you're not listening, because you don't belong to god."*

⁴⁸ The Ioudaioi answered and spoke to him: "Aren't we right
in saying that you're a Samaritēs and have a demon in you?"
⁴⁹ Iēsous answered, "I *don't* have a demon in me; on the contrary,
I honor my father: but you dishonor me. ⁵⁰ I'm not seeking my
own glory. There's someone who does seek it, and who does
judge. ⁵¹ *Amēn amēn* I tell you, if someone safeguards what I say, he
will, for all of time, never look on death." ⁵² [So] the Ioudaioi said
to him, "Now we *know* that you have a demon in you. Abraam
died, and so did the prophets, but you tell us, 'If someone safeguards what *I* say, for all of time he will never taste death.
⁵³ You're not greater than our father Abraam, who died, are you?
And the prophets also died. Who are you making yourself out to
be?" ⁵⁴ Iēsous responded, "If I glorify myself, my glory is nothing.
But it's my father who glorifies me, and you claim that he's our
god, ⁵⁵ but you haven't recognized him, whereas I do know him;
and if I were to say that I don't know him, I would be like you all,
a liar; but I do know him, and I safeguard what he's spoken. ⁵⁶
Your father Abraam was elated that he would see my day; and he
saw it, to his joy." ⁵⁷ Then the Ioudaioi said to him, "You're not

---

* The gist of this contention is that traditional Judaism understands God's
fatherhood only symbolically. If what Jesus says is blasphemous, the punishment
is stoning (Leviticus 24:13–15).

fifty years old yet, and you've seen Abraam?" ⁵⁸ Iēsous said to them, "*Amēn amēn* I tell you, before Abraam came into being, I have been." ⁵⁹ They then picked up stones to throw at him, but Iēsous hid and left the temple precinct.

CHAPTER 9

¹ Then as he went along, he saw a man who had been blind from birth. ² And his students questioned him, saying, "*Rabbí*, who did wrong, this man or his parents, so that he was born blind?" ³ Iēsous answered, "Neither this man nor his parents did anything wrong: the purpose was that the work of god should show brightly and clearly in his case. ⁴ We need to be working at the work of the one who sent me while it's still daytime. The night is coming, when no one can work. ⁵ While I'm in the world, I'm the light of the world."* ⁶ Having said this, he spat on the ground and made some mud with the spit, then wiped the mud onto the man's eyes,† ⁷ and said to him, "Get moving and wash in the pool of Silōam (which translates as "the one who has been sent").‡ He then went away and washed, and came back seeing.

⁸ Now the neighbors and those who had observed him before, because he was a beggar, said, "Isn't this the one who sat begging?" ⁹ Others said, "It's not him," and still others said, "No, but he looks like him." He, however, said, "It *is* me." ¹⁰ Then they said to him, "[So] how were your eyes opened?" ¹¹ He answered, "The

---

* In late antiquity, the hyper-learned Alexandrian school of literature touted the motif of diligent late-night study by lamplight; ordinary people worked only by natural light.

† See Mark 7:33 and 8:23 for other instances of saliva, which had magical associations, being used for healing.

‡ This pool in the southwestern part of Jerusalem was fed by a spring and was used for ritual purification.

man called Iēsous made some mud and wiped it on my eyes and said to me, 'Get moving, go to the Silōam and wash.' So I went and washed, and then I was able to see again." [12] And they said to him, "Where is he?" He said, "I don't know."

[13] They took this man, who'd been blind before, to the Farisaioi. [14] Now the day on which Iēsous had made mud and opened the man's eyes was the *sabbaton.* [15] So the Farisaioi as well subjected him to an interrogation, a second one, as to how his sight was healed. He said to them, "He put mud on my eyes, and I washed, and now I can see." [16] So some of the Farisaioi said, "This man isn't from god, because he doesn't observe the *sabbaton.*" [But] others said, "How can anyone who's in the wrong perform such signs?" Hence there was a split among them. [17] So they spoke to the blind man again: "What do *you* say about him, since it's your eyes he opened?" And he said, "He's a prophet."

[18] The Ioudaioi didn't believe that he had been blind and that his sight had been restored, until they called in the parents of the man whose sight had been restored. [19] And they questioned them, saying, "This is your son, who you say was born blind? So how does it come about that he can see now?" [20] His parents then answered by saying, "We know that this is our son and that he was born blind. [21] But how it comes about that now he can see, we don't know; and as to who opened his eyes, we don't know that either. Ask him; he's an adult, he'll speak for himself." [22] His parents said this because they were afraid of the Ioudaioi, as the Ioudaioi had already decided among themselves that anyone who agreed Iēsous was the anointed one would be expelled from his synagogue. [23] This is why his parents said, "He's an adult, ask him."

[24] So for a second time they called in the man who'd been blind, and they said to him: "Give glory to god. We know this man is a wrongdoer." [25] Then he answered, "Whether he's a wrongdoer, I don't know. I know one thing: I was blind, but now I can see." [26] So they said to him, "What did he do to you? How

did he open your eyes?" ²⁷ He answered them, "I already told you, and you didn't listen. Why do you want to hear it again? You don't want to become his students too, do you?" ²⁸ And they spoke to him abusively, saying, "You're a student of his yourself! *We*'re students of Mōüsēs. ²⁹ We *know* that god spoke to Mōüsēs.* We don't even know where this man is from." ³⁰ The man answered and spoke to them: "Now here's something amazing: you don't even know where he's from—but he opened my eyes! ³¹ We know that god doesn't listen to wrongdoers, but if someone is a worshipper of god and does what god wants, god does listen to him. ³² Since the beginning of time, it was never heard of that anyone opened the eyes of a person born blind. ³³ If this man weren't from god, he couldn't have done anything." ³⁴ They answered by telling him: "You were born in the middle of so much wrongdoing that there's nothing else to you,† and you're trying to teach *us*?" And they threw him out.

³⁵ Iēsous heard that they'd thrown him out, and he found him and said, "Do you trust in the son of mankind?" ³⁶ He answered by saying, "But who is it, sir, so that I can trust in him?"‡ ³⁷ Iēsous said to him, "But you *have* seen him, and he's the one speaking with you." ³⁸ He said, "I do trust, lord," and prostrated himself in worship.§

³⁹ Then Iēsous said, "I came into this world for the case to be decided, so that those who don't see will be able to see, and those who do see will become blind." ⁴⁰ The Farisaioi who were with him heard this and said to him, "*We*'re not blind, are we?" ⁴¹ Iēsous

* Moses is the purported author of the Pentateuch or Torah, the first five books of the Hebrew Bible.

† Euphemistically: You are a bastard.

‡ See pp. xxix–xxxi in the Introduction; this man may be confused as to what "son of mankind" means.

§ The *kurie* of Verse 36 must be "sir," but two verses later, it seems to mean "lord," a divinity in the flesh. See "lord" in the Glossary.

said to them, "If you *were* blind, you wouldn't be in the wrong. But as it is, because you say, 'We can see,' you're stuck in your wrongdoing."

CHAPTER 10

———

[1] "*Amēn amēn* I tell you all, whoever doesn't come through the gate into the yard where the sheep are kept, but instead climbs in some other way, he's a thief and a bandit. [2] No, the one coming in through the gate is the sheep's shepherd. [3] The gatekeeper opens up to him, and the sheep listen to his voice, and he calls his own sheep by their names and leads them out. [4] When he's brought out all that are his own, he makes his way ahead of them, and the sheep follow him, because they know his voice. [5] They'll never follow a stranger; they'll run from him instead, because they don't recognize strangers' voices." [6] Iēsous gave them this analogy, but they didn't understand what he was saying to them.*

[7] Then Iēsous spoke again: "*Amēn amēn,* I tell you that I am the gate to the sheep. [8] All the people who have come [before me] are thieves and bandits; but the sheep didn't listen to them. [9] *I* am the gate. If anyone goes in through me, he'll be kept safe, and will come in and go out and find pasture. [10] The thief doesn't come except to thieve and slaughter sheep and destroy.† I came so that they could have life, and have it in profusion.

---

* This characterization of a responsible leader is much older even than the Twenty-Third Psalm. Very early Middle Eastern leaders used the same kind of expression, and their staffs were analogous to the combined tool and weapon some shepherds still carry.

† See "thief" in the Glossary. Judas of Galilee had led a major rebellion against the imposition of tax registration by the Roman governor Quirinius in 6 C.E. The insurgents stole animals and burned homes of those who did not withhold their registration.

¹¹ "I am the real shepherd. The real shepherd lays down his life for the sake of the sheep. ¹² If it's just a hired man and not the shepherd, and the sheep aren't his own, he sees the wolf coming and abandons the sheep and runs away—and the wolf snatches them and scatters them—¹³ because he's just a hired man, and he doesn't care about the sheep.

¹⁴ "I am the real shepherd, and I know my own, and my own know me. ¹⁵ As the father knows me, I also know the father, and I lay down my life for the sake of the sheep.* ¹⁶ But I have other sheep that don't belong to this yard; I need to lead those too, and they'll listen to my voice, and they'll all become one flock, with one shepherd.†

¹⁷ "Because of this the father loves me: I lay down my life, so that I can have it back again. ¹⁸ No one takes it from me, but rather I lay it down of my own accord. I have the power to lay it down, and the power to have it back again; I received this command from my father."

¹⁹ There was a split among the Ioudaioi again because of these things he said. ²⁰ Many among them said: "He has a demon in him, and he's out of his mind. Why are you listening to him?" ²¹ But others said, "These aren't the statements of someone possessed by a demon. A demon can't open the eyes of the blind, right?"

²² At that time the festival of the rededication‡ was going on in Hierosoluma; it was winter, ²³ and Iēsous was walking around in the temple precinct in the portico of Solomōn.§ ²⁴ So the Ioudaioi

---

* The most reliable herder would be the only son of the house, who expected to inherit all the animals.

† At the time of the Gospel of John's appearance, Christianity was a multi-ethnic religion spreading through much of the Roman Empire.

‡ Hanukkah, the eight-day celebration commemorating the Maccabean re-dedication of the Temple after it had been profaned by the Greek ruler Antio-chus Epiphanes in the second century B.C.E.

§ This was on the eastern side of the Temple's outer court, a public place where even women were permitted. It is named after Solomon, but the original

surrounded him and said to him, "How long are you going to keep us in this terrible suspense? If you're the anointed one, tell us openly." ²⁵ Iēsous answered them, "I told you and you still don't believe. The work I carry out in the name of my father—this testifies for me. ²⁶ But you don't believe, because you're not any of my sheep. ²⁷ My sheep listen to my voice, and I know them, and they follow me. ²⁸ And I give them life that lasts for all time, and for all time they'll never be destroyed, and nobody's going to tear them from my hand. ²⁹ What the father has given me is greater than everything else, and no one can tear it from the father's hand. ³⁰ I and the father are one being."*

³¹ Again the Ioudaioi picked up stones in preparation for stoning him. ³² Iēsous responded to them: "I've shown you many good works that came from the father. Which work are you stoning me for?" ³³ The Ioudaioi answered him: "We're not stoning you for any good work, but because of blasphemy, and because, even though you're just a human being, you make yourself out to be a god."† ³⁴ Iēsous answered them, "Hasn't it been written in your law, 'I said, "You are gods"?'‡ ³⁵ If he called those people gods, and they're the people to whom god's utterance came—and what's written can't lose its force—³⁶ can you say of the one the father made holy and sent into the world, 'You're blaspheming!' because I said, 'I am god's son'? ³⁷ If I don't carry out the work of my

---

Temple attributed to him was built in the tenth century, whereas the basis for Herod's recent renovation dated from the sixth century.

  * Again, the pragmatic analogy would be a father and only son's equal material interests; the motif will be developed at length in the discourse of Chapters 13 through 17.

  † See Leviticus 24:16 concerning blasphemy.

  ‡ One relevant verse is Psalms 82:6, but the next verse confirms the distance between the deity and mortals in traditional Jewish thought. The two verses read: "I say, 'You are gods, children of the Most High, all of you; nonetheless, you shall die like mortals, and fall like any prince.'" Exodus 7:1 reads (with my emphasis), "See, I have made you *like* God to Pharaoh . . ."

father, then don't trust me. [38] But if I do carry it out, and you still don't trust me, trust in that work, so that you know and understand that the father is in me and I am in the father." [39] [Then] they tried again to seize him, but he went out and escaped their hands.

[40] Then he went away, back to the other side of the Iordanēs, to the place where Iōannēs had been baptizing people at the start,* and he remained there. [41] And many people came to him and said, "Iōannēs didn't perform a single sign, but everything that Iōannēs said about this man was true." [42] And many people came to trust in him there.

CHAPTER 11

———

[1] A certain man was ailing, Lazaros from Bēthania, the same village Maria and Martha her sister lived in. [2] Now, Mariam was the one who spread perfume over the master and wiped dry his feet with her hair,† and it was her brother Lazaros who was ailing. [3] So the sisters sent a message to Iēsous, saying, "Master, look, your dear friend is ailing." [4] When he heard this, Iēsous said, "This ailment won't lead to death; on the contrary, it's for the glory of god, so that god's son can be glorified through it." [5] But Iēsous did love Martha and her sister and Lazaros. [6] So when he heard that the man was ailing, he stayed in the place where he was for two days, [7] and only after that did he say to the students, "Let's get back to Ioudaia." [8] His students said to him, "*Rabbí,* now the Ioudaioi are looking to stone you, and you're heading back there again?" [9] Iēsous answered, "Aren't there twelve hours in the day? If someone walks around during the day, he doesn't collide with

---

  * See the note at Mark 1:5 concerning the general geography.

  † See 12:3–8 below.

anything, because he sees the light of this world. ¹⁰ But if someone walks during the night, he *does* collide with things, because
the light isn't *inside* him."*

¹¹ He said these things, and next he told them, "Lazaros our
dear friend has fallen asleep. But I'm on my way there so that I
can rouse him from sleep." ¹² So the students said to him, "Master, if he's fallen asleep, he'll be cured." ¹³ But Iēsous had spoken
about his death, whereas the others thought he spoke about ordinary sleep. ¹⁴ But then Iēsous spoke to them openly: "Lazaros
has died. ¹⁵ And I'm happy for your sake: this will lead you to
believe, because I wasn't there when it happened. But let's get to
him." ¹⁶ Then Thōmas who was called the Twin said to his fellow
students, "Let's get there ourselves as well, so that we can die
with him."†

¹⁷ So when Iēsous arrived, he found that Lazaros had already
been in the tomb for four days. ¹⁸ Now Bēthania was near Hierosoluma, about fifteen stades away.‡ ¹⁹ And many of the Ioudaioi
had come to Martha and Mariam to console them about their
brother. ²⁰ So when Martha heard that Iēsous was coming, she
went out to meet him. Meanwhile, Mariam was sitting in the
house. ²¹ So Martha said to Iēsous, "Master, if you'd been here,
my brother wouldn't have died. ²² [But] even now I know that
whatever you ask god for, god will give you." ²³ Iēsous told
her, "Your brother will rise to his feet." ²⁴ Martha said to him, "I
know that he'll rise to his feet in the rising, on the last day."
²⁵ Iēsous said to her, "I myself am the rising, and life.§ Whoever

---

* Daylight hours are normally the only time for active life. But Jesus, *being* the
light, is not restricted in his activities by time and place.

† Are Thomas' words here sarcastic? See below at 14:5 and 20:24–29.

‡ The West Bank village al-Eizariya has been identified with Bethany; the
distance is perhaps two miles.

§ Martha has expressed a belief in the afterlife apparently both embraced by
mainstream sectarians (the Pharisees) and purveyed by existing apocalyptic lit-

trusts in me, even if he dies, will live. ²⁶ And whoever lives and trusts in me will, for all of time, never die.* Do you believe this?" ²⁷ She said to him, "Yes, master. I've come to believe that you're the anointed one, the son of god who is coming into the world."†

²⁸ Then, having said this, she went away and called Mariam her sister, saying to her discreetly, "The teacher's here, and he's calling for you." ²⁹ And when Mariam heard, she got up quickly and came to him. ³⁰ Īēsous hadn't yet come into the village, but was still in the place where Martha had met him. ³¹ But the Ioudaioi who were with Mariam in the house, consoling her, saw that she got up quickly, so they went out and followed after her, thinking that she was headed to the tomb to cry there.

³² Then when Mariam arrived where Īēsous was and saw him, she fell down at his feet, saying to him, "Master, if you'd been here, my brother wouldn't have died." ³³ Then Īēsous, when he saw her crying, and the Ioudaioi who were accompanying her crying too, howled within, with his very life-breath, and was greatly distressed. ³⁴ Then he said, "Where have you laid him?" They said to him, "Master, come and see." ³⁵ Īēsous shed tears.‡ ³⁶ Then the Ioudaioi said, "See how loving a friend he was to

---

erature. Jesus, with an extra, emphatic pronoun (*egō* for "I myself"), declares that he personally—God is not mentioned—embodies the afterlife.

  * These two verses apparently reflect a generational problem that is also addressed by Paul in 1 Thessalonians 4: since the Second Coming has proved to be long delayed, assurance is needed that both those who are living when it eventually happens and those who are deceased can be resurrected.

  † This echoes the beginning of the Gospel of John, at 1:9, and has messianic overtones.

  ‡ This three-word, shortest verse of the Bible employs a verb that depicts the tears on his face, whereas the verb used elsewhere in the episode, and familiar in scenes of mourning and other suffering, is for ordinary crying or wailing. Even Jesus' expressions of grief are special. In Verses 33 and 38, he makes a rare, animal-like sound, and the verb is in an intensive compound form.

him." [37] But some of them said, "He opened the blind man's eyes: couldn't he keep this man from dying?"

[38] So Iēsous, again howling deep within, came to the tomb. It was a cave,* and a stone was lying against it. [39] Iēsous said, "Lift away the stone." Martha, a sister of the dead man, said to him, "Master, by now he smells: he's been dead four days." [40] Iēsous said to her, "Didn't I tell you that if you believed, you'd see god's glory?" [41] So they lifted the stone away, and Iēsous lifted his eyes upward and said, "Father, I give thanks to you because you heard me. [42] I knew that you hear me at all times, but because of the crowd standing around, I said it, so that they believe it was you who sent me." [43] And having said these things, he yelled with a loud voice, "Lazaros, come out of there!" [44] And the dead man came out, his hands and feet bound with strips of cloth and his face bound up in a napkin. Iēsous said to them, "Untie him and let him go."

[45] Then many of the Ioudaioi who had come to Mariam and seen what he did trusted in him. [46] But some of them went to the Farisaioi and told them what Iēsous had done.

[47] Then the high priests and the Farisaioi convened their high council† and said, "What do we do, since this man performs so many signs? [48] If we let him go on like this, everyone will trust in him, and the Romans will come and do away with our country and our nation." [49] But one among them, Kaïaphas, who was chief priest for that year, said to them, "You all don't know anything. [50] You don't even figure that it's better for you if a single man dies for the people and the whole nation isn't destroyed." [51] He didn't say this on his own authority; instead, in his capacity as chief priest for that year, he prophesied that Iēsous was about to die

---

* From at least the time of Abraham, caves, because of their rarity and the large spaces some could provide, were prestigious family burial places. (See Genesis 23.)

† The Sanhedrin.

for the nation, [52] and not only for the nation, but also to bring together as one the scattered children of god. [53] From that day onward, therefore, they plotted to kill him.*

[54] So Iēsous no longer walked around openly among the Ioudaioi, but instead went away from there to a neighborhood close to the wilderness, to a town called Efraim,[†] and there he stayed with his students.

[55] But the *pascha* of the Ioudaioi was close, and many went up to Hierosoluma from the countryside for this festival in order to purify themselves.[‡] [56] So they looked for Iēsous and spoke to each other while standing in the temple precinct: "What do you all think? He certainly won't come to the festival—will he?" [57] The high priests and the Farisaioi had given orders that whoever knew where he was needed to report it so that they could seize him.

CHAPTER 12

———

[1] Then, six days before the *pascha,* Iēsous came to Bēthania, where Lazaros lived, the man Iēsous had awakened from among the

---

* Caiaphas' tenure is verified by the later historian Josephus, and this account confirms the highly politicized nature of the high priesthood at this time. Nonetheless, prophetic power is here attributed to this priest because of his position. The speech seems to allude to the Jewish Diaspora (literally "scattering"), which was a major incubator of early Christianity—but this stage was apparently over by the time the Gospel of John appeared.

† If Ephraim is the modern Taybeth in remote hill country, it would have been a one- or two-day journey northeast of Jerusalem, in the direction of Galilee.

‡ At least since the Temple was rebuilt in the sixth century B.C.E., essential religious obligations were concentrated there; those who did not conform through periodic attendance could be ostracized.

dead. ² So they prepared a dinner for him there, and Martha waited on them, and Lazaros was one of those reclining with him.*

³ Then Mariam took a pound of perfume—which was genuine, extremely costly nard—and spread it on Iēsous' feet and wiped them dry with her hair. And the house was filled with the scent of the perfume. ⁴ But Ioudas the Iskariōtēs,† one [of] his students, who was going to hand him over, said, ⁵ "Why wasn't the perfume sold for three hundred denarii and the money given to the destitute?" ⁶ But he said this not because he cared about the destitute, but because he was a thief: he kept the money-box and used to pilfer what was put into it. ⁷ But in answer Iēsous said, "Let her alone. She bought it to keep for the day I would be prepared for burial. ⁸ Surely you people are going to have the destitute among you forever, but you're not going to have *me* forever."

⁹ A large crowd of the Ioudaioi learned he was there, and they came not because of Iēsous only, but also to see Lazaros, whom he'd awakened from among the dead. ¹⁰ But the high priests plotted to kill Lazaros too, ¹¹ because, due to him, many of the Ioudaioi were defecting and trusting in Iēsous.

¹² On the next day, the large crowd that had come for the festival heard that Iēsous was coming into Hierosoluma, ¹³ and they took the branches of palm trees‡ and came out to meet him, yelling,

> *"Hōsanna!*
> *Blessed is the one coming in the name of the lord,§*
> *[And] the king of Israel."*

---

* At least among the Greeks and Romans, a well-to-do lady of the house would never serve (or help serve) the meal (though among the Romans she could be included as a diner). This may be Martha's special gesture of thankfulness for her brother's resurrection.

† See the note at Mark 3:19.

‡ Fertility, victory, and eternal life were among the things that evergreen palm branches symbolized.

§ See Psalms 118:25–26. *Hōsanna* means "Rescue, please," in Hebrew.

¹⁴ Having found a little donkey, Iēsous mounted on it—as it has been written:

> ¹⁵ *"Don't be afraid, daughter Siōn:*
> *Look, your king is coming,*
> *Mounted on a donkey's colt."**

¹⁶ His students didn't recognize all this at first, but when Iēsous was glorified, then it occurred to them that this had been written about him, and that people had done these things for him. ¹⁷ Thus the same crowd was testifying that had been with him when he summoned Lazaros out of the tomb and awakened him from among the dead. ¹⁸ Hearing that he had performed this sign was [another] reason for the crowd coming to meet him. ¹⁹ So the Farisaioi said to each other, "You all can see it: you're achieving nothing. Look, the whole world has gone away, following after him."

²⁰ Now there were some Greeks among those who had come up to worship at the festival. ²¹ So these people approached Filippos from Bēthsaïda in Galilaia and made inquiries with him, saying, "Sir, we want to see Iēsous." ²² Filippos went and told Andreas; Andreas and Filippos went and told Iēsous. ²³ But Iēsous responded to them by saying, "The time has come for the son of mankind to be glorified. ²⁴ *Amēn amēn* I tell you, unless a grain of wheat falls onto the ground and dies, it remains nothing but a single grain. But if it dies, it brings a large harvest. ²⁵ Whoever clings to his living self† like a dear friend will lose it, but whoever hates his living self in this present world will keep it safe, and it will be life for all time. ²⁶ Whoever tends to me had better follow me, and where I am, my attendant will be there too. And if someone tends to me, my father will honor him.‡

---

* See the note at Matthew 21:5.

† See "soul" in the Glossary.

‡ See the note at Mark 3:19 concerning the Greek names of certain disciples as

[27] "As things are, my living self has been thrown into confusion, but what should I say? 'Father, rescue me, now that the time has come'? But this is the reason I came to this time. [28] Father, bring glory to your name." Then there came a voice from the sky: "I have both glorified it and will glorify it again." [29] So the crowd standing there and listening to him said thunder had sounded; others said, "A messenger's spoken to him." [30] Iēsous responded by saying, "It wasn't because of me that the voice came, but because of you. [31] Now the judgment of this world is here; now the ruler of this world will be thrown clear out of it.* [32] And I myself, if I'm raised up above the earth, will draw all people to myself." [33] He said this to signal the kind of death he was about to undergo.†

[34] So the crowd responded to him: "We've heard from the writings of the law that the anointed one will remain for all time, so what do you mean by saying that the son of mankind must be raised up? Who's this 'son of mankind'?"‡ [35] Iēsous then said to them, "For a short time longer the light is among you. Walk while you have the light, so that the darkness doesn't overtake you. Someone walking in darkness doesn't know where he's headed. [36] While you have light, trust in the light, so that you

---

possible indicators of Hellenistic cultural influence. Here two disciples with such names are go-betweens for "Greeks" who seek a meeting with Jesus. Are these Diaspora Jews or pagan admirers of Judaism, known elsewhere in the New Testament as "God-fearers" and "God-worshippers"?

* The ruler of most of the known world at this time was the Roman emperor Tiberius, but when the Gospel of John was completed, it may have been the tyrannical emperor Domitian (assassinated in 96 C.E.), whom some ancient authors implicate in major persecutions of Christians. However, the deposing of earthly authority was a commonplace of apocalyptic literature. This passage could also refer to a supernatural being.

† Once again, wordplay for "raising [on the cross/to the sky]."

‡ The Messiah as David's successor was expected to reign on earth forever to protect and glorify his people. See, for example, Psalms 89:35–37, Ezekiel 37:24–25, and Daniel 7:13–14.

become sons of the light." Iēsous said these things, then went away and hid from them.

³⁷ But though he'd performed so many signs before their eyes, they didn't trust in him, ³⁸ so that what was spoken by Ēsaïas the prophet would be fulfilled, when he said:

> *"Lord, who believed what they heard from us?*
> *And to whom was the arm of the lord uncovered?"**

³⁹ For this reason they weren't able to believe: Ēsaïas also said,

> ⁴⁰ *"He blinded their eyes,*
> *And made their hearts calloused and unfeeling,*
> *So that they couldn't see with their eyes*
> *Or perceive with their hearts*
> *And turn around and let me heal them."*†

⁴¹ Ēsaïas said these things because he saw his glory, and he spoke about him. ⁴² Nevertheless, even many of the leaders trusted in him, but because of the Farisaioi they didn't admit it, fearing they would be banned from their synagogues. ⁴³ They loved the glory of human beings more than god's glory.

⁴⁴ Iēsous shouted out, saying, "Whoever trusts in me doesn't trust in *me*, but instead in the one who sent me. ⁴⁵ And whoever gazes on me gazes on the one who sent me. ⁴⁶ I came into the world as light, so that everyone who trusts in me won't stay in darkness. ⁴⁷ And if anyone hears the things I say and doesn't guard them and carry them out, I'm not going to judge him, since I didn't come to judge the world, but instead to rescue the world. ⁴⁸ Whoever rejects me and doesn't accept the things I say

---

* Isaiah 53:1; the arm of God stands for his strength.

† Isaiah 6:10.

has someone else to judge him: the true account I've given—*that* will judge him on the last day. ⁴⁹ That's because I haven't said anything on my own behalf; instead, the father himself who sent me gave me a command as to what to talk about and how to say it. ⁵⁰ And I know that his command is life for all time. So what I talk about, I talk about it in just the way the father said it to me."

CHAPTER 13

———

¹ Before the festival of the *pascha,* Iēsous knew that his time had come to cross over out of this world to the father. But because he had loved his own people who were in the world, he kept loving them until the end. ² And when the banquet was taking place, and the slanderer had already put it into the heart of Ioudas the son of Simōn Iskariōtēs to hand him over, ³ Iēsous, knowing that the father had given everything into his hands and that he had come from god and was heading back to god, ⁴ got up from the banquet, put aside his outer clothing, took a towel, and tied it around his waist. ⁵ Then he poured water into the washbasin and proceeded to wash his students' feet and to wipe them dry with the towel he had around his waist. ⁶ Then he came to Simōn Petros, who said to him, "Master, are *you* washing *my* feet?" ⁷ Iēsous answered by saying to him, "What I'm doing you don't realize right now, but you'll understand afterward." ⁸ Petros said to him, "You must never wash my feet, as long as time lasts." Iēsous answered him, "If I don't wash you, you'll have no share along with me."* ⁹ Simōn Petros said to him, "Master, don't just wash my feet, but also my hands and my head." ¹⁰ Iēsous said to him, "Someone who's had a bath has no need to wash, except for his feet; no, he's clean all over. And you people are

———

* *Meros* is a word for a share of an inheritance.

clean—but not every one of you." [11] He knew, in fact, who was handing him over, and that is why he said, "Not every one of you is clean."*

[12] Then when he had washed their feet [and] put on his outer clothing and reclined again, he said to them, "Do you understand what I've done for you? [13] You call me 'the teacher' and 'the master,' and those are proper things to say, since that's what I am. [14] So if I've washed your feet, and I'm the master and the teacher, you also ought to wash each other's feet. [15] I've set you an example, so that what I did for you, you in turn should do. [16] *Amēn amēn* I tell you, there's no slave who's greater than his master, and no envoy who's greater than the one who sent him. [17] If you know these things, you'll be happy if you practice them.

[18] "I'm not talking about all of you. *I* know the ones I singled out. Instead, it's so that what's written can be fulfilled: 'The one who ate my loaf has lifted his heel against me.'† [19] But right now I tell you this, before it happens, so that when it happens you believe that *it's me.*‡ [20] *Amēn amēn* I tell you, the one who takes in whoever I'm going to send takes me in, and the one who takes me in takes in the one who sent me."

[21] After saying these things, Iēsous was agitated clear to his life-breath, and he testified by saying, "*Amēn amēn* I tell you, one of you is going to hand me over." [22] The students looked at each

---

* This cannot be a species of proper Jewish ritual washing before eating, because that did not single out the feet, and this meal has already begun. Peter tries at least to move Jesus' ministrations to more respectable parts of his body. (Note that "feet" is a Hebrew euphemism for the penis; and Jesus' word choices may allude to instructions in Leviticus 15 for cleansing in the case of a male genital discharge.) Thematically, the focus moves from the "whole" body (*holos:* my "all over") to the whole community of Jesus' followers (*pantes:* "every one of you"), with the exception of Judas.

† Psalms 41:9; the meaning is probably a kick or a contemptuous turning of the back.

‡ Possibly (another) reference to Exodus 3:14, "I AM THAT I AM," God's naming and definition of himself.

other, at a dead end in guessing which one he meant. ²³ There was one of his students, reclining in Iēsous' arms, whom Iēsous loved. ²⁴ Therefore Simōn Petros gestured to him to ask who it was Iēsous meant. ²⁵ So the man reclining against Iēsous' chest said to him, "Master, who is it?"* ²⁶ Iēsous answered, "It's the man for whom I dip this piece of bread, and give it to him."† He then dipped the bread [took it] and gave it to Ioudas the son of Simōn Iskariōtēs. ²⁷ And then, after that piece of bread, satanas entered into him. Iēsous then said to him, "What you're about to do, do it quickly." ²⁸ [But] no one among those reclining at the table knew why he said this to him. ²⁹ Some of them in fact thought, since Ioudas kept the money-box, that Iēsous had said to him, "Buy the things we need for the festival," or that he wanted him to give something to the destitute. ³⁰ At any rate, he took the piece of bread and went out right away. But it was night-time.‡

³¹ Then when he'd gone out, Iēsous said, "Now the son of mankind has been glorified, and god has been glorified in him. ³² [If god has been glorified in him,] god will also glorify him in himself, and will glorify him right away. ³³ Little children, I'm with you for a little while longer. You'll look for me, and what I said to the Ioudaioi, I say to you as well now: where I'm headed, you can't go. ³⁴ I give you a new command, to love each other; just as I have loved you, you must love one another as well. ³⁵ By this,

---

* The Greek- or Roman-style dining couch was wide enough to allow two diners to lie parallel, on their sides, the one in front leaning on the chest of the one behind. (The *kolpos* mentioned in Verse 23 is the "bosom," where a baby was held and nursed.) By tradition, the "beloved disciple," John, is the purported author of this Gospel. See also Chapter 21 and the note at its end.

† Bread would be dipped in relishes, condiments, gravy, or stew in common bowls.

‡ Merchants and beggars alike would not be available at this late hour, especially on a holiday. Beyond this, the little sentence is sinister; ancient authors tended to agree that any business transacted at night was likely to be criminal or conspiratorial.

everyone will know that you're my students, if you show love for one another."*

³⁶ Simōn Petros said to him, "Master, where are you headed?" Iēsous answered [him], "Where I'm headed, you can't follow me now, but you'll follow afterward." ³⁷ Petros said to him, "Master, why is it that I can't follow you right now? I'll lay down my life for you." ³⁸ Iēsous responded, "You'll lay down your life for me? *Amēn amēn* I tell you, the rooster definitely won't crow before you deny three times that you know me."

CHAPTER 14

——

¹ "Don't let your hearts be troubled. Trust in god, and trust in me. ² In my father's house, there are many places to stay; if there weren't, would I have told you that I'm on my way to get a place ready for you? ³ And if I'm on my way and get a place ready for you, I'm coming back, and I'll take you along to join me, so that where I am, you all will be too.† ⁴ And where I'm headed [myself], you know the way."

⁵ Thōmas said to him, "Master, we *don't* know where you're headed. How can we know the way?" ⁶ Iēsous said to him, "*I* am the way, and the truth, and life; no one comes to the father except through me. ⁷ If you've come to know me, you'll also know my father. And from now on, you know him and you've seen him."

⁸ Filippos said to him, "Master, show us the father, and it will be enough for us." ⁹ Iēsous said to him, "I've been with all of you

---

* It does not seem to be a new commandment at all, as the Synoptic Gospels all indicate (Mark 12:28–31, Matthew 22:35–40, and Luke 10:25–28).

† These are almost certainly dedicated guest quarters, not mere rooms; in any case, the King James Version's "mansions" is an outdated term for a place to stay.

for such a long time—and you didn't recognize me, Filippos? Anyone who's seen me has seen the father. What do you mean by 'Show us the father?' ¹⁰ Don't you believe that I am in the father and the father is in me? In the things I say to you, I'm not talking on my own account; no, the father, who lives in me, carries out his work. ¹¹ Believe me because I am in the father and the father is in me. Or if not, have trust because of the work itself.

¹² "*Amēn amēn* I tell you, whoever trusts in me will carry out himself the work I do, and will do even greater work than this, because I'm on my way to the father. ¹³ And whatever you ask for in my name, I'll do it, so that the father is glorified in the son. ¹⁴ If you ask me for anything in my name, I'll do it.

¹⁵ "If you love me, you will guard and carry out my commands. ¹⁶ And I'll ask the father, and he will give you another advocate, so that he'll be with you for all time, ¹⁷ as the life-breath of truth, which the world isn't able to take in, because it doesn't see it or recognize it. You recognize it, because it lives with you and will be in you.* ¹⁸ I won't leave you orphaned; I'm coming to you. ¹⁹ A little longer, and the world won't see me anymore, but you'll see me, because I live, and you will live. ²⁰ On that day you'll know that I am in my father, and you in me, and I in you.† ²¹ Whoever possesses my commands and guards

---

* Jesus speaks here and in Verses 26 and 16:7–11 below of a being sometimes referred to in English as the Comforter, but the Greek word *paraklētos* usually means an advocate, which suggests defense during persecutions or a role in the apocalyptic final judgment. These are important passages underlying the theology of the Holy Trinity (from the Latin for "three in one"), consisting of the Father, the Son, and the Holy Spirit. I will not dilate on the final formulation, which probably would have made no sense to the Gospels' authors, let alone to people in the time and place where the story happens. But I do state that to Jews of the Second Temple period, the world was richly populated with supernatural functionaries, and a divine helper and supporter of pious mortals would not have needed any explaining.

† This is a key passage concerning the Second Coming, or the *parousia* ("presence" or "arrival"), Jesus' return to the world at the end of ordinary history.

them, that's the one who loves me. And the one who loves me will be loved by my father, and I'll love him and reveal myself clearly to him."

²² Ioudas (not the one called Iskariōtēs) said to him, "Master, [and] how has it come about that you're going to reveal yourself to us but not to the world?" ²³ Iēsous answered him by saying, "If someone loves me, he'll keep safe what I speak of, and my father too will love him, and we'll come to him and make our home with him. ²⁴ But whoever doesn't love me won't keep safe the things I speak of. But what I speak of, which you hear, isn't mine; instead, it belongs to the father who sent me.

²⁵ "I've told you these things while I remained with you. ²⁶ But the advocate, the holy life-breath, which my father will send in my name—*he* will teach you everything and remind you of everything I [myself] said to you.

²⁷ "Peace I leave to you, my peace I give to you. Not as the world gives, I give to you. Don't let your hearts be troubled, and don't let them be cowardly. ²⁸ You've heard me say to you: 'I'm heading off—and coming to you.' If you loved me, you'd be full of joy that I'm making my way to the father, because the father is greater than I am. ²⁹ And now I've said this to you before it happens, so that when it happens, you'll believe. ³⁰ I'll no longer talk much with you, since the ruler of the world is coming; but he has no power over me. ³¹ Nevertheless, so that the world can know that I love the father, I'm doing as the father commanded me. Get up—let's get out of here."*

---

* Many of Jesus' assertions in this speech would have sounded more worldly and familiar to contemporary readers. For a young man to claim that none of his friends could approach his powerful father (especially as guests), except through him, is mere common sense. The passage concludes with the mention of another essential feature of the father-son relationship, obedience. There was no age of majority or expected assertion of independence.

CHAPTER 15

---

[1] "I'm the true grapevine, and my father is the farmer. [2] Every branch on me that doesn't bear fruit, he prunes, and every branch that does bear fruit, he prunes clean so that the vine bears more fruit. [3] You yourselves are already made clean* by the discourse I've shared with you. [4] Live in me, and I'll live in you. Just as the branch can't bear fruit by itself if it doesn't live on the vine, so you also can't bear fruit if you don't live in me. [5] I'm the vine, and you're the branches; whoever lives in me, while I live in him, will bear a lot of fruit, because apart from me all of you can't do anything. [6] If someone doesn't live in me, he's thrown out like a branch and withers, and they gather him and the others together and throw them into the fire, and they burn. [7] If you all live in me, and if the things I say live in you, whatever you want, ask for it, and it will be done for you. [8] My father is glorified in this: that you bear a large harvest and become my students.†

[9] "Just as the father has loved me, I have also loved you: live in my love. [10] If you guard and observe my commands, you'll stay in my love, as I've observed the father's commands and stay in his love. [11] I've said these things to you so that my joy can be in you and your joy can be made complete. [12] This is my command, that

---

* Verbs for pruning: *airō* and the emphatic *kathairō;* the similar-sounding adjective for "clean" or "pure": *katharos.* The semantic connection is that the useless branches are cleaned away by a thorough pruning—but the rhetorical figures are not about any accurate description of vine-dressing. A branch is a *klēma,* and fruit is *karpos,* so the alliteration is piled on.

† The imagery of cutting down to size also underlies the idea of hubris in Classical tragedy; "hubris" began as a technical term for the excessive leafy growth that saps a fruit-bearing plant's productivity. The protagonist of tragedy has typically acquired too much power, which unbalances him and leads to disaster. Violence operates on him to restore the whole society through a process analogous to pruning.

you love each other as I've loved you.* ¹³ No one has greater
love than this, the love that makes him lay down his life for his
close friends' sake. ¹⁴ You're my close friends if you do what I
command you to. ¹⁵ I don't call you slaves any longer, because a
slave doesn't know what his master's doing. I've called you
friends instead, because everything I've heard from the father
I've made known to you. ¹⁶ You didn't choose me—I chose you,
and I assigned you to go and bear a harvest, and your harvest
needs to last, so that whatever you ask the father for in my name,
he'll give you. ¹⁷ I give you these commands so that you love each
other.†

¹⁸ "If the world hates you, you should know that it hated me
before it hated you. ¹⁹ If you were part of the world, the world
would love you the way it loves its own. But because you're not
part of the world, because instead I picked you out and set you
apart from the world—for this reason, the world hates you.‡
²⁰ Remember what I said to you: 'There's no slave greater than his
master.'§ If they hounded me, they'll hound you too. If they've
safeguarded what I said, they'll safeguard what you say. ²¹ But
they'll do all these things to you on account of my name, because
they don't know the one who sent me. ²² If I hadn't come and
spoken to them, they wouldn't be in the wrong. But as it is, they
have no excuse for what they've done wrong. ²³ Whoever hates
me hates my father too. ²⁴ If I hadn't, right in the midst of them,
carried out works that no one else ever carried out, they wouldn't
be in the wrong; but as it is, they've seen and hated both me and
the father. ²⁵ It was necessary, however, so that what was said, and

---

* See 13:35 and the note.

† Here, it is close friends, *filoi,* who are the objects of *agapaō,* the verb for less
privileged love—not the cognate verb *fileō,* as might be expected. It is as if family
and nonfamily relationships are merging.

‡ The language is playful. The preposition *ek,* "out of," is used first for being
"a part of." Then it appears in the compound verb *eklegomai,* "choose out of," and
then in the sense of "apart from."

§ Above, 13:16.

written down in their law, be fulfilled: 'They hated me for no reason.'*

²⁶ "When the advocate I'll send comes to you from the father—the life-breath of truth that makes its way from the father—he will testify about me.† ²⁷ But you also must testify, because you were with me from the beginning."

CHAPTER 16

¹ "I've told you these things to keep you from falling away. ² They'll ban you from the synagogues. More than that, the time is coming when everyone who kills you will think that he's offering a service to god. ³ And they'll do these things because they never knew the father or me. ⁴ But I've spoken of these things so that when the time comes for them, you'll remember I told you about them. I didn't tell you these things from the beginning, because I was with you. ⁵ But now I'm headed to the one who sent me, and not one of you asks me, 'Where are you headed?' ⁶ Still, because I've said these things, grief has filled your hearts. ⁷ Yet I tell you the truth: it's better for you that I go away. If I didn't go away, the advocate wouldn't come to you. If I'm on my way, I'll send him to you. ⁸ And when he comes, he'll cross-examine the world about wrongdoing, and about doing right, and about what the verdict must be. ⁹ About wrongdoing: people do not trust in me. ¹⁰ About doing right: I'm headed to the father, so that you no longer perceive me. ¹¹ About the verdict: the ruler of this world will be subject to the verdict.

¹² "I have many more things to say to you, but you can't endure

---

* Psalms 35:19 and 69:4.

† See the note at 14:15–17.

them just now. ¹³ When *he* comes, the life-breath of truth, he'll lead you on the journey in all truth. He won't speak on his own behalf; instead, he'll bring you a message about the things to come. ¹⁴ He'll glorify me, because he'll take a message from me and bring it to you. ¹⁵ Everything the father has is mine. For this reason, I've said he's going to take a message from me and bring it to you.*

¹⁶ "A little while, and you'll no longer perceive me; a little while more, and you'll see me." ¹⁷ Then some of his students said to each other, "What's this he's talking to us about? 'A little while, and you won't perceive me; a little while more, and you'll see me'? And 'I'm headed to the father'?" ¹⁸ So they said, "What is this 'a little while' [that he's talking about]? We don't understand what he's saying."

¹⁹ Iēsous knew they wanted to ask him, so he told them, "You're asking each other what it meant when I said, 'A little while, and you won't perceive me; a little while more, and you'll see me'? ²⁰ *Amēn amēn* I tell you, you'll cry and mourn, but the world will be delighted. You'll have pain, but your pain will become joy. ²¹ When a woman is in labor, she has pain, because her time has come, but when she gives birth to the child, she no longer remembers her grinding suffering, because of her joy that a human being has been born into the world. ²² So you have pain now, but I'll see you again, and your hearts will be full of joy, and no one will take your joy from you.†

²³ "And on that day, you won't have any requests to make of me. *Amēn amēn* I tell you, whatever you ask the father for in my name, he'll give it to you. ²⁴ Until now, you asked for nothing

---

* See 14:17 and the note. Here the helper sent fills an explicitly forensic function but also acts as a messenger, which suggests that he is a kind of angel (on which see the Glossary). See 12:31 and the note concerning "the ruler of this world."

† The Greek word *lupē* covers both emotional and physical suffering. The Septuagint uses the plural of the word for the curse of difficult human childbearing.

in my name. Ask, and you'll get it, so that your joy can be complete.

²⁵ "I've told you these things through figures of speech. The time is coming when I'll no longer speak to you through figures of speech; no, in all openness I'll give you the news about the father. ²⁶ On that day, you'll ask in my name, but I'm not telling you that I'll ask the father on your behalf. ²⁷ The father himself, you see, is your loving friend, because you've been my loving friends,* and you've come to believe that I came from god. ²⁸ I came from the father, and I've come into the world. I'm leaving the world again and making my way to the father."

²⁹ His students said, "Look, now you're speaking in all openness, and not using any figure of speech. ³⁰ Now we know that you know everything and don't need anyone to question you. This is why we believe that you came from god." ³¹ Iēsous responded to them: "Just now you believe? ³² Look, the time is coming, and it's come, for you to be scattered, each one to his own home, and to leave me by myself. But I'm not by myself, because my father's with me. ³³ I've said these things to you so that you can have peace in me. In the world, you have grinding suffering, but be brave: I've conquered the world."

CHAPTER 17

¹ Iēsous finished saying these things. Then, lifting his eyes to the sky, he spoke: "Father, the time has come. Glorify your son, so that your son can glorify you; ² insofar as you gave him authority

---

* The verb *fileō* indicates that because the disciples have a privileged, special relationship with Jesus, they have it with God too.

over all mortal life, so that he could give life for all time to all those you gave to him. ³ And this is life without end, so that they know you, the only true god, and Iēsous, the Anointed One, whom you sent. ⁴ I glorified you on the earth, completing the work you gave me to do. ⁵ And now you must glorify me, father, by your side, with the glory I had by your side before there was a world.

⁶ "I showed your name clearly to those you gave to me out of the world. They were yours, and you gave them to me, and they've safeguarded what you spoke. ⁷ Now they know that everything you gave to me is from you; ⁸ because the words you gave to me, I gave to them; and they accepted them, and they know in truth that I came from you, and they believe that you sent me.

⁹ "I ask you for their sake; I don't ask for the sake of the world, but for the sake of those you gave me, because they're yours. ¹⁰ And everything I have is yours, and everything you have is mine, and I have been glorified in these things. ¹¹ But I'm no longer in the world, whereas they *are* in the world, and I'm going to you. Holy father, keep watch over them in your name, which you gave me, so that they can be one, as we're one. ¹² When I was with them, I kept watch over them in your name, which you gave me, and I kept on guard, and not one of them was destroyed except for the son of destruction, so that what was written could be fulfilled.* ¹³ But now I'm going to you—yet I say these things in the world so that they have my joy fulfilled in themselves. ¹⁴ I gave them what you've spoken, and the world hated them, because they're not part of the world, just as I'm not part of the world. ¹⁵ I don't ask for you to take them out of the world, but that you keep them safe from the malicious one.† ¹⁶ They're not part of the world, as I'm not part of the world. ¹⁷ Make them pure and holy

---

* "Son of destruction" is a distinctly Hebrew- or Aramaic-like epithet.

† See "evil" and "devil" in the Glossary.

in the truth; what you speak is truth. ¹⁸ As you sent me into the world, I sent them into the world. ¹⁹ And on behalf of them I make myself holy, so that they can also be made holy in the truth.

²⁰ "But I don't ask on behalf of them alone, but also on behalf of all those trusting in me through what they say, ²¹ so that they can all be one; just as you, father, are in me and I am in you, may they also be in us, so that the world believes you sent me. ²² And I gave them the glory you gave me, so that they could be one, just as we are one. ²³ I am in them and you are in me, so that they can be completed as one; so that the world knows that you sent me, and that you loved them just as you loved me.

²⁴ "Father, I want also those you gave me to be with me where I am, so that they look on my glory, which you gave me because you loved me before the foundations of the universe were laid. ²⁵ Just and lawful father, the world hasn't known you, but I've known you, and these men have known you sent me. ²⁶ And I made your name known to them, and I'll keep making it known, so that the love with which you have loved me can be in them, and I can be in them."

CHAPTER 18

¹ Once he'd said these things, Iēsous went out with his students across the Kedrōn, a brook that flows only in winter, to where there was a cultivated grove, and he and his students went into the grove.

² Now Ioudas, who was handing him over, also knew the place, because Iēsous had often met there with his students.* ³ So Iou-

---

* The specification of a "grove" or "garden" in John calls to mind the famous "groves of Academe" for teaching philosophy in Athens.

das, taking a military division, and retainers from the high priests and the Farisaioi, came there with lanterns and torches and weapons.* [4] So Iēsous, noting everything that was coming at him, came forward and said to them, "Who are you looking for?" [5] They answered him, "Iēsous the Nazōraios." He told them, "That's me." Ioudas, the one handing him over, was standing with them. [6] So when he told them, "It's me," they backed up and fell to the ground. [7] Again he asked them, "Who are you looking for?" And they said, "Iēsous the Nazōraios." [8] Iēsous responded, "I told you it was me. So if it's me you're looking for, let these people get out of here." [9] He said this so that what he had said would be borne out: "I didn't lose a single one of those you gave me."† [10] Then Simōn Petros, who had a sword, drew it and struck the chief priest's slave and cut off his right ear. And the name of the slave was Malchos. [11] Then Iēsous said to Petros, "Put that sword back in its sheath. My father gave me a drinking cup— don't I have to drink out of it?"

[12] Then the division and its officer and the retinue of the Ioudaioi seized Iēsous, tied him up, [13] and led him to Annas first. He was the father-in-law of Kaïafas, who was the chief priest for that year; [14] and Kaïafas was the one who had advised the Ioudaioi that it was better for one man to die for the sake of the whole people.‡

[15] Simōn Petros and another student followed after Iēsous. But that student was known to the chief priest, so he went with Iēsous into the chief priest's palace. [16] But Petros stood outside by the gate; so the other student, the one known to the chief priest,

---

* John is the only Gospel writer who records Roman involvement in the arrest. See the note at Mark 14:43. It is absurd that Judas is shown with Roman soldiers at his disposal.

† John 6:39 and 17:12.

‡ Annas, the father-in-law of the chief priest Caiaphas, and—according to Josephus, a historian a couple of generations later—deposed in favor of him, is shown acting in close coordination.

came out and spoke to the girl who was gatekeeper, and brought Petros inside.* ¹⁷ Then that slave girl, the gatekeeper, said to Petros, "Aren't you one of this man's students too?" He said, "I'm not." ¹⁸ The slaves and the retainers were standing there. They had made a coal fire, because it was cold, and they were warming themselves. And Petros was standing with them and warming himself.

¹⁹ Meanwhile the high priest interrogated Iēsous about his students and his teachings. ²⁰ Iēsous answered him, "I've spoken openly to the world. I've always taught in a synagogue and in the temple precinct, where all the Ioudaioi assemble, and I've said nothing in secret. ²¹ Why are you interrogating me? Interrogate the people who heard what I said to them! Look, they know what I said." ²² Once he said this, one of the retainers who was standing near Iēsous gave him a slap and said to him, "Is this how you answer the high priest?" ²³ Iēsous answered him, "If I've said something wrong, give your testimony that it's wrong. But if I'm right, why do you beat me?" ²⁴ Then Annas had him tied up and sent him to Kaïafas the chief priest.

²⁵ Meanwhile, Simōn Petros was standing and warming himself. So they said to him, "Aren't you one of his students too?" He denied it, saying, "I'm not." ²⁶ One of the high priest's slaves spoke up, as he was a relative of the one whose ear Petros had cut off: "Didn't I see you in the grove with him?" ²⁷ Again Petros denied it, and right away the rooster crowed.

²⁸ Then they led Iēsous from Kaïafas to the governor's headquarters.† By now it was early morning. But they themselves didn't go into the headquarters, for fear of being defiled; they

---

* The man who knows the priest may be Judas, but it could be someone else, in parallel to the streaking young man mentioned in Mark (14:51–52), who is also not named. Or it might be Jesus' follower John (to whom this Gospel is attributed), repeatedly but discreetly depicted in important roles.

† See the note at Mark 15:16.

needed, on the contrary, to be able to eat the *pascha.** [29] So Pila-tos† came out to them and said: "What charge are you bringing [against] this man?" [30] They answered him by saying, "If he hadn't been up to no good, we wouldn't have turned him over to you." [31] So Pilatos said to them, "Take him yourselves and judge him under your law." The Ioudaioi said to him, "It's not permitted to us to kill anyone." [32] This was so that the statements Iēsous had made could be borne out: he'd indicated the kind of death he was about to undergo.‡

[33] So Pilatos went back into the governor's headquarters again, called Iēsous before him, and said to him, "You're the king of the Ioudaioi?" [34] Iēsous answered: "Do you say this on your own, or have other people told you about me?" [35] Pilatos answered: "What? Am I a Ioudaios? Your own nation and the high priests handed you over to me. What did you do?" [36] Iēsous answered: "My kingdom isn't part of this world. If my kingdom were part of this world, *my* retinue would fight to keep me from being handed over to the Ioudaioi. But as it is, my kingdom isn't part of here." [37] So Pilatos said to him, "Then you *are* a king?" Iēsous answered, "*You* say I'm a king. I was born for this, and for this I came into the world: to testify to the truth. Everyone partaking in the truth listens to my voice." [38] Pilatos said to him, "What's truth?"

Having said this, he came out again to the Ioudaioi and told them: "I find no guilt in him. [39] But it's your custom that I release

---

* I.e., a second evening's celebration, but this appears only ever to have been a Diaspora custom.

† See the note at Mark 15:1.

‡ Perhaps the Jewish leaders are alluding to the latitude allowed them under the Roman regime, as the death penalty *is* prescribed in the Torah for a number of offenses, including blasphemy (Leviticus 24:16), and the Book of Acts (7:58) shows a stoning for blasphemy being carried out in roughly the prescribed manner. But nowhere do the Hebrew scriptures prescribe crucifixion. A "lifting up" execution must therefore be carried out by the Romans according to Jesus' prediction.

one person to you on the *pascha.* So do you want me to release to you the 'king of the Ioudaioi'?" ⁴⁰ Then they screamed back at him the words "Not him! Barabbas!" Now, Barabbas was a bandit.*

CHAPTER 19

¹ So at this point Pilatos took Iēsous and had him flogged.† ² And the soldiers wove a garland out of thorny branches and put it on his head,‡ and they draped a purple robe over him. ³ And they came up to him, saying, "Joy to you, king of the Ioudaioi!" And they slapped him around. ⁴ And Pilatos came out again and said to the people, "Look, I'm bringing him out again to you, to let you know that I don't find any guilt in him." ⁵ So Iēsous came outside again, wearing the thorny garland and the purple robe. And Pilatos said to them, "Look at this guy."§

⁶ So when the high priests and their retinue saw him, they screamed the words "Hang him on the stakes, hang him on the stakes!"¶ Pilatos said to them, "Take him yourselves and hang him there, as I don't find any guilt in him." ⁷ The Ioudaioi answered him: "We have a law, and according to that law he has to die, because he presented himself as the son of god." ⁸ So when Pilatos heard this statement, he became more fearful. ⁹ Then he went into the headquarters again and said to Iēsous, "Where are you from?" But Iēsous didn't give him any answer. ¹⁰ So Pilatos said to him, "You're not talking to me? Don't you know that I

---

* See the notes at Mark 15:6 and 7.

† The verb indicates that small sharp objects are attached to the whip's thongs.

‡ A garland, not a metal crown, signified honor in Greek and Roman culture.

§ See p. xxxi of the Introduction concerning this famous statement.

¶ See the note at Mark 15:13.

have the power to let you go and the power to hang you on the stakes?" [11] Iēsous answered [him], "You don't have any power over me, unless it's been given to you from above. This is why the one who handed me over to you is more in the wrong."* [12] After this, Pilatos kept trying to let him go. But the Ioudaioi screamed, saying, "If you let him go, you're no friend of Kaisar. Anyone presenting himself as king opposes Kaisar."† [13] So once he heard them say these things, Pilatos brought Iēsous out and sat on the platform in the place called the Stone Pavement, but in Hebrew Gabbatha.‡ [14] But it was the day of preparation for the *pascha*,§ and it was about the sixth hour of the day, so he said to the Ioudaioi, "Look, it's your king." [15] Then they screamed, "Get rid of him! Get rid of him! Hang him on the stakes!" Pilatos said to them, "I'm supposed to hang your king on the stakes?" The high priests answered, "We don't have any king but Kaisar." [16] So then he handed him over to them to be hung on the stakes.

Then they took Iēsous over from him.¶ [17] And taking on the load of the stake,** he went out to what is called the Place of the Skull, which in Hebrew is called Golgotha,†† [18] where they hung

---

* That is, Pilate, but not Judas, is part of the providential plan for the crucifixion.

† Again, the emperor Tiberius. Ironically, he was a morose, reclusive, scholarly man who likely would have viewed these events in Judea with boredom and exasperation.

‡ *Bēma* ("thing you step up on"; my "platform") and *gabbatha* ("raised place"; as usual, an Aramaic word is identified as Hebrew) are essentially the same thing. The stone pavement, however, would be the floor of the room, and was probably a striking mosaic. There is a good archaeological contender for this exact place.

§ This does not look correct; that would have been the day before. Again, the Second Seder or repeated celebration is a Diaspora tradition.

¶ Pilate is shown handing Jesus back to the Jewish authorities, whereas nothing is conceivable but that he kept him in his own custody, to be executed at his command in the Roman manner.

** The condemned person might carry only the horizontal crosspiece.

†† Traditionally identified with the site of the Church of the Holy Sepulcher, and next to a busy road even during antiquity.

him up, and with him two others, one on either side; he was in the middle. ¹⁹ And Pilatos wrote the notice and put it on the stake; and this was written there:

Iēsous the Nazōraios, the king of the Ioudaioi.*

²⁰ Many of the Ioudaioi read this notice, because the place where Iēsous was hung on the stakes was near the city, and the writing was in Hebrew, Latin, and Greek. ²¹ Now, the high priests of the Ioudaioi said to Pilatos, "Don't write 'the king of the Ioudaioi'; write, 'He *said,* I'm the king of the Ioudaioi.'" ²² Pilatos answered, "I wrote what I wrote."

²³ Now the soldiers, when they had Iēsous hung on the stakes, took his clothes and made four portions, a portion for each soldier; but there was also his tunic. The tunic was a seamless one, woven in a single piece from top to bottom. ²⁴ So they said to each other, "Let's not tear it—we can draw lots for who gets it." This was so that what was written could be fulfilled, [which says,]

> *"They divided up my clothes among themselves,*
> *And they threw lots for my clothing."*

Accordingly, the soldiers did this.†

²⁵ Beside Iēsous' stake were standing his mother and his mother's sister, and Maria the wife of Klōpas, and Maria the Magdalēnē.‡ ²⁶ So Iēsous, seeing his mother and the student he

---

* This is the *titulus,* or sign of shame, posted at the top of the cross.

† The quotation is from Psalms 22:18. Jesus, about to be crucified naked, was presumably arrested in a tunic, a cloak, and sandals. It is unlikely that the soldiers each took a quarter of the cloak and half a sandal, before considering the valuable tunic. Another reason to doubt the account here is that the other executed men's clothing would have come into the reckoning from the start.

‡ It seems impossible that two sisters have the same given name, but to show this more clearly I have had to massage the editors' version of the text, adding

loved standing next to her, said to his mother, "Woman, look, it's your son"; [27] then he said to the student, "Look, it's your mother." And from that time onward, the student took her into his own home.*

[28] After this, seeing that everything was at an end, Iēsous said—so that what was written could be fulfilled—"I'm thirsty." [29] Lying there was a container full of vinegar, so they stuck a sponge full of the vinegar on a branch of hyssop and put it to his mouth. [30] Then, after he took in the vinegar, Iēsous said, "It's at an end," and he let his head fall and gave over his life-breath.†

[31] Then the Ioudaioi, because it was the day of preparation, were unwilling to let the bodies remain on the stakes during the *sabbaton*—and in fact that *sabbaton* was an even more solemn day—they asked Pilatos for the legs of the men on the stakes to be broken and the bodies removed. [32] So the soldiers came and broke the legs of the first man, and then of the second who had been hung on the stakes along with him. [33] But when they came to Iēsous and saw that he was already dead, they didn't break his legs; [34] instead, one of the soldiers pricked him in the side with his spear, and blood and water burst out.‡ [35] And the one who saw

---

"and" after "mother's sister." In either case, there are three Marys, not the kind of situation found in fiction, except comedy.

* The "beloved disciple," representing the pseudoauthorial "John" (see 13:23–25 and the note) is again in a special position, as the only male follower near the cross. The adoption of Jesus' mother is not historically likely, as Jesus appears to have had several siblings. (See, for example, Mark 6:3.)

† The scripture is Psalms 69:21: "They gave me poison for my food, and for my thirst they gave me vinegar to drink." Vinegar was the on-duty, nonalcoholic drink of Roman soldiers. The hyssop plant had medicinal and ritual uses. The manner of death is clinically convincing: as soon as the head drops at a sharp angle, the airway closes.

‡ Breaking the legs of the crucified on their stand could be an act of mercy, hurrying death, because the body could not then be held straight enough to breathe. John uniquely testifies that this measure was taken, for ritual reasons, at Jesus' crucifixion; the bodies could not be removed and buried on the Sabbath (and especially not on Passover falling on a Sabbath, as depicted in John). Also

it testified to it—and his testimony is true, and he knows he's telling the truth—so that you can all believe too.* ³⁶ These things happened so that what is written would be fulfilled: "None of his bones are to be shattered." ³⁷ And yet another thing that was written says, "They'll look at the one they stabbed."†

³⁸ After these things, Iōsēf of Arimathaia, as a student of Iēsous—a secret one, because of his fear of the Ioudaioi—asked Pilatos to let him take the body of Iēsous; and Pilatos allowed it; so he came and took his body. ³⁹ And Nikodēmos—who had first come to him at night‡—came also, bringing a mixture of myrrh and aloes weighing about a hundred pounds. ⁴⁰ They then took the body of Iēsous and wrapped it tightly with the aromatic spices in linen cloths, according to the custom of the Ioudaioi in burying their dead. ⁴¹ And in the place where he was hung on the stakes there was a cultivated grove, and in the grove was a new tomb where no one ever had been laid. ⁴² So there, as it was the day of preparation for the Ioudaioi, and because the tomb was close by, they laid Iēsous.§

Deuteronomy 21:22–23 forbids corpses of the executed ever to be hung on display overnight.

* The author of the Gospel of John is again identified as the disciple who was present at the cross. See above at Verses 26–27.

† Exodus 12:46 forbids the bones of the Passover sacrifice to be broken. See Psalms 34:20 for an allusion in a human connection. Zechariah 12:10 is the source of the second quotation.

‡ See 3:1–21 above.

§ This passage shows the body not merely anointed, wrapped up, and placed in an exclusive tomb, but also encased with an amount of chemically active substances that might have weighed half as much as the body did. (The Roman pound was about eleven and a half ounces.) Though Jews acculturated to Egypt (and a large and influential community lived there) may have practiced the elaborate, laborious local type of embalming, I can't find that this was ever the case in Judea. And what about the considerable evidence that washing and anointing a corpse for interment was, among the Jews, a women's job?

CHAPTER 20

––––

¹ On the first day after the *sabbaton,* Maria the Magdalēnē came early in the morning, when it was still dark, to the tomb and saw that the stone had been taken from the tomb. ² So she ran and found Simōn Petros and the other student, who was Iēsous' dear friend, and said to them, "They've taken the master out of the tomb, and we don't know where they put him."* ³ So Petros and the other student went out and were coming toward to the tomb. ⁴ The two ran together, but the other student ran more quickly, ahead of Petros, and came to the tomb first. ⁵ Then, leaning in, he saw the linen bands lying there; nevertheless, he didn't go in. ⁶ Now Simōn Petros came too, following him, and went into the tomb, and observed the linen bands lying there. ⁷ But the napkin that had been on his head wasn't lying with the bands, but was rolled up and set apart, in another spot. ⁸ So then the other student as well, the one who'd come first to the tomb, entered it and saw and believed.† ⁹ They didn't yet understand what was written, that it was necessary for him to rise from among the dead.‡ ¹⁰ Then the students returned to where they were staying.

¹¹ But Maria stood outside the tomb, close to it, crying. Then, while she was crying, she leaned down into the tomb ¹² and saw

––––

* See the end of the previous chapter, and the note. What is left for Mary to do here? Her "we" suggests that this scene is adapted from versions in which several women make the visit.

† Peter and the "beloved" John (both the disciple and the purported author of this Gospel) are at it again, in detailed competition. There is more forensic detail here than in the Synoptic Gospels. If mischievous persons removed the body, why did they bother to neatly roll up and put aside the face covering?

‡ There are a number of such *spoken* predictions in the Gospels, but of course within this present narrative economy, nothing at all has yet been written down about Jesus directly and specifically. Perhaps the author is thinking of Job 19:25, about the resurrection of a redeemer.

two messengers in white clothing,* sitting one at the head and one at the foot of the place on which Iēsous' body had been lying. ¹³ And they said to her, "Woman, why are you crying?" She told them, "They've taken my master, and I don't know where they've put him." ¹⁴ Once she'd said this, she turned around and saw Iēsous standing there, but she didn't know that it was Iēsous. ¹⁵ Iēsous said to her, "Woman, why are you crying? Who are you looking for?" Thinking it was the gardener, she said to him, "Sir, if it was *you* who carried him away, tell me where you put him, and I will take him."† ¹⁶ Iēsous said to her, "Mariam!" Turning around, she said to him in Hebrew, *"Rabbouni!"* (which means "teacher").‡ ¹⁷ Iēsous told her, "Don't hang on to me, because I haven't yet gone up to the father.§ Be on your way to my brothers and tell them I'm going up to my father and the father of you all, and to my god and the god of you all." ¹⁸ Mariam the Magdalēnē went to take the message to the students: "I've seen the master"; and she told what he'd said to her.

¹⁹ When it was evening on that day, the first after the *sabbaton*, and the doors were locked where the students were staying, out of fear of the Ioudaioi, Iēsous came and stood among them and said to them: "Peace to you!" ²⁰ And once he'd said this, he showed

---

* Again, it was difficult and expensive to make and keep cloth pure white. (Woolen togas were whitened with chalk in Rome to mark out the "whitened ones," or *candidati*, in elections.) White linen robes were associated with royalty, grandeur, and ritual.

† See Luke 24:16 and the note concerning normal hooding for protection from the sun that hides the face outdoors.

‡ See "rabbi" in the Glossary. *Rabbouni* (or *rabbōni*) occurs elsewhere in the Gospels only at Mark 10:51. In other sacred literature, it can be an epithet for God. "Hebrew" can, as usual, refer to the Aramaic dialect Jesus and his circle very likely spoke.

§ There are several nonridiculous theories for why Jesus tells Mary not to, probably, "hang on to" him, rather than the traditional "touch." To me, it seems commonsensical that Jesus is extricating himself from her embrace so that he can ascend to God.

his hands and his side to them, and the students were overjoyed to see the master. ²¹ [Iēsous] then said to them again, "Peace to you! Just as my father has dispatched me in his service, I'm sending you." ²² And having said this, he puffed air into them and told them, "Take the holy life-breath. ²³ If people do wrong and you pardon them, they *will* be pardoned; but if people do wrong and you hold on to it, those wrongs *will* be held on to."*

²⁴ But Thōmas, one of the twelve, who was called the Twin, wasn't with them when Iēsous came. ²⁵ So the other students told him, "We've seen the master." He, however, said to them, "Unless I see in his hands the holes from the nails and put my finger into those holes, and put my hand on his side, I'll never believe." ²⁶ Then, eight days later, his students were again indoors, and now Thōmas was with them. And even though the doors were locked, Iēsous came and stood among them and said, "Peace to you." ²⁷ Next he said to Thōmas, "Let's have your finger here, so you can check my hands, and let's have your hand so you can put it on my side: become a believer, instead of an unbeliever." ²⁸ Thōmas answered by saying to him, "You are my master and my god." ²⁹ Iēsous said to him, "Because you've seen me, you've come to believe? They're happy people who didn't see, yet still believed."

³⁰ Now Iēsous performed many other signs before [his] students' eyes, signs that haven't been written about in this book. ³¹ But what's written here is meant to lead you all to believe that Iēsous is the anointed one, the son of god; and to allow you, by believing, to have life in his name.†

---

* Taking someone's dying breath in one's mouth was a folk ritual of the time. Here the resurrected Jesus seems to reverse such a ritual, and of course his breath partakes of immortality. The verb is the same as for playing the flute.

† This looks a lot like the ending of one version of the book, an ending that is, unlike that of the other Gospels, explicitly authorial.

CHAPTER 21

¹ After these things, Iēsous revealed himself again to his students at the Sea of Tiberias;* and this is how he revealed himself. ² There together were Simōn Petros and Thōmas, who was called the Twin, and Nathanaēl from Kana in Galilaia, and the sons of Zebedaios, and two other of Iēsous' students. ³ And Simōn Petros said to them, "I'm going off to fish." They told him, "We're coming with you." Then they went out and boarded the boat, but during that night they caught nothing. ⁴ But soon after dawn arose, Iēsous stood on the shore; the students, however, didn't recognize that it *was* Iēsous.† ⁵ So Iēsous said to them, "You don't have anything to nibble, youngsters?" They replied to him, "No." ⁶ Then he said to them, "Throw in the net to the right side of the boat, and you'll find something." They threw it in accordingly, and discovered they no longer had strength enough to drag it back, there were so many fish in it. ⁷ Hence the student Iēsous loved‡ said to Petros, "It's the master!" Simōn Petros, hearing it was the master, tied his outer garment around his waist (as he had stripped)§ and threw himself into the sea. ⁸ But the other students came in the small boat, as they weren't far from land— only about two hundred cubits¶—dragging the net full of fish. ⁹ Then as they climbed out onto the land, they saw a charcoal fire laid, and a cooked relish lying on that, and a loaf. ¹⁰ And Iēsous said to them, "Bring some of the relish you've caught just now." ¹¹ So Simōn Petros climbed into the boat and dragged the net

* The same as the Sea of Galilee.

† See the note at Luke 24:15, and 20:14–15 above.

‡ See 13:23–25 above, and the note.

§ Working naked or seminaked was normal, but putting on the heavy outer garment for a plunge into the water—unless it is done for decorum's sake—looks odd.

¶ About three hundred feet, if this is a Roman cubit.

onto the dry land; the net was full of large fish, a hundred and fifty-three of them. But even though there were so many, the net didn't tear.* ¹² Iēsous told them, "Come and have breakfast." But none of the students dared to ask him, "Who are you?" knowing as they did that it was the master. ¹³ Iēsous came up and took the bread and gave it to them, and likewise the relish. ¹⁴ This was now the third time Iēsous was revealed to the students after he rose from among the dead.†

¹⁵ Then when they'd had breakfast, Iēsous spoke to Simōn Petros: "Simōn, son of Iōannēs: do you love me more than these others do?" Simōn said to him, "Yes, master, you know I'm your close friend." Iēsous said to him: "Pasture my lambs." ¹⁶ Iēsous spoke to him again, a second time: "Simōn, son of Iōannēs, do you love me?" Simōn said to him, "Yes, master, you know I'm your close friend." Iēsous said to him, "Shepherd my sheep." ¹⁷ Iēsous spoke to him a third time: "Simōn, son of Iōannēs, are you my close friend?" Petros was aggravated that Iēsous had spoken to him a third time, now saying, "Are you my close friend?" Now Petros said to him, "Master, *you* know everything; *you* recognize that I *am* your close friend." [Iēsous] said to him, "Pasture my sheep.‡ ¹⁸ *Amēn amēn*, I tell you: when you were a young man,

* There appears to be a joke in this passage involving two nouns: *prosfagion* (apparently "little eatable," or a relish; my "anything to nibble") in Verse 5, and, to follow that word up, *opsarion* ("little cooked food," also a relish, and I call it that in my translation). The food designated by both words is commonly, but not necessarily, fish. Jesus visibly offers food that is in accordance with both words' strict meanings: the food is prepared, and in the proper limited amount, and to be eaten with bread. Peter, a step behind events as usual and never the most subtle disciple, hears only the loose and colloquial meaning of both words, "fish," and so can prankishly be sent to the netful of large raw fish, as if they were needed for breakfast.

† That is, only the two appearances to the male disciples in the previous chapter count.

‡ The humor here hangs on the difference between the verbs *agapaō* (more about benevolence, the quality of the famous 1 Corinthians 13) and *fileō* (more about personal attachment). One or the other of these very verbs has been applied to the apostle John at critical moments: 13:23–25 (*agapaō*), 19:26–27 (*agapaō*),

you belted up your clothes and walked around wherever you wanted. But when you get old, you'll stretch out your hands, and someone else will truss you in a belt and take you where you don't want to go." [19] He said this to signal the kind of death with which Petros was going to glorify god.* And having said this, he told him, "Follow me."

[20] Turning around, Petros saw the student Iēsous loved, who was following them; during the banquet he had reclined against Iēsous' chest and had said, "Master, who's the one who's going to hand you over?"† [21] Seeing this man, Petros said to Iēsous, "But Master, what about *him*?" [22] Iēsous told him, "If I want him to stay until I come back, what does that have to do with you? *You*, follow me." [23] Thus the story arose among the brothers that this student wouldn't die. But Iēsous didn't say to him that he wouldn't die; he only said, "If I want him to stay until I come back, [what does that have to do with you]?"

[24] This is the student who is testifying about these things, and

---

20:2 (*fileō*). Now Jesus first seems to be describing *fileō* as a superior sort of *agapaō*, and to be offering Peter this role, but when Peter repeatedly uses the verb *fileō* of himself, trying to pin down the distinction, Jesus keeps trivially changing the metaphoric terms of the missionary assignment. It is as if Jesus is asserting in a roundabout way that the kind or degree of affection an associate has for him makes no difference—which was hardly the usual attitude in the ancient world, so naturally Peter is confused and hurt. By the time Jesus uses the verb *fileō* of Peter, Peter loses his temper, only to hear the language of shepherding changed again. It sounds like a mercilessly teasing lesson that personal feelings do not matter, a lesson from a leader who has shown another follower striking personal favoritism.

* Tradition says that Peter was crucified (upside down). The belt that gives freedom of movement by tying up garments becomes the "belting up" (an unusual way to put it, so the pun is rather labored) of a prisoner. A prisoner's hands that are stretched out in supplication double as arms that are spread out on a cross (and may be tied in place, so the belt image may apply here too): "stretch" and "spread" are different meanings of the single verb used here.

† Again, see 13:23–25 above, and the note.

the one who's written them down, and we know his testimony is true. [25] But there are many other things Iēsous did, and if every one of them were written down, I don't think that even the whole universe would have room for the books that would be written.*

* This whole final chapter looks added on, and mainly for the purpose of dignifying John at Peter's expense, probably reflecting conflicts among Jesus' followers and their successors. At last, the "beloved disciple" is firmly identified as the author of the Gospel, but as before, the actual name is not given.

ACKNOWLEDGMENTS

This book would not exist without a phalanx of champions. Leading the phalanx are Gail Hochman, my agent; Parisa Ebrahimi, my editor; and Sam Nicholson, who obtained the title for the Modern Library. I owe heartfelt thanks to the Robert B. Silvers Foundation, Pendle Hill Quaker Study Center, and the University of Pennsylvania for help in the completion of the manuscript. Much gratitude is due to Robert Cousland of the University of British Columbia for his learned, insightful, and tactful advice. Vincent La Scala applied virtuoso expertise and immense care to an unusually demanding manuscript. Most of all, I thank my husband, Tom Conroy, who champions me every day of my life.

My debt to monuments of modern Bible scholarship is enormous, and I mention here only the most essential works. The Greek text of the Gospels from which I translate is the twenty-eighth edition of the Nestle-Aland *Novum Testamentum Graece* (German Bible Society, 2012). I have had frequent recourse to the third edition of Frederick William Danker's *Greek-English Lexicon of the New Testament* (University of Chicago Press, 2000).

ABOUT THE TRANSLATOR

SARAH RUDEN was educated at the University of Michigan, Harvard, and Johns Hopkins. She has translated several books of ancient literature, among them Vergil's *Aeneid* and Augustine's *Confessions,* and is the author of *Paul Among the People: The Apostle Reinterpreted and Reimagined in His Own Time* and *The Face of Water: A Translator on Beauty and Meaning in the Bible.* She is the past recipient of Guggenheim and Whiting awards, and completed this translation of the Gospels with the help of a grant from the Robert B. Silvers Foundation. Formerly a scholar-in-residence at Yale Divinity School, she is currently a visiting researcher at the University of Pennsylvania.

sarahruden.com   ·

ABOUT THE TYPE

The principal text of this Modern Library edition was set in a digitized version of Janson, a typeface that dates from about 1690 and was cut by Nicholas Kis (1650–1702), a Hungarian working in Amsterdam. The original matrices have survived and are held by the Stempel foundry in Germany. Hermann Zapf (1918–2015) redesigned some of the weights and sizes for Stempel, basing his revisions on the original design.